Law, Knowledge, Culture

This book is dedicated to my sister and dear friends
Sophie, Steve, Kirstie, Craig and Carol.
Future leaders.

Law, Knowledge, Culture

The Production of Indigenous Knowledge in Intellectual Property Law

Jane E. Anderson

Visiting Research Scholar, Institute for Law and Society, School of Law, New York University, USA

Edward Elgar

Cheltenham, UK • Northampton, MA, USA

Published by
Edward Elgar Publishing Limited
The Lypiatts
15 Lansdown Road
Cheltenham
Glos GL50 2JA
UK

Edward Elgar Publishing, Inc.
William Pratt House
9 Dewey Court
Northampton
Massachusetts 01060
USA

A catalogue record for this book
is available from the British Library

Library of Congress Control Number: 2009921518

Mixed Sources
Product group from well-managed forests and other controlled sources
www.fsc.org Cert no. SA-COC-1565
© 1996 Forest Stewardship Council
FSC

ISBN 978 1 84542 485 5

Printed and bound by MPG Books Group, UK

Contents

Acknowledgements

This book was written in order to demystify key elements of legal discourse, and to illustrate the inner mechanics of an increasingly powerful body of law. Importantly this is not a book about defining indigenous knowledge, rather it is about the capacity of western law to make and remake that very category. The politics of the book is simple – unmasking the history, function and operation of intellectual property law actually provides the possibility for re-imagining how it could be used to advance indigenous interests in knowledge control, access and use. Given the complexity of colonial relationships within Australia as elsewhere, I firmly believe that finding a productive way forward in law and politics is not a task for indigenous people alone. It is the responsibility of us all.

This book initially developed out of my PhD thesis completed in the Faculty of Law at the University of New South Wales. Since then it has been reworked and informed by all my experiences working with indigenous people, families and communities in Australia, the United States and Indonesia.

My greatest debt is to Kathy Bowrey who has been an intellectually stimulating supervisor, but more than this, an incredibly generous and supportive friend at all points in this journey.

A four-year research fellowship at the Australian Institute of Aboriginal and Torres Strait Islander Studies (AIATSIS) provided new perspectives crucial for this work. Indeed it was within this context that the possibility for extending the work practically became a reality. The resulting experiences within contemporary indigenous political contexts have been invaluable and inevitably have been woven into the arguments in the book. The time at AIATSIS was the most formative period for me and it would not have been possible without the generosity in time and thought provided by Steve Kinnane, Craig Greene, Kirstie Parker, Carol Ryan, Luke Taylor, Peter Veth, Barry Cundy, Dianne Hosking, Patrick Sullivan, Toni Bauman, Lisa Strelein, Glen Kelly, Donna Oxenham and Mick Dodson at AIATSIS, as well as the support of those beyond the Institute namely, Martin Nakata, Jill McKeough, Brad Sherman, Leanne Wiseman, Colin Golvan, Charles Prouse, Terri Janke, Peter Drahos, Mark McMillan and Megan Davis.

A Rockefeller Fellowship at the Smithsonian Institution in 2005 enabled me to re-position my thoughts within a context beyond Australia. For this opportunity and the engaging conversation that ensued I would like to thank Richard Kurin, Sita Reddy, Lesley Fordred-Green, Atesh Sonneborn, James Early and Carla Borden.

My last year as a Fellow at the International Center for Advanced Studies at New York University provided the time I needed to complete the manuscript and to reflect upon the necessity of inter-disciplinary conversations within this field. This was a particularly stimulating experience and I would like to thank Tom Bender and Tim Mitchell for the opportunity, as well as all the 2006–7 Fellows. In particular Maimuna Huq, Diana Yoon, Deb Cowen, Wei-ha Wu, Xying Wang, Julia Elyachar, Alondra Nelson, Miriam Ticktin, Peggy Summers, Ella Shohat, Ulla Berg, Sherene Seikaly and Chris Otter.

Outside these fellowships, my work would not be possible without the ongoing support and encouragement of Fred Myers, Faye Ginsberg, Haidy Geismar, Wend Wendland, Peter Jaszi, Arun Agrawal, Sally Engel Merry, Elspeth Probyn, Tim Rowse, John Frow, Sonia Smallacombe, Bina D'Costa, Beth Povinelli, Rizaldi Saigian, Agus Sardjono and Ignatias Harianto.

Finally, my family and friends have been a constant support in providing space to test new ideas. For the love and laughter that has kept me going I am particularly indebted to Sophie Anderson, Sue Anderson, Ron Anderson, Brenden McCumstie, Wayne Deans, Lidia Tamplenizza, Courtney Botfield, Annie Lee, Smokey Forrester, Sally Heckel, Matt Giffin, TJ Volonis, Mel O'Hanolan, Rich Baz, Andy Russell, Peter Mahomet, Sarah-Jane Clarke and Andrea Geyer.

Cases

BRITISH CASES

AUSTRALIAN CASES

We decided to go and look at the site that was the subject of the painting. These were the waterhole paintings, right, and I thought that this waterhole was like, down the street, and it turned out it was in the most remote place. . .the waterhole that he [John Bulun Bulun] depicts, and has depicted throughout his whole artistic career. . .and others have depicted too was in fact a site he had never been to. . .it had never dawned on me before that for some of the artists, the first time that they saw the waterhole that they were depicting was with me from an aeroplane when we finally found it, using maps to locate it. We never landed, couldn't land there, it was in the most remote place. . .and I only realised then that what they were depicting was from their own sense of, you know, their own imagery. . .they had incorporated it into their own sense of the present and the real, something that they didn't know at all. . .it was amazing, that aspect of the Bulun Bulun case was amazing. I only realised that day that he had not actually been to the waterhole.

Colin Golvan (2002)

But the property here claimed is all ideal; a set of ideas which have no bounds or marks whatever, nothing that is capable of a visible possession, nothing that can sustain any one of the qualities or incidents of property. Their whole existence is in the mind alone; incapable of any other modes of acquisition or enjoyment, than by mental possession or apprehension; safe and invulnerable, from their own immateriality: no trespass can reach them; no tort affect them; no fraud or violence diminish or damage them. Yet these are the phantoms which the Author would grasp and confine to himself: and these are what the defendant is charged with having robbed the plaintiff of.

Justice Yates, *Millar v Taylor* (1769) 98 ER 233

To know the cause of a phenomenon is already a step taken in the direction of controlling it.

Ranajit Guha (1988)

Introduction

In 1983 Aboriginal artist Yanggarrny Wunungmurra and the Aboriginal Arts Agency commenced action for copyright infringement against a fabric designer/manufacturer and the proprietor of a retail shop.[1] The argument was that the copyright in the bark painting 'Long necked fresh water tortoises by the fish trap at Gaanan' had been infringed when reproduced onto fabric without the artist's consent. The case was settled with the first defendant, the designer, being ordered to pay damages and to supply a list of all persons to whom he had supplied fabric. The second defendant, the retailer, was ordered to deliver all the remaining material to the plaintiff. The case hardly made a ripple in the vast waters of increasing copyright litigation within Australia. In hindsight this is a surprise considering that, at the time, an emerging issue in the Australian political environment was a concern for the protection of 'expressions of folklore', namely Aboriginal art.[2]

Eleven years later another copyright case unfolded in the Northern Territory Federal Court that generated significantly more attention.[3] *Milpurrurru & Others v Indofurn Pty Ltd* involved the unauthorised reproduction of Aboriginal art as the designs for a series of impressive carpets intended for the art market. The significance of the case lay in the perception that it presented a clear judicial affirmation that Aboriginal art could legitimately secure copyright protection, and the collective interests of Aboriginal owners could be somehow legally secured. While some commentators in the popular media hailed the case as the '*Mabo* of copyright'[4], others argued that the case demonstrated the inherent irreconcilability between intellectual property law and indigenous beliefs and knowledge structures.[5]

Importantly this case drew attention to the profound problem of securing intellectual property protection for intangible indigenous subject matter and cultural expression.[6] The case also demonstrated how the 'uniqueness' of Australian indigenous cultures, expressed through cultural products such as art, were increasingly marketable commodities. This, in turn, increased the potential for these objects to be considered as legitimate entities for the deployment of western legal frameworks that control and protect certain kinds of knowledge.

Notably, the presiding judge, Justice von Doussa found that a 'cultural harm' had been sustained against the Aboriginal artists and awarded additional damages accordingly. The very idea and articulation that a 'cultural harm' had taken place, indicated how issues of 'culture' and cultural difference were being interpreted and translated into a legal framework.[7] Moreover, the case validated a narrative of the law as adaptable and responsive to changing political environments and the needs of the new 'indigenous' stakeholders. Thus with the finding of copyright infringement and the award of significant damages, the *carpets case* made legal history.[8]

* * *

Indigenous interests and rights in intellectual property has become a very popular area of contemporary concern.[9] Consideration is no longer confined to specialist legal interest or academic disciplines.[10] Questions about rights in intellectual property are raised throughout local communities, indigenous organisations, centres for policy co-ordination, as well as national and international bureaucracies.[11] Indeed the networks through which discussions of intellectual property flow have generated a wealth of material describing the 'problems' of intellectual property.[12] These include the global challenge of adequately protecting specific 'types' of knowledge and a questioning of the utility of international legal instruments, as well as what they may or may not address. However, given how diverse the contexts are in which conversations about intellectual property and indigenous knowledge are occurring, it is surprising that there has been limited attention directed to the emergence of this field. That it is virtually impossible to consider expressions of indigenous interests in knowledge control and protection *outside* legal discourse raises fundamental questions about the constitution of this subject in law and policy, and in particular, the specific effects of its location within legal frameworks of meaning. Indeed the discourse is so large, with so many participants, at so many levels of political engagement and with varying levels of agency, that the subject itself has become its own referent. That is to say that discussions often oscillate around themselves as if contained by their own references, repetitions and points of identification.[13]

The focus of this book is on the emergence of claims about the protection of 'indigenous knowledge' within Australia and the effects of the placement of such claims within an intellectual property discourse. My point in looking to this appearance is to illuminate the range of networks and influences – political, cultural, economic, personal – that are always-already working to produce meaning about indigenous interests in IP. In particular the book pushes boundaries in terms of understanding how a range of individuals, agencies, governments, bureaucracies have acted, and continue to act, on the problem of indigenous knowledge and intellectual property protection. Of significance here are the kinds of meanings about indigenous rights in intellectual property which are being constructed, articulated, mobilised and mediated, and how these effect the kinds of remedies and/or possibilities for action which are being made available.[14]

My interest in this issue began ten years ago. Concerned with the ways in which knowledge about Aboriginal and Torres Strait Islander people and epistemology was circulated and authorised in a neoliberal colonial settler state like Australia, I became engaged in locating the conditions for the emergence of the concept of intellectual property within an indigenous context.[15] In other words, what was its point of departure as a subject of law; a topic of attention in bureaucracy; a concept creating new languages and expectations within Aboriginal communities and policy arenas; and something of discussion in the general media? What became clear, and even more so when I began working with colleagues in Aboriginal organisations, communities and policy arenas was that this emergence did not exist in isolation to any of the other political and social dynamics that were occurring in relation to Aboriginal rights in Australia. Indeed, the production of something named as 'indigenous intellectual property' was thoroughly imbued with, and hence also a product of, sophisticated discourses of national and international indigenous rights, specifically rights in land, rights of sovereignty and rights of citizenship.[16]

This is clearly going to be quite a particular perspective, and at all moments in this book I claim responsibility for how the issues are interpreted, the networks are understood and the links drawn. The discussion is theoretical and philosophical in scope but it derives not only from archival-theoretical engagement with scholarship about law and the conditions under which legal authority operates, but practical experiences working with Aboriginal artists, communities and indigenous bureaucracies predominately within Australia.[17] Whilst my theoretical influences are a combination of legal, critical legal and postmodern insight, it is the practical work for the last five years at the Australian Institute of Aboriginal and Torres Strait Islander Studies, (currently the only federal indigenous-run organisation within Australia),[18] that has provided fresh impetus towards making sense of the complexities and importantly, contradictions, that characterise this field and the possibilities for action and agency that now need to be developed and extended.

The book in no way seeks to posit a definitive truth about a matter as politically complicated as indigenous interests in intellectual property. Simply – there is no one truth here, no singular problem and conversely no singular solution. In that sense, I will not be using the book as a forum for arguing about greater rights in intellectual property for indigenous people, nor for the inevitable failure of law to address indigenous interests on indigenous terms. Nor do I seek to present a position about the extent that these rights could and should be protected, if only they were articulated in more simple and streamlined ways that greater nation state governments and sweeping international bureaucracies could tolerate. Rather, the book argues that what is happening at the intersection of indigenous rights and intellectual property law is of critical importance for how we understand the social effects of law: indigenous expectations of intellectual property and the emerging relationships and decision-making frameworks being generated around the notion of knowledge as a naturally occurring type of property, both within communities and in political/policy arenas. Understanding these often competing and contradictory dynamics matters if the diverse range of indigenous interests in intellectual property are going to be supported and thoughtfully progressed at local, regional and international levels.

Intellectual property law came to the subject of indigenous knowledge with a self-conscious appraisal of its need to be more socially responsive in the construction of legal relations of culture. Intellectual property academics are now almost self-congratulatory in their attention to indigenous matters as a 'special' kind of concern.[19] This is despite a disinclination to consider the history of intellectual property law and its function as an instrument fashioned through a particular kind of colonial politics that facilitated the historical exclusion of indigenous interests from broader policy developments in this field to start with.[20] Understanding the history of intellectual property law reframes the current debates and helps us understand the extent that the relationship between intellectual property law and indigenous knowledge is regulatory. For law is critically involved in managing how 'indigenous knowledge' is conceptualised, constructed and typologised within legal, bureaucratic, policy and increasingly more localised contexts.[21] This affects how the problem of indigenous rights in intellectual property is configured and understood, and what kinds of possibilities for protecting knowledge can be imagined. For legal paradigms of intellectual property law are functioning as fundamental mechanisms of governance, producing new ways of authorising knowledge, new frameworks for engaging with knowledge circulation, new kinds of knowledge authorities and new kinds of legal communities.[22]

A key problem with this field is that while there has been considerable (anthropological) focus on the indigenous dimensions and interpretations of the 'intangible', debates around cultural heritage and indigenous knowledge protection tend to endorse the authorised master narrative of intellectual property law's history.[23] That is, that it is consistent, *a*historical, *a*political, *a*cultural and unchanging. To properly understand why indigenous ownership claims challenge the congruency of law it is important to consider the literary property debates of the eighteenth and nineteenth centuries and the development of 'design' as part of the intellectual property network.[24] It is here that the disputes about intangible property, the problem of identifying the 'property' and justifying the 'right' first really emerge and are fleshed out in courts and through broader social networks.[25] Following this history one finds that ownership and 'property' in something that is intangible has never been clear for intellectual property law. Indeed law still struggles with exactly the same problems today: determining the metaphysical dimensions of the 'property' and justifying the 'right'.[26] The messy, inconsistent and unstable nature of intellectual property law is herein exposed. This leads to an inevitable fracture in the dominant narrative of intellectual property and with it the assumptions about how law works, and how it responds to new kinds of cultural/political issues as they emerge.[27]

In order to develop new possibilities for the protection of indigenous knowledge and knowledge practices, there must be a reframing of what intellectual property does and how it functions to manage the always already complicated social relationships around knowledge use and access. My point of departure is that 'indigenous intellectual property' is not an ahistorical *subject* to which the law responds. Rather, it is a very specific *category* that has been made and remade through various social, cultural, political and economic interventions including the struggles that are internal to law.

THE PROBLEMS AND POLITICS OF TERMINOLOGY

For this work, engaging in discussions about the position of indigenous knowledge (and its analogues including traditional knowledge, traditional ecological knowledge, cultural knowledge and folklore)[28] in intellectual property law requires an appreciation of how the term indigenous knowledge will be employed, as well as how other concepts of indigenous knowledge are currently circulated from indigenous, governmental and academic perspectives. In this work indigenous knowledge is the preferred term. This is owing to the circumstances within Australia where indigenous knowledge is predominately utilised in reference to intellectual property and indigenous interests. However, from the outset it is crucial that the very politics of the term 'indigenous' is recognised. For it is not only within intellectual property contexts that definitions of 'indigenous' present difficulties. There remain lively debates within Aboriginal, Torres

Strait Islander and indigenous contexts about the effects of classifying colonial systems, and the impact on group/community/self identification, as well as the implications of definitions arising from legislative contexts.[29] In Australia for example, there is ongoing debate amongst indigenous people about the difficulties of the labels 'Aboriginal' and/or 'Torres Strait Islander' and/or 'indigenous peoples'. These are extended to include debates about the constraints of the terminology, its vagaries, the dangers of papering over diversity and the inherent problem of minimising significant issues of identity and subjectivity.[30] As Marcia Langton has explained,

> Who is Aboriginal? What is Aboriginal? For Aboriginal people, resolving who is Aboriginal and who is not is an uneasy issue, located somewhere between the individual and the state. They find white representations of Aboriginality disturbing because of the history of forced removal of children, disenfranchisement from civil rights, and dispossession of land.
>
> The label 'Aboriginal' has become one of the most disputed terms in the Australian language. There are High Court decisions and opinions on the 'term' and its meaning. Legal scholar John McCorquodale tells us that in Australian law there have been sixty-seven definitions of Aboriginal people, mostly related to their status as wards of the state and to criteria for incarceration in the institutional reserves. These definitions reflect not only the Anglo-Australian legal and administrative obsession, even fixation, with Aboriginal people, but also the uncertainty, confusion and constant search for the appropriate characterisation: 'full blood', 'half caste', 'quadroon', 'octoroon', 'such and such a admixture of blood', 'a native of Australia', 'a native of an admixture of blood not less than half Aboriginal', and so on. . . . The fixation on classification reflects the extraordinary intensification of colonial administration of Aboriginal affairs from 1788 to the present.[31]

Owing to this history, the classification of Aboriginality is contested and this is precisely what will always make it a difficult category in law and politics.[32] These key problems and politics have significant effects in how indigenous issues are even conceptualised, let alone played out, within law and policy.

In the context of this work, whilst I remain concerned about the use and deployment of terms, I will not be explicitly engaging in the debates about which terminology is better, and for whom. At a later point in the work and in light of the problems of marginalising issues of politics and subjectivity within broader intellectual property debates I will discuss the manner in which indigenous issues are classified within international and bureaucratic discussion papers.[33]

For my purposes the concept of 'indigenous knowledge' requires a certain level of demystification. By demystification I mean exposing certain conditions that have enabled indigenous knowledge to be constructed as a coherent entity and, most importantly, significantly different from 'western' knowledge. Recognising that indigenous knowledge like all knowledge is changeable and permeable is often overlooked in discussions of this subject because it disrupts a dichotomy between indigenous and western knowledge which is dependent upon discourses of difference and exclusion.

If we are to understand the process of positioning indigenous knowledge in intellectual property law, it is at first instance integral to appreciate how the term 'indigenous knowledge' is itself a construct that limits what can be understood within the diverse range of indigenous experience, ontology and epistemology. My interest here is not what constitutes indigenous epistemology but more the use of terminology – specifically how the construct 'indigenous knowledge' circulates within intellectual property discussions. Intellectual property law seeks to produce indigenous knowledge (and the analogues of traditional knowledge, folklore etc) as coherent entities – that is, the same unto themselves, but different in relation to any other kind of knowledge practice, embodiment and transference. This affects how indigenous interests are understood, and significantly, how indigenous interests are classified as the 'same' in their identification as 'indigenous' despite vastly different social and cultural experiences, ontologies and epistemologies. The mystification of indigenous knowledge has led to mistaken conclusions about the dynamic intersections permeating indigenous ways of knowing. Implicitly and explicitly, a reflection on the instability of the category 'indigenous knowledge' will be at all stages of this work. Indeed it is this instability, which mirrors the instability of intellectual property law in general, that makes the category difficult to manage, and to develop appropriate solutions (that accord with problems experienced at more localised levels) for.

In 1995 Arun Agrawal challenged the way in which indigenous knowledge was discussed in contemporary anthropological and social theory research.[34] The article traced the increased interest in indigenous knowledge from a variety of sectors, including international and national institutions, and for a variety of purposes including indigenous participation in development strategies, aid objectives and scientific research.[35] Agrawal's argument is that the making of indigenous knowledge as a specific 'target' within these discourses signaled a profound shift in appreciating the content (and hence value) of indigenous ways of knowing. Agrawal goes on to argue that consequently there is a tendency in such studies to construe indigenous knowledge as 'somehow' fundamentally different to other forms of knowledge. Here the questions are about the 'validity and even the possibility of separating traditional or indigenous knowledge from western or rational/scientific knowledge.'[36] The point is twofold. Firstly, that the intersections of all knowledge are potentially permeable, whatever the genesis; and secondly that the dichotomy generally assumed between indigenous knowledge and 'western' knowledge is produced through historically informed networks of power.[37]

The classification between 'indigenous' and 'western' knowledge, as bounded wholes can never be effectively established. This is because such classification 'seeks to separate and fix in time and space (separate as independent, and fix as stationary and unchanging) systems that can never be thus separated or so fixed.'[38] Knowledge, and its expression and practice is more complicated than any form of binary allows and fundamental concerns about the intersections of relations of power in the production and circulation of knowledge are often understated or ignored.[39] Labelling and classifying knowledge as 'types' ultimately produces organisational categories that bare little resemblance to practical utility and the interchangeability of experience.[40]

Martin Nakata has extended these observations within an Australian indigenous context.[41] Nakata explains contentions in the current debate about the utility of indigenous knowledge: primarily that the use of the term 'indigenous knowledge' seldom engages in any contextualisation of knowledge use and tends to indicate quite particular interests.[42] As he remarks, 'the Indigenous Knowledge enterprise seems to have everything and nothing to do with us'.[43] Indigenous people function as the subjects from which the 'indigenous knowledge enterprise' develops. This is at the expense of continued appreciation of the changing uses of knowledge systems.[44] It is this observation that holds particular resonance to what follows in this book. Nakata is certainly correct, discussions of indigenous knowledge seldom engage in contextual usage and this is clearly a problem for areas like intellectual property law. But if one looks more closely at the history of intellectual property, which is where Part One of this book begins, it is clear that intellectual property law isn't interested in contextualising *any* kind of knowledge, indigenous or otherwise. This is because knowledge has always been difficult for law to name, identify, classify and then protect.[45] After long contention around this very issue, intellectual property law sidestepped the problem by ultimately focusing the form of the protection on the product of the knowledge (that is, a book, artwork, database), rather than the knowledge itself. It is therefore somewhat ironic that it is the problem of decontextualising indigenous knowledge, and thus not being able to fully grasp either its metaphysical makeup or contextual utility in order to make clear frameworks for protection, that re–exposes contingencies that go to the very heart of our current intellectual property law frameworks.

Nakata makes the further observation that the increasing discussions of indigenous knowledge remake it as 'a commodity, something of value, something that can be value added, something that can be exchanged, traded, appropriated, preserved, something that can be excavated and mined'.[46] Becoming a term that can be used by a variety of groups to support partisan interests, it runs the risk of losing meaning and context. Following Nakata then, the position of indigenous knowledge in intellectual property law is significant because it indicates quite a particular interest. Intellectual property law has become a key site in constructing indigenous knowledge as a stable subject and further, in producing it as a 'type' of distinct knowledge to be documented and managed through networks of legal power.[47] This is, however, at the expense of complicated contexts and contested politics which ultimately mean that indigenous knowledge will never be 'securely' or fully captured in registries, in legislation or in policy.

THE INSISTENCE ON INDIGENOUS KNOWLEDGE AS 'TRADITIONAL' KNOWLEDGE

Despite these obvious problems of history, politics and locating a stable indigenous subject, the 'indigenous knowledge' category in intellectual property law functions through several terms that are often used interchangeably. I highlight the usage of these additional terms, in particular 'folklore' and 'traditional knowledge', for two reasons. Firstly, I want to suggest that the ways by which indigenous knowledge is equated to 'traditional knowledge' is representative of the way that indigenous knowledge structures and thus indigenous people continue to occupy uneasy positions in relation to contemporary cultural practice. The problem is that the pervading emphasis on the 'traditional' component of indigenous knowledge facilitates a perception of incompatible differences between indigenous and western knowledge.

Secondly, the emphasis on the traditional component of indigenous knowledge significantly affects how it can be understood and made intelligible before the law. This therefore also affects how realistic outcomes in intellectual property law are envisaged. The question that remains is this: can utilisation of the term 'tradition', as it is evoked in reference to indigenous people and knowledges, ever be really re-conceptualised outside the meaning making contexts that established the relationship between the 'traditional' and the 'primitive' and the 'modern' in the first place? At best, it would be naïve to think that in the context of intellectual property law a term like 'tradition' occupies a more neutral space, where history and politics informing the term remain in abeyance. Inevitably, through its utterance, repetition and circulation amongst legal academics, as well as bureaucratic and centres for policy development, 'tradition' (and more latterly 'culture')[48] functions as the key trope for the identification of the metaphysical dimensions of indigenous knowledge – such an identification being crucial for an intellectual property right to be justified.[49] In an inspired yet unpredictable twist, with the repetition of tradition as the key element of indigenous differentiation and necessary inclusion, intellectual property law again must face itself and the difficulties of identifying the metaphysical dimensions of property.

The Report *Intellectual Property Needs and Expectations of Traditional Knowledge Holders*[50] emanating from the intellectual property standard setting organisation World Intellectual Property Organisation, aptly demonstrates the interchangeability of the terms used in reference to indigenous knowledge. The document starts in the following way;

> Traditional knowledge is created, originated, developed and practiced by traditional knowledge holders. . . From WIPO's perspective, expressions of folklore are a subset of and included within the notion of traditional knowledge. Traditional knowledge is in turn, a subset of the broader concept of heritage. Indigenous knowledge being the traditional knowledge of indigenous peoples, is also a subset of traditional knowledge. As some expressions of folklore are created by indigenous persons there is an overlap between expressions of folklore and indigenous knowledge, both of which are forms of traditional knowledge.[51]

The struggle to adequately describe indigenous knowledge, as a singular and relatively bounded entity, is reflected in this quote. It is a problem I have sympathy with, if only because of its inevitability. The difficulty of finding terminology that can capture the myriad of experiences that draw on and utilise, often at the same time, all these 'types' of knowledges and more, will continue to exist. The challenge remains to recognise these as historically and politically derived difficulties, and then to reconsider how they might meaningfully be overcome.

The dilemma indicated through the WIPO Report, and others that draw on WIPO's authority, in positioning indigenous knowledge within the sphere of intellectual property reflects both uncertainty and insecurity. Law manages indigenous categories because a cultural identity is recognised (with indigenous knowledge, an assumed difference means that the cultural identity is disclosed). Yet intellectual property is generally disinterested in the cultural identity of any of its categories. To this end, a 'special' position is established that allows space for a connection between knowledge and identity and is applied to denote unique properties and legal positioning. This specialness becomes identified as 'cultural' in nature.[52] 'Culture', then, becomes the primary trope for identifying and explaining the unique concerns that are brought to intellectual property law by indigenous people.[53]

Ivison, Patton and Sanders have emphasised the need for urgent reflection in the making of categories that depend upon abstract binaries. For 'when we evoke a mysterious otherness or radical difference in referring to indigenous cultures we are in danger of replaying prejudices that assume the inherent inferiority of indigenous peoples and their practices'.[54] The emphasis on the 'traditional' lifestyles and 'traditional' peoples misunderstands colonial realities and the commonality of indigenous engagement with information management and markets.[55] The insistence on the 'traditional' as the key marker of difference obscures contemporary indigenous practice and the reality that indigenous knowledge also undergoes transformation overtime in usage and circulation both within family or community contexts and/or between families, the community and external parties.[56]

The anxiety for intellectual property law in reconciling indigenous interests becomes heightened by a reliance upon an unreal indigenous subjectivity that is cloaked in a sense of antiquated tradition.[57] For claims of cultural difference have to be balanced against the dynamic ways in which cultures borrow and import practices and the extent that cultural identities are constantly reforming and renegotiated.[58] What is potentially destabilising for the position of indigenous knowledge within networks of intellectual property is a reliance on notions of a 'traditional culture' that evoke particular romanticised and singular perceptions of indigenous culture, experience and community.[59] The phantoms of romanticism that underpin much of intellectual property law and its consequent development are never too far away.[60] Appeals to a romantic past are repeated in new ways in the present.[61] This inevitably affects how indigenous knowledge is produced, positioned and managed through an intellectual property regime and how indigenous people negotiate positions in relation to these laws. Thus my key interest is in how intellectual property law constructs the indigenous category, and how it seeks to manage indigenous interests and relationships to law. To this end, it is the partial successes, moderate failures and potential dangers within intellectual property law with respect to the challenge of indigenous knowledge that is the focus of the book.

* * *

In Australia, the copyright cases involving Aboriginal art that developed through the 1980s and 1990s, generated debate and discussion within political, academic and more localised contexts. These discussions extended arguments that addressed legal inclusivity, the rights and legitimacy of indigenous voices before the law and the recognition of the aesthetic nuances of Aboriginal cultural products. The cases did signify a genuine attempt within legal liberalism to accommodate the claims of indigenous people. For the Aboriginal artists involved, the cases represented a consolidation of the view that their art could be protected through western intellectual property laws, specifically copyright and that this was interconnected with sovereign claims and land ownership.

The *carpets case* was significant as it explicitly included aspects characterised as 'indigenous difference' within the fabric of the law. Whilst this will be explained in more depth in Part Two through a close reading of the cases themselves, in the main, the previous copyright cases included indigenous issues on the same terms as the non-indigenous. However when debate relating to cultural differences arose it was positioned at the margins of the law and aroused a range of hitherto unexplored notions.[62] Thus the *carpets case* is important because it spurred debate about the terms of inclusion and questioned how indigenous concerns about protecting intangible cultural heritage were to be addressed. Explicitly the authority of the law was engaged to address indigenous interests, thereby exposing the power of legal discourse to produce the category and inform how it could be managed successfully and adequately.

However, the immediate challenge for intellectual property law in protecting indigenous knowledge resonates with tensions that characterise intellectual property law as a whole. As 'new' subject matter, indigenous knowledge requires an identification of the boundaries or marks that established its 'property' for protection.[63] The greatest surprise is the familiarity of the task, for the central problematic of intellectual property law is the way in which it justifies a property right in *any* intangible subject matter.[64] Yet the law generally fails to acknowledge that this is problematic in non–indigenous cases. Indigenous knowledge provides an example of how intellectual property law still grapples with determining the metaphysical dimensions of intellectual property subject matter.

The problem is that the unauthorised use of intangible indigenous subject matter involves an intersection of elements, not all of which can be remedied through the intellectual property framework. The danger in assuming intellectual property law has the capacity to provide just solutions to the appropriation of indigenous knowledge limits an understanding of the broader issues associated with the political and social impetus of naming and identifying instances of cultural appropriation. Intellectual property is evoked as the strategy for securing cultural integrity.[65] However, claims for protecting cultural integrity and stopping cultural appropriation are highly political. This is the difficulty of reconciling sovereign claims, minority rights and the preservation of 'culture' within the context of intellectual property law.

Consequent to the success of indigenous claims involving visual artwork, certain critical legal and philosophical analyses from the debates surrounding Aboriginal art are used as a point of departure for developing the arguments in this book. As the Australian case law has grappled with the inclusion of Aboriginal art as legitimate subject matter, and the attention of the Australian Government has been focused on this area in particular, copyright forms the key focus. However I will extrapolate beyond the category of copyright in order to understand how intellectual property law more generally constructs and subsequently treats intangible indigenous subject matter. To this end the book is occupied by the following core questions:

- what are the cultural, political and legal shifts that have produced the category of indigenous knowledge within the field of intellectual property law?
- how does legal power produce a domain specifically occupied by a concept of 'indigenous knowledge' and how does it seek to manage such a domain?

The focus here is on the philosophical issues that surround the process of imbuing an object with property rights, exploring how this process replicates liberal possessive individualism in both indigenous and non-indigenous cases and how this functions as a means to manage indigenous difference.[66] Property relations are understood as an instance of governmental management however, in the context of indigenous intellectual property, the management and outcome is far from predictable.[67] This is because how the law actually deals with any intangible subject matter is not as consistent or stable as is generally believed. Indigenous claims expose the contingency and instability of intellectual property law and this is crucial for understanding law's difficulties in managing the direction and closure of the category.

As already stated, the book is divided into three parts. Each explores a broad theme that is integral to the making of the indigenous category within intellectual property. Part One begins with a consideration of the history of intellectual property law. In particular it considers both the early development of controls for managing relationships around knowledge use and circulation in the United Kingdom, and the more 'modern' manifestation that we have come to understand as a body of law named as 'intellectual property'. This first part will also explore the cultural functions of law, that law does not function in isolation, but is always-already informed by a range of political, social, economic and cultural relationships. A combination of these elements will always drive the 'discovery' of new areas of legal focus and categorisation.

Part Two takes the identification of a new 'indigenous' category within Australian intellectual property law as its point of departure. A close reading of the initial bureaucratic interventions leading to the actual cases and the subsequent bureaucratic, academic and indigenous responses, provides a structure for understanding how knowledge about indigenous interests in intellectual property emerged. This analysis makes the relationships between legal authority, bureaucratic intervention and the significance of individual action clearer. It establishes a framework for understanding the extent that intellectual property law functions as a regulatory mechanism for managing relationships between people and legal authority, and that this has effects upon how solutions to the problems of indigenous control of knowledge are phrased, and how they have become dependent upon further legal expertise and legal authority.

Part Three explores how 'culture' has been produced in intellectual property law as a singularised and reified trait possessed only by indigenous people. Through the prism of current policy and legislative initiatives within Australia, this section discusses what the limitations and future possibilities for this field might be. It argues that attention must be given to more localised strategies, emboldening already existing (and those in the process of being developed) community based approaches to knowledge management. Whilst this may appear to be in conflict with global intellectual property governing strategies, practical experience has shown how more local focused activities provide new possibilities in this area. This is because they enable space for diverse indigenous histories and experiences, as well as problems with sovereignty and legal autonomy to be engaged more meaningfully. Part Three directly addresses the tension between theory and policy development that haunts this field. It concludes with suggestions for how this tension may be overcome so that indigenous people and communities can mediate knowledge management contexts on their own terms.

Increasingly indigenous knowledge is, for the purposes of governmental intervention, being generated and identified as a 'type' existing within a legal domain, produced through case law, governmental reports, academic interest and international concern. In reality, indigenous knowledge is not ahistorical and uniformly coherent. The objective of this book is to consider how this field of knowledge has been produced, including how other disciplines and forms of analysis have become subordinate to the legal questions that the intersection of indigenous knowledge and intellectual property generate.[68]

The variety of demands made to include indigenous knowledge as an intellectual property category reflect the complex motivations, networks and interests of all stakeholders. It also highlights the positions that shape what can be known about the dimensions of indigenous knowledge, and the extent to which it can be recognised and incorporated within this legal framework. This book seeks to unpack fundamental problems in reconciling both intellectual property law and indigenous knowledge as categories of law and subjects of governance. Significantly it seeks to highlight a remarkable irony, that efforts to include indigenous knowledge in intellectual property in effect (re)expose contingencies in intellectual property law that are constant and have remained relatively undisclosed. In positioning indigenous knowledge within an intellectual property regime, the law produces a category that is difficult to manage, but it is this very difficulty that provides the possibility for more localised approaches to be justified and further developed.

NOTES

1. *Yanggarrny Wunungmurra v Peter Stipes* (1983) Federal Court, unreported. See: N. Stevenson, 'Case Note: Infringement in Copyright in Aboriginal Artworks', (1993) 17 *Aboriginal Law Bulletin* 5.
2. We can tell the case provoked little comment for several reasons. Firstly it was not reported in the intellectual property case reports and secondly, there is very little reflection on the case in the wealth of literature dealing with Aboriginal art and copyright. Vivien Johnson makes the note that 'the case was not seen as important because the focus was on folklore not copyright.' V. Johnson, *Copyrites: Aboriginal Art in the Age of Reproductive Technologies*, National Indigenous Arts Advocacy Association and Macquarie University: Sydney, 1996.
3. *Milpurrurru & Others v Indofurn Pty Ltd* [1994] 30 IPR 209, 130 ALR 659 (hereafter the *carpets case*). Also see: T. Janke (1995) 'Copyright: The Carpets Case', (1995) 3 (72) *Aboriginal Law Bulletin/Alternative Law Journal* (Joint Issue) 36.
4. For instance: V. Trioli, 'Record Damages for Illegal Aboriginal Images', *The Age*, 14 December 1994. The perception of the *carpets case* as the *Mabo* of copyright was subsequently raised in academic circles. This followed literature examining how the *Mabo* decision provided possibilities for recognising 'common law native title intellectual property'. For example see: K. Puri, 'Copyright Protection for Australian Aborigines in the Light of Mabo' in Stephenson, M. A., and S. Ratnapala (eds), *Mabo: A Judicial Revolution*, The University of Queensland Press: Brisbane, 1993; K. Puri, 'Cultural Ownership and Intellectual Property Rights Post-Mabo: Putting Ideas into Action', (1995) 9 (3), *Intellectual Property Journal* 293; D. Ellinson, 'Unauthorised Reproduction of Traditional Aboriginal Art', (1994) 17 (2) *University of New South Wales Law Journal* 327; N. Lofgren, 'Common Law Aboriginal Knowledge', (1995) 3 (77) *Aboriginal Law Bulletin*, 10; M. Blakeney, '*Milpurrurru & Ors v Indofurn Pty Ltd & Others* – Protecting Expressions of Aboriginal Folklore Under Copyright Law', (1995) *elaw: Murdoch Electronic Law Journal* at www.murdoch.edu.au/elaw/issues/v2n1/blakeney.txt; D. Bennett, 'Native Title and Intellectual Property', (1996) 10 *Land, Rights, Laws: Issues of Native Title* 2; S. Gray, 'Wheeling, Dealing and Deconstruction: Aboriginal Art and the Land Post Mabo', (1993) 3 (63) *Aboriginal Law Bulletin* 10; S. Gray, 'Squatting in

Red Dust: Non-Aboriginal Law's Construction of the 'Traditional' Aboriginal Artist', (1996) 14 (2) *Law in Context* 29.

5. See: T. Davies, 'Aboriginal Cultural Property?', (1996) 14 (2) *Law in Context* 1; M. Dodson (1996), 'Indigenous Peoples and Intellectual Property Rights', in *Ecopolitics IX – Conference Papers and Resolutions*, Northern Land Council: Casuarina 1996; M. Davis, 'Indigenous Peoples and Intellectual Property Rights', (1996) *Parliamentary Library Research Paper* 20; M. Blakeney, 'Bioprospecting and the Protection of Traditional Medicinal Knowledge of Indigenous Peoples: An Australian Perspective', (1997) 6 *European Intellectual Property Review* 298; C. Eatock and K. Mordaunt, *Copyrites*, Australian Film Finance Corporation Limited, 1997; J. McKeough and A. Stewart 'Intellectual Property and the Dreaming', in E. Johnstone, M. Hinton, and D. Rigney (eds), *Indigenous Australians and the Law*, Cavendish Publishing: Sydney, 1997.
6. See the following reports in the media: 'Aboriginal Art Copyright Win', *The Advertiser*, 14 December 1994; 'Aboriginal Art on Carpets Costs Importer $188,000', *Townsville Bulletin*, 15 December 1994; M. Lang, 'Artists win copyright case', *West Australian*, 14 December 1994; R. Macklin, 'Court Moves to Stop Rip-off of Aboriginal Art', *The Canberra Times*, 17 December 1994; R. Hessey, 'Designs on the Future', *The Sydney Morning Herald*, 15 December 1994; C. Egan, 'Tickner to Protect Aboriginal Artists', *The Australian*, 15 December 1994.
7. This is an example of what Stanley Fish calls the 'amazing magic trick' of law – 'when a new movement in law or precedent is made but it is possible to claim that there is nothing innovative or new being done or said even while new departures are being taken.' In A. Sarat and T. Kearns (eds), *History, Memory and the Law,* University of Michigan Press: Ann Arbor, 1999. In this context, Justice von Doussa made a significant intervention through introducing a new remedy in copyright law but claimed that it was only an elaboration of what already existed in precedent. This will be elaborated in Part Two.
8. The damages amounted to $188,000. At the time this was the largest sum ever awarded in an Australian copyright case.
9. How and why it is so popular remain as questions of ongoing interest.
10. Initially it was indigenous spokespeople and the legal discipline that took a special interest in indigenous intellectual property issues. This was followed later by anthropology, postcolonial studies, history, sociology, political science, archaeology, development studies, linguistics, philosophy and more recently science studies. The literature on the subject currently exceeds expectations. For space constraints it cannot be fully documented here. For a selection of writings initially produced in Australia and then becoming more international in scope see: W. Marika, 'Copyright on Aboriginal Art', (1976) 3 (1) *Aboriginal News* 7; R. Bell, 'Protection of Aboriginal Folklore: or Do they Dust Reports?', (1983) 17 *Aboriginal Law Bulletin* 5; J. Weiner, 'Protection of Folklore: A Political and Legal Challenge', (1987) 18 (1) *International Review of Industrial Property and Copyright Law* 56; K. Maddock, 'Copyright and Traditional Designs: An Aboriginal Dilemma', (1988) 34 *Aboriginal Law Bulletin* 8; V. Johnson, 'A Whiter Shade of Paleolithic: Aboriginal Art and Appropriation', (1988) 34 *Aboriginal Law Bulletin* 11; C. Golvan, 'Aboriginal Art and Copyright: The Case for Johnny Bulun Bulun', (1989) 10 *European Intellectual Property Review* 346; C. Golvan, 'Aboriginal Art and the Protection of Indigenous Cultural Rights', (1992) 7 *European Intellectual Property Review* 227; S. Harrison, 'Ritual as Intellectual Property', (1992) 27 *Man* 225; B. Sherman, 'From the Non-original to the Ab-original' in B. Sherman, and A. Strowel (eds), *Of Authors and Origins: Essays on Copyright Law*, Clarendon Press: Oxford UK, 1992; R. Gana Oekediji, 'Has Creativity Died in the Third World? Some Implications of the Internationalization of Intellectual Property', (1995) 24 (1) *Denver Journal of International Law and Policy* 109; C. Hawkins, 'Stopping the Rip-offs: Protecting Aboriginal and Torres Strait Islander Cultural Expression', (1995) 20 (1) *Alternative Law Bulletin* 7; C. Golvan, 'Court Provides Strong Protection for Aboriginal Artwork', (1995) 8 (1) *Australian Intellectual Property Law Bulletin* 6; H. Fourmile,

'Protecting Indigenous Intellectual Property Rights in Biodiversity', in *Ecopolitics IX – Conference Papers and Resolutions*, Northern Land Council: Casuarina, 1996; D. Posey, 'Indigenous Peoples and Traditional Resource Rights: A Basis for Equitable Relationships' in *Ecopolitics IX – Conference Papers and Resolutions*, Northern Land Council: Casuarina, 1996; D. Posey and G. Dutfield, *Beyond Intellectual Property*, International Development Research Centre: Ottowa, 1996; K. Wells, 'The Cosmic Irony of Intellectual Property and Indigenous Authenticity', (1996) 7 (3) *Culture and Policy* 45; F. Dawson, 'The Importance of Property Rights for Biodiversity Conservation in the Northern Territory', (1996) 3 (2) *The Australian Journal of Natural Resources Law and Policy* 179; C. Golvan, 'Aboriginal Art and Copyright Infringement' in L. Taylor and J. Altman (eds), *Marketing Aboriginal Art in the 1990s*, Aboriginal Studies Press: Canberra, 1996; M. Strathern, 'Potential Property: Intellectual Rights and Property in Persons', (1996) 4 (1) *Social Anthropology* 17; S. Brush, 'Whose Knowledge, Whose Genes, Whose Rights?' in S. Brush and D. Stabinsky (eds), *Valuing Local Knowledge: Indigenous Peoples and Intellectual Property Rights*, Island Press: Washington DC, 1996; M. Mansell, 'Barricading Our Last Frontier – Aboriginal Cultural and Intellectual Property Rights' in *Land Rights: Past Present and Future – Conference Papers*, Northern and Central Land Councils: Canberra, 1997; M. McMahon, 'The Intellectual Property Regime and the Protection of Indigenous Cultures' in *Land Rights: Past Present and Future – Conference Papers*, Northern and Central Land Councils: Canberra, 1997; M. Blakeney, 'Bioprospecting and the Protection of Traditional Medicinal Knowledge of Indigenous Peoples: An Australian Perspective', (1997) 19 (6) *European Intellectual Property Review* 298; S. Gray, 'Vampires around the Campfire', (1997) 22 (2) *Alternative Law Journal* 60; B. Ziff and P. Rao (eds), *Borrowed Power: Essays on Cultural Appropriation*, Rutgers University Press: New Jersey, 1997; M. McMahon, 'Indigenous Cultures, Copyright and the Digital Age', (1997) 3 (90) *Aboriginal Law Bulletin* 14; A. Barron, 'No Other Law? Author-ity, Property and Aboriginal Art' in L. Bently, and S. Maniatis (eds), *Perspectives on Intellectual Property Volume 4: Intellectual Property and Ethics*, Sweet and Maxwell: London UK, 1998; D.E. Long, 'The Impact of Foreign Investment on Indigenous Culture: An Intellectual Property Perspective', (1998) 23 *North Carolina Journal of International Law and Competition Regulation,* 229; M. Brown, 'Can Culture be Copyrighted?', (1998) 39 (2) *Current Anthropology* 193; R. Coombe, *The Cultural Life of Intellectual Properties: Authorship, Appropriation and the Law*, Duke University Press: Durham NC, 1998; K. Aoki, 'Neocolonialism, Anticommons Property and Biopiracy in the (Not-So-Brave) New World Order of International Intellectual Property Protection', (1998) 6 *Indiana Journal of Global Legal Studies* 11; M. Strathern, *Property, Substance and Effect: Anthropological Essays on Persons and Things*, Athlone Press: London UK, 1999; M. Sunder, 'Intellectual Property and Identity Politics: Playing with Fire', (2000) 4 (1) *Journal of Gender, Race and Justice* 69; M. Blakeney, 'The Protection of Traditional Knowledge under Intellectual Property Law', (2000) 6 *European Intellectual Property Review* 251; S. Kirsch, 'Environmental Disaster, 'Culture Loss' and the Law', (2001) 42 (2) *Current Anthropology* 167; V. Shiva, *Protect or Plunder? Understanding Intellectual Property Rights*, Zed Books: India, 2001; J. Gibson, 'Justice of Precedent, Justness of Equity: Equitable Protection and Remedies for Indigenous Intellectual Property', (2001) 6 (4) *Australian Indigenous Law Reporter*1; P. Drahos and R. Mayne (eds), *Global Intellectual Property Rights: Knowledge Access and Development*, Palgrave Macmillan: Hampshire UK, 2002; F.W. Grosheide and J.J. Brinkhof (eds), *Intellectual Property Law 2002: The Legal Protection of Cultural Expressions and Indigenous Knowledge*, Intersentia Publishers: Antwerp, Oxford, New York, 2002; S. Harrison, 'The Politics of Resemblance: Ethnicity, Trademarks: Head-Hunting', (2002) 8 *Journal of the Royal Anthropological Institute* 211; E. Hirsch, 'Malinowski's Intellectual Property', (2002) 18 (2) *Anthropology Today* 1; R. Sackville, 'Legal Protection of Indigenous Culture in Australia', (2003) 11 *Cardozo Journal of International and Comparative Law* 711; C. Hayden, *When Nature Goes Public: The Making and Unmaking of Bioprospecting in Mexico*, Princeton

University Press: Princeton, 2003; S. Greene, 'Indigenous People Incorporated? Culture as Politics, Culture as Property in Pharmaceutical Bio-prospecting', (2004) 45 (2) *Cultural Anthropology* 211; M. Brown, *Who Owns Native Culture?*, Harvard University Press: Cambridge MA, 2004; G. Nicholas and K. Bannister, 'Copyrighting the Past?', (2004) 45 (4) *Cultural Anthropology* 327; M. Mundy and A. Pottage, *Law, Anthropology and the Social*, Cambridge University Press: Cambridge UK, 2004; H. Geismar (2005), 'Copyright in Context: Carvings, Carvers and Commodities in Vanuatu', (2005) 32 (3) *American Ethnologist* 437; E. Coleman, *Aboriginal Art, Identity and Appropriation*, Ashgate Publishing: Aldershot UK, 2005; S.W. Bunting, 'Limitations of Australian Copyright Law in the Protection of Indigenous Music and Culture', (2000) 18 *Context: Journal of Music Research* 15; M. Strathern, *Kinship, Law and the Unexpected: Relatives are Always a Surprise*, University of Cambridge Press: Cambridge UK, 2005; J. Gibson, *Community Resources: Intellectual Property, International Trade and the Protection of Traditional Knowledge*, Ashgate Publishing: Aldershot UK, 2005.

11. For example, international lobby groups include the International Indian Treaty Council [www.treatycouncil.org]; Third World Network [www.twnside.org]; Intellectual Property Watch [www.ip-watch.org]; Africa Action [www.africaaction.org]. Also consider the increased funding by philanthropic organisations in the United States such as the Rockefeller Foundation and the Ford Foundation.
12. In this area the work of Rosemary Coombe has been the most prolific and widely cited. In particular see: 'The Properties of Culture and the Politics of Possessing Identity: Native Claims in the Cultural Appropriation Controversy', (1993) 6 (2) *Canadian Journal of Law and Jurisprudence* 249; 'Intellectual Property, Human Rights and Sovereignty: New Dilemmas in International Law Posed by the Recognition of Indigenous Knowledge and the Conservation of Biodiversity', (1998) 6 *Indiana Journal of Global Legal Studies* 59; 'The Recognition of Indigenous People's and Community Traditional Knowledge in International Law', (2001) 14 *St Thomas Law Review* 275; 'Fear, Hope and Longing for the Future of Authorship and a Revitalized Public Domain in Global Regimes of Intellectual Property', (2003) 52 *De Paul Law Review* 1171.
13. G. Delueze, *Difference and Repetition* (translated by P. Patton), Columbia University Press: New York, 1997.
14. These possibilities are usually articulated as policy and/or legislative reforms in national and international forums. For a discussion of the inter-penetration of strategies between the international and national see: J. Anderson, 'The Politics of Indigenous Knowledge: Australia's Proposed Communal Moral Rights Bill', (2004) 23 (4) *University of New South Wales Law Journal* 585; and J. Anderson, 'Chapter Nine – Globalising Indigenous Rights in Intellectual Property' in *The Production of Indigenous Knowledge in Intellectual Property Law*, PhD Dissertation, Law Faculty, University of New South Wales 2003.
15. I was frustrated by the apparent simplicity and similarity of the debates in Australia in the 1980s and 1990s. My initial interest in the repetition of utterances about the incommensurability of the law in regard to indigenous interests moved me to a space where I began considering how they had become an issue 'worthy' of substantial debate and discussion in legal academic circles.
16. In particular, research that reflected upon postcolonial politics pointed to the significant relationships between power and legal authority within colonial states and hence problems of appropriation and the making of legal categories. For example see: N. Dirks, G. Eley and S. Ortner (eds), *Culture/Power/History: A Reader in Contemporary Social Theory*, Princeton University Press: New Jersey, 1994; B. Ziff, and P. Rao (eds), *Borrowed Power: Essays on Cultural Appropriation*, Princeton University Press: New Jersey, 1997; R. Gana Okediji, 'The International Relations of Intellectual Property: Narratives of Developing Country Participation in the Global Intellectual Property System', (2003) 7 *Singapore Journal of International & Comparative Law* 315.
17. Over the last two years, I have been involved in a significant intellectual property project in Indonesia. The first part of the project in 2004 was conducted through the Social Science Research Council and the Ford Foundation. The second and third part of the

project was conducted between the Ford Foundation and American University. For an initial summary of the project see: www.ssrc.org. The final report, 'Intellectual Property and Traditional Arts in Indonesia' will be released in 2008.

18. On March 24 2005, the Aboriginal and Torres Strait Islander Commission (ATSIC) was abolished. *The Aboriginal and Torres Strait Islander Commission Amendment Act* 2005 was passed through the Australian parliament. ATSIC (1990–2005) was the elected indigenous body through which Aboriginal and Torres Strait Islander people were formally involved in the processes of government affecting their lives. See:, 'Extraordinary Forum: The Future of Australian Indigenous Governance', (2004) 8 (4) *Indigenous Law Reporter*; L. Strelein, J. Anderson and S. Bradfield, *Submission to the Senate Select Committee on the Administration of Indigenous Affairs by the Australian Institute of Aboriginal and Torres Strait Islander Studies*, 2004.
19. There are clear traces of romanticism in how legal academics have discussed indigenous people and culture in relation to intellectual property law. This predominately relates to presumptions of indigenous sameness and homogeneity, relationships to nature and communal existence.
20. There are very few histories that show the unique development of intellectual property law in colonial contexts. For an exception see L. Bently, 'Copyright and the Victorian Internet: Telegraphic Property Laws in Colonial Australia', (2004) 38 *Loyola Los Angeles Law Review* 71. For a discussion of this absence see: J. Anderson and K. Bowrey, 'The Imaginary Politics of Access to Knowledge: Whose Cultural Agendas are Being Advanced?', Conference Paper, *Con/Texts of Invention Conference* Case Western Reserve University, 20–22 April 2006.
21. See: J. Anderson, *Intellectual Property and Indigenous Knowledge: Access, Ownership and Control of Cultural Materials – Final Report*, Australian Institute of Aboriginal and Torres Strait Islander Studies: Canberra, 2006.
22. This argument will be extended throughout the book and is made in reference to insights on the workings of discourse, power, authority and governance provided by Michel Foucault in his work 'On Governmentality' in G. Burchell, C. Gordon and P. Miller (eds), *The Foucault Effect: Studies in Governmentality*, The University of Chicago Press: Chicago, 1991. While Foucault's interlocutors are many, I restrict myself here to those who have been fundamental in setting possible trajectories for work on issues of governmental rationality. These include Colin Gordon, Nikolas Rose, Peter Millar, Barry Hindess, Mitchell Dean, Pasqualle Pasquino, Francois Ewald, Jacques Donzelot, Ian Hunter and Pat O'Malley.
23. Michael Brown's work is representative of this approach to intellectual property law. See M. Brown, *Who Owns Native Culture?*, Harvard University Press: Cambridge MA, 2004.
24. See K. Bowrey (1994), 'Don't Fence Me In: The Many Histories of Copyright', Doctor of Juridical Studies, University of Sydney, 1994 and K. Bowrey, 'Who's Writing Copyright's History?', (1996) 18 (6) *European Intellectual Property Review* 322; B. Sherman, and L. Bently, *The Making of Modern Intellectual Property: The British Experience 1760–1911*, Cambridge University Press: Cambridge UK, 1999.
25. For a recent exploration of the dynamics of the eighteenth century copyright regime see R. Deazley, *On the Origin of the Right to Copy: Charting the Movement of Copyright Law in Eighteenth Century Britain (1695–1775)*, Hart Publishing: Oxford and Portland, 2004. For earlier influential discussions see: M. Woodmansee, 'The Genius and the Copyright: Economic and Legal Conditions of the Emergence of the Author', (1984) 17 *Eighteenth Century Studies* 425; M. Rose, 'The Author as Proprietor: *Donaldson v. Becket* and the Genealogy of Modern Authorship' in B. Sherman and A. Strowel (eds), *Of Authors and Origins: Essays on Copyright Law*, Clarendon Press: Oxford UK, 1994; M. Rose, *Authors and Owners: The Invention of Copyright*, Harvard University Press Cambridge MA, 1993.
26. It is worth considering the mirroring of problems that intellectual property law has with identifying the 'property' and managing relationships in the new digital communications and technology environment.

27. Following Sherwin, this would constitute a moment when law goes 'pop' – where we find new opportunities to expand the ways in which we think and talk about law. See R. Sherwin, *When Law Goes Pop: The Vanishing Line Between Law and Popular Culture*, The University of Chicago Press: Chicago, 2000.
28. A. Agrawal, 'Indigenous Knowledge and the Politics of Classification', (2002) 54 (173) *International Social Science Journal* 287 at 293.
29. Native title is the most recent legislative reform that has placed demands on Aboriginal and Torres Strait Islander people in terms of conforming to relatively fixed self and group identification frameworks in Australia. See the *Native Title Act* 1993 (Cth), and the *Native Title Amendment Act* 1998 (Cth). For discussion of the effects and ongoing challenges of presuming stable categories as identity markers within law see: E. Povinelli, *The Cunning of Recognition: Indigenous Alterities and the Making of Australian Multiculturalism*, Duke University Press: Durham NC, 2002; G. Edmond, 'Thick Decisions: expertise, advocacy and reasonableness in the Federal Court of Australia', (2004) 74 (3) *Oceania* 190.
30. Eric Michaels notes, 'Colonial Australian administration has always refused to recognize that there is no-one Aboriginal culture but hundreds of them, as there are hundreds of distinct languages, all insistently autonomous. Local political systems promoted no 'leader' to be taken to, a problem that apparently stymied Captain Cook and has plagued 200 years of subsequent race relations. The overarching class 'Aboriginal' is a wholly European fantasy, a class that comes into existence as a consequence of colonial domination and not before (although Aborigines will make concessions to this fantasy seeing possibilities thereby for political and economic power).' E. Michaels, *Bad Aboriginal Art: Tradition, Media and Technological Horizons*, Allen and Unwin: Sydney, 1994 at 150. For a further elaboration on the implications of these continuing constructions of Aboriginality and 'tradition' in the Access to Knowledge/Public Domain political legal movements see: J. Anderson and K. Bowrey, 'The Imaginary Politics of Access to Knowledge: Whose Cultural Agendas are Being Advanced?', supra n.20 and A. Chander and M. Sunder, 'The Romance of the Public Domain', (2004) 92 *California Law Review* 1331.
31. M. Langton, 'Aboriginal Art and Film: The Politics of Representation', (2005) 6 *Rouge*.
32. See: A. Haebich, *Broken Circles: Fragmenting Indigenous Families 1800–2000*, Fremantle Arts Centre Press: Fremantle, 2000 and N. Dirks, *Castes of Mind: Colonialism and the Making of Modern India*, Princeton University Press: New Jersey, 2001.
33. See: P. Nadasdy, *Hunters and Bureaucrats: Power, Knowledge and Aboriginal State Relations in the Southwest Yukon*, University of British Columbia Press: Vancouver, 2003.
34. A. Agrawal, 'Dismantling the Divide Between Indigenous and Scientific Knowledge', (1995) 26 *Development and Change* 413. For another version of this article see: 'Indigenous and Scientific Knowledge: Some Critical Comments', (1995) 3 (3) *Indigenous Knowledge and Development Monitor*, which generated varying and considered responses. For my purposes I will be referencing the initial citation above.
35. The *Indigenous Knowledge and Development Monitor* provided a strategic place to voice Agrawal's argument, as it also functions as a journal exploring the potential articulations of indigenous knowledge within a 'development' discourse.
36. A. Agrawal, 'Dismantling the Divide Between Indigenous and Scientific Knowledge' n.34 at 414.
37. See also: R. Drayton, *Nature's Government: Science, Imperial Britain and the Improvement of the World*, Yale University Press: New Haven, 2000; D.W. Chambers, and R. Gillespie, 'Locality in the History of Science: Colonial Science, Technoscience and Indigenous Knowledge', (2000) 15 *Osiris* 221; 'Focus: Colonial Science', (2005) 96 (1) *Isis*. As a key early text influencing these debates see: B. Cohn, *Colonialism and its Forms of Knowledge: The British in India*, Princeton University Press: New Jersey, 1996.
38. A. Agrawal, n.34, at 422.

39. For a good discussion regarding the problem of knowledge, culture and property from a Nietzschean perspective see T. Flessas, 'Aphorisms, Objects and Culture' in P. Goodrich and M. Valverde, *Nietzsche and Legal Theory: Half-Written Laws*, Routledge Press: New York, 2005.
40. See: J. Rappaport, *Intercultural Utopias: Public Intellectuals, Cultural Experimentation, and Ethnic Pluralism in Columbia*, Duke University Press: Durham NC, 2005.
41. M. Nakata, 'Indigenous Knowledge and the Cultural Interface: Underlying Issues at the Intersection of Knowledge and Information Systems', (2002) 28 *International Federation of Libraries Association Journal* 281.
42. Nakata notes that these interests include 'fields of ecology, soil science, veterinary medicine, forestry, human health, aquatic resource management, botany, zoology, agronomy, agricultural economics, rural sociology, mathematics, management science, agricultural education and extension, fisheries, range management, information science, wildlife management, and water resource management.' Ibid., at 282.
43. Ibid., at 282.
44. A. Agrawal, n.34 at 292.
45. Understanding what knowledge is and how we recognise it and convey it has been a pre-occupation of western philosophy. See for instance the work of Scottish Enlightenment thinker David Hume.
46. M. Nakata, n.41 at 283.
47. In this context also consider the increased calls for new documentary practices such as inventories and lists of indigenous knowledge. Such documentary practices extend the field of intellectual property intervention, as they automatically engage with regimes of copyright and raise further questions of ownership, the extent of protection and access.
48. This will be explored in more depth in Part Three.
49. This will be expanded in Part One.
50. World Intellectual Property Organisation, *Intellectual Property Needs and Expectations of Traditional Knowledge Holders: WIPO Report on Fact-finding Missions on Intellectual Property and Traditional Knowledge (1998–1999)*, Geneva, Switzerland, 2001.
51. Ibid., at 26.
52. Shelley Wright has argued that part of the problem for the law in recognising indigenous demands can be understood by what is perceived to be the 'untrustworthy' nature of indigenous knowledge: 'The real problem is that indigenous peoples are not seen to as trustworthy guardians of wisdom because they are so different in European eyes . . . it is illustrative of the relationship between European literate cultures and the oral cultures of colonised peoples. . . Speech is usually seen as less trustworthy than written evidence; experience to be valuable must be recorded; history does not become "history" until human narrative is transformed from oral mythology into written "fact" and lived experience is transformed into detached experience that can be objectively analysed.' S. Wright, *Becoming Human: International Human Rights, Decolonisation and Globalisation*, Routledge: New York, 2001 at 106–107.
53. The problem that this generates is the subject of Part Three.
54. D. Ivison, P. Patton and W. Sanders, 'Introduction' in D. Ivison, P. Patton and W. Sanders (eds), *Political Theory and the Rights of Indigenous Peoples*, Cambridge University Press: Cambridge, 2000 at 4.
55. Intellectual property law remains surprisingly impervious to the substantial critical literature on the invention of tradition. See: E. Hobsbawm and T. Ranger (eds), *The Invention of Tradition*, Cambridge University Press: Cambridge, 1992.
56. For a contemporary Australian example, consider the feature film *Ten Canoes* (2006) by Rolf de Heer and members of the Ramingining community in Northern Australia. In film also see *Atanarjuat (The Fast Runner)* (2001) by Iglook Isuma Productions – the first independent Inuit production company formed in 1990.
57. Peter Brosius has made the observation that the concept of 'tradition' and its emphatic equation with indigenous peoples is not exclusively the work of non-indigenous agencies and institutions. Indigenous people have also sought to use 'traditional' representations

to secure particular ends. Brosius uses the example of conservation campaigns as a key site to understand how 'traditional' is re-appropriated by indigenous people. In this way, power and resistance are seen as mutually engaged. See: P. Brosius, 'Anthropological Engagements with Environmentalism', (1999) 40 (3) *Current Anthropology* 277; and, P. Brosius, 'Green Dots, Pink Hearts: Displacing Politics from the Malaysian Rain Forest', (1999) 101 (1) *American Anthropologist* 36. See also T. Li, 'Articulating Indigenous Identity in Indonesia: Resource Politics and the Tribal Slot', (2000) 42 (1) *Comparative Studies in Society and History* 149.

58. See J. Beckett (ed), *Past and Present: The Construction of Aboriginality*, Aboriginal Studies Press: Canberra, 1988. More recently see: M. Dodson, 'The end in the beginning: re(de)finding Aboriginality', (1994) 1 *Australian Aboriginal Studies* 2; M. Langton, *'Well I heard it on the radio and saw it on the television. . .': an essay for the Australian Film Commission on the politics and aesthetics of filmmaking by and about Aboriginal people and things*, The Australian Film Commission, 1993. See also: M. Barcham, '(De) Constructing the Politics of Indigeneity' in D. Ivison, P. Patton and W. Sanders (eds), *Political Theory and the Rights of Indigenous Peoples* n.54.
59. This has been most explicitly played out in native title cases. In particular see the literature surrounding the emphasis on tradition in the Yorta Yorta case: *Members of the Yorta Yorta Community v State of Victoria* [1998] FCA 1606; *Members of the Yorta Yorta Community v State of Victoria* [2001] FCA 45 and *Members of the Yorta Yorta Community v State of Victoria* [2002] HCA 58. For example: V. Kerriush and C. Perrin, 'Awash in Colonialism', (1999) 24 (1) *Alternative Law Journal* 3; S. Young, 'The Trouble with 'Tradition': Native Title and the *Yorta Yorta* Decision', (2001) 30 (1) *The University of Western Australia Law Review* 28; J. Weiner, 'Diaspora, Materialism, Tradition: Anthropological Issues in the Recent High Court Appeal of the Yorta Yorta', (2002) 2 (18) *Land, Rights, Laws: Issues of Native Title* 1; L. Strelein, 'Members of the Yorta Yorta Aboriginal Community v Victoria [2002] HCA 58 – Comment', (2003) 2 (21) *Land, Rights, Laws: Issues of Native Title* 1; R. Bartlett, 'The Obsession with Traditional Laws and Customs Creates Difficulties Establishing Native Title Claims in the South', (2003) 31 (1) *The University of Western Australia Law Review* 35.
60. J. Anderson and K. Bowrey, n.33.
61. 'Paradoxically, however, the concepts of "traditional knowledge", "the public domain" and "cultural environmentalism" are now proving to be obstacles to understanding poor people's knowledge as intellectual property.' M. Sunder, 'The Invention of Traditional Knowledge', University of California Davis Legal Studies Research Paper Series, Paper 75, 2006.
62. For instance see: *Yumbulul v Reserve Bank of Australia & Others* (1991) 21 IPR 481; and, *Foster v Mountford & Rigby Ltd* (1977) 14 ALR 71.
63. 'Subject matter' is utilised in this work in order to be consistent with standard legal referencing in intellectual property law, specifically within copyright. I am nevertheless mindful of the problems of subject/object descriptors more generally.
64. I will be examining this problematic in Part One.
65. See: R. Coombe, 'The Properties of Culture and the Possession of Identity: Postcolonial Struggle and the Legal Imagination' in B. Ziff, and P.V. Rao (eds), *Borrowed Power: Essays on Cultural Appropriation*, Rutgers University Press: New Jersey, 1997.
66. See also: P. Drahos, *A Philosophy of Intellectual Property*, Dartmouth Press: Sydney, 1996 and, B. Bryan, 'Property as Ontology: On Aboriginal English Understandings of Ownership', (2000) 13 *Canadian Journal of Law and Jurisprudence* 3.
67. Identifying the unpredictability of governing strategies is a feature of governmentality literature. In particular it refers to the inevitable failure of programmes of government. As Peter Miller and Nicholas Rose explain, 'Programmes constitute a space within which the objectives of government are elaborated, and where plans to implement them are dreamed up. But the technologies which seek to operate on activities and processes produce their own difficulties, fail to function as intended.' P. Miller, and N. Rose, 'Governing Economic Life', (1990) 19 (1) *Economy and Society* 1 at 14. See also N. Rose and P. Miller, 'Political Power Beyond the State: Problematics of Government',

(1992) 43 (2) *British Journal of Sociology* 172; C. Gordon, 'Governmental Rationality: An Introduction' in G. Burchell, C. Gordon and P. Miller (eds), *The Foucault Effect: Studies in Governmentality*, The University of Chicago Press: Chicago, 1991; M. Dean, *Governmentality: Power and Rule in Modern Society*, Sage Publications: London, 1999; N. Rose, *Powers of Freedom: Reframing Political Thought*, Cambridge University Press: Cambrige, 1999.

68. For instance, the requirements of originality and questions of authorship have pre-occupied many writers in this area.

PART I

Law

Introduction

> Viewing law as the mutual interpenetration of the formal legal system and daily life invites us to consider the interaction of the legal and the non-legal as sources of both self-conscious and unself-conscious action.[1]

In all the writing that has been produced about indigenous interests in intellectual property law there is a notable absence. This absence is of a jurisprudential and critical reading of the history and development of intellectual property law as a specific cultural form, one integrally involved in managing relationships around knowledge use and circulation. This absence explains why intellectual property is repetitively understood and interpreted as a relatively naturally occurring and stable area of law. This, of course, is not so. Intellectual property is historical, political and contested, and this is ultimately what makes for its messiness in dealing with particular issues when they arise. This messiness within IP law is consistent regardless of whether the concern raised is one of regulating emerging digital technologies or protecting indigenous knowledge. Understanding the history fundamentally alters how we interpret what is going on when indigenous knowledge enters an intellectual property discourse. Thus, in responding to an urgent need for a little history work, this first part of the book will reflect on the making of intellectual property law.

When it comes to indigenous interests in intellectual property law, it is readily assumed that the problem is with the law. For example, that it doesn't protect collective interests, doesn't recognise the legitimacy of oral cultures, and can't accommodate alternate views of property and ownership. These perspectives seek to locate the particular places where law fails and lets indigenous people down. I want to move beyond these particular readings of law's inadequacies and instead explore them as necessary and inevitable instances that reveal the complex relationships and embedded networks functioning within law. In this sense, and following James Boyd White, law should be understood as a 'social and cultural activity, as something we do with our minds, with language and with each other'.[2] Law is not some abstract bounded entity. Rather, it is fluid and dynamic. When faced with new kinds of claims, like indigenous interests in intellectual property, critical legal scholars and cultural theorists are provided with an opportunity to understand the intricate operations of law. Importantly, in these contested instances it is possible to uncover the extent that law has also been intrinsically involved in making, and effecting relations between, the very problems that are generating new claims to law and requiring legal attention and remedy.

This first part of the book 'Law' will be divided into three separate chapters. The first chapter sketches out a framework for understanding law – not as a body of rules but as a network of interpretation and operation that influences and conversely, is influenced by, individual, social, cultural, political and economic dimensions. Here the focus is on problems of jurisprudence and the contingency of law, where rather than a unitary phenomenon, law, legal institutions and legal power are shown as deeply imbued within, and dependent upon, networks of political and social influence. Thinking through law in relation to society and individuals focuses attention on how law is informed and constituted by cultural production, where law is simultaneously an object and subject of culture. The example that will be used to illustrate the cultural forms that law takes will be drawn from the socially and legally developed concepts and expectations of property. This is important for understanding the historical and philosophical relationships between 'real' property law and intellectual property law, and the way in which indigenous claims to intellectual property challenge legal categories of identification of property rights, and simultaneously endorse them.

After establishing that law is not above or beyond politics and social influence, the second chapter will move to an examination of a specific instance of law's development: the making of modern intellectual property law. This section will consider the disparate and inconsistent history and philosophy of intellectual property. In particular it will highlight how what appears as a distinct field of law is actually a relatively recent phenomenon. In order to appreciate the general operation of intellectual property law on knowledge and knowledge 'objects', and more specifically, how this impacts upon how issues of indigenous knowledge are identified and treated, this history matters considerably. As will become clearer at later stages of the book, this kind of jurisprudential reading of intellectual property's history opens the space of interpretation and reframes the struggles around indigenous knowledge protection as ones that are also internal to the development of intellectual property law as a whole.

Destabilising the narrative of intellectual property as a cohesive unit provides the context for the final chapter in this first part of the book. This chapter will constitute an examination of the creation of copyright as a sub-category of intellectual property law. As copyright is characterised by its influence from early enlightenment and romantic notions of possessive individualism, the chapter will explore the extent that these influences continue to underpin the two categories that identify legitimate copyright subject matter: authorship and originality. These categories function to maintain the limits and boundaries of copyright and as such it is at these points that the dilemma of including indigenous knowledge within this framework is most starkly exposed. In concluding with a consideration of the subjectivity of copyright, prompted through postmodern critiques, what is developed is an appreciation that the intersection of indigenous knowledge in intellectual property law is defined, and in response to, the characteristics of intellectual property law that include its complex history, its categories of measurement and the inevitable influence of political and economic discourses.

Overall, Part One argues that the difficulties facing intellectual property law in securing indigenous knowledge as a category that it can recognise, rather than being 'new' are actually part of a continuum. In this sense, law should be understood as working through an ongoing series of problems that it has been addressing for years. The past histories of intellectual property inform the present. The dominant problem set for intellectual property law – and this affects the inclusion of indigenous knowledge – is how law grants property status to intangible knowledge and how it 'identifies' the 'property' and the 'right'. In this sense it is argued that what many intellectual property laws share is this central problematic, manifested in various legal forms and practical negotiations of authorised identifications of property.

NOTES

1. F. Munger, 'Mapping Law and Society' in *Crossing Boundaries: Traditions and Transformations in Law and Society Research*, in A. Sarat, M. Constable, D. Engel, V. Hans, S. Lawrence (eds), Northwestern University Press, 1998 at 43.
2. J. Boyd White, *Heracles' Bow: Essays on the Rhetoric and Poetics of the Law*, University of Wisconsin Press: Wisconsin at x.

1. The cultural life of law

'Intellectual property' has become internationally recognised as a term covering a collection of intangible rights and causes of action developed by western nation states at various times to protect particular aspects of artistic and industrial output – copyright, designs, patents, trade secrets, passing off, aspects of competition law and trade marks. A description of, purpose for and scope of intellectual property law has been defined internationally through *The Convention Establishing the World Intellectual Property Organisation 1967* (WIPO).[1] In general, intellectual property laws seek to 'promote investment in, and access to, the results of creative effort, and extend to protecting the marketing of goods and services'.[2] As a signatory to the Convention, Australia promotes the protection of intellectual property in Australia and throughout the world through a variety of conventions and agreements. One reason for this is that intellectual property is increasingly an important mechanism of world trade.[3] Thus the regime of intellectual property law in Australia is in keeping with the definitions provided through the WIPO Convention and subsequent agreements made through this international body.[4]

With a direct relationship between intellectual property, economics and trade becoming more explicit critical evaluation of intellectual property and its history have emerged.[5] Critical interest has been facilitated in part by concern for new and emerging technologies and related practices, such as developments with digital technology and biotechnology.[6] Much of this commentary has involved an evaluation of the role of intellectual property laws in facilitating commodification and the development of new markets.[7] As part of the developing discourse, attention has also been directed to the implicit cultural elements (and hence cultural prejudices) of intellectual property law, wherein cultural products are increasingly circulating as commodities within networks of private property relations.[8]

Recently Peter Drahos (with Braithwaite) observed that, '[i]ntellectual property rights are, in essence, government tools for regulating markets in information'.[9] With the continuing global redefining of intellectual property standards and the animated trade bargaining pivoting around the Agreement on Trade Related Aspects of Intellectual Property Rights (TRIPs) a variety of publications by governments and non-government organisations (NGOs) echo concerns about the control over knowledge markets facilitated through intellectual property laws.[10] For example, in many 'developing' countries intellectual property is increasingly considered as a mechanism providing new techniques of control, authority and knowledge management in the post-colonial era. We are now located at a specific point in time when the field of intellectual property law is undergoing transformation both in circulation and exposure.[11] 'Intellectual property rights have gone global.'[12]

LAW AND THE SOCIAL

That intellectual property law has become a subject of discussion within so many diverse forums and by so many people with different levels of access to law and legal agency tells us something broader about law itself: that it occupies a myriad of social spaces. It is not restricted to law books, courtrooms, institutions or bureaucracies. It is instead something that we negotiate everyday. For 'legal meaning is found and invented in the variety of locations and practices that comprise culture, and that those locations and practices are themselves encapsulated, though always incompletely, in legal forms, regulations and symbols'.[13] Law, in all its functions, is deeply imbued in a social nexus, and it is this nexus that provides the law with fluidity and changeability. For intellectual property this means that it is informed and influenced by changing social and political movements as much as by new court based judgments and determinations.

This way of understanding law really emerged in the latter part of the twentieth century. Critical attention to problems of jurisprudence grew from dissatisfaction with understanding law as a regime of abstract rules.[14] This was because legal power was a much more dynamic process than an argument relying on abstract rules could accommodate. For example, the way in which these rules were interpreted played a significant role in how legal power was exerted, and upon whom. Further, as a focus on the circulations of legal meaning increased, it was clear that such meaning was not communicated in a one-directional way: that the direction changed depending on who was communicating, interpreting, and in which kinds of contexts. Indeed, much critical attention continues to explore key assumptions underpinning the authority of the legal discipline. For instance:

> in what sense law is objective (determinate, impersonal) and autonomous rather than political and personal; the meaning of legal justice; the appropriate and actual role of the judge; the role of discretion in judging; the origins of the law; the place of social science and moral philosophy in law; the role of tradition in law; the possibility of making law a science; whether law progresses; and the problematics of interpreting legal texts.[15]

Certainly, it was consideration of the relations between law and politics that provided the initial frame for an analysis of the indeterminacy of legal thought and legal outcomes. In this way a fundamental critique of law was directed against legal formalism and objectivism.[16] Critical reflection upon differences between 'law making and law application' exposed the extent of thought where formalism and objectivism were assumed in each process. In this context, formalism should be understood as a 'commitment to, and therefore a belief in the possibility of, a method of legal justification that contrasts with open ended disputes about the basic terms of social life . . . [t]his formalism holds impersonal purposes, policies and principles to be indispensable components of legal reasoning'.[17] In other words, it is only through a rational, undemonstrative and apolitical framework of analysis that legal dogma is possible. Objectivism insists on the authority of legal material – cases, statutes and accepted legal rationale – as they display 'always imperfectly, an intelligible moral order'.[18] What characterises legal formalism and objectivism is the presumption that it is possible for law to function in an abstract space beyond people and politics.

In particular, it was these two specific characteristics of law which came under increased scrutiny, for their inability to provide an accurate account of legal process and function.[19] The fuzzy boundaries between law, individuals and practice also heightened the necessity for reflection that made links between legal processes and their effects on social relationships. This critical work illustrated how law *never* functions above or beyond politics.[20] Both the 'law-in-context movement' and critical legal jurisprudence challenged the belief in the naturalness, efficiency and fairness of the structure of the legal profession. It revealed the hidden characteristics and political life of legal reasoning.

As well as arguing for a broader understanding of the contingency of law and highlighting the impossibility of objectivism, critical legal scholarship also questioned how it was then, that the legitimating and constitutive operation of law, on all levels of social and individual engagement, could be seen to be natural.[21] The progression of this line of inquiry revealed that underlying particular legal doctrines rested categories of legal analysis that distributed particular and subtle effects. In short, this meant that law, positioned within a political location, was partial, contingent and specific. Law responded to politics and politics enhanced the position of law, particularly in situated and localised centres of conflict. Critical legal theory unmasked the 'universalism' of traditional legal jurisprudence, rejecting the premise that law exists in a political and social vacuum.

However, this kind of legal thinking developed a critique of law that was difficult for mainstream jurisprudence and legal teaching to absorb.[22] Nonetheless, sympathetic to the broader general critique of law, dedicated readings of feminism and law,[23] race and law,[24] and law and discourse[25] endured, drawing upon political theories of feminism, critical race theory and postmodernism.[26] This new interdisciplinary scholarship has revealed contingencies and limits within the law that were previously undisclosed and hidden. Rethinking the construction of categories of law with regard to differing subjectivities has produced new and diverse ways of thinking about law, legal process and legal power that reflect upon the complexity of legal engagement within any social context. Through this thinking indigenous claims to self-determination and human rights have taken on a new resonance, displacing the mythology of modern law as autonomous, distinct, unified and internally coherent.[27] Understanding the complex and intricate relationships between law, power and authority is urgently required. This necessitates an appreciation of the ways in which law shapes and influences how people think and act, and conversely how different kinds of actions can influence the direction that law takes on a particular issue.

LAW AND INDIGENOUS PEOPLE

Critical attention to the subject positions that indigenous people occupy within the law (and within society) has been crucial for locating and identifying modes of historical injustice. It has also provided a context for understanding the amalgam ways through which law treats difference.[28] Indeed it is impossible to consider the position of indigenous people in relation to western law without also recognising the historical circumstances of colonisation to which indigenous people have been subjected. This includes the way in which legal precedent has established Anglo-Australian jurisdiction over indigenous people.[29] While arguments by indigenous people fundamentally question the legitimacy of the jurisdiction of Australian courts, inevitably leading to opposing sovereignty claims, the continuing over-representation of indigenous people in the criminal justice system, for example, reflects the power of legal apparatus to continue to exert its effects upon indigenous people.[30]

In Australia, the 1967 referendum where 'full' citizenship rights were established for Aboriginal and Torres Strait Islander people implied the 'application of the principle of equality before the law'.[31] This included dismantling the discriminatory legislation and policies directed towards indigenous people during the prolonged period of colonisation.[32] However, as Irene Watson and Chris Cuneen, amongst others, have argued, the colonial optic for viewing and managing indigenous people through the legal system has not changed very substantially.[33] The significant *Royal*

Commission into Aboriginal Deaths in Custody[34] highlighted the severe failings of the Australian legal system to respond to cultural differences and recognise the effects of colonial power structures on colonised people.[35]

The way in which indigenous people have been constructed and produced before the Anglo-Australian legal system is a product of social and political influence in which the law has been integrally engaged.[36] This itself draws attention to the extent that politics is embedded within the law: that it does not function in an isolated sphere. The recent push to recognise the 'special' circumstances under which indigenous subjects enter the legal discourse has prompted consideration of the extent to which law can accommodate difference. For example, the recent exploration by the Western Australian government on potential ways of incorporating customary law is illustrative of the ways in which indigenous difference (as custom/culture) is treated.[37] Here indigenous culture is deployed in the law as a problematic – there is a real question about the accommodation of difference in law, for instance that indigenous people can make for differing legal subjectivities.

The tension for law is that indigenous people can also make for similar legal subjects owing to changing cultural experience, circumstance and relations. The problem is that indigenous differences in relation to certain kinds of law can be localised and particular – it is not always possible to generalise from local to broader national Aboriginal contexts. For example, with the overturning of the doctrine of *terra nullius* through the *Mabo* decision in 1992, new dilemmas in accommodating indigenous difference have arisen. Specifically these are in terms of recognising indigenous proprietary rights to land. As the Australian High Court found that such rights continued to exist after colonisation and British sovereignty,[38] questions of land ownership, native title and the presumption of generic land 'ownership' initially formed the frontier for illustrating how law treats difference presented through indigenous legal subjects.[39]

At this point it is useful to move to an examination of how individual and group claims to 'real' property have provided a platform that challenge (once revered) legal frameworks. Property provides a vantage point to consider a number of intersecting elements including the traditions of western philosophy of property and rights in property; legal frameworks through which social relations between people are engaged; and, how different indigenous perceptions of property disrupt traditional western jurisprudence.

The consideration of how such difference is treated in 'real' property terms is crucial to developing an appreciation of the implications in intellectual property. It is worth remembering that the ways in which 'real' property justifies a right in property differs considerably to that in intellectual property.[40] However, a conception of property, here understood as a principle of social organisation, was intrinsic to some of the emergent arguments justifying intellectual property.[41] The real value in understanding the concept of property and its subsequent deployment is not only to demonstrate how law accommodates differing indigenous conceptualisations of property rights, but as will be the focus on the following chapter, how law works simultaneously to extend and enhance its own categories and boundaries of identification and classification.

WHY 'REAL' PROPERTY MATTERS

> Property is nothing but a basis of expectation: the expectation of deriving certain advantages from a thing which we are said to possess, in consequence of the relation in which we stand towards it. There is no image, no painting, no visible trait, which can express the relation that constitutes property. It is not material, it is metaphysical, it is a mere conception of the mind.[42]

The language of property underpins the way that indigenous knowledge and expression have come to be positioned within the law. This is not only in regard to 'intellectual' property but follows a trajectory set first by land rights and subsequently followed by claims to the ownership material cultural products.[43] Discussions that pinpoint notions of cultural 'ownership' and 'theft' denote exclusive relations of private property. For my purposes here, it is certainly a significant moment when social issues are positioned for remedy through legal means, and raises questions about the influence of the law in managing particular sites of discontinuity, for instance indigenous property rights.[44] At the same time it also makes for challenging legal positions.

It could be argued that western law is preoccupied with property rights and their protection.[45] Importantly in Australia, *Mabo* (1992) addressed in part, the injustice of colonisation (expropriating property) and the historical legal denial of indigenous customary rights. It is significant that this political watershed was achieved through a case specifically centred on property. For the indigenous claimants, western property law, or 'real' property, provided a vehicle to argue for a set of rights, one of which could be understood because of the familiar phrasing of the claim through this legal jurisdiction – ownership of land.[46] Together, the politics of law and the justice claims made to the law, expressed in terms of expectation following Bentham, create a tension in dealing with indigenous property. For indigenous property is not confined to a claim restricted by real property law but incorporates other categories of law such as intellectual property.[47]

Both modern 'real' property law and intellectual property law developed significantly in the eighteenth and nineteenth centuries.[48] Yet, both bodies of law experienced profound difficulties in securing agreement on foundations and principles, despite various statutory reforms. Challenged in terms of addressing their own cultural specificity and history, it is unsurprising that both fields of law are stretched by indigenous 'real property' and 'intellectual property' claims. In both spheres, western notions of property have come under increased scrutiny. Property is 'an expression of social relationships because it organises people with respect to each other and their material environment'.[49]

The power of property is that it resides simultaneously within the law and outside it. It is both a legal and social trope. Where indigenous people have adopted the property discourse to challenge precepts of *terra nullius*, for example, property demarcates competing political interests: for example in the instance of the *Mabo* case between the Murray Islanders and the Australian Commonwealth Government. It also points to the ways in which, inescapably, property mediates the world in which people interact and the possible relationships between individuals and communities as well as legal and governmental institutions. Arguably, property is an essential organising principle around which liberal ideals of ownership and possession are circulated and authorised. Law is an important vehicle in distributing and circulating perceptions of property relations within social, political and economic networks, but as property theory illustrates, law remains unclear about what property is or means.

The concept of property has evolved over time. However the modern political conception of property owes a considerable debt to John Locke and it is therefore important to sketch briefly his approach to property.[50] Locke's thinking on property was instrumental in shaping how successors such as Blackstone,[51] Bentham,[52] Hohfeld[53] and Reich[54] reinterpreted and reinscribed concepts that have become central tenets in modern liberal political contexts.

John Locke's labour theory justified private property in a unique and somewhat oblique way which explains the subsequent contrary interpretations of his theory of natural rights.[55] Locke's concern with property is identified as existing in *Two Treatises of Government*.[56] The explanatory passage in 'Of Property' commonly cited to clearly locate this position is:

> Though the Earth, and all inferior Creatures be Common to all Men, yet every Man has a *Property* of his own *Person*. This nobody has any right to but himself. The *Labour* of his body and the *Work* of his hands, we may say are properly his. Whatsoever then he removes out of the State that Nature hath provided, and left it in, he hath mixed his *Labour* with, and joyned to it something that is his own and thereby makes it his *Property*.[57]

Locke's justification of private property rests upon three key principles that can be elicited from this passage. Firstly, that 'every Man has a *Property* of his *Person*', and that '*Labour* of his body and *Work* of his hands' are therefore part of this property of the person. Secondly, mixing individual labour with the state of nature, produces something new which will be a person's property. Thirdly, it is labour that adds the value to land (the common state of nature), making it worth something, rather than nothing; as Locke asserts 'for it is labour indeed that puts the difference of value on everything'.[58] The key factor in this argument is that man's labour is an exertion of action exercised upon an object or thing previously inactive, for example while fruit grows it has to be picked and therefore labour exerted to become the property of the picker. Labour must be used to cultivate, extract and to make value out of something that would otherwise be worthless. Locke's natural rights theory assumes the inherent action of human endeavour which is juxtaposed to the contexts of the inactive state of nature: 'commons' provided by God for the use of 'Man'. Further, as property is thus imbued with the qualities of a natural right, it does not emanate from social relations but exists 'prior to the social order'.[59]

Notably, Locke's conception of natural rights requires a specific interpretation of 'labour' and the definition of the labourer entitled to property. There is an implicit hierarchy within Locke's natural rights theory – not only relating to who is a legitimate 'person' but also what the act of labour and cultivation entails. Cultivation is closely wedded to notions of civilisation, the presumption being that labour 'improves' the land and enables progress to be sustained. This presumption as well as those about the inferiority of certain kinds of people are demonstrated most aptly later in his account where Locke makes the distinction between labour and cultivation and the wastelands of America untilled (in the European sense) by the Indians: the logic extends via the implication that there is no property held by the Native Americans in America because there has been no labour exerted to cultivate and improve the land, especially given that: 'Nature [has] furnished as liberally as any other peoples with the material of plenty'.[60]

It can, however, be misleading only to consider this brief part of Locke's work to understand his natural rights theory of property.[61] For Locke's theory of property was also positioned within a larger discourse about government – in the justification of the English Revolution of 1688 and to invalidate the doctrine of absolute monarchy presented by Robert Filmer in *Patriarcha: or The Natural Order of Kings* (1680).[62] That such selective readings from Locke's work have been so influential is curious – even more so if we then consider how Locke's natural rights theory has also been used to authorise property in intellectual property, a connection that Locke himself never made as he did not support a perpetual right of authors in a work.[63]

Whilst Lockean labour theory is discussed in some accounts of intellectual property law,[64] other prominent histories trace no such derivations.[65] The absence is interesting considering that a justification for modern intellectual property law, argued initially in the context of the English literary property debates of the eighteenth century, is that all authors have a natural pre-existing (and perpetual) private property right to the text because of the labour exerted. The position of 'labour' to justify property in abstract objects is significant but raises the question of boundaries, '[l]abour creates the property right, but what identifies the object of that property right?'.[66]

It was William Blackstone, an English common law theorist in the eighteenth century, that adapted and modified Locke's position on rights and labour in the particular context of the literary property debates of that same period. To this end, Blackstone pioneered a natural rights approach to ideas and knowledge, arguing the common law right to literary property arose through the natural labour exerted in the production of the expression. As Deazley notes, 'Blackstone was clearly influenced by Locke's second treatise on government, but had obviously failed to acquaint himself with Locke's personal views as to what property did exist in books'.[67] Whilst Locke did not support a perpetual common law right in an expression because of the unlikely 'essential representation of an identity in a work' nevertheless, in intellectual property circles Blackstone's interpretation has become synonymous with Locke's position and emphasises the rationality beginning to be utilised for the identification of property relationships.[68]

Nevertheless, by the end of the following century, Blackstone's conception of property originally equating to absolute dominion over things, was replaced by a newly defined form of property. The features that characterised this new form of property were that it had been dephysicalised, consisting not of rights over things but of any valuable right.[69] Value thus became the key to identifications of property, serving both the tangible realm of property and intangible property. Value, although relying on arbitrary judgement, linked formulations of property and secured judicial autonomy. Importantly measuring value was increasingly tied to the market and this meant that new forms of property could be constituted and protected.[70]

Whilst Blackstone embraced and reinterpreted Locke's account of natural rights theory and its justification for property, intermingling it with common law theories of entitlements, Jeremy Bentham, as Blackstone's predecessor, rejected natural law and natural rights. Subsequently Bentham's influence in dismissing any claim to 'naturally' occurring rights in law, resonate from considerations of the relationship, generated by property, as being between persons, rather than between a person and a thing. However, whilst scorning natural rights and claiming to have replaced them with utility (or the greatest happiness of the greatest number), Bentham still rested the property right on labour. Bentham presents a case that relations of property are constitutive of social relations. Property then is not a pre-existing concept of law rather it is a socially constructed concept embodying questions of power and social relations. Thus property is not objectively definable or identifiable.[71]

Law provides the frameworks whereby an expectation of property is constructed and disseminated. In this sense, while property is a medium for social organisation, it is nevertheless regulated through legal parameters which govern that expectation. Bentham's position that 'property is nothing but an expectation' is significant precisely because expectation is fundamentally developed through human relations. It is not a pre-existing concept. What is integral to expectation is the extent to which such anticipation has been generated. The grounds for expectation need to be first established so that there is a sense of probability. This makes claims of entitlement possible. Expectation arises because of changing systems of value and the political circumstances for the voicing of rights claims. But expectation is also positioned within a field where it is legitimate to have expectation to begin with, that there is some form of precedent for such expectation to be recognised. If property is nothing more than expectation, then this is contingent upon the legal avenues that produce and uphold this 'expectation'. Expectation then can be shaped and sculpted so that what is expected is not beyond delivery.

Bentham's interpretation of property makes a different linkage between real property and intangible property possible to that assumed by Blackstone. Rather than treat the expression of ideas – the book (literary property) – as a kind of pre-occupied land, Bentham's approach obliterates the physicality of property altogether, relocating the gaze to the classificatory distinctions and boundaries produced by law itself. Law produces the legal subject/object. This is later understood by Charles Reich to also involve ceding an authority of the marketplace, to the extent that the law itself practically engages 'expectation'.[72]

The economic transformation of property is an equally important element of contemporary social relations especially in its capacity to generate new forms of expectation. Thus property relations become imbued with an intent to generate revenue, where governmental influences readily demarcate political domains of interaction. The economic utility of property generates new forms of expectation that law inevitably regulates.[73]

Changing interpretations of value inform property relations and influence how law identifies a distinction between exclusive possession and economic value.[74] Kevin Gray has argued that seeing property as generating a power relationship significantly increases the range of interests wherein property can be claimed.[75] As the limits on property are not fixed, judicial processes, for example through the courts and in the making of legislation, have the power to 'create property'.[76] The direct implication for intellectual property, at least, is that if there are no natural limits, and the politics of determining the boundaries of property are acknowledged, how can indigenous claims be denied?

Indigenous claims that directly target legal frameworks and institutions of law are made because an expectation has been developed that the law can recognise and respond to indigenous people's claims to property, both tangible and intangible.[77] Indigenous claims to cultural property evoke an expectation, not only in recognising a proprietary right, but also on the level of expecting justice. The politics of recognition here also illustrate how certain kinds of claims resonate within law itself, forcing law to respond in new ways. The example is in the resulting production of indigenous knowledge as a distinct category within law. Thus the nature of the expectation is marked by the boundaries of law that can respond and deliver a legally recognisable 'property' right.

Noel Pearson, Aboriginal spokesperson in Australia and Team Leader of Cape York Partnerships in northern Queensland, has recognised the utility and possibility for action wherein legal frameworks can be adopted for purposeful strategies of recognition.[78] As he states, indigenous people 'need to be realistic about the following: first about the content and the nature of the tools which are available to us; second about what these tools can positively achieve. They are limited tools and to optimise results we must use them wisely and skillfully'.[79] Pearson indicates the possibility of utilising law as a strategic vehicle, through which indigenous interests might be advanced. Certainly then, re–imagining a concept of property so that it can be adapted to differing conceptions of ownership, and relations between people, is a necessary element in voicing an expectation of law. In this context, the expectation is for a guarantee of justice through equitable treatment in recognising the legitimate rights and interests indigenous people have in controlling culturally specific knowledges and products. This strategy contests the language of the law and the power of property within it.

The legal claims for (indigenous) property rights become a powerful vehicle in advancing indigenous self-determination claims. Claims for property ownership in intangible material raise an agenda and present an expectation for legal action. Indeed, the increasing indigenous claims to intellectual property frameworks within national and international contexts, speaks to the power of the broader intellectual property discourse. Intellectual property has provided a platform to which other indigenous issues can be attached and made more visible. In harnessing intellectual property as a powerful regime crucial to the function of liberalism, capital flow and modern trade relations, indigenous claims strategically demand legal attention and response.

Despite this optimism, there is a legitimate point to critical work that reveals how phrasing indigenous interests in knowledge protection and control within an intellectual property discourse necessarily reduces indigenous concepts of ownership and property to a western framework at the expense of a more nuanced understanding of historical and contemporary pressures and contexts. For example Michael Dodson has argued that;

> Certainly neither the Copyright Act, nor any other acts are able to provide for the complexities and subtleties of the ownership of indigenous art. The roles and obligations of our artists, the relationships between the artist as an individual and as a member of the society in which he or she works finds little accommodation within the existing legal framework.[80]

In a similar way, Michael Blakeney has argued that;

> Indeed a major problem, which has been identified in analysing traditional knowledge and cultural expression in conventional intellectual property terms is the observation that 'indigenous people do not view their heritage in terms of property at all. . .but in terms of community and individual responsibility'.[81]

Both Dodson and Blakeney emphasise how the existing legislative framework, in particular that of property, fails to take account of the diversity of positions held by indigenous people in relation to expressions of intangible cultural material.[82] Both suggest that a property discourse reduces indigenous concepts and community values. In reflecting upon these difficulties, Valerie Kerruish has observed that;

> Private property within a historical and cultural context that transforms such property, at the level of normative discourse into rights of persons (moral subjects, citizens) is a mode of social organisation which has exhausted its emancipatory potential.[83]

Kerruish's point is that it is capital that protects its power as property at all costs, therefore there can be no emancipatory power for the poor. But the conflict in the context of indigenous intellectual property is of a different nature. There is not a direct confrontation with capital versus labour. In fact it is the potential of indigenous cultural expressions as capital that encourages the law to engage with the subject. This links back precisely to Pearson's point that there is emancipatory potential within the law, because there is nowhere else to go: the law can provide realistic expectations of what is possible, and not in a disciplinary arena of pre-ordained values imposed on indigenous people. The opportunity to expose the limits of the law comes from within law itself.

When indigenous people make the claim that intellectual property laws should protect their cultural integrity and cultural expressions, the challenge has been set for the law in a familiar framework. For law moderates difference when presented through the guise of its own categories and frameworks. Nevertheless, the irony remains that it is because indigenous interests were not seen as property proper, that this new appeal to property can be made. Other pressures, such as political influence and individual advocacy, also force changes in recognition and hence in the scope of the law. To change the terms of the debate necessitates initially beginning on these terms. The assumption that indigenous people are unable or unwilling to employ such strategic engagement misunderstands the ways by which multiple resistances to circulations of power can be or are imagined and enacted by individuals as well as generating new kinds of political impetus. As Michel de Certeau has argued, it is possible to subvert dominant representations and laws, 'not by rejecting or altering them, but by using them with respect to the ends and references foreign to the system. . .'.[84] de Certeau's point is that it is possible to deflect the power of the dominant social order, and I would add, that in this current context even the phrase, 'indigenous intellectual property', illustrates the particular kinds of deflection of property as power at play.

The primacy of law and legal frameworks in mediating certain kinds of political struggles is of fundamental interest here. In the context of property, law functions as a location where challenging positions are circulated. This is not only in regard to competing sovereignty claims but also contested value systems and intellectual traditions regarding knowledge use, management, access and circulation. It seems at least in intellectual property, incommensurable differences in knowledge production, ownership and protection are the familiar arguments that constitute the circularity of contemporary debate. However, if we keep in mind the complex relationship of dependency between knowledge and power, what is revealed is how the new subject of 'indigenous intellectual property', once created, starts to produce its own frameworks of understanding and regimes of truth. Further, these are not only the apparatus of the coloniser, but also tools adopted and modified by indigenous people and consequently a feature of indigenous governance. For whilst 'property' and 'ownership' might not fully encompass indigenous aspirations and perceptions, they do provide an easily recognised and accepted terminology through which indigenous interests can be elevated.

So, whilst law reduces (cultural) differences so that they are barely noticeable, at the same time it also relies upon them to understand the differing demands brought for legal interpretation, mediation and importantly, remedy. This is part of the necessarily cultural functions of law. While law rejects difference presented to it in a radical way, it accommodates difference when it is presented through the guise of its own categories and terms of reference.[85] This is the reality of legal engagement with differentials, cultural or political, as law mediates a space that does not destablise its own narrative of internal cohesion. As Elizabeth Povinelli has explored in the context of land rights and native title in Australia, this can result in the construction of specific categories of cultural difference – where a criteria of *authenticity* is established that demands a specific 'performance' of legal subjectivity.[86] In this sense, law becomes intimately engaged in establishing how certain legal subjectivities are recognized – to the extent that this then effects how individuals behave within legal as well as other social contexts. At the same time however, this is never completely predictable, as individuals also use and modify law for their own strategic purposes.[87] This means that legal frameworks can also be adapted for purposeful strategies of recognition.[88]

Voicing a concern for indigenous property within a legal framework of intellectual property strategically works to alert the law to a concern to which it may have otherwise been blind. Because the challenge is set within the law's own terms of reference it must engage the challenge. Not to do so would undermine the legal narrative of 'universalism'. Thus a possibility for utilising law also depends upon recognising the emancipatory potential of property.[89] Indeed it is important to acknowledge that whilst indigenous advocates have been at the forefront of pointing to the limitations of western law, the very language of and expectations of intellectual property have not been abandoned as potentially useful political tools. In the communities, organisations and bureaucracies where I have worked, the current expressions and expectations around the protection of knowledge do not advocate an abandonment of 'property' *per se*.[90] Instead, the anticipation is of a reworked property regime that accommodates differing interests and expectation. Property, and hence legal networks remain the primary vehicles through which indigenous interests are being expressed.

It is because intellectual property is being evoked as the primary vehicle to secure indigenous interests in knowledge control and management that it is imperative that we look at the emergence of a body of law specifically engaged with managing expectations of property in intangible things like knowledge. The next section explores the foundational jurisprudential contests that characterize intellectual property law. This is because these are almost always left out of the literature and debates on indigenous knowledge and intellectual property. Yet they are critical to understanding both the operation of legal authority and the function of law in fashioning new kinds of categories and interests. The absence of this jurisprudence limits what we can understand about the politics of this domain of law and the emergence of indigenous knowledge within it. What follows sets the frame for a more nuanced engagement of the extent that law constructs a space of interpretation for indigenous knowledge and indigenous culture(s). In more plain terms, what will become apparent is the manner in which intellectual property law actively makes an 'indigenous' category that it can identify, incorporate and respond to through new treaties, policies and legal reforms.[91]

NOTES

1. Prior to 1967, international standards for intellectual property protection were established through the *Paris Convention for the Protection of Industrial Property* (1884) and the *Berne Convention for the Protection of Literary and Artistic Works* (1886).
2. J. McKeough, K. Bowrey and P. Griffith, *Intellectual Property: Commentary and Materials* (third edition), The Lawbook Company: Pyrmont, Sydney, 2002 at 3.
3. This has been made explicit through the 1994 *Agreement on Trade Related Aspects of Intellectual Property Rights* (TRIPs). As McKeough, Bowrey and Griffith note 'TRIPs is one of a system of agreements which make up the World Trade Organisation (WTO). TRIPs links intellectual property rights to GATT or WTO rights and obligations'. J. McKeough, K. Bowrey and P. Griffith, *Intellectual Property: Commentary and Materials*, supra n.2 at 4. See also: M. Blakeney, *Trade Related Aspects of Intellectual Property Rights: A Concise Guide to the TRIPs Agreement*, Sweet and Maxwell: London, 1996; P. Drahos with J. Braithwaite, *Information Feudalism: Who Owns the Knowledge Economy*?, Earthscan Publications Ltd: London, 2002; P. Drahos and R. Mayne (eds), *Global Intellectual Property Rights: Knowledge Access and Development*, Palgrave MacMillan: Hampshire and New York, 2002.
4. In particular see the *WIPO Performances and Phonograms Treaty* (1996) and the *WIPO Copyright Treaty* (1996).
5. See for example: B. Sherman and L. Bently, *The Making of Modern Intellectual Property: The British Experience 1760–1911*, Cambridge University Press: Cambridge, 1999; P. Drahos, *A Philosophy of Intellectual Property*, Dartmouth Press: Sydney, 1996; R. Deazley, *On the Origin of the Right to Copy: Charting the Movement of Copyright Law in Eighteenth-Century Britain (1695–1775)*, Hart Publishing: Oxford and Oregon, 2004.
6. See: P. Drahos, 'Capitalism, Efficiency and Self-Ownership', (2003) 28 *Australian Journal of Legal Philosophy* 215.
7. C. Lury, *Cultural Rights: Technology, Legality and Personality*, Routledge: London and New York, 1993; J. Boyle, *Shamans, Software and Spleens: Law and the Construction of the Information Society*, Harvard University Press: Cambridge MA, 1996; L. Lessig, *The Future of Ideas: The Fate of the Commons in an Interconnected World*, Random House: New York, 2001; D.E. Long, 'The Impact of Foreign Investment on Indigenous Culture: An Intellectual Property Perspective', (1998) 23 *N.C.J. Int'l L.& Com.Reg.* 229; M. Ryan, *Knowledge Diplomacy: Global Competition and the Politics of Intellectual*

Property, Brookings Institution Press: Washington DC, 1998; S. Sell, 'Industry Strategies for Intellectual Property and Trade: The Quest for TRIPS and Post-TRIPS Strategies', (2002) 10 *Cardozo Journal of International and Comparative Law* 79; C. May, *A Global Political Economy of Intellectual Property Rights: The New Enclosure?*, Routledge: London and New York, 2000; C. May and S. Sell, *Intellectual Property Rights: A Critical History*, Lynne Rienner Publishers: UK, 2005.

8. For example: P. Drahos with J. Braithwaite, *Information Feudalism: Who Owns the Knowledge Economy?*, supra n.3; P. Drahos and R. Mayne (eds), *Global Intellectual Property Rights: Knowledge Access and Development*, supra n.3; R. Coombe, *The Cultural Life of Intellectual Properties: Authorship, Appropriation and the Law*, Duke University Press: Durham and London, 1998; K. Aoki, 'Neocolonialism, Anticommons Property and Biopiracy in the (Not-So-Brave) New World Order of International Intellectual Property Protection', (1998) 6 *Ind. J. Global Leg. Stud.* 11; J. Gaines, *Contested Culture: The Image, the Voice and the Law*, The University of North Carolina Press: Chapel Hill, 1991; V. Shiva, *Protect or Plunder? Understanding Intellectual Property Rights*, Zed Books: India, 2001; D.E. Long, '"Globalization": A Future Trend or a Satisfying Mirage', (2001) 49 (1) *Journal of the Copyright Society of the USA* 313; R. Gana, 'Has Creativity Died in the Third World? Some Implications of the Internationalization of Intellectual Property', (1995) 24 (1) *Denv. J. Int'l L. & Pol'y* 109; P.E. Geller, 'Copyright History and the Future: What's Culture Got to Do With It?', (2000) 48 (1) *Journal of the Copyright Society of the USA* 209; D.E. Long, '"Democratizing" Globalization: Practicing the Policies of Cultural Inclusion', (2002) 10 *Cardozo Journal of Interternational and Comparative Law* 217.
9. P. Drahos with J. Braithwaite, *Information Feudalism: Who Owns the Knowledge Economy?*, supra n.3 at 3.
10. For example see the Canadian NGO, Rural Advancement Foundation International (RAFI) at [http://www.rafi.org.au]. See also the Third World Network, *The Need for Greater Regulation and Control of Genetic Engineering: A Statement by Scientists Concerned about Current Trends in the New Biotechnology*, Penang, Malaysia, 1995. Released articles include 'Feared reviewed science: contaminated corn and tainted tortillas – Genetic Pollution in Mexico's centre of maize diversity' (2002) 74 *RAFI Communique* at http://www.rafi.org/article.asp?newsid=287; 'GM Fallout from Mexico to Zambia: the great containment', RAFI press release, October 25, 2002 at http://www.rafi.org/article.asp?newsid=366; 'Sovereignty or Hegemony: Africa and security, Negotiating from reality' May 30 1997 at http://www.rafi.org/article.asp?newsid=192. For a discussion of implications for patents on plants like neem and tumeric see: Commission on Intellectual Property Rights, *Integrating Intellectual Property Rights and Development Policy*, London, 2002; E. Martin, 'The Neem Tree Patent: International Conflict over the Commodification of Life', (1999) 22 *B.C. Int'l & Comp. L. Rev.* 279; V. Shiva, *Monocultures of the Mind: Perspective on Biodiversity and Biotechnology*, Zed Books: India, 1993.
11. Knowledge about intellectual property rights is always undergoing transformation, however in recent times the interpretation has shifted again owing to the increasing globalisation of such rights. See D.E. Long, 'The Impact of Foreign Investment on Indigenous Culture: An Intellectual Property Perspective', supra n.7.
12. P. Drahos 'Introduction' Drahos, P., and R. Mayne (eds), *Global Intellectual Property Rights: Knowledge, Access and Development*, supra n.3 at 1. See also C. May, *A Global Political Economy of Intellectual Property Rights: The New Enclosures?*, Routledge: London, New York, 2000.
13. A. Sarat and J. Simon, 'Beyond Legal Realism?: Cultural Analysis, Cultural Studies and the Situation of Legal Scholarship', (2001) 13 (35) *Yale Journal of Law and the Humanities* 1 at 21.
14. See for instance: J. Austin, *The Province of Jurisprudence Determined* and *Lectures on Jurisprudence* (3 vols) John Murray: London, 1861–3; H.L.A. Hart, *The Concept of Law*, Clarendon Press: Oxford, 1961; R. Dworkin, *Law's Empire*, Fontana Press: London, 1986.

15. R.A. Posner, *The Problems of Jurisprudence*, Harvard University Press: Cambridge MA, 1990.
16. R. Unger, *The Critical Legal Studies Movement*, Harvard University Press: Cambridge MA, 1986.
17. R. Unger, *Law in Modern Society: Toward a Criticism of Social Theory*, Free Press: New York, 1976 at 1.
18. Ibid., at 2. See also the debate about the relationship between law and morals, in particular, M. Sandel (ed), *Liberalism and its Critics*, New York University Press: New York, 1984. Also see: A. Young and A. Sarat (eds), (1994) 3 (3) *Beyond Criticism: Law Power and Ethics, Social and Legal Studies* 1.
19. See the discussion in F. Munger, 'Mapping Law and Society' in Sarat, A., M. Constable, D. Engel, V. Hans and S. Lawrence (eds), *Crossing Boundaries: Traditions and Transformations in Law and Society Research*, Chicago: Northwestern University Press: 1998 at 43.
20. In other disciplines, such as anthropology, the social relationships generated through law were also of increasing interest. However, owing to alternate histories and philosophies underpinning each discipline the object of interest differed. For instance, anthropologists focused more on the social relationships generated through law and legalism often in non-western contexts, whereas legal scholars tended to focus more on internal legal questions and, increasingly how law functioned and was affected by political influences like feminism or socialism. For examples of the work of legal anthropologists emanating around the same time as the critical legal movements see the collection in L. Nader (ed), *Law in Culture and Society*, Aldine Publishing Company: Illinois, 1969.
21. M. Tushnet, 'Critical Legal Studies: A Political History', (1991) 100 (5) *The Yale Law Journal* 1515 at 1526. Also see: J. Derrida, 'Force of Law: The Mystical Foundation of Authority', (1990) 11 *Cardozo Law Review* 919.
22. The antagonism against critical legal scholars highlighted the threat that such ideas posed to the establishment. In Australia, the controversy was contextualised at the Law Faculty of Macquarie University. See *Report of the Committee to Review Australian Law Schools, A Discipline Assessment*. Commonwealth Tertiary Education Commission: Australian Government Publishing Service, 1987. In America, critical legal theorists were sacked and denied tenure. For an account of this see M. Tushnet, 'Critical Legal Studies', supra n.21 at 1530–1534.
23. For feminist critiques challenging traditional jurisprudence see: C. Smart, *Feminism and the Power of Law*, Routledge: London, 1989; C. MacKinnon, *Feminism Unmodified: Discourses on Life and Law*, Harvard University Press: Cambridge MA, 1987; T. S. Dahl, *Women's Law: An Introduction to Feminist Jurisprudence*, Oxford University Press: Oxford, 1987; M. Thornton, *The Liberal Promise: Anti-Discrimination Legislation in Australia*, Oxford University Press: London and Sydney, 1990.
24. For race and law see: P. Williams, *The Alchemy of Race and Rights*, Harvard University Press: Cambridge MA, 1991; C. Cunneen and T. Libesman, *Indigenous People and the Law in Australia*, Butterworths: Sydney, 1995; P. Fitzpatrick, 'Racism and the Innocence of Law' in Fitzpatrick, P. and A. Hunt (eds), *Critical Legal Studies*, Basil Blackwell: Oxford, 1991.
25. For law and discourse: R. Cotterrall, *Law's Community: Legal Theory in Sociological Perspective*, Clarendon Press: Oxford, 1995; H. Stacey, 'Legal Discourse and the Feminist Political Economy: Moving Beyond Sameness/Difference', (1996) 6 *The Australian Feminist Law Journal* 115.
26. See for example: P. Fitzpatrick, *The Mythology of Modern Law*, Routledge: London and New York, 1992.
27. Ibid., from 10.
28. For critical readings that examine the position of indigenous people within the law see generally: C. Cuneen, 'Judicial Racism', (1992) 2 (58) *Aboriginal Law Bulletin* 9; P. Dodson, *Royal Commission into Aboriginal Deaths in Custody: Regional Report of the Inquiry into Underlying Issues in Western Australia*, Australian Government Printing Service: Canberra, 1991; P. Hanks and B. Keon-Cohen, *Aborigines and the*

Law, George Allen and Unwin: North Sydney, 1984; G. Bird, G. Martin and J. Nielson (eds), *Majah: Indigenous Peoples and the Law*, The Federation Press: Sydney, 1996; R.L. Barsh, 'Indigenous Peoples: An Emerging Object of International Law', (1986) 80 *The American Journal of International Law* 369; I. Watson, 'Indigenous Peoples' Law-Ways: Survival against the Colonial State', (1997) 8 *Australian Feminist Law Journal* 39; E. Johnson, M. Hinton and D. Rigney (eds), *Indigenous Australians and the Law*, Cavendish Publishing: Sydney, 1997; C. Cuneen and T. Libesman, *Indigenous People and the Law in Australia*, Butterworths: Australia, 1995.

29. C. Cuneen, *Conflicts, Politics and Crime*, Allen and Unwin: Sydney, 2001 at 5. Cunneen has more recently extended his argument about the limits of litigation in the case of the Stolen Generations. See C. Cuneen and J. Grix, 'The Limitations of Litigation in Stolen Generation Cases' *AIATSIS Research Discussion Paper* No. 15 2004.
30. In Australia many indigenous people are in custody for minor offences. See: J. Walker and D. McDonald, *The Over Representation of Indigenous Peoples in Custody in Australia*, Australian Institute of Criminology – Issues Paper 47, August 1995; Aboriginal and Torres Strait Islander Social Justice Commissioner *Fifth Report*, HREOC, 1997; Aboriginal and Torres Strait Islander Social Justice Commissioner, *Social Justice Report 2001*, J.S. McMillan Publishing: Sydney 2001; Aboriginal and Torres Strait Islander Social Justice Commissioner, *Social Justice Report 2002*, J.S. McMillan Publishing: Sydney, 2002.
31. C. Cuneen, supra n.29 at 7.
32. For two important narratives see: S. Kinnane, *Shadow Lines,* Fremantle Press: Fremantle, 2004; and A. Haebich, *Broken Circle: Fragmenting Indigenous Families 1800–2000*, Fremantle Arts Centre Press: Fremantle W.A., 2000.
33. This is neo-colonialism. I. Watson, 'There is No Possibility of Rights Without Law: So Until Then Don't Thumb Print or Sign Anything!', (2000) 5 *Indigenous Law Bulletin* 4; I. Watson, 'Buried Alive', (2002) 13 (3) *Law and Critique* 253; C. Cuneen, supra n.29 at 10. See also: G. Bird, '*The Civilising Mission': Race and the Construction of Crime*, Contemporary Legal Issues No.4, Monash University, 1987; J. Purdy, 'British Common Law and Colonised Peoples: Studies in Trinidad and Western Australia' in Bird, G., G. Martin and J. Nielson (eds), *Majah: Indigenous Peoples and the Law*, The Federation Press: Sydney, 1996; J. Purdy, 'Postcolonialism: The Emperor's New Clothes?' in Darian-Smith, E., and P. Fitzpatrick (eds), *Laws of the Postcolonial*, The University of Michigan Press: Michigan, 1999.
34. *Royal Commission into Aboriginal Deaths in Custody – National Report*, AGPS: Canberra, 1991. Also see: *Royal Commission into Aboriginal Deaths in Custody – Interim Report*, AGPS: Canberra, 1988.
35. See: P. Dodson, *The Wentworth Lecture 2000 – Beyond the Mourning Gate: Dealing with Unfinished Business*, AIATSIS: Canberra, 2000; M. Langton, *Too Much Sorry Business: The Report of the Aboriginal Issues Unit of the Northern Territory*, AGPS: Canberra, 1991; H. Wootten, 'Deaths in Custody', Paper delivered at the Coronial Inquest Seminar, Sydney University Law School, 1992; T. Rowse, 'The Royal Commission, ATSIC and Self-Determination: A Review of the Royal Commission into Aboriginal Deaths in Custody', (1992) 27 (3) *Australian Journal of Social Issues* 153; M. Langton, 'Dumb politics wins the day', (2000) *Land Rights Queensland* 11.
36. See for example: J. Clarke, 'Law and Race: The position of Indigenous people', Bottomley, S., and S. Parker (eds), *Law and Context* (second edition), Federation Press: Annandale, 1997.
37. *Aboriginal Customary Laws: Final Report*, Western Australia Law Reform Commission, 2006.
38. *Mabo v Queensland* [No.2] (1992) 175 CLR 1.
39. P. Patton, 'The Translation of Indigenous Land into Property: The Mere Analogy of English Jurisprudence. . .', (2000) 6 (1) *parallax* 25.
40. How intellectual property law justifies a right in property will be examined in the following chapter.
41. These formed part of the literary property debates.

42. J. Bentham, 'Chapter VIII – Of Property', reprinted in Macpherson, C.B (ed), *Property: Mainstream and Critical Positions*, University of Toronto Press: Toronto, 1978 at 51.
43. Debates about material cultural objects (for instance what is now commonly referred to as cultural property) has informed intellectual property discussions in Australia.
44. P. O'Malley, 'Indigenous Governance' in Hindess, B. and M. Dean (eds), *Governing Australia: Studies in Contemporary Rationalities of Government*, Cambridge University Press: Australia, 1998; P. O'Malley, *Law Capitalism and Democracy*, Allen and Unwin: Sydney, 1983.
45. See: K. Bowrey 'The Outer Limits of Copyright Law – Where Law Meets Philosophy and Culture', (2001) 12 *Law and Critique* 75; P. Drahos with J. Braithwaite, *Information Feudalism: Who Owns the Knowledge Economy?*, supra n.3.
46. See: N. Loos and K. Mabo, *Edward Koiki Mabo: His Life and Struggle for Land Rights*, Queensland University Press: St Lucia, 1996.
47. See: K. Howden, 'Indigenous Traditional Knowledge and Native Title', (2001) 24 (1) *UNSW Law Journal* 60;
48. See: B. Sherman and L. Bently, *The Making of Modern Intellectual Property: The British Experience 1760–1911*, supra n.5; D. Leiberman, *The Province of Legislature Determined: Legal Theory in Eighteenth Century Britain*, Cambridge University Press: Cambridge, 2002; P. Drahos, *A Philosophy of Intellectual Property*, supra n.5; J. Litman, 'The Public Domain', (1990) 39 (4) *Emory Law Journal* 965 at 970–972.
49. B. Bryan, 'Property as Ontology: On Aboriginal and English Understandings of Ownership', (2000) 13 *Can. J. L. & Juris.* 3.
50. For more detailed approaches see: R. Ashcraft, *John Locke: Critical Assessments*, Routledge: London, 1991; C. Fox, *Locke and the Scriblerians: Identity and Consciousness in Early Eighteenth Century Britain*, University of California Press: Berkeley, 1988; J. Dunn, *The Political Thought of John Locke*, Cambridge University Press: Cambridge, 1969.
51. W. Blackstone, *Commentaries on the Laws of England*, Facsimile of the First Edition (1765–1769) Chicago University Press: Chicago, 1979.
52. J. Bentham, *The Theory of Legislation* in Ogden, C.K. (ed), Keagan Paul Publishers: London, 1931. This text draws from Bentham's *Principles of the Civil Code* which was first published in French in 1802 and in English in 1830.
53. W.N. Hohfeld, 'Some Fundamental Legal Conceptions as Applied in Juridical Reasoning', (1913) 23 *Yale Law Journal* 16. See also: J.E. Penner, 'The Bundle of Rights Picture of Property', (1996) 43 *UCLA Law Review* 711.
54. C. Reich, 'The New Property', (1964) 73 *Yale Law Journal* 733. Reich's work focused on the function of property and the changing social relations effecting the construction of property.
55. I will consider this shortly, however for interests sake compare J. Tully, *A Discourse on Property: John Locke and his Adversaries*, Cambridge University Press: Cambridge, 1980, and C. B. Macpherson, *The Political Theory of Possessive Individualism: Hobbes to Locke*, Clarendon Press: Oxford, 1962. Also see: P. Drahos, *A Philosophy of Intellectual Property*, supra n.5 for a discussion of these dissenting views.
56. *Two Treatises of Government* was first published in 1689. J. Locke, *Two Treatises of Government* (reprint) J.M. Dent & Sons Ltd: London, 1990.
57. Ibid., at 136.
58. Ibid., at 136.
59. M. Rose, *Authors and Owners: The Invention of Copyright*, Harvard University Press: Cambridge MA, 1993 at 6.
60. J. Locke, *Two Treatises of Government*, supra n.56 at 136.
61. K. Bowrey, *Don't Fence Me In: The Many Histories of Copyright*, Doctor of Juridical Studies, University of Sydney, 1994 (unpublished). Peter Drahos also notes that it is too simple a view of the natural law tradition in which Locke worked to depict him as a 'labour theorist of property'. P. Drahos, *A Philosophy of Intellectual Property* supra n.5 at 48. James Tully argues that Locke's philosophy is deeply embedded within a religious

context that is impossible to ignore in understanding Locke's conception of nature, law and the commons. See J. Tully, *A Discourse on Property: John Locke and his Adversaries*, supra n.55.

62. Whilst published after Filmer's death, it was the most complete expression of his ideas.
63. Ronan Deazley also traces this history in *On the Origin of the Right to Copy: Charting the Movement of Copyright Law in Eighteenth Century Britain (1695–1775)*, Hart Publishing: Oxford and Portland, 2004.
64. See for instance: P. Drahos, *A Philosophy of Intellectual Property*, supra n.5; J. Hughes, 'The Philosophy of Intellectual Property' (1988) 77 *The Georgetown Law Journal* 287; M. Rose, *Authors and Owners*, supra n.59; D. Saunders, *Authorship and Copyright*, Routledge: London, 1992; B. Sherman and L. Bently, *The Making of Modern Intellectual Property*, supra n.5; E. Hettinger, 'Justifying Intellectual Property', (1989) 18 (1) *Philosophy and Public Affairs* 31.
65. See for instance: B. Kaplan, *An Unhurried View of Copyright*, Columbia University Press: New York, 1967; R. Patterson, *Copyright in Historical Perspective*, Vanderbilt University Press: Nashville, 1968; V. Bonham-Carter, *Authors By Profession, Volume One and Two*, The Society of Authors: London, 1978; J. Feather, *The Provincial Book Trade in Eighteenth Century England*, Cambridge University Press: Cambridge, 1985.
66. P. Drahos, supra n.5 at 51.
67. R. Deazley, supra n.5 at 42.
68. M. Rose, supra n.59 at 5.
69. K. Vandervelde, 'The New Property of the Nineteenth Century: The Development of the Modern Concept of Property' (1980) 29 *Buffalo Law Review* 325.
70. This will be elaborated in the context of the changing value of Aboriginal art in Part Two of this book.
71. See: C. Reich 'The New Property' (1964) 73 *Yale Law Journal* 733. Reich's argument focuses on the function of property and the changing social relations effecting the construction of property.
72. Thus overcoming the dead hand of legal 'tradition'. (This was understood as Bentham's critique of Blackstone.)
73. T. Mitchell, 'The Properties of Markets: Informal Housing and Capitalisms Mystery', Cultural Political Economy Working Paper Series, Institute for Advanced Studies in Social and Management Sciences, University of Lancaster, 2004; J. Elyachar, *Markets of Dispossession: NGOs, Economic Development and the State in Cairo*, Duke University Press: Durham, 2005.
74. D. Graeber, *Toward an Anthropological Theory of Value: The False Coin of Our Own Dreams*, Palgrave Press: New York, 2001.
75. K. Gray, 'Property in Thin Air', (1991) 50 *Cambridge Law Journal* 252 at 307. See also: M. Radin, *Reinterpreting Property*, University of Chicago Press: Chicago, 1993; C. Harris, 'Whiteness as Property', (1993) 106 (8) *Harvard Law Review* 1709 at 1730.
76. K. Gray, 'Property in Thin Air', Ibid. at 307.
77. The cultural property movement illustrates this nicely.
78. See also: C. O'Faircheallaigh, *Negotiating Major Agreements: The 'Cape York Model'*, Discussion Research Paper No. 11, AIATSIS: Canberra, 2000.
79. N. Pearson, 'Aboriginal law and Colonial Law since Mabo' in Fletcher, C. (ed), *Aboriginal Self-determination in Australia*, Aboriginal Studies Press: Canberra, 1994, at 158.
80. M. Dodson, 'Indigenous Peoples and Intellectual Property Rights' *Ecopolitics IX – Conference Papers and Resolutions*, Northern Land Council: Sydney, 1995 at 31.
81. M. Blakeney, 'Bioprospecting and the Protection of Traditional Medical Knowledge of Indigenous People: An Australian Perspective', (1997) 6 *European Intellectual Property Review* 298 at 300.
82. See: A. Weiner, *Inalienable Possessions: The Paradox of Keeping While Giving*, University of California Press: Berkeley, 1992.
83. V. Kerruish, 'Reconciliation, Property and Rights' in Christodoulidis, E., and S. Veitch (eds), *Lethe's Law: Justice Law and Ethics in Reconciliation*, Hart Publishing: Oxford, 2001 at 195.

84. M. de Certeau, *The Practice of Everyday Life* (trans S. Rendall), University of California Press: Los Angeles, 1984 at xiii.
85. See G. Edmond, 'Thick Decisions: Expertise, Advocacy and Reasonableness in the Federal Court of Australia' 74 (3) *Oceania* 190–230; P. Fitzpatrick, *Mythology of Modern Law*, Routledge: London and New York, 1992; P. Fitzpatrick, *Modernism and the Grounds of Law*, Cambridge University Press: Cambridge, 2001.
86. E. Povinelli, *The Cunning of Recognition: Indigenous Alterities and the Making of Australian Multiculturalism*, Duke University Press: Durham, 2004.
87. K. Bowrey, *Law and Internet Cultures*, Cambridge University Press: Cambridge, 2005; J. Litman, *Digital Copyright: Protecting Intellectual Property on the Internet*, Prometheus Books: New York, 2001 at 195.
88. H. Geismar, 'Copyright in Context: Carvers, Carving and Commodities in Vanuatu', (2005) 33 (3) *American Ethnologist* 437–459.
89. V. Kerruish, 'Reconciliation, Property and Rights', supra n.83 at 195; N. Pearson, 'Aboriginal Law and Colonial Law since Mabo', supra n.79; C. O'Faircheallaigh, 'Negotiating Major Agreements: The 'Cape York Model', supra n.78.
90. J. Anderson, L. Aragon, I. Haryanto, P. Jaszi, A. Nababan, H. Panjiatan, A. Sardjono, R. Siagian, R. Suryasaladin, *Traditional Arts: A Move Towards Protection in Indonesia* (forthcoming).
91. I thank Tim Rowse for discussion with me about this point.

2. The making of intellectual property law

The appearance of intellectual property has been largely tackled in terms of an exploration of the emergence of its particular, distinctive categories and subject matter. As a subject of history, the most studied category has been copyright. Though not necessarily claiming the story of copyright as somehow representative of the history of all intellectual property laws, copyright historians have suggested a model of truth about intellectual property laws and a method of historical inquiry in general, directing historians towards discovering the origins of the relevant laws.

What the origins of copyright have been taken to be has differed, reflecting diverse disciplinary approaches and interests. Publishers and booksellers put forward a version,[1] legal historians have presented an account,[2] literary theorists have offered another version,[3] different from the Marxist perspective[4] that, in turn, differs from the 'postmodern' perspective.[5]

In an overview of such histories, Kathy Bowrey notes how many of these histories fail to engage meaningfully with each other.[6] Bowrey's point is to highlight the striking reluctance in generating inter-disciplinary conversations.

> History shows that our understanding of copyright develops out of the interaction of a number of perspectives, even though few writers seem prepared to acknowledge this. At first each discipline wanted to pursue their own definition of the subject. Later on definitions were built in reaction to those earlier territorial claims. The argument was over deciding *what the legitimate interests and concerns of copyright are* and *who is authorised to speak for them*. There was an unwillingness to make space for the diversity of experiences and interests involved with copyright.[7]

What Bowrey advocates is a cross disciplinary approach to understanding copyright and its significance within legal relations of power.[8] Her point about the difficulty of achieving such a perspective is indicative of how the borders of copyright and more generally intellectual property law are patrolled. Under such circumstances knowledge about how copyright is constituted is limited. This helps guarantee the authority of the legal voice to speak about copyright through the language of law, leaving the other narratives as partial and contingent to accessing the domain of legal discourse.[9] In this sense, there is also a tendency to ignore political and social contexts and the effects of these in shaping the law. The histories tend to remain abstract rather than situated in historical epochs. What is at stake here is the fluidity of disciplinary exchange and the recognition of diverging historical accounts according to different sources, agendas and points of view. Further, the legal narrative of intellectual property's history assumes access and legal competence to understand and reproduce this discourse.[10] This secures the legitimacy of the discourse to distribute an 'authentic' meaning and thus perpetuate the ways in which debates about intellectual property are able to engage with new (and differing) subject matter.

HISTORICAL INFLUENCE

Few histories speak to the space that now constitutes intellectual property by extending analyses through a particular history of copyright to intellectual property law as a whole. One notable exception is Brad Sherman and Lionel Bently's work *The Making of Modern Intellectual Property.*[11] This book addresses the imbalance in histories of copyright, patents, designs and trademarks in order to explain how the whole legal field of intellectual property has been constructed.

What is different in this appreciation of the history of intellectual property is that the writers locate the production of the category of 'intellectual property' with jurisprudential concerns about the making of 'modern' laws. By modern law Sherman and Bently refer specifically to the *form* of the law, namely its abstract and *a*historical representation in legislation, spoken through the language and logic of political economy and utilitarianism.[12] They reject the view that an understanding of intellectual property can be derived from a concern for the origins of particular laws that are now recognised and encompassed by the rubric 'intellectual property law'. In suggesting that the domestic and specialist considerations of intellectual property, such as a history of copyright, do not explain its genesis, their analysis leads to an argument that it is the struggles of making 'modern law' that has significantly contributed to the evolution of the category in law that came to be termed 'intellectual property'.[13]

Sherman and Bently begin their history by noting the distinction between pre-modern intellectual property law and modern intellectual property law. The distinction, which they are the first to admit is 'somewhat artificial',[14] is nevertheless a useful way for considering the differences in identifying what we now understand as intellectual property law. For example, they note that the period around the 1850s marks the historical moment when intellectual property law, with its relatively bounded figure and specific categories including internal logic and language, emerged. Prior to this period, intellectual property law was haphazard and incomplete. Far from being readily determined and uniform, the development of intellectual property law as a distinct category of law has been slowly developed over a period of time, namely as law came to grapple with a series of issues that threatened its coherence. For until the 1850s there was no discernable law of copyright, patents or designs: the subcategories now recognised under the general axiom of intellectual property. Instead, prior to this period, there was an agreement that 'law granted property rights in mental labour, although the nature of this legal category was itself uncertain.'[15] Thus prior to the 1850s there was no clear or discernable way of managing intellectual property law. The pre-modern was subject specific and reactive as it tended to respond to particular problems when they were presented. The literary property debates in the eighteenth and nineteenth centuries are an example on point. In comparison what characterises modern intellectual property law from the 1850s is that it is more abstract and forward looking. Importantly the focus of the law was shifted *away* from measuring the *labour embodied in the subject matter* to concentrate more on the *object produced by the subject matter*.

Sherman and Bently's approach is to cut through the social and cultural histories of copyright, patents and designs to locate the struggles with which law was intrinsically engaged. For example, they suggest that what the eighteenth century contest over literary property really demonstrated was laws inability to determine effectively the metaphysical dimensions of intangible property (for instance how to designate the boundaries for the property).[16] Whilst relatively unsurprising, as this specific problem was not to be solved easily, it became a constant point of legal consideration and contestation throughout the eighteenth and nineteenth centuries. The crisis this created, in understanding the order and function of copyright law, was handled by shifting the sphere of legal concern away from its internal disorder, to the more general meaning and concerns of intellectual property law.[17] Thus in the late nineteenth century intellectual property law started to take on a new and recognisable shape closer to that which we currently understand, where the main concern settled on defining the object of legal protection. In this sense law was able to shift its gaze from the problem of determining the metaphysical dimensions of intangible property (for example, what was an original work), and focus instead on the object or commodity. For example discussing the original in terms of what is worth copying is worth protecting.[18]

Through moderating the perspective, the problem of determining the metaphysical dimensions of intangible property appeared resolved. The shift of the gaze also meant that the internal logic of copyright law was withdrawn from view. This left within the body of the law incremental disputes about the object of legal protection. Whilst the question of determining the foundational basis of the law was sidestepped, the issue of defining the protected intangible property in copyright still persisted. Moreover, struggles to identify and measure knowledge through a prism of mental labour still troubles intellectual property law today. However such problems, if noticed at all, are attributed to unusually challenging facts and circumstance, rather than generated through the legal processes of definition inherent to the law.[19]

It is significant that the framing of intellectual property law often excludes consideration of its own historical contingency.[20] Of specific importance to this process are the narratives that intellectual property law has produced of its own history. For instance, the preoccupation with narratives that locate the emergence of copyright with the 1710 *Statute of Anne* or patents with the 1624 *Statute of Monopolies* present intellectual property law as an increasingly coherent and stable body of law derived from Statutes.[21] The cost of such narratives is the marginalisation of discussion about the complexity in the emergence of the concept of intellectual property law. Intellectual property laws are (only) presented as unsettled and complex in the historical past. Those problems are 'resolved' through time via various key reforms. Thus current laws are largely *a*historical in the sense that they only contextualise the past in order to show problems having been overcome. The face with which such laws front the future is comparatively featureless and capable.

The difficulties in granting property rights in mental labour were central to the development of a body of law named intellectual property. It is significant that as the eighteenth century became marked with new concerns, economic and industrial, these were also integral to the changing form of law; from subject specific law to a general 'body' of law replete with coherent and universal categories of assessment. What such a change achieved was to shift the attention away from the problems that threatened the coherence and universality of the law. This is not to say that with a shift in the focus such a problem disappeared, for indeed on closer examination intellectual property law is still characterised by how it reconciles and rearticulates proprietary rights in creative endeavour. In this way intellectual property still maintains the primary difficulties that marked its 'premodern' form. Thus the most profound and certainly lingering issues for intellectual property law revolve around the problem of understanding the metaphysical dimensions that constitute intangible property.

THE LITERARY PROPERTY DEBATES

The English literary property debates of the eighteenth century are important because they provide contextualisation for the initial struggles with which the law was externally and internally engaged.[22] Not only do they illustrate difficulties that are still paramount to intellectual property law, but also reveal how, in a variety of ways, law sought to resolve these complexities. Inevitably individuals (jurists and advocates) also played significant roles in directing the path that the law could take in response to such difficulties. The literary property debates provide a space for considering not only how the law responded to the challenge of metaphysical property, but also that the arguments by proponents, opponents, jurists and others influenced the shape the law took. In these early debates it is possible to discern arguments that attempt to grapple with, and understand, intangible property. These arguments inevitably expose the struggles as being within the law itself. Sherman and Bently's point is that far from only happening within literary property and copyright, the struggle that law was intrinsically engaged also extended into other areas that would later be grouped under the axiom, intellectual property.

Thus the literary property debates provide a focal point where the concept of intangible property was thrashed out and as such predominately included devising a method for appreciating the *nature* of intangible property. Within these arguments for literary property the notion of property rights in mental labour was at the forefront of the debate. As discussed in reference to Locke earlier, the arguments also exposed how notions of 'property' were translated into the debates and how the natural right through an individual's labour was adapted, developed and justified.[23] What the literary debates also signal is how a corresponding key process for the law was in identifying what the limits and boundaries of the intangible subject matter could be.

At first instance, the struggle for the law began as one of identification.

In terms of identifying intangible property, there were three key points, raised by opponents and supporters alike, that highlighted the difficulty for the law in recognising intangible property. The first involved the circumstances in which such property could be legitimately 'acquired'; the second involved the problem of identifying mental labour in literary property; and the third concerned the 'economic and cultural consequences of recognizing a perpetual textual monopoly.'[24]

Inevitably, arguments for perpetual common law rights in intangible property raised the question of how title in property arises. At this period in time, and as I discussed in the previous chapter, property was commonly conceived in political theory as being acquired through first occupancy.[25]

However, as intellectual ideas could not be 'occupied' in the same sense as land, it therefore followed that intellectual ideas could not be seen as property. One jurist, Justice Yates, who constantly argued against the common law right, highlighted the difficulty with equating property rights with ideas. As he noted '[t]he occupancy of a thought would be a new kind of occupancy indeed' for an object of property 'must be capable of distinct and separate possession.'[26] For an example of the difficulty in grasping a property right in an intangible form, consider the following argument made by Justice Yates in the case *Millar v Taylor* (1769).

> But the property here claimed is all ideal; a set of ideas which have *no bounds* or *marks* whatever, nothing that is capable of a *visible possession*, nothing that can sustain any one of the *qualities* or *incidents of property*. Their whole existence is in the mind alone; incapable of any other modes of acquisition or enjoyment, than by mental possession or apprehension; safe and invulnerable, from their own immateriality: no trespass can reach them; no tort affect them; no fraud or violence diminish or damage them. Yet these are the phantoms which the Author would grasp and confine to himself: and these are what the defendant is charged with having robbed the plaintiff of.[27]

In response to this kind of reasoning and fearing that it would undermine the common law right, the Stationers[28] and their supporters, all keen to see perpetual common law rights in intangible property as it guaranteed their monopoly, argued that a different concept of property was required; one that was 'appropriate for the case at hand.'[29]

As an alternative position, the Stationers, who had Blackstone as their counsel, presented the case that there was property in *mental labour* based on Locke's *Two Treatises of Government* in which the natural rights thesis functioned as the (familiar) marker of property. As already discussed, this was a strategic and selective reading of Locke.[30] While Locke was a supporter of an author's literary property, he was not concerned with defining what it is that an author 'owns' and justifying that as a 'right'. Nevertheless, those who favoured perpetual common law literary property focused on labour as the source of the property right.[31] To enhance the legitimacy of this position they argued that it was the *style* and *sentiment* of the author which 'occupied' the text.

At this stage it is worth noting that the difficulty in conceiving the nature of the property right was not unique to the literary debates and to the formation of copyright.[32] It would however be dangerous to generalise this problem as occurring throughout all regimes currently grouped under the axiom of intellectual property. What makes the problem worth commenting upon is that while other areas of intellectual property did not have the same crisis in defining the property right as copyright did, the shift to understanding the property as a right in labour subsequently influenced the other regimes that were to come to be grouped as laws of intellectual property. For copyright, at least, the dilemma in defining the property right for literary property was (partially) resolved with the increasing reliance upon possessive individualism.[33]

Certainly a primary element that emerged from the literary property debates was this reliance upon an individual's labour as denoting a property right. There were those who argued for and against such positions. Indeed Yates J saw that the right was more of a personal right than a property right. As Mark Rose recounts, Yates 'insisted on maintaining the distinction between a personal right and an object of property. He did not deny that a personal right might be incorporeal but he did deny that anything incorporeal could be treated as property, in the same sense as a house or land.'[34] To countenance such opposition, proponents for the common law right, advocated that the property was neither in the physical books nor the ideas expressed, but actually 'something else entirely, that consisted of style and sentiment.'[35] Thus the argument circled back to identifying the intangible dimensions of the subject matter. This moved the law in a direction where identification of the intangible became central to ascertaining the right.

That the intangible domain was not marked by boundaries in the same manner as physical objects, led the early jurists to compare the right in literary property to that of patents. In this sense measuring the obvious tangibility of property in one area of law to the perceived intangibility of that which makes a literary work. In *Tonson v Collins* (1760) Blackstone J, argued that 'one essential requisite of every subject of property was that it must be a thing of value'[36] and that for literary property the thing of value was 'sentiment'. Influenced by Yates' J dissenting position that there was no distinction between copyright and patents, Blackstone moved his discussion to the subject of property where, evoking the earlier differentiation between literary and mechanical invention by another jurist, he stated that 'where two engines might resemble each other, they could never be identical because materials and workmanship must differ. But every duplicate of a literary text was the same text because its essence was immaterial.'[37] Herein lay the development that was to affect significantly the shape the law took – pushing the law to focus on the object produced by the intangible subject matter and defining copyright in terms of its points of differentiation to patents.

These questions about the nature of property were philosophical in the sense that they were about justifying the origin of the right. However, in practice only a partial explanation of the nature of the property was provided. This was because it was difficult in practice to identify the boundary to such a right. This problem was played out in questions over the derivative works such as translations and abridgements. If the text was not identical – was it an infringement of the owner's right? As well as this, and because of disagreements over the appropriate justification argument to apply, the legal questions focused relationally on the problems that law was likely to have in identifying the existence of such property rights, rather than establishing the boundary. Traditionally, property was seen to demarcate definitively a zone of exclusion, at which point it became necessary to show that with a concept of intangible property there was something that was 'capable of being visibly and distinctly enjoyed.'[38] Thus, the challenge was to provide certain markers that would enable literary property to be identified and distinguished thereby making the zone of exclusion clear. It is hard to say how and when precisely this issue was resolved, however it was consistently argued in terms of literary property, that the words in print provided the marker necessary to identify property.[39] As Rose notes '[d]ressed in language, the writer's ideas became a property that could be conveyed from owner to owner.'[40]

Whilst the initial decision by the King's Bench in *Donaldson v Becket* (1774) found for an author's common law right in property, the reversal of the decision by the House of Lords, declaring that copyright was a limited term right, highlighted that the answer to the question of literary property was far from clear.[41] As the case presented a failure to endorse *any* particular foundation for the literary property right it also highlights the indeterminacy of the law in this area. In the following decades, owing to the lack of clarity in determining property in mental labour, the law was developed and interpreted by competing demands. This indeterminacy was what made law subject specific. Interestingly, the objections to a perpetual literary property right raised in *Donaldson v Becket* (1774) laid the foundations for a shift to a different kind of analysis of intangible property rights.

THE MAKING OF MODERN LAW

As well as foundational issues about the origin and boundaries of the 'right', it was also argued, from analysis following *Donaldson v Becket* (1774), that literary property could not be considered as 'property' proper because no harm could be made against the owner in the taking of the property. That is, the nature of the intangible property meant that the harm to the owner through taking the property was difficult to measure and identify. This point was persuasively argued against by highlighting the future financial benefits that the owner would not be able to share. Economic concerns thus became an adequate means for measuring and identifying the loss of this unique form of property. Hence translation, abridgements and other derivative markets slowly came within the purview of protection to justify this extension of the private right. The following line of reasoning was established: that inadequate legal protection of the economic value of the work would provide little incentive to produce. That this argument relied upon the importance of economics is significant; for the argument is only possible in a period where the liberal democratic form of an economy was beginning to have its own status and regimes of logic.[42] In a parallel development the law became an integral vehicle for upholding that logic.[43] Being deprived of the potential rewards from an economic realm was how the harm against the owner was to be understood in regards to this new form of property relationship. The development in intellectual property law of an integral relationship between property and economics has been dynamic and, as will be considered in more depth at a later stage of this work, significant: specifically in the way in which modern intellectual property law approaches and evaluates an object for protection.[44]

A further problem, after these considerations about identifying the property relation in intangibles, was how to *describe* the subject matter in law itself. Such a problem existed for literary property, patents and design and arose because it was the intangible dimension – not the product (for instance the book) that was supposedly protected in the law. Specifically, when describing intangible property, law spoke of the intangible in dynamic terms, as something that required action through the function of mental labour.[45] However when it came to dealing with the product, the law was unable to represent it in a way that reflected the process of intellectual and metaphysical origin. The 'law lacked the language with which to reproduce the nature of the intangible.'[46] This was a difficulty in phrasing the difference between the 'creation' or intellectual labour and the shaping of that labour into a tangible product.[47]

To this end, the identity of the abstract object became known to the law through the physical object that was produced. Peter Drahos explains the necessity of the transition, where '[a]t some point before property rights attach to the abstract object, the various regimes require(d) some kind of corporealisation of the abstract object.'[48] Inevitably, the *product* which could be named and identified, became the *object* of intellectual property law. For copyright this meant the artistic work or book; for patents, the invention; and, for design, the tangible reproduction (through documentation) of the design. This logic, coupled with economic discourse, further justified an expansion of literary property-like subject matter to include a very diverse array of cultural/industrial objects.[49]

If exclusive possession was to be granted to a product of intellectual labour, it thus became necessary to establish a means of identifying a reproduction of that product. In this sense, for a property right to be granted, *the intangible had to be reproducible*: for the copy would generate an infringed right in the original property. In addition, the property had to be identifiable, insofar as it was possible to identify to what extent it had been reproduced. Thus the law took on a further change when it recognised that the object of intellectual property law could be infringed beyond the immediate form expressed. To this end, legal protection was extended to non-identical copies of the expression. In order to highlight this point, it is useful to consider the case of translation, which provides an example of how important it was to identify a work in order to further identify a copy or an infringement.

In *An Unhurried View of Copyright*, Benjamin Kaplan explains that the first substantial question to arise under the *Statute of Anne* (1710) was that of alleged infringement by translation.[50] In 1720, Dr Thomas Burnett brought an action against the translator of his Latin work, *Archaeologaie Philosophicae*. The defendant argued that the translation was in fact a 'different book'[51] and therefore the translator was the author of the 'new' book. In this sense, because the translator had put the book into another form, the defendant argued that it was not the same as reprinting because it required the 'translator to bestow his care and pains upon it'.[52] The judge appeared to accept this reasoning from the defendant, that, if the translation was a work of authorship (and importantly mental labour), at the same time it could therefore not be a copy. The issue of identifying a copy and identifying authorship recurred throughout this period as the law sought to establish means of identifying infringement. Other key cases that sought to clarify this issue involved maps, abridgements and histories.[53] However, the issue of copying was resolved by not looking at what had been *taken*, but what he/she had *added* to make it a work distinct from the copy.[54]

As Kaplan highlights through these early cases, the eighteenth century law was caught in judgments of identity. The subject specific nature of these meant that identification of the subject matter became necessarily linked with a concern for aesthetics. In this sense, aesthetic judgments in the form of identifying whether or not a work was infringed relied upon judicial interpretation, as there was no singular underlying principle of the law that could determine an infringement. What this shows is that the direction that the law took was in fact in response to all the underlying issues whose genesis resided in the identification of metaphysical dimensions of intangible property.

FROM COPYRIGHT TO DESIGN

Despite these considerable challenges, and the multiple efforts within copyright law aimed at their resolution, it is actually design law, codified as a particular category within an intellectual property framework, that produced the first significant transition for intellectual property law.[55] Of importance are the reforms in design legislation that occurred between 1839–1843.[56] Developed in conjunction with design legislation, there were two elements that had a significant effect upon the production of intellectual property law generally. The first concerns the introduction of a system of registration, known as the Designs Register. The second involves a shift in the way in which law concerned itself with the 'aesthetics of law' whereby law itself became interested in the future shape that it was was to take.[57] This attention to the aesthetics of law was specifically demonstrated in the organisational mechanism employed by law to move from subject specific analysis to more abstract formation. Thus the abstraction of legal categories influenced the way in which problems were to be resolved, categories organised and boundaries patrolled.[58]

With the challenge to British design from other trading nations, a variety of initiatives were developed specifically to improve the state of British design. Of these, the *Designs Registration Act* (1839), one of two acts[59] aimed to extend the scope of current design protection through the process of registration. Through the Act, the length of time offered for protection for designs was extended. This was premised on the prerequisite that the design was registered.

The introduction of a process of registration is an important moment in the history of intellectual property law. For registration effectively enabled the centralisation of particular forms of knowledge by recording the characteristics of the (protectable) product. This meant that the law was increasingly able to rely on institutionalised characteristics and avoid subject specific judgments. Culturally specific modes of identification were normalised as the key characteristics required for registration – and obviously anything that fell outside these markers did not qualify for registration and consequent protection.

A primary feature of the registration system, as was developed for designs, was that it regulated and managed specific information. The Register became the institution for accumulating, monitoring and distributing information about the various forms that mental labour could take. Moreover, the process of registration intrinsically established a means of producing proof about the nature of a design. For example, if an image was registered as a design, it could not later be claimed that it was instead a patent.[60] In addition the burden of proof fell to the creator rather than the law to establish what protection it deserved. Essentially, the system of registration facilitated a way of categorising and cataloguing the product of intellectual labour, the work itself.

The role of registration in controlling certain kinds of information was central to the development of the categories of intellectual property law. Further, through the development of this system of recording and documenting knowledge, bureaucratic power took on a new dimension. Importantly this was because the system of registration became 'publicly' controlled (through government) rather than privately regulated as had been the case through specific entities such as guilds.

Publicly controlled knowledge (through registries and archives for example) is an intrinsic mechanism of government.[61] The changes in categorising and regulating specific knowledges also occurred at a time when bureaucratic power in the form of modern European governance was consolidating itself.[62] It is not a coincidence that in the same period that this form of governance begins to take on its contemporary shape that intellectual property law also begins to take its current form. Both develop parallel systems of understanding and conceptualising the power of knowledge and the importance of developing programmes that monitor its progress. For intellectual property law this was achieved through registration. For governance this was increasingly achieved through law. Both facilitated a means for the future direction of the other: a bureaucracy seemingly acting in response to individual initiative. Such controls were also self-regulatory, in the sense that the onus was on the creator to conform to the conditions of registration in order to secure protection. In this way then it is possible to see a specific mode of governance occurring wherein the creator elects to participate in their own governance in return for legal protection. Further, the legal actor becomes simultaneously an object of the law and a self-actualising subject where the blurring between the two categories, rather than destabilising the unity of the opposition, enhances the inter-relations.

The registration process effectively contributed to the closure of debates concerning the nature of intangible property over the second half of the nineteenth century. As Sherman and Bently note, 'creations were not only radically detached from their creators, they also acquired a degree of juridical autonomy they had not previously experienced.'[63] Registration provided a means of decontextualising the product, effectively affirming the product as a 'legal object'. Further, registration effectively centralised specific kinds of knowledge that were deemed appropriate for intellectual property protection through establishing offices in centres of production such as London and Paris. With the increase in processes of centralising government occurring in Europe in the mid-nineteenth century, registration became a necessary vehicle of governance. The spread of modern registration systems was itself instrumental in providing possibilities for managing the identification of specific categories of knowledge.

A further feature that influenced the shape of intellectual property law was the way that the registration process codified protection through its representation of the intangible on paper. As the process for registration became more refined and rationalised, it led to patterns of standardisation that could be applied across a variety of locales. For if the process of standardisation could be applied in varying countries, intellectual property law could take on an almost universal status where the same protection could be guaranteed as if there was a standard normative mode of measurement. Consequently registration could become an end in itself.

Registration thus proved to be one of the most profound techniques in the organisation of certain kinds of legal categories and the production of modern intellectual property law. Without such systematised processes of documenting, archiving and managing specific categories of knowledge, it is unlikely that intellectual property law would have gained the reified status and power that it currently sustains. For intellectual property, registration allowed the codification of 'types' of knowledge to became one of the necessary mechanisms for producing an effective 'body' of intellectual property law (potentially global in scope) that could identify specific 'types' of knowledge through universal categorical indices whilst also promoting the benefits of an extensive intellectual property regime.

CONCLUSION

The key point to this overview of the emergence of intellectual property law is that the law was not pre-existing, nor was it a coherent entity with an underlying logic. Rather, intellectual property law functioned disparately, responding to specific issues as and when they arose. There was no obvious line connecting an author to property in the work (indeed, the very concept of authorship was also emerging at this time) and the legal principles that identify intangible property were slowly and partially assembled in response to specific concerns. In this sense law was deeply involved in its ongoing creation and thus instrumental in creating its own categories and developing processes of recognition and identification.

Consequently, these factors averted attention away from the destabilising potential of the laws inability to fully describe or justify the 'right'. As there was no pre-existing conception of a work, only the law itself could establish the means and process for understanding intangible property. The resulting dynamism of the law is often overshadowed but it is useful to keep in mind that in present day intellectual property law, the difficulties about 'the essence of intangible property continue to appear when law is confronted with new subject matter.'[64] Moreover, rather than highlighting the cohesion, it brings to the fore the complexity and messiness of the law both within its construction and its modern function.

In recognising the importance of the past in shaping present law, the next chapter considers the individuation of copyright as a subset of intellectual property law. Concepts of authorship and originality become the key tools for identifying the intangible property within copyright. The point is to consider how these categories function to influence the shape of the law and the judgments that are subsequently made in relation to identifying new 'types' of knowledge – for instance indigenous knowledge. Through such an analysis the structure of the law as messy and incomplete is exposed, where the struggles of modern law to determine the metaphysical dimensions of intangible property are revealed as still actively functioning and directing the way in which the law responds to the introduction of new kinds of cultural knowledge.

NOTES

1. J. Feather, *The Provincial Book Trade in Eighteenth Century England*, Cambridge University Press: Cambridge, 1985; and, V. Bonham-Carter, *Authors by Profession Volume One and Two*, The Society of Authors: London, 1978.
2. B. Kaplan, *An Unhurried View of Copyright*, Columbia University Press: New York, 1967; and, R. Patterson, *Copyright in Historical Perspective*, Vanderbilt University Press: Nashville, 1968.
3. E. Eisenstein, *The Printing Revolution in Early Modern Europe*, Cambridge University Press: Cambridge, 1983.
4. B. Edelman, *Ownership of the Image: Elements for a Marxist Theory of Law* (transl. by Kingdom, E.), Routledge and Keegan Paul: London, 1979. Edelman was strongly influenced by the early Soviet Jurist Evgeny Pashukanis writing in the 1920's. See: E. Pashukanis, *Law and Marxism* Arthur, C. (ed), Ink Links: London, 1978.
5. The postmodern perspective is strongly influenced by Foucault. See: M. Rose, 'The Author as Proprietor: *Donaldson v Becket* and the Genealogy of Modern Authorship' in Sherman, B. and Strowel, A (eds), *Of Authors and Origins: Essays on Copyright Law*, Clarendon Press: Oxford, 1994; M. Rose, *Authors and Owners: The Invention of Copyright*, Harvard University Press: Cambridge MA, 1993; M. Woodmansee and P. Jaszi (eds), The *Construction of Authorship: Textual Appropriation in Law and Literature*, Duke University: Durham and London, 1994; R. Coombe, *The Cultural Life of Intellectual Properties: Authorship, Appropriation and the Law*, Duke University Press: Durham and London, 1998. For a cultural studies perspective see: J. Gaines, *Contested Culture: The Image, The Voice and The Law*, University of South Carolina Press: Chapel Hill, 1991.
6. K. Bowrey. 'Who's Writing Copyright's History?', (1996) 18 (6) *European Intellectual Property Review* 322. See also: C. May 'Why IPRs are a Global Political Issue', (2003) 1 *European Intellectual Property Review* 1.
7. K. Bowrey, 'Who's Writing Copyright's History?', ibid. at 329 [emphasis in the original].
8. This advocacy has been taken up recently in C. May and S. Sell, *Intellectual Property Rights: A Critical History* Lynne Reiner: UK, 2005.
9. See also: R. Deazley, 'Re-reading Donaldson (1774) in the Twenty First Century and Why It Matters', (2003) 25 (6) *European Intellectual Property Review* 270; and R.

Deazley, *On the Origin of the Right to Copy: Charting the Movement of Copyright Law in Eighteenth Century Britain (1695–1775)*, Hart Publishing: Oxford and Portland, 2004.
10. S. Almog, 'From Sterne and Borges to Lost Storytellers: Cyberspace, Narrative and Law', (2002) 13 *Fordham Intellectual Property, Media and Entertainment Law Journal* 1.
11. B. Sherman and L. Bently, *The Making of Modern Intellectual Property: The British Experience 1760–1911*, Cambridge University Press: Cambridge, 1999.
12. Ibid., at 3–4.
13. Ibid., at 1–10.
14. Ibid., at 3.
15. Ibid.
16. Ibid., at 5.
17. Ibid., at 4.
18. The examples given here are mine.
19. See for example *Desktop Marketing Systems Pty Ltd v Telstra Corporation Ltd* [2002] FCAFC 112, concerning the subsistence of copyright in a telephone directory. A discussion of the case will be made later in the chapter.
20. B. Sherman and L. Bently, *The Making of Modern Intellectual Property*, supra n.11 at 6.
21. Ibid., at 206–212.
22. The literary property debates argued for and against common law literary property. The litigation was between the London and Scottish booksellers. The key cases were: *Millar v Kinkaid* (1750) 4 Burr. 2319, Eng. Rep. 210; *Tonson v Collins* (1760) 1 Black. W 301, 96 Eng. Rep. 169; *Osborne v Donaldson* (1765) 2 Eden. 328, 28 Eng. Rep. 924; *Millar v Taylor* (1769) 4 Burr. 2303, 98 Eng. Rep. 201; *Donaldson v Becket* (1774) 4 Burr. 2408, 98 Eng. Rep. 257.
23. See: R. Deazley, *On the Origin of the Right to Copy*, supra n.9.
24. B. Sherman and L. Bently, *The Making of Modern Intellectual Property*, supra n.11 at 21. See also: K. Bowrey *Don't Fence Me In: The Many Histories of Copyright*, Doctor of Juridical Studies, University of Sydney, 1994 (unpublished).
25. Locke discussed this concept, it was one he developed from Roman law, but it did not justify property in itself, except so far as occupation equalled cultivation. As I discussed in the previous chapter it was re-popularised by Blackstone in the late eighteenth century.
26. *Millar v Taylor* (1769) 4 Burr. 2303, 98 Eng. Rep. 201, at 230.
27. *Millar v Taylor* (1769) 4 Burr. 2303, 98 Eng. Rep. 201, at 233. I have added the italics to point to the ways in which property was to be known and the future elements that were used to help understand intangible property: this involved making the intangible into a visible possession that had its own marks of identification which could therefore become property.
28. The Stationers Guild was established in 1405 in London. Printmakers began to join the guild after printing was introduced.
29. B. Sherman and L. Bently *The Making of Modern Intellectual Property*, supra n.11 at 22.
30. See Chapter 1.
31. B. Sherman and L. Bently, *The Making of Modern Intellectual Property*, supra n.11 at 23.
32. The difficulty of conceiving the nature of the property rights was also debated in 'real' property too, for example in regards to custom, squatting and aristocratic inheritance claims. While the 'real' property debates were similarly philosophical they were grounded in corporeality.
33. It is worth remembering that the notion of possessive individualism was not a stable theory either, as it changed through its application in a variety of cases, depending on any number of individuals who utilised and manipulated it to justify the point or argument at hand.
34. M. Rose, 'The Author as Proprietor', supra n.5 at 39.

35. Ibid., at 39.
36. *Tonson v Collins* (1760) 96 ER 180.
37. M. Rose, *Authors and Owners*, supra n.5 at 89.
38. B. Sherman and L. Bently, *The Making of Modern Intellectual Property*, supra n.11 at 25.
39. This was reaffirmed by Blackstone where he states: 'Now the identity of a literary composition consists entirely in the sentiment and the language; the same conceptions, clothed in the same words, must necessarily be the same composition: and whatever method be taken of conveying that composition to the ear or to the eye of another, by recital, by writing, or by printing, in any number of copies or at any period of time, it is always the identical work of the author which is so conveyed.' See M. Rose, *Authors and Owners*, supra n.5 at 89–90.
40. Ibid., 91.
41. M. Rose, 'The Author as Proprietor', supra n.5. See also: R. Deazley, 'Re-reading Donaldson (1774) in the Twenty First Century and Why It Matters', supra n.9.
42. P. Miller and N. Rose, 'Governing economic life', (1990) 19 (1) *Economy and Society* 1.
43. Brevity of space does not allow for an in-depth exploration of this parallel development for law and economics.
44. I will be examining the importance of value in measuring objects for protection with respect to Aboriginal art in Part Two.
45. Remembering Locke's discussion and how rights to property are bestowed primarily through action.
46. B. Sherman and L. Bently, *The Making of Modern Intellectual Property*, supra n.11 at 49.
47. Interestingly at the same period in which the difficulty of describing the difference between the idea and its expression was contested, the same problem arose in relation to paper money. 'Currency had traditionally been solid and material: gold and silver refined to an established standard of purity and parceled into specified weights stamped into coins . . . but coinage of this sort was inadequate to meet the demands of a developing commercial nation and during the course of the century . . . forms of commercial paper were absorbed into the economic system as a legitimate form of currency. Thus money also became phantasmic, a matter of circulation of signs abstracted from their material base.' M. Rose, *Authors and Owners*, supra n.5 at 129.
48. P. Drahos, *A Philosophy of Intellectual Property*, Dartmouth Press: Sydney, 1991 at 151. See also comments on the model of 'real' property being used for intellectual property in J. Litman, 'The Public Domain', (1990) 39 (4) *Emory Law Journal* 965 at 970–972.
49. 'Another social development that must be mentioned is that copyright has on one hand become more and more the concern of enterprises and institutions, and has on the other hand developed into a legal instrument for the regulation of the transfer of cultural information. Cultural information has, speaking in economic terms, made the step from product to raw material.' F.W. Grosheide, 'When Ideas Take the Stage' (1994) 6 *European Intellectual Property Review* 219 at 219.
50. B. Kaplan, *An Unhurried View of Copyright*, supra n.2 at 9.
51. Ibid., at 9.
52. Ibid., at 10.
53. For the key case involving whether maps or charts were copyright subject matter see *Sayre v Moore* (1785) 1 East 361, 102 Eng. Rep. 139; and for abridgement, *Dodsley v Kinersley* (1761) Amb. 403, 27 Eng. Rep. 270.
54. B. Kaplan, *An Unhurried View of Copyright*, supra n.2 at 17. Of course, non-protection of translations as well as underdeveloped international protection gave a boost to the British publishing industry at the expense of the French, Flemish and German publishers. National laws did not generally recognise the copyright of foreign nationals nor the rights of colonial subjects.
55. Sherman and Bently, *The Making of Modern Intellectual Property*, supra n.11 at 63–76.
56. Ibid., at 64–65.

57. Ibid., at 73–74.
58. Ibid., at 62.
59. The other was the *Copyright of Design Act* (1839) which offered shorter periods of protection (3 months) and registration was not necessary.
60. B. Sherman and L. Bently *The Making of Modern Intellectual Property*, supra n.11 at 79–82.
61. There is a burgeoning literature on archives as key mechanisms for facilitating the making of new kinds of categories and therefore new forms of governance. See N. Dirks, *Castes of Mind: Colonialism and the Making of Modern India*, Princeton University Press: New Jersey 2001; L. Stoler, 'Colonial Archives and the Arts of Governance' (2002) 2 (1–2) *Archival Science*, 87–109; T. Osborne, 'The Ordinariness of the Archive', (1999) 12 (2) *History of Human Sciences* 51.
62. See: M. Foucault, 'Governmentality' in Burchell, G., C. Gordon and P. Miller (eds), *The Foucault Effect: Studies in Governmentality*, The University of Chicago Press: Chicago, 1991.
63. B. Sherman and L. Bently, *The Making of Modern Intellectual Property*, supra n.11 at 177.
64. Ibid., at 58.

3. Copyright and the categories of identification

It is surprising that copyright law still retains much of its pre-modern form, in that it is still relatively subject specific. One significant reason for this is because copyright law in the United Kingdom and its subsequent colonies, did not historically entertain prolonged engagement with the process of registration. Instead in 1911, copyright secured automatic protection for works. Prior to this period copyright protection had also been conditional on registration.[1] The problem and the reason for moving beyond the registration for copyright works was that the process of registration did little beyond determine 'title' to a text and perhaps unlike patents, trademarks and design, registration could not resolve the underlying difficulty of determining a property in a text.[2] The ellipse in the differential way in which copyright law emerged can also be explained through the hierarchical status that literary and artistic work held in relation to 'industrial property.' For continental copyright, the argument that justified automatic protection for literary works as against registration arose because it became extremely difficult to minimise a literary or artistic work into a representation of that work: the representation constituting the necessary form for registration. Significantly, the literary work retained its 'original' form and hence protection rather than shifting – as a consequent of registration – to acquiring protection through a representation of the subject matter.

This is not to say that copyright law didn't have its own modes of regulating knowledge through forms of categorisation. The categories of originality and authorship have functioned to maintain a perception of coherence within copyright law and established firm boundaries around its subject matter through determining what a work was and how it could be transformed. In this way authorship and originality became the key categories that provide the means for making identifications of what constitute 'legitimate' copyright subject matter.

As copyright did not require registration, it did not need to reproduce the intangible subject matter into an object of representation. However, copyright law was influenced by this way of understanding the intangible object, where the focus of the law was set upon the tangible 'creation' produced by the intangible subject matter – thus making the 'work' (the book, the artwork) itself a decontextualised legal object. But copyright took on a unique form to the other categories of intellectual property where the actual intangible subject matter continued to exert pressure in determining its nature. Thus copyright law was never totally able to exist solely on the abstraction of its categories: the specific subject matter in each case was and remains ever present and ever influential. Indeed the dependence upon both abstract categories and subject specific concerns characterises modern copyright. To this end the effectivity of copyright law still actively involves negotiating the extent to which the nature of the intangible property can be determined.

The importance of authorship and originality in characterising the nature of the copyright is evident in many examinations of copyright.[3] Both notions have determined the specificity of copyright and facilitated the distinct modes of categorisation pertaining to the subject matter afforded through copyright. The following discussion of authorship and originality foregrounds the subsequent latter examination of indigenous knowledge: specifically its inclusion and making as a discrete category within law. This is because the two key concerns that were initially raised (and continue to exist) in relation to the inclusion indigenous knowledge (known to law at first instance through the tangible product, Aboriginal art) centrally engage(d) questions of authorship and originality. Both authorship and originality are considered specifically in relation to a work presented as if it were a closed entity, not to the more fluid dynamics constitutive and determining the existence of the work. It is in this way that criteria of the identifiable 'author' and the 'original' work facilitate the idea/expression distinction that underpins the copyright regime.[4] Importantly, both categories have also incorporated an economic rationale of measurement integral to the internal coherence of intellectual property law as a whole.

AUTHORSHIP

Mark Rose and Martha Woodmansee have done much to facilitate an appreciation of the importance of authorship to the emergence of copyright.[5] As has been exposed through their work it was ostensibly relations between booksellers and publishers that pushed the law to consider the category of the author, even though ironically, in the literary property debates, authors were noticeably absent.[6] As such, law became deeply involved in constructing how this subject (the author) was to be understood before the law and consequently within society.

Early histories of copyright, such as the work by Feather and Bonham-Carter[7] primarily sought to explain 'why the priority of the law was not that of protecting the author's private property rights in the text'.[8] In such circumstances it was assumed that the law was relatively disinterested in the changing social status of the 'author'. The prevailing philosophical movement of romanticism in the eighteenth and nineteenth centuries however, meant that law did become concerned and quite instructive in the modern formation of the notion and identity of the 'author'. While certainly it is accurate to suggest that this was not a primary concern for the law, it was inevitably an effect of the law. By this I mean that because of the multiplicity of factors influencing law and its relationship with the legal idea of the 'author', an inevitable byproduct was the transference of characteristics identifying the 'author' within law to the wider society. The focus on questions of literary property in law could not help but be influenced by romantic assertions of 'natural rights': subsequently effecting how the concept of the author as an individual and also as a legal entity was seen before law as the agent determining status and authority within society.

Defining the category of the 'author' was the means for establishing the legitimacy of property in a 'work.' As Foucault has highlighted, the rise of the author in western liberal societies was intrinsically tied to relationship between the text and a system of property relations.[9] In authorising such property relations, law necessarily affected the functionality of the subject named as the 'author'. Foucault's interest was in the operation of what he calls the 'author-function'. Importantly, the first of the four general characteristics that Foucault identifies as marking the author-function is how it is 'linked to the juridical and institutionalized system that encompasses, determines and articulates the universes of discourses'.[10] Whilst Foucault was never particularly interested in law, and at times discussing it in ways that ignore and underplay the fluid power relations that make law a fundamental mechanism of governing, in this essay he does recognise the instructive relationship between the emergence of the entity named as an author, and the legal and institutional networks that uphold and endorse that same entity.

As discussed in the previous chapter, the *Donaldson v Becket* (1774)[11] case functions as the historical location where law begins to negotiate categories that identify specific kinds of intangible subject matter and in doing so produces legal authority, both in relation to law and society. With no 'authoritative legal precedent that endorsed the purported theory of right'[12] the power to define and limit copyright was left with parliament, through which statutes regulating the period of the right were endorsed. Through *Donaldson v Becket* (1774) copyright was affirmed as a creature of positive law,[13] whereby the power to limit and define the right rested within the statute, rather than existing as a common law right.[14] Through this judgment copyright was also affirmed as providing an 'economic right'.

Rose's particular interest is in how the case conveys the emergence of the author as a proprietor.[15] This is in order to highlight the historical emergence of the concept of an author, which began and was effectively completed in the eighteenth and nineteenth centuries. In this way Rose disputes the narrative of the ahistorical 'author-myth' positioned as a naturally occurring legal subject. He specifically points to *Donaldson v Becket* (1774) as a case that shows that there was no automatic connection between authors and texts. Instead, Rose points to a variety of factors, both cultural and legal, that were required before the notion of an author could be established. For example, 'before the modern author could come into being there had to exist a market for books to sustain a commercial system of cultural products'.[16] Rose observes that 'the concept of an *author* as an *originator* of a literary text, rather than a reproducer of traditional truths' had to be realised in society, before it could be actualised.[17] The notion of the author was also influenced by cultural specificities where writing and recording were understood as necessary processes of civilisation, progress and individuation.[18] In contrast, traditional truths were seen to circulate much more prolifically in oral cultures that were identified as 'communal'. This in part speaks to the dilemma of identifying and individuating indigenous works, as indigenous people are still largely seen to be reproducing traditional truths within an alternative paradigm of 'community' to that relied upon by intellectual property law. I will return to this in more depth in the second part of the book when considering how Aboriginal artists were interpreted in relation to their works in the Australian copyright cases of the 1980s.

Law was certainly responsive to the cultural influence of possessive liberalism in shaping the notion of an author. Nevertheless there were other ruptures and discontinuities that also facilitated the production of the author and the category of authorship before the law.[19] It is these multiple vectors that help configure the notion of authorship in the abstract, where the 'author' as an individuated subject, becomes known to law only in its abstraction. In this way authorship also becomes a legal category in its own right that can measure and identify a 'work'. Rose's insights about the rise of modern authorship expose the complexity of the law and the difficulty in locating a specific period where the law was seen to arrive at a particular definition of the author in relation to a text. In its abstraction authorship becomes a self-justifying concept that averts attention away from the problem of boundaries and importantly, subjectivity. In conjunction with the new economic logic of the law, authorship provides a useful (if not also self-fulfilling) category through which identification of legitimate legally identified and defensible works can be made.

It is precisely the lack of clarity in the terms that seek to identify the intangible, that still makes copyright susceptible to concerns regarding definitions of what constitutes the property. According to modern copyright the author is seen as the first owner of the property. While 'author' is not defined in *Copyright Act 1968* (Cth),[20] the concept does imply that the author is the originator of the ideas expressed in a material form. The connection between authorship and originality remains important in modern copyright and it is in this way that the two terms function to identify copyright subject matter, for if there is no identifiable author, then there is no copyright. Likewise, if there is no originality invested in the work, then there is no protection. Of course the boundaries here are not as clear as they seem, for there is no definition of an author or of originality in the statute, therein providing the possibility for a range of cultural objects to be considered as legitimate copyright subject matter.

ORIGINALITY

Originality, like authorship, remains undefined in the (Australian) *Copyright Act 1968* (Cth). Similarly, originality has historically helped determine the nature of the intangible property. In the literary property debates, originality helped identify, to some extent, the process of individuating an idea and expressing it in a tangible work. In this way originality was concerned with a *judgment of the relationship* between the work and the creator.[21] It also functioned in the nineteenth century as a means of determining whether a work infringed another work.[22]

Through this early period, originality served as a means to identify the defendant's work from the plaintiff's, and inquiry into originality was not directed towards the plaintiff's work alone – this was a shift that occurred in the twentieth century.[23] Thus originality was used as a mechanism to consider the equilibrium of interests invested in a determination of an 'original' work. For example this was a key element in early cases involving sea charts,[24] road maps[25] and the French dictionary.[26] Drawing a balance between protection and access did not involve a determination between private property rights.[27] The key question was how to balance the original effort of both parties, rather than upholding the private rights of the plaintiff. In this way broad social considerations were imbued in determining a copyright, including the benefits to the public and the existing market for works of an informational nature.

The importance of the concept of originality in determining copyright is evident where the term functions as the means for identifying both the mental labour or 'creativity' of the 'author' and the nature of the property. Through a perception, consolidated in the literary property debates, that ideas come from an 'intellectual commons',[28] the notion of originality was developed as a way to individuate and understand the distinct transformation of the 'ideas in common' as the unique expression of an individual who has a right to its ownership. In this way individualisation occurs when the idea is extracted from the shared space of knowledge and independently expressed. Originality then, performs a dual role as it not only pertains to the individual but also identifies the nature of the expression manifest in the intangible subject matter. The abstract notion of originality functions as a mechanism for identification, through which the work itself becomes knowable and individuated.

In the early period of copyright law, prior to the *Imperial Copyright Act* of 1911 that, on adoption by commonwealth legislature, extended British copyright law to colonies and dominions including Canada, New Zealand, Australia and South Africa,[29] originality was implicit within the concept of creativity: each act by an individual in producing a unique object required creativity and was necessarily original. Following 1911, originality was written into the statute as the *Copyright Act 1912* (Cth) confirmed that every work that was claimed as copyright must be original. In Australia, by the *Copyright Act 1968* (Cth), subsistence of copyright existed in 'every *original* literary, dramatic, musical and artistic work'.[30] One of the outcomes of this interpretative process was that the originality requirement came to be read as a reference to the plaintiff's work alone, with the question of the originality of the defendant's work only arising as a sub-issue under the issue of infringement – in relation to whether or not an alleged taking of the plaintiff's work was substantial, given the changes that the defendant may have made to the work.[31] For example, in the Australian case, *Victoria Park Racing and Recreation Grounds Co Ltd v Taylor* (1937), protection was denied to the compilation of horse racing details written on a display board justified through the extent that,

> some original result must be produced. This does not mean that new or inventive ideas must be contributed. The work need show no literary or other skill and judgment. But it must originate with the author, and be more than a copy of other material.[32]

In another case that illustrates the difficulty with originality, *Kalamazoo (Aust) Pty Ltd v Compact Business Systems P/L* (1985), Thomas J determined that copyright subsists in the pegboard systems constructed by employees of Kalamazoo. The point of comparison is with the plaintiff's work alone. He states:

> while I refuse to find that the authors showed great skill, I did find that their preparation required a degree of concentration, care, analysis, comparison . . .

> In each case some awareness of contemporary developments and the marketability of such forms played a part in their creation.[33]

The shift in how originality is used to identify a plaintiff's work rather than a defendant's work speaks to the reprioritisation of interests in defining 'original'. Remembering the eighteenth century case of translation, it was the defendant's work that was considered closely to see what new elements had been added, not what had been taken from the plaintiff's 'original' work. Part of this shift in the twentieth century is due to concern that defining originality must be done as objectively and fairly as judicially possible, and this meant considering the plaintiff's work over that of the defendant's without reference to the work's value in aesthetic terms.[34] As the early twentieth century case (which underpins current Australian judicial interpretation), *University of London Press Ltd v University Tutorial Press Ltd* (1916) demonstrates, the formulation was:

> The originality which was required relates to the expression of the thought. But the Act does not require that the expression must be in an original or novel form, but that the work must not be copied from another work – that it should originate from the author.[35]

The difficulty of determining the boundaries of originality in particular cases however, demonstrates the challenge of applying such an abstract concept as a legally imposed standard. For the standard is ambiguous. It is difficult to determine who 'wins' through the indeterminacy of the law. Attention then, must be directed at specific instances of case law – for example what actually happens with the ambiguity of the categories in the actual practice of the law? The importance of judicial determination highlights the position of case law in informing the more 'abstract' theory.

Recent Australian case law highlights the extent to which a work constitutes originality has required questions of judgment by the court for which there is no clear point of reference.[36] This has pushed law to a space where the Court decides the merit of originality in works on a case by case basis, the law still being subject specific and case specific in its determination of 'originality'.[37] It also shows that issues about the nature of copyright and its justification and boundaries were not resolved clearly in the nineteenth century, despite the management discussed by Sherman and Bently of intangible rights.[38] The problems were merely hidden beneath a superficial classification of interests and impoverished definitional rubrics.

The Australian case law aptly demonstrates the difficulties facing the Court in deciding on matters of originality. Commenting in his judgment from the initial hearing of *Telstra v Desktop Marketing Systems* (2001), a case that, at first instance, involved determining whether the compilation of names, addresses and phone numbers found in the white or yellow pages constituted copyright subject matter, Finkelstein J states;

> In precisely what sense a work must be original is not clear and the resolution of that question lies at the heart of this case. A work will lack originality if it is copied or adapted from another. This does not mean that the subject matter of copyright must be new or novel, as is the case of an invention the subject of patent protection. To the contrary, much of what is found in literature, drama or music is not new, but nevertheless it is proper subject matter for copyright.
>
> Originality means at least, that the work has been created by the author.[39]

The issue of originality underpins this case, but the indeterminacy of the term poses real difficulties in deciding both on the subsistence of copyright and consequently, infringement. As noted above, Finkelstein J and subsequently Chief Justice Black and Justices Lindgren and Sackville in the Full Federal Court appeal, recognise that it is the slippery question of originality that underpins the case.

Establishing the originality of the telephone book speaks to the problem central to intellectual property law: the difficulty in determining what the intangible element actually is within the product brought before the court. Within Australian copyright legislation, the phone book comes under protection as a special kind of literary work: as a compilation.[40] In this regard the question of arranging the information becomes one of labour rather than creativity. Desktop Marketing argued that as copyright cannot exist with facts, and as names, phone numbers and addresses found in the white pages are constituted as facts that freely circulated in the public domain, copyright did not exist and by virtue of its non-existence, was not infringed. Alternatively, Telstra argued that by way of the *intellectual labour* exerted in the directories, the product was an industrious collection of factual data sufficient to attract copyright protection as a compilation. The extent of the labour, mental and physical, exerted in compiling the phone book, became the measure of its originality. Finkelstein J seems genuinely astonished when he comments that '[a] casual reader of a directory might be surprised to learn of the complexities involved in its preparation'.[41]

The stability of the category of originality is maintained by shifting the way in which originality is determined. Intellectual labour becomes the signifier for originality and is justified through considering the plaintiff's work in isolation. It is in this way that the surety of the category is upheld. Indeed, it could be argued that the position taken in regards to originality functions as an institutionalised justification that maintains the coherence of legal categories of originality and authorship, because copyright depends upon them for its own perpetuation.[42] The legal principle of originality is decontextualised, elevating it to a more universal and abstract, rather than specific, level and the law maintains the appearance of objectivity, even if it has to decide on a case by case basis what constitutes an 'original' work. However, for those who remain unsatisfied with the judicial claims of objectivity, it is clear, as with most legal classifications, 'originality is not natural and secure, but culturally and historically determined'.[43]

The decision by the Full Bench of the Federal Court in *Desktop Marketing*[44] demonstrates how the linkages are made that connect authorship and originality but also points to how copyright law depends upon the specific, in this case the technological facts that led to the creation of the database, for confirmation of the abstract, that is, the production of an 'original' work. The case also highlights how low the Australian threshold for originality actually is. Chief Justice Black and Justices Lindgren and Sackville in the appeal follow the precedent set in the first instance by Finkelstein J. In his judgment Lindgren J cites from *Halsbury's Laws of England* that:

> Only original works are protected, but it is not requisite that the work should be the expression of thought, for Copyright Acts are not concerned with the originality of the ideas, but with the expression of thought, and in the case of a literary work, with the expression of thought in print and writing. The originality which is required relates to the expression of the thought. It is not required that the expression should be in an original or novel form but that the work should not be copied from another work; it should originate from the author.[45]

The argument linking authorship to originality is nicely demonstrated in this citation. Its utilisation in *Desktop Marketing* highlights two points. The first is that it represents the standard judicial argument that justifies both the property right and the work as property through categories of copyright. The second is the reluctance of the law and the courts to recognise the difficulty that evoking the abstraction of such categories perpetuates an inability within the law to fully grasp the problem. Jane Ginsburg has also argued that the law 'encounters far more difficulty accommodating works at once high in commercial value but low in personal authorship'.[46] In the silences brought into the law with its modern 'development', what is made possible is the reification of the author and work, giving both a suggestion of secure, self-evident meaning. When proprietal claims challenge the status of either the author or the work by a competing commodity, it is necessary to affirm the priority of the legal precepts of the author and the original, so that the stability of the categories and the law itself is maintained. As McKeough, Bowrey and Griffith observe;

> To some extent the concept of what constitutes a work within the Act and the concept of originality are intertwined. It is difficult to discuss what amounts

> to a work without discussing originality, since without a sufficient degree of originality, a work will not come into existence.[47]

Thus the problem still remains one of determining and identifying what the intangible element is for copyright protection through abstract categories and circular relations of justification. In this way, legal argument functions as a powerful forum, 'in which dominant narratives of social reality are produced and alternative discourses silenced'.[48]

The category of originality, because of ambiguities in definition, depends upon the judgment of the court to translate and apply the abstraction into contextual meaning. The function of the court then becomes one that manages categories of copyright and inevitably the stability of the law. In short, the court plays a fundamental role in upholding the legitimacy of categories that measure and identify copyright. The court governs the way in which interpretations of the law are made. To this end, each judgment of originality that the court makes in order to contextualise the abstract term becomes a matter of fact and degree determined differently in every case.[49] Recognising that judges do not exist in a vacuum but are social and cultural beings very much like the rest of the population then means that if each case is measured by fact and degree and each judge has their own interpretation and methods of applying the law, then it is possible to argue that these methods are not and have never been 'objective'. Instead such decisions and questions of degree embody cultural influences. Inevitably when making a decision, the law will be influenced by cultural factors emanating from the subjective position of the judge in applying the abstract principle upon which the stability of the law depends. The abstract principle primarily being the singularity of an author/original identification as a substitute for a more metaphysical determination of ownership.

THE SUBJECTIVITY OF COPYRIGHT

The argument that has been built so far is that the authoritative narrative that promotes law as abstract and *a*historical fails to engage meaningfully with the reality of subjective decisions that shape the direction taken by law. Indeed it could be argued that the key failing of the literature accounting for the emergence of intellectual property law (which the previous section has drawn from) is characterised by an absence of political and economic discourses within the theory. The legal literature, although informed by critical legal sensibilities, addresses the jurisprudence of copyright and literary property and its philosophical pretensions whilst scaling over the practice and contemporary nineteenth century politics. The stance is justified because of difficulties in factoring in law's indeterminacy. For instance, because the actual emergence of intellectual property is so discordant and diversely expressed, the tendency for legal historians and theorists has been to look to a way of encapsulating the broad sweep, with little focus on the existing cases. However, as McKeough, Bowrey and Griffith observe,

> In reading copyright case law it is important to consider whether theories like romanticism have influenced judicial understandings. Though copyright is . . . a creature of positive law, despite *Copyright Act 1968* (Cth) s8, not all important copyright principles are expressed in the text of legislation. Further, in many places the legislation relies upon 'ordinary' or 'common sense' meaning of terms. There is ample space for romantic and other values coming into the body of copyright law. *Therefore understanding copyright law requires an interpretation of case law in view of many possible social and cultural influences and prejudices, including romanticism.*[50]

As already discussed, it is a combination of postmodern and critical legal critiques that has led to dissatisfaction with the authority of legal reasoning in copyright case law. Such critiques point out that the law does not function in isolation, but produces and is produced by cultural values and perspectives. This is in particular regard to 'common sense' decisions that are made in any number of ways by the court when applying a principle that is not explicitly defined in the legislation. This complexity highlights the discontinuity of the law, for cultural and political factors inevitably influence the shape that the law takes.

While Mark Rose's work pointed debate in this direction, he maintained a strong interest in the particular category of authorship. Indeed, the cultural production of the author and the twinned concepts of authorship and originality in intellectual property law are among the many potential sites for the recognition of the cultural influence and production of categories within the law. Following from Rose's work and also influenced by Foucault, Rosemary Coombe has written extensively on the inevitable influence of cultural factors on the law.[51] With an interest in the peculiar political intersections that legitimate intellectual property laws, Coombe has also pointed to the dynamism of contemporary cultural practices that promote individual resistance to monopoly privileges extant within an intellectual property regime. Thus Coombe highlights the multiplicity of experience through which individuals and the law are interconnected.[52] Rather than the spheres being abstract and separated, they are intertwined and contingent upon the other for future development and direction. As a result of cultural influence, the possibilities for shaping the direction that the law takes function within a network of multiple relations, where the constant process of reshaping the law is in direct response to multiple cultural productions.

The inevitability of the engagement of law with cultural functions is, in part, due to the difficulty of people as legal subjects who do not necessarily behave in a predictable manner for law or governance. Thus one of the difficulties for the law is that it must be dealing constantly with the complexity of individuals and how they perform as legal subjects.[53] It is almost impossible to speculate upon the specificity of action undertaken by individuals as legal subjects.[54] For certain legal subjects, the law intersects their lives at an extreme rate, almost to the extent that individual lives embody a *performativity* in relation to law and legal bureaucracy.[55] In short, there is no certainty in how individuals relate to the law, and this makes for complex legal subjects. One of the reasons why law is so messy and disorderly is that 'citizens make challenging legal subjects'.[56] A snapshot of the broader landscape of litigation law points to such difficulties.

This dilemma is also present in copyright law, where the law has also attempted to accommodate demands raised through the increase in new and different technologies. How individuals negotiate around new knowledge and new knowledge industries and lay claims of ownership to knowledge affect the response of the law. In this way then, copyright is influenced by relationships between individuals, as legal subjects who intersect the law through an engagement with cultural products, for instance, those increasingly produced through information technologies and digital communications.

Notably Coombe engages with a variety of theoretical and philosophical positions in order to more fully understand the dynamics generated by the law in contemporary cultural practice. Avoiding traditional jurisprudential thought that considers the law through positions that have been historically favoured by the law to the exclusion of others, she notes the tendency within scholarship devoted to intellectual property to limit consideration to legal doctrine and legal rationality.[57] Such literature accounts for the function of the law without critically examining its operation. Coombe continues her point through emphasising that:

> [t]here has been too little consideration of the cultural nature of the actual forms that intellectual property laws protect, the social and historical contexts in which cultural proprietorship is (or is not) assumed, or the manner in which these rights are (or are not) exercised and enforced to intervene in every day struggles for meaning.[58]

The particular effects of the law need to be considered not in isolation, but with regard to the individual and cultural products generated through the intersection of law and 'culture'.

These critical cultural legal frames point to the role that individuals play in exercising autonomy from the law and also generating new and productive ways of intersecting with law. Individual interpretative agency constitutes an embodied approach to the effects of law and how these effects impact in a variety of dispersed locales. For when judges make decisions based on 'common sense', they are only one in a number of players that duly influence the cultural shape that the law takes: multiple parties push and wrestle, influence and negotiate the form of the law. These influences occur through particular resistances to law, but also in the cases that are tested through law. For cases do not exist in abstraction either, but are generated from a particular time and space, and as reaction to a particular incident or against the law. Recognising this inherent politics allows for alternate readings of the emergence of discrete categories within law.

As new knowledge and knowledge products come before law, increasingly law must determine the extent of the protection it can grant and the identifying characteristics of the material. But this exposes a challenge, whereby calls for protection of new material – an expectation of legal action – increasingly mean that the law must employ its principles of measurement and identification and ultimately widen the scope of what is considered to be intellectual property. Thus the difficulties are part of a continuum, where the law can be seen to be working through an ongoing set of concerns. The problems are however modified through the changing nature of the intangible subject matter and the multiple levels of expectation generated through individual actors.

It is the widening of the scope of what comes under and can be protected as intellectual property that has become a focus for critical inquiry. The increased power of intellectual property to protect cultural products has facilitated such a focus.[59] In a social environment where trademarks circulate to designate ownership of a product, where digital technology pushes for rethinking the concept of the author and where an individual is exposed to endless merchandising protected by intellectual property laws, critiques of intellectual property seek to point to how such laws are functioning to increasingly control the flow of information.[60]

Contemporary theoretical critiques also point to what is excluded from intellectual property and have prompted a reflexivity regarding these exclusions. For instance, this includes indigenous and/or local knowledge. In this regard the process for inclusion evokes a sustained and prolonged rethinking of how and to what extent these 'new' knowledges can be incorporated. The process is not an instantaneous one. Rather it evolves from a political location that develops and produces itself as a category to be known before the law. The process is sustained and draws on multiple actors and employs a network of relations that eventually produce the 'new' knowledge as a category in its own right.

It was through postmodern and related critiques that intellectual property law became sufficiently self-reflexive to address the exclusion of indigenous knowledge from its sphere. Yet indigenous knowledge is still seen as a kind of 'special' case for the law. The perception has developed through a reflection of the cultural specificity of the law in regards to indigenous people and the effects of colonisation. It is also perhaps because there has been hesitancy in moving beyond the social construction of indigenous people as 'reproducers of traditional truths', rather than as 'authors' (albeit in different forms) of contemporary narratives.

CONCLUSION

Recognising the plurality of relations that have contributed to the production of the category of the 'indigenous' within intellectual property provides a space to understand the connections between legal scholarship, history, politics and legal practice. In this way, there is no singular factor that could explain the emergence of a concept of indigenous knowledge within an intellectual property discourse, but rather a multiplicity of factors pushing, constructing and producing indigenous knowledge as a distinct issue to be taken up and advanced and hence as a category to be known before the law. Perhaps as Martin Nakata suggests, it is the 'Indigenous Knowledge enterprise'[61] and the increased national and international inquiries into indigenous knowledge[62] that help locate concerns and generate levels of expectation for the legal protection of indigenous knowledge. But what characterises the position of indigenous knowledge within intellectual property law (as within other discourses) is how it is unproblematically assigned a 'different' status. The challenge then is to recognise the extent that law is also dependent upon other authoritative discourses, such as anthropology, in its identification of the indigenous as 'other'. This position directly affects the way in which the law treats the inclusion of indigenous knowledge.[63] Thus the law becomes deeply involved in constructing how this new category of subject matter is to be understood both in law, and as suggested through the case of the 'author', also in society. Law is involved in making an 'indigenous knowledge' category as well as responsible for distributing this new category within social and political contexts.

The purpose of this first part of the book has been to expose the complexity and messiness of the law – specifically, that intellectual property law, far from being a coherent body of law, is characterised by internal struggles to identify and determine the nature of the intangible elements that it seeks to protect. In this regard, the history of intellectual property law that has been provided, functions to illustrate that what we currently know as intellectual property is a relatively recent phenomenon. Indeed, it is the difficulties within modern law itself that have led to the construction of categories that identify the subject matter of the law. This work has followed from Sherman and Bently in locating a history of intellectual property law that speaks to the construction of intellectual property law as a whole, rather than subject specific interests.

In looking at the characteristics of copyright law, the point has also been to show how a range of cultural factors also engage and intersect with law, ultimately influencing the direction that the law takes. This approach is integral to an appreciation of how and to what extent indigenous knowledge has been produced as a category in its own right within intellectual property law. My point is to show the extent of elements that push, negotiate and construct indigenous knowledge within an intellectual property framework, and that this framework imposes conditions of possibility in regards to outcomes and discussions of property rights in indigenous knowledge.

The second part of the book will now consider more closely the concomitant factors that have been involved in making the category of indigenous knowledge within intellectual property law. Importantly, it considers the conditions of existence for government intervention articulated through the key governmental reports which function as important precursors for the case law. Ultimately, as we move into the second phase of the book, it is important to remember that the production of indigenous knowledge within intellectual property discourse is still actively occurring, as the law continues to grapple with the difficulty and difference of the subject matter; particularly in specific circumstances that demand the functionality of the law while also pointing to its complexity.

NOTES

1. The *Copyright Act 1911* (UK) was adopted in Australia through the *Copyright Act 1912* (Cth). The main reason for adopting the law in Australia was that, as the new Imperial legislation was designed to apply to members of the Berne Convention (1886), it was argued that if Australia adopted the Act, Australian copyrights would automatically be respected in France, Belgium, Germany and Spain (amongst others). In addition the Imperial legislation offered a longer period of protection. The *Copyright Act 1968* (Cth) is Australia's current copyright act.
2. For example, in the registration of patents a precise description of the invention was necessary in order to limit the specific right to a graphical and textual description available for public inspection. If copyright had kept to the 'title' rationality, copyright claims would have been limited to exact/precise reproductions.
3. For example see: M. Rose *Authors and Owners: The Invention of Copyright*, Harvard

University Press: Cambridge MA, 1993 at 113–129; and, D. Saunders, *Authorship and Copyright*, Routledge Press: UK, 1992.

4. The basis for the idea/expression distinction is that property cannot be vested in ideas themselves, only the expression of those ideas that is conveyed in some tangible form.
5. M. Rose, *Authors and Owners*, supra n.3.
6. Whilst the author was the focal point of the literary property debates, they were argued between the different booksellers, hence the term 'battle of the booksellers'. The author provided both sides with a vehicle to mobilise arguments. For example the author became representative of the argument of a common law right, even though it was the booksellers who were arguing for this right.
7. J. Feather, *The Provincial Book Trade in Eighteenth Century England*, Cambridge University Press: Cambridge, 1985; and, V. Bonham-Carter, *Authors by Profession, Volume One and Two*, The Society of Authors: London, 1978.
8. J. McKeough, K. Bowrey and P. Griffith, *Intellectual Property: Commentary and Materials* (third edition), The Law Book Company: Sydney, 2002 at 17.
9. M. Foucault, 'What is an Author?', in Rabinow, P. (ed), *The Foucault Reader: An Introduction to Foucault's Thought*, Penguin Books: London, 1984.
10. Ibid., at 162.
11. *Donaldson v Becket* (1774) 4 Burr 2408, 98 Eng. Rep. 257.
12. J. McKeough, K. Bowrey and P. Griffith, *Intellectual Property. Commentary and Materials*, supra n.8 at 20.
13. Ibid., at 20.
14. R. Deazley, 'Re-reading Donaldson (1774) in the Twenty First Century and Why It Matters', (2003) 25 (6) *European Intellectual Property Review* 270; and R. Deazley, *On the Origin of the Right to Copy: Charting the Movement of Copyright Law in Eighteenth Century Britain (1695–1775)*, Hart Publishing: Oxford and Portland, 2004.
15. M. Rose, 'The Author as Proprietor: *Donaldson v Becket* and the Genealogy of Modern Authorship', Sherman, B., and Strowel, A. (eds), *Of Authors and Origins: Essays on Copyright Law*, Clarendon Press: Oxford, 1994.
16. Ibid., at 29.
17. Ibid., at 29. Emphasis mine.
18. S. Wright, *International Human Rights, Decolonisation and Globalisation: Becoming Human*, Routledge: London and New York, 2001 at 99.
19. Most obviously these include significant economic and political changes. See M. Rose, 'The Author as Proprietor' supra n.15. Also see: M. Woodmansee, 'The Genius and the Copyright: Economic and Legal Conditions of the Emergence of the Author', (1984) 17 *Eighteenth Century Studies* 425.
20. Except for photographs where the author is the person who takes the photograph, *Copyright Act 1968* (Cth) s.10(1).
21. B. Sherman, 'From the Non-original to the Ab-original', in Sherman, B., and A. Strowel (eds), *Of Authors and Origins: Essays on Copyright Law*, Clarendon Press: Oxford, 1994 at 119.
22. See my earlier comments about the case of translation.
23. The early twentieth century case that signals this shift is *University of London Press Pty Ltd v University Tutorial Press Ltd* [1916] 2 Ch 602.
24. *Sayre v Moore* (1785) 1 East 361, 102 Eng. Rep. 139.
25. *Cary v Kearsley* (1802) 4 Esp. 168, 170 Eng. Rep. 679.
26. *Spiers v Brown* (1858) 6 WR 352.
27. K. Bowrey, 'Originality in Copyright: How low can you go?' UNSW Seminar Paper, 11 September, 2001 [on file with author]. As Bowrey explains, 'Many nineteenth century cases do not see originality as referring to a question about the subsistence of copyright – in terms of testing what the plaintiff has done to produce the expression. They understand originality as involving a contextual and relational judgment about this works position to the marketplace. Whether copyright should protect this 'original' work depends upon the consequences of its protection for others.'

28. For a useful discussion on the concept of intellectual commons see: P. Drahos, *A Philosophy of Intellectual Property*, Dartmouth Press: Sydney, 1991 from 54.
29. S. Wright. *International Human Rights, Decolonisation and Globalisation: Becoming Human*, supra n.18 at 119.
30. *Copyright Act 1968* (Cth) s.32.
31. K. Bowrey 'Originality in Copyright: How low can you go?' UNSW Seminar Paper, Sept 11, 2001.
32. *Victoria Park Racing and Recreation Grounds Co Ltd v Taylor* (1937) 58 CLR 479 at 511 (Dixon J).
33. *Kalamazoo (Aust) Pty Ltd v Compact Business Systems P/L* (1985) 5 IPR 213.
34. This corresponds with laws own concern with aesthetics that marks its modern development. See Chapter Two.
35. *University of London Press Ltd v University Tutorial Press Ltd* (1916) 2 Ch 602.
36. The recent Australian case law is *Desktop Marketing Systems Pty Ltd v Telstra Corporation Limited* [2002] FCAFC 112.
37. This is further illustrated by the different decisions and rationales utilised in other jurisdictions faced with the same problems of originality, fixation and phone books. Whilst the Australian case followed the English case *Walter v Lane* [1900] AC 539, the decision in the United States case, *Feist Publications, Inc., v. Rural Telephone Service Co.*, 499 U.S. 340 (1991) found that there was no copyright in Rural's telephone book.
38. B. Sherman and L. Bently, *The Making of Modern Intellectual Property: The British Experience 1760–1911*, Cambridge University Press: Cambridge, 1999 at 101–128.
39. *Telstra Corporation Limited v Desktop Marketing Systems Pty Ltd* (2001) FCA 612.
40. In the *Copyright Act 1968* (Cth) s.10(1) a *literary work* includes:
    a. a table, or compilation, expressed in words, figures or symbols; and,
    b. a computer program or compilation of computer programs.
41. *Telstra Corporation Limited v Desktop Marketing Systems Pty Ltd* (2001) FCA 612.
42. J. Gaines, *Contested Culture: The Image, the Voice and the Law*, University of North Carolina Press: Chapel Hill, London, 1994 at 13–17.
43. B. Sherman, 'From the Non-original to the Ab-original' supra n.21 at 120.
44. *Desktop Marketing Systems Pty Ltd v Telstra Corporation Limited* [2002] FCAFC 112.
45. *Halsbury's Laws of England Second Edition*, 1932, vol 7 at 521 cited in *Desktop Marketing Systems Pty Ltd v Telstra Corporation Limited* (2002) FCAFC 112.
46. J. Ginsburg, 'Creation and Commercial Value: Copyright Protection of Works of Information' (1990) 90 *Columbia Law Review* 1865 at 1866. However the United States has adopted a different standard see: *Feist Publications v Rural Telephone Service* (1991) 499 U.S. 340.
47. J. McKeough, K. Bowrey and P. Griffith, *Intellectual Property: Commentary and Materials*, supra n.8 at 55.
48. D. Otto, 'Subalterity and International Law: The Problems of Global Community and the Incommensurabilty of Difference' in Darian-Smith, E., and P. Fitzpatrick (eds), *Laws of the Postcolonial*, University of Michigan: United States, 1999 at 162.
49. The notion of 'fact and degree' in originality cases was developed by Lord Atkinson in *Macmillan & Co Ltd v K & J Cooper* (1923) LR 51 Ind. App. 109 at 125 where he states, 'In every case it must depend largely on the special facts of the case, and must in each case be very much a question of degree.'
50. J. McKeough, K. Bowrey and P. Griffith, *Intellectual Property: Commentary and Materials*, supra n.8 at 23 [emphasis mine].
51. Much of her earlier work has been collected in the book, R. Coombe, *The Cultural Life of Intellectual Properties: Authorship, Appropriation and the Law*, Duke University Press: Durham and London, 1998.
52. Ibid., see generally the 'Introduction'.
53. K. Bowrey and M. Rimmer, 'Rip, Mix, Burn: The Politics of Peer to Peer', (2002) 7 (8) *First Monday*.
54. I have explored this elsewhere in relation to community based legislation. See: J.

Anderson, 'The Politics of Indigenous Knowledge: Australia's Proposed Communal Moral Rights Bill', (2004) 27 (3) *New South Wales Law Journal* 585.

55. In this way I mean that lives become acted out and mediated through law in multiple contexts. For many individuals much daily life is played out or performed in spaces of legal influence such as courts, prisons or mediated through legal officers such as police and lawyers. I describe this as being the 'performativity' of the law, following from Judith Butler's work on the performance of gender. See: J. Butler, *Gender Trouble: feminism and the subversion of identity,* Routledge: New York, 1990. Thoughts in this context have developed through consideration of the legal performativity of indigenous youth in north west New South Wales. It prompts questions about what the effects of this are for a variety of (social and cultural) futures. I thank my sister, Sophie Anderson, Senior Solicitor, Western Aboriginal Legal Service, for extended discussions with me on this subject.
56. K. Bowrey and M. Rimmer, 'Rip, Mix and Burn' supra n.53.
57. R. Coombe, *The Cultural Life of Intellectual Properties: Authorship, Appropriation and the Law* supra n.51.
58. Ibid., at 7.
59. See for instance: P. Drahos with J. Braithwaite, *Information Feudalism: Who Owns the Knowledge Economy?*, Earthscan Publications: London, 2002.
60. For a varying opinions regarding this subject: P. Drahos with J. Braithwaite *Information Feudalism*, ibid; L. Lessig, *The Future of Ideas: The Fate of the Commons in an Interconnected World*, Random House: New York, 2001; M Ryan, *Knowledge Diplomacy: Global Competition and the Politics of Intellectual Property Future*, Brookings Institution: Washington DC, 1998; S. Shulman, *Owning the Future*, Houghton Mifflin: Massachusetts, 1999; J. Litman, *Digital Copyright*, Prometheus Books: New York, 2001; J. Boyle, *Shamans, Software and Spleens: Law and the Construction of the Information Society*, Harvard University Press: Cambridge MA, 1996; S. Vaidhyanathan, *Copyrights and Copywrongs: The Rise of Intellectual Property and How it Threatens Creativity*, New York University Press: New York, 2001.
61. M. Nakata, 'Indigenous Knowledge and the Cultural Interface: Underlying Issues at the Intersection of Knowledge and Information Systems', (2002) 28 *International Federation of Libraries Association Journal* 281 at 282.
62. A. Agrawal, 'Dismantling the Divide Between Indigenous and Scientific Knowledge', (1995) 26 *Development and Change* 413 at 415.
63. This will be taken up in Part Three.

PART II

Knowledge

Introduction

> [t]o identify a problem as a legal need is to make a particular judgment about appropriate solutions to that problem and then to recast the conception of the problem to accord with the nature of the proposed solution.[1]

Law has established certain pre-eminent boundaries in addressing the problem of indigenous knowledge. This includes the way in which concepts of indigenous knowledge are positioned within the law and the extent that protecting a diversity of indigenous interests in controlling and disseminating knowledge systems is secured through an expectation of legal remedy. The challenge of how to stop the unauthorised use of indigenous knowledge is now firmly constituted as a problem to be solved by and managed in the legal domain.

The possibility for legal frameworks to deliver important entitlements and recognition that, whilst partial and incomplete, would nevertheless be difficult to gain elsewhere recognises that within law, certain politics of demand are at play which emanate from discursive positions not necessarily (at least initially) informed by law or bureaucracy. In this sense, while law may have a central role in making meaning about a particular subject, there is a range of other elements involved in bringing a particular issue to the attention of law. For instance, in Australia, changing political environments, the rise of an international Aboriginal art market and the advocacy of key individuals were all instrumental factors in alerting law to the problem of inappropriate use of Aboriginal artistic designs. Indeed, it is significant that the copying of Aboriginal artistic styles had been encouraged and endorsed for at least a century. This leads to the fundamental question: what was the shift that saw this copying as a legal problem, rather than a state and socially sanctioned process informing a nationalist aesthetic? The point to remember is that the making of this problem within a legal space was not necessarily predictable and thus suggests a range of changing circumstances that influenced how law came to identify the 'problem' of copying Aboriginal art.

The early reaction of the law was promising but uncertain.[2] There was hesitancy in regards to the 'appropriateness' of reconciling western legal principles to indigenous concepts of knowledge and ownership. However, the subsequent developments in the production of indigenous knowledge within the law were not achieved through further litigation. It was governmental action. For law is not just court determined (directly applying the law). It is also managed through bureaucratic intervention, as law establishes and defines new spaces of intervention which may ultimately lead to legislative reform.

However, within legal bureaucracy the culturally specific nature of indigenous knowledge continues to present challenges regarding the position of 'culture'. As I discussed in the last chapter, how the law treats difference is on its own terms, that is, what it can admit is mediated through its own modes of identification and categorisation, largely established through precedent. As indigenous intellectual property is not a 'legal' category in the sense that it is not derived from a specific piece of legislation in synthesis of common law, how did indigenous knowledge come to be firmly grounded in the legal sphere? Does the nature of its fabrication affect how the issue is talked about and constituted as a problem? To what extent do the discussions present the possibility of an outcome? What, if any, potential remedies exist beyond the law?

This second part of the book is divided into four chapters. The opening chapter picks up from the previous discussion on the making of intellectual property law and extends it into the context of identifying and classifying Aboriginal art. It begins with an appreciation of the importance of economic incentive and the commodity production of Aboriginal art in constituting indigenous knowledge as a distinct entity for law reform. Drawing upon insights provided by Bernard Edelman, my argument is that law takes on and forwards legal problems with significant economic implications. Paralleling the incorporation of photography and cinema as intellectual property subjects with Aboriginal art and hence indigenous knowledge provides a useful vantage point for understanding how law first identifies, and then classifies new kinds of cultural/economic products.

The second chapter is a site-specific study of the paradoxical enclosure and openness of the bureaucratic agenda targeting indigenous interests in intellectual property. To this end my argument will consider the two leading governmental reports dealing specifically with the protection of Aboriginal art and cultural expressions released within Australia: the 1981 *Report of the Working Party on the Protection of Aboriginal Folklore*; and the 1994 *Stopping the Rip Offs: Intellectual Property Protection for Aboriginal and Torres Strait Islander Peoples*. These two reports are significant precisely because they have been instrumental in directing the legal approach in Australia to protecting indigenous knowledge. However, the difficulty of negotiating an agreed purpose for the protection of indigenous knowledge undermines each report. This affects how indigenous knowledge is produced and made knowable as a legal subject. The importance of these bureaucratic reports lies in the way they have functioned simultaneously to set the legal trajectory and affirm the authority of intellectual property. As such they have been instructive in the development of a specific kind of governable space, where debates concerning intellectual property and indigenous knowledge may be heard, phrased and understood.[3]

Following from this study, the third chapter will provide a close examination of how this 'new' issue of bureaucratic attention and management was dealt with in case law. The chapter will consider the two cases: *Milpurrurru & Others v Indofurn Pty Ltd*[4] (hereafter the *carpets case*) and *Bulun Bulun & Others v R & T Textiles Pty Ltd.*[5] While both these cases involve the unauthorised reproduction of Aboriginal art each is distinctive owing to the differing elements of copyright law that constitute their focus, and the extent to which the recognition of cultural differences is incorporated into the law through the decisions made. The *carpets case* (1994) sets the precedent that enables *Bulun Bulun v R & T Textiles* (1998) to push the limits of the law with regards to 'difference'. Fundamentally exposed through this case law is how the function of the law is influenced by cultural expectations of how the law should react in specific circumstances, for instance those of misappropriation of Aboriginal cultural imagery and products. Nevertheless, the inability of intellectual property law to secure successfully the closure of 'indigenous' as a category, consequently reflects the power of certain kinds of knowledge to elude standardised systems of organisation and management. This also suggests that the possibilities for recognition and protection are not solely dependent upon legal processes of identification and classification.

The politics of law are revealed through instances of case law. Thus the final chapter illustrates how the category 'indigenous intellectual property' exposes the real difficulties for the law – precisely to what extent cultural difference can be accommodated and how the law treats indigenous difference. In particular it will consider how cultural difference is positioned, and how it is absorbed and treated within legal regimes. The terms of inclusion are rendered visible, even if they remain at the margins. Judicial decisions reveal gaps in the law that also constitute limits. However, the limits of the law are political in construct as they are dually informed and established by specific networks of power.[6] In this way the law does not function in isolation but produces and is produced by cultural values and perspectives.[7] Thus understanding copyright law requires an 'interpretation of case law in view of many possible social and cultural influences and prejudices'.[8]

The corollary drawn between early literary property debates in the eighteenth century and the difficulties presented by indigenous knowledge highlight how the problems of identifying indigenous knowledge are part of a continuum; where intellectual property law must revisit earlier difficulties concerning knowledge as property and the extent to which the right in intangible property can be determined. Indigenous knowledge surprises the law by how familiar these problems are. It does however present the law with difficult cultural contexts providing challenges that demand a new and timely response. In particular, this plays into the shift at a national and international level that has underpinned consideration of indigenous people as 'special' legal subjects. The complexity of legal subjectivity reveals that the law is not a coherent stable entity, but a product of social and political construction. It is precisely the messiness and complexity of the law that reveals the possibility for the law to respond to subject specific issues. What follows is a sustained examination of governmental process of engagement: recognising the multiple vectors that have effectively come to produce the category we now know as indigenous intellectual property.

NOTES

1. P. O'Malley, *Law Capitalism and Democracy*, Allen and Unwin: Sydney, 1983 at 104.
2. See my earlier discussion in regards to *Yanggarrny Wunungmurra v Peter Stipes* (1983) Federal Court, unreported and *Bulun Bulun v Nejlam Pty Ltd* (1989) Federal Court, unreported.
3. Here I draw on the work of Peter Miller and Nikolas Rose in 'Governing Economic Life', (1990) 19 (1) *Economy and Society* 1. This is expanded in N. Rose, *Powers of Freedom: Reframing Political Thought,* Cambridge University Press: London, 1999.
4. *Milpurrurru & Others v Indofurn Pty Ltd* (1994) 30 IPR 209.
5. *Bulun Bulun & Others v R & T Textiles Pty Ltd* (1998) 41 IPR 513.
6. M. Davies, *Delimiting the Law: Postmodernism and the Politics of the Law*, Pluto Press: Chicago and London, 1996 at 57.
7. See Chapter 1. Also R. Coombe, *The Cultural Life of Intellectual Properties: Authorship, Appropriation and the Law*, Duke University Press: Durham and London, 1998.
8. J. McKeough, K. Bowrey and P. Griffith, *Intellectual Property: Commentary and Material* (third edition), The Lawbook Company: Sydney, 2002 at 23.

4. Aboriginal art and the economic currency of law

It is clear that the purpose and function of intellectual property is historically and politically tied to promoting economic incentives. This explains why intellectual property laws are increasingly important components of world trade and the subject of world trade arguments. Beyond the classificatory indices of authorship and originality discussed previously, intellectual property is inescapably deeply imbued with commercial dynamics that dually function to inform and identify intangible subject matter.

Modern intellectual property law approaches and evaluates an object for protection through an integral relationship between property and economics.[1] As discussed earlier, following the eighteenth century literary property case *Donaldson v Becket* (1774),[2] the argument was made that one could identify the harm of taking the property of intellectual labour through the financial benefits that would be deprived to the 'originator' of the work.[3] Economic concerns thus became incorporated as a means for measuring and identifying the loss and thereby worth, of this unique form of commodity.

EDELMAN AND THE COMMODITY FORM

In the last few decades, knowledge itself has become valuable in new kinds of ways. Grosheide explains, that '[c]ultural information has, speaking in economic terms, made the step from product to raw material. This also explains why national governments are now more than ever alert to matters of intellectual property rights. Trade in cultural information or intellectual property rights has become a substantial part of national economies . . .'[4]

Debates and discussions about the knowledge economy, and how to enhance and protect it proliferate. As Drahos suggests:

> We have seen lying at the heart of the knowledge economy are intangible assets – for example, algorithms that drive computers and formulae that underpin chemical processes of production. The intellectual property rules governing the ownership of these assets have been globally and profoundly changed in the last

> twenty years. These rules impact on who can and cannot be an entrepreneur in the knowledge economy.[5]

These debates have taken many forms including: the proliferation of information technologies; the proactive collection and archiving of knowledges; questions regarding the social and cultural impact of knowledge economies; and, most importantly for our discussion here, who 'owns' knowledge in this new economy.

As one instance in the growing awareness of the value of knowledge, Agrawal has considered the privileged position that indigenous knowledge has come to occupy in scientific and development discourses.[6] This reversal of fortunes for indigenous knowledge has led to the development of multiple efforts aimed at collecting, recording and classifying such knowledge as well as the development of extensive and sophisticated storage mechanisms, for instance in digital databases.[7] With the changing recognition of the 'value' and currency of knowledge, the desire to make such knowledge privately and exclusively owned simultaneously increases.

Under such circumstances, critical attention has been directed to understanding the multiple ways in which, owing to the changing modes of recognising the value of knowledge, legal structures have been (re) deployed as strategic mechanisms that establish new forms of control and monopoly privileges over certain forms of knowledge and information. *Information Feudalism: Who Owns the Knowledge Economy?* by Peter Drahos, provides an interpretation of the politics and the effects of increasing economies of knowledge. Information is a valuable resource, and therefore the ownership stakes are high.

> Intellectual property rights are a source of authority and power over informational resources, on which the many depend – information in the form of chemical formulae, the DNA in plants and animals, the algorithms that underpin digital technologies and the knowledge in books and electronic communities. These resources matter to communities, to regions and to the development of states.[8]

It is a reinvigorated knowledge economy that enables the management of increasingly valuable forms of knowledge whilst also positioning such knowledge within a discourse of currency, commodity and law.

The dynamic between intellectual property and the economic process of valuation has been examined by scholars seeking to explain how commodity forms of production function as key informing elements of intellectual property law.[9] Certainly economic considerations were an important element in elevating the concerns of competing booksellers in the literary property debates of the eighteenth century. Not surprisingly in 1920s

Marxist scholars were developing analyses that considered the production of the commodity through the law.[10] In 1979 Bernard Edelman revisited early concerns in the context of intellectual property, considering the development of photography and cinema as new and legitimate kinds of subject matter deserving protection.[11] Edelman was concerned with producing a general theory of the production of such legal categories showing how their inclusion is dependent upon processes of capitalism whereby all aspects of creation are reduced to a commodity form intrinsic to market production.[12]

Edelman's work illustrates how the expansion of property rights is made to new commodity forms. He considers the inclusion of the photograph as a new kind of subject matter in copyright law in France, and argues that it is only through a change in the accepted value of this kind of 'knowledge' and its product (the photograph) that enabled the production of a new category. This changing value was directly tied to its market potential.[13] The strength and utility of Edelman's argument for considering both the inner workings of intellectual property and its social implications is in his exploration of how new subject matter is fashioned to fit into categories for intellectual property protection. Thus from the perspective of economic advantage and the commodity value within the marketplace, interesting parallels can be drawn between Edelman's analysis of the inclusion of the photograph and the inclusion of indigenous knowledge, specifically through the commercial considerations influencing and enhancing the value of Aboriginal art (as the product) in a marketplace of relations. For intellectual property law, Aboriginal art represents a new commodity form, albeit one that plays on its 'age-old' pre-market status.

Edelman's initial concern when considering the development of the law covering photography and cinema, is in understanding how the photographic form 'appropriates the real',[14] that is, it involves the taking of an image that would otherwise exist within the public domain and invests it with property rights. For instance a photograph of a lake or a monument is a reproduction of something that existed as 'real' prior to the photograph capturing it as an image. The image, re-appropriated from the real, then becomes the property of the photographer executed through the mechanical process of taking a photo (where labour has been exerted). Thus the re-appropriated 'real' becomes a recognisable object to the law, which is 'always-already invested with property'[15] because the law anticipates that ownership of the image invariably belongs to someone.

Property is of primary importance here, for it is through the notion of property that creation can be understood: property makes the invisible (creation) visible (through the product – the photograph). In this sense Edelman argues that property as a concept of law is a juridical fiction.

As a fiction it permits the transition from the intangible – 'creation', 'intelligence'; to the tangible – the photograph, the painting, or the work.[16] The tangible is characterised in terms of private property: it can be owned. The presumption here is that the public domain is public property. By capturing an image of the public domain through an act of invisible creation, the negative becomes the private property of the owner. Moreover, the 'real' becomes an object, made into a specific category before the law. For instance copyright legislation recognises the 'photograph' as a particular kind of artistic work.

Analogous to issues of locating the 'original' component of indigenous knowledge and hence satisfying categories of identification within copyright, there was considerable debate as to whether photography constituted an act of 'creative endeavour'. The mechanical process implicit in photography has separated it from previously assumed 'creativity' that produced the tangible painting or literary work. That the camera was a machine disrupted the linearity that had previously constructed the association between the 'creator' and the 'creation' that had been integral to understandings of what constituted an artistic form. As Edelman explains,

> The law recognised only 'manual' art – the paintbrush, the chisel – or 'abstract' art – writing. The irruption of modern techniques of the (re)production of the real – photographic apparatuses, cameras – surprises the law in its quietude of its categories.[17]

To this end, Edelman considers the historical stage wherein the juridical birth of photography and the cinema is made possible. In doing so, he points to the importance of socially bestowing photographers and film makers as 'creators' thus providing the cinematic industry with the benefit of legal protection whereby economic value is invested in the photographer or film maker as a 'creator' and 'owner' of the work. This can be paralleled to Rose's comments about the social production of the 'author' for the purposes of the literary property debates.[18] In short, for the purposes of the law there must be an identifiable individual that can be pinpointed as the legitimate 'owner' of the private property.

Edelman recognises that the economic importance of photography and the cinema lead to a fundamental revision of them within the law. His point is not to describe the economic process but more the way in which 'this process is reproduced within the law and the way in which the law makes it effective'.[19] Thus the law presents itself as responsive to economic demands and capable of reconstructing itself in response. The artistic recognition of the photographer and the recognition that the photographer is a 'creator' was a necessity of the industry. The effectivity of processes making this possible was by proceeding through the 'aesthetic'.[20] The outcome being that the pseudo-aesthetic is subtly mixed with commercial considerations or as Edelman phrases it 'the aesthetic is subordinated to commerce'.[21]

Like the difficulties with identifying indigenous knowledge as intangible subject matter, photography needed to carry identifiable marks necessary for legal protection. In other words, photography must be made an 'artistic' activity where 'creative labour' has been invested. Photography needs to become understood socially as an artistic product and as all artistic products are always-already subject to the market, the commodity form of the product becomes the production of the artifact. This point can equally be applied to the recognition of Aboriginal art as an artistic product and thus a commodity form. This leads Edelman to observe that, 'art is both "product" and "moment" of capital'.[22]

Edelman's analysis reveals an astute awareness for how the law functions to produce categories that it can understand and work with and how the law is also responsible for circulating these within society. In this sense, the law is not only responsive to the market but also to the cultural conditions that render the applicability of the law in a particular context important. For it is not only the development of the cinematographic industry that makes the production of 'creativity' of the object of photography important, but also that at the time of such debates, there were '50,000 people who live by photography in France'.[23] In this way the law is responsive to the cultural context that facilitates the market. It does not produce the market alone but is implicitly involved with it and its perpetuation.

It follows then that the production of art as commodity is also an act of law and jurisprudence. It is thus unsurprising that legal values regarding Aboriginal art support the social production of economic value in Aboriginal art. Following Edelman's argument, the real that is re-appropriated to produce the product, Aboriginal art, is understood through the intangibility of indigenous knowledge. As Martin Nakata has noted, indigenous knowledge is now understood as an enterprise, an industry, and this social production demands legal response.[24] The commonality in legal approach to photography and Aboriginal art belies the challenge of identifying indigenous subject matter. All the elements that the law needs to classify new subject matter are here, however they are disguised by more prominent concepts of 'tradition', 'indigenous as culture' and perceptions of incommensurate cultural positions. As Colin Golvan comments;

> It had never dawned on me before that for some of the artists, the first time that they saw the waterhole that they were depicting was with me from an aeroplane when we finally found it, using maps to locate it . . . and I only realised then that what they were depicting was from their own sense of, you know, their own imagery . . . they had incorporated it into their own sense of present and the real.[25]

It is this 'real', this imagery, that is precisely what the law works upon to make a subject of property. A key differential however, is that the real – indigenous knowledge, and the product – Aboriginal art, have not been securely abstracted and decontextualised as legal objects. What this then means is that cultural values beyond the economic currency of knowledge continue to exert pressure in how this subject is identified. This generates alternate affects, for example, political issues of cultural identity and integrity become intertwined with the protection of Aboriginal art, the protection of indigenous knowledge and the function of intellectual property law. As a result, these techniques of valuation make it difficult for law to develop reflexivity toward different cultural positions and contexts especially ones indifferent or opposed to the commodification process.

At this stage it is worth further developing a consideration of how Aboriginal art circulates within a commodity discourse: for it is the historical emergence of Aboriginal art into western art spaces that effectively produced Aboriginal art as a commodity replete with new markers of value. Deriving an economic value enables Aboriginal art to be presented as a legitimate form to be protected through intellectual property law. The production of Aboriginal art as a commodity however, complicates the cultural context of the art and consequently means that the cultural differences are only engaged in any legitimate form at the margins of the law. Moreover, concepts such as 'tradition' and 'culture' are emboldened as they help identify and locate the key features that comprise the 'value'. Underlying the protection of Aboriginal art through copyright is its economic value, which has been both culturally and historically produced. Appreciating the varying intersections that inform this position of Aboriginal art as a commodity enables both an understanding of bureaucratic unwillingness to engage fully with the extent of cultural differences in indigenous knowledge as intangible property and the anxiety for the law that this inevitably generates. It is to these further considerations that we will now turn.

Developing a means for calculating the value of the intangible property is a crucial feature that underpins the identification of categories for intellectual property protection. Economic values are implicit within the legal identification of Aboriginal art, justifying its admission within this body of law.[26] In a significant way Aboriginal art is measured through the lens of the western market. Judicial reasoning relies upon and replicates this process of valuation. Interestingly it is the increased commodification of Aboriginal art, culminating in instances of infringement that highlights its newly acquired economic value and status within the market. As Edwin Hettinger explains;

> market value is a socially created phenomenon, depending on the activity (or non activity) of other producers, the monetary demand of producers and the kinds of property rights, contracts and markets the state has established and enforced. The market value of some fruits of labour will differ greatly with variations in these social factors.[27]

Thus, even when the law depends on the economic as a mode of valuing intangible subject matter, it is still culturally and socially produced. Clearly the market value of Aboriginal art has changed over time and it is this change that produced a shift in seeing Aboriginal art in a context of intellectual property protection. This economic rationale provides a means for appreciating the way in which copyright law identifies and embraces 'new' forms of subject matter. It also forms a point by which strategies to contest inappropriate use of Aboriginal art in the marketplace are imagined.

As noted earlier, an important development in the making of modern intellectual property law was in establishing distinct categories for intellectual property protection – for example copyright for artistic expression – where closed and bounded definitions of these categories facilitated their abstraction. Additionally, instead of focusing on the subject matter in the form of the intangible property or the idea because of the difficulty this presented in justifying the right in the property, the law shifted its gaze to consider the visible form that the subject matter created, such as the book or the machine, in other words the tangible expression or product. If we consider indigenous knowledge as the intangible subject matter and Aboriginal art as the product produced through this subject matter, it is the product, the expression of indigenous knowledge in a material form of art, that is the key focus for copyright law.[28] This shifts the process of identification to characteristics held in the tangible form. Nevertheless determining the metaphysical dimensions of the property right still influence the composition of categories despite the fact that this remains an implicit component.

Central to the making of modern intellectual property law was the development of a means to measure the value of the tangible form produced by the intangible subject matter. This was due to the closure of the intangible property owing to the displacement of mental labour in the second half of the nineteenth century.[29] Such a closure brought a shift from the 'doctrine of intellectual property law towards questions of political economy and policy'.[30] The identification of the unique properties of mental labour affected both the categories of intellectual property law and how these categories were explained.[31] On one hand this meant that qualitative judgments about the boundary between categories was rendered ineffective, and for example, the law could no longer sustain an inherent identification process of what characterised a literary process and consequently what properly belonged as copyright and what didn't.[32] This difficulty, arising from the displacement of mental labour, also impacted on how the separate categories were explained. Intangible property remained a pivotal consideration in organising the categories as they retained distinction through their relative 'value'.[33] The point to emphasise is that there was a modification in how to measure this relative value, that is, through the 'macro-economic value of property rather than, as had been the case previously, the quantity of the mental labour embodied in the property in question'.[34] It became possible to measure value based on the contribution that the intangible 'property' offered to society, a quality increasingly measured through commercial considerations.

This change meant that what was to become important to modern intellectual property law was not the creativity (remembering its displacement) contained within the work, but rather the contribution the work, as property, made within society. This was judged through the language and logic of the economy. Thus value becomes a term associated and circulated within a quasi-natural realm named as 'economic'. To this end, the value of the object was rendered into a form that was calculable through the language and logic of property within the economy.[35] Following these thoughts then, the value of Aboriginal art becomes calculable through its position as property within the marketplace and consequently takes on a commodity form where its movement within the market can be readily traced.

The emergence of Aboriginal art into the market is part of a process of social construction and production wherein the increase in the demand and popularity of indigenous cultural products is a direct effect. Significantly, as Aboriginal art emerged into a western art space two important things occurred. Firstly as part of its engagement with the market the value of Aboriginal art becomes calculable. Secondly, the concept of an (individual) 'artist' or 'creator' in relation to a work is developed. These two factors influence later arguments for Aboriginal art, as artistic work, to be eligible for copyright. Namely the market provided the necessary means for measuring the value of the work and within such a market, Aboriginal art could be classified according to categories of intellectual property law where there was an artistic work and an identifiable artist. As Shelley Wright explains however, this has been at the expense of an appreciation of indigenous subjectivity and experience – for the marketing of indigenous cultural products relies heavily upon imaginary constructions of Aboriginality.[36] I would also add that the concept of an Aboriginal artist has not been fully secured in relation to Aboriginal art. This has much to do with the way in which Aboriginal art has moved from ethnographic spaces into economic frameworks. The value is still dependent upon, and in some circumstances enhanced by, ethnographic and anthropological readings of Aboriginal cultures and societies.

Aboriginal art has increasingly become marked as a *cultural* commodity. This invisible intangible cultural dimension of indigenous knowledge remains pivotal in the organisation of the tangible product, Aboriginal art, through categories of copyright. The influence of the intangible is dually exerted in the making of the 'cultural' commodity through, for instance, relying upon essential readings of spirituality and tradition. The economic production of Aboriginal art is still dependent upon a complicated, abstract and romantic relationship between indigenous people and their cultural products, where indigenous people are present, but experience, context and subjectivity are reimagined within the market providing complimentary markers of 'authentic' and 'traditional' Aboriginal culture. Certainly the economic potential of indigenous cultural products provides new modes of regulation and increased ways of governing the production of these cultural products and their circulation within a market.[37] However the irony is that with the emergence of Aboriginal art within the commodity market, there remained initially no clear or identifiable artist/author. This was peculiar to the Australian circumstance whereby economic value was generated before the other categories governing the legitimacy of the subject matter, for instance originality and authorship, could be developed and applied.

THE EMERGENCE OF AN ABORIGINAL ART MARKET

The location of Aboriginal art as 'art' within a marketplace has been a relatively recent inscription.[38] As Fred Myers has explored, the making of the Aboriginal art industry is complex because it has been dependent upon a range of interactions between governmental and individual initiatives.[39] Indeed the making of 'Aboriginal art' was integral to its subsequent recognition by laws of intellectual property. For prior to this transformation indigenous artistry was constructed by anthropological and ethnographic knowledges as 'objects' of culture, constituted as non-art captured through the term 'folklore'. Importantly, these historical markers are still powerfully active and have been absorbed into a popular market indirectly influencing the current value of Aboriginal art.[40]

Colonisation in Australia, like in other areas of the Empire, engaged in the active collection of ethnographic and anthropologic 'data' that documented what was then perceived to be 'primitive' cultures and lifestyles thought to be on the wane.[41] While many 'cultural objects' were collected throughout this early colonial period it is notable that in 1910, anthropologist Baldwin Spencer began collecting Aboriginal bark paintings predominately from Arnhem Land in northern Australia.[42] Over the course of the next ten years, he accumulated over two hundred paintings collected on behalf of the National Museum of Victoria.[43] Spencer actively encouraged art and craft workers in Victoria to visit the museum and 'copy some of the designs of the Australian aborigine [sic]'.[44] In part this was to encourage the generation of a distinctive Australian aesthetic art style that differentiated Australia from Britain.[45] By the 1930s, indigenous styles were apparent in graphic design, fabrics, murals, ceramics and rubber floors. In this period Aboriginal 'art' accompanied by art that copied Aboriginal styles and forms began to appear in cultural spaces other than the museum.

The history of the emergence of Aboriginal art illustrates the extent that the process of copying Aboriginal styles and designs was governmentally and socially endorsed for nearly a century. For example, in 1941, an exhibition was prepared by the Museum of Victoria that sought to demonstrate the application that could be achieved by artists using inspiration from Aboriginal art. The exhibition *Aboriginal Art and its Applications* began with Aboriginal bark paintings and concluded with examples of the application of these styles including work by Margaret Preston and many ceramicists.[46] The art by Preston and others was referred to as 'new' Aboriginal art which was juxtaposed to 'old' Aboriginal art, that is, art done by Aboriginal people. There was a notable distinction between the 'new' author/artist and the communal Aboriginal group featuring little differentiation. 'Old' Aboriginal art was perceived to be timeless and ahistorical: such a construction of 'traditional' Aboriginal culture embodied in Aboriginal art possible because of the absence of the figure of the Aboriginal artist. Significantly this unindividualised (read as communal) character also became an important marker of its commercial value.

In the mid to late 1940s, Albert Namatjira from the Hermannsburg mission in Central Australia gained national recognition as a talented artist. Through his style of watercolour landscapes, Namatjira was individuated from his community.[47] To this end, Namatjira was one of the first Aboriginal people to be positioned as an identifiable individual artist and significantly, an 'author' of his 'artistic' work.[48] In this context it helped that Namatjira was utilising what were popularly held as 'western' aesthetic styles such as watercolours and was thus also participating within a largely European artistic tradition that had already set the relationship between the individual and the work.

In the 1950s the State Gallery of New South Wales began to buy Aboriginal artwork, and in the 1960s Aboriginal art and design appeared on stamps and banknotes. Ironically, while Aboriginal art was beginning to become representative of 'Australianess', indigenous people were still not citizens of the country.[49] Thomas' observations are pertinent as he observes that cultural colonisation perpetuates itself,

> not by the theft of motifs or art styles that are reproduced . . . but through forging national narratives that situate indigenous people firmly in the past, or in a process of waning; while settlers are identified with what is new and flourishing and promising.[50]

Thus the use of Aboriginal motifs on stamps[51] and banknotes[52] points to an unstable disjuncture. Indigenous artwork is used to create and establish a unique cultural identity, which at the same time denies contemporary indigenous subjectivity precisely because the indigenous subject is constructed as 'traditional' or in the past, unidentifiable from the homogenised group or community.[53] As Marcia Langton explains:

> Although ideas about Aboriginal culture are constantly recirculated and renegotiated in Australian society, many non-indigenous Australians continue to hold to the trope of a 'Stone Age' Aboriginal culture frozen in time. Aboriginal society had been deemed throughout colonial and much of post-Federation Australia to be limited, inflexible, utilitarian, animist and above all, a primitive way of life inexorably doomed to extinction.[54]

The 1970s marked a period of distinct change in the desirability of Aboriginal artwork. This was paralleled by a change in governmental policy: from assimilation to self-determination. The change specifically saw an increased market for Aboriginal artwork by indigenous people as opposed to the style of Aboriginal artwork done by non-indigenous people.[55] With the interest generated out of the Papunya art movement and new kinds of governmental incentives, indigenous artists began to be associated with their own works and emerged as the faces behind the perpetually constructed 'timeless' genre of Aboriginal art. What was also important about this period of Aboriginal art was that the economic value of Aboriginal artworks began to change.[56]

James Clifford has made pertinent observations about the way in which non-western objects have moved from the space of ethnographic specimens to that of major art creations.[57] Clifford's comments provide insights into the processes that have enabled indigenous artistry to be produced as culturally and economically valuable. Clifford aptly notes:

> The 'beauty' of non-western art is a recent discovery. Before the twentieth century many of the same elements were collected and valued for different reasons. In the early modern period, their rarity and strangeness were prized . . .

> the value of exotic objects was their ability to testify to the concrete reality of an earlier stage of human culture, a common past confirming Europe's triumphant present.[58]

Herein lies a central point crucial to understanding the transformation of indigenous objects from ethnographic *specimens* to *works* of artistic merit, facilitating their incorporation as objects of intellectual property protection. This is the shift in register of value: from anthropological and ethnographic specimens to a different economic realm of art/value and inevitably a new kind of commodity. Arguably however, the former is displaced only to return and exert influence in the market where the exotic representation of 'otherness' becomes integral to the economic value of such cultural products. In this light, it could be posited that one of the initial reasons for the increased value of 'traditional' Aboriginal art is that it embodies a perception of otherness, that is it conveys significant mythologised and romantic features of Aboriginal culture to 'outsiders' through an indefinable *essence* of 'tradition'. Wally Caruana points to this factor stating:

> [t]he art of Aboriginal Australia is the *last great tradition* of art to be appreciated by the world at large. Despite being one of the longest traditions of art in the world, *dating back to at least fifty millennia, it remained relatively unknown* until the second half of the twentieth century.[59]

Aboriginal art is valued on one level for its representation of cultural difference. That is, Aboriginal art is art in the western sense, but simultaneously more than art because it is, at least within the market, represented as inherently connected in its context to a religious and spiritual domain. The centrality that Aboriginal art has to Aboriginal life, land and spirituality contributes to how the 'beauty' of the art is produced for the western gaze. A complex interplay exists here, wherein the distinction between the 'aesthetic' value and the anthropological value of Aboriginal art actively contributes to the production of indigenous art in the market. Cultural institutions such as art galleries transformed indigenous 'objects' into artworks, displayed for their aesthetic qualities; by contrast, in museums the same indigenous objects were exhibited in their cultural contexts, maintaining the construction of 'exotic' or 'primitive' peoples. Notably in art galleries explicit cultural background and context is not essential to aesthetic appreciation. It would be a mistake however, to assume that this cultural context is irrelevant to such aesthetic appreciation. Rather it has an implicit function; for the value of Aboriginal art is in its powerful evocation of the religious or Dreaming, a sense of spirituality unknown and difficult to translate. While in museums such an association may have been achieved through the positioning with other 'artifacts' and ethnographic specimens, in art galleries however, the accompanying 'story' or narrative fulfils such a role by lending an 'authentic spirituality' to the product.

All commodities have markers of value. These markers of value are explicitly linked to economic markets and importantly to popular demand. Once something becomes popularised, its economic value increases which can be demonstrated through the price. Thus over the last twenty years, Aboriginal art has increased in value both nationally and internationally. Initially the value of Aboriginal art could be linked to romantic notions of 'primitive' art and also understanding that the art was representative of Aboriginal traditions existing for 'over a thousand years'. Subsequently the value of the art increased, partly due to production in colonial discourse of markers of Aboriginal art such as its representation of 'tradition'. In this way then Aboriginal art was perceived as authentic if it replicated notions of the 'traditional' artistry and community, and assumed a position that was predominately *a*historical, abstract and imaginary.

Once a product becomes a commodity however, it is standardised to the market. The product, in this case Aboriginal art, enters a realm of economics where it is abstracted from the cultural and physical associations of people and place. Ironically these physical associations sustain the abstraction. In this way, the marker of value reflecting the 'cultural significance' of the art or the cultural differences that it embodies, function to maintain it as a commodity but separated from the context and indeed the actual life of the creative artists themselves. To some extent this explains the striking absence of a speaking voice of the indigenous artists. The creators of the very objects deemed 'powerful' are located outside the discussion; subjectivity is put at the margins as the art is extracted from its social context. This is a perpetuation of what Thomas observed about early use of Aboriginal art where the 'natives were called upon to be present on the walls through their artifacts, but required to be absent in their persons'.[60]

THE IMAGINARY ABORIGINAL

The positioning of art in 'western' society as highly valued cultural artifact is important to the historical emergence and appreciation of Aboriginal artwork as 'good' art.[61] Nevertheless, it remains that underlying such a transition for 'traditional' Aboriginal art is the trope of the 'primitive'.[62] Furthermore in the movement from ethnographic specimens to aesthetic form, the trope is reconstructed and repositioned so that it continues to exert power in art spaces. This is primarily evoked through the evocation of tradition. As George Marcus and Fred Myers observe,

> the art world has largely gone on constructing the 'primitive' even in its post-modern dislocations. At least part of the appeal of Aboriginal acrylic paintings continue to rely on the sense of Aborigines as 'primitives'.[63]

The trope of the 'primitive' denotes difference and otherness. Indeed it is the unique cultural differences presented as underpinning Aboriginal art that contributes to the value of indigenous artwork within the art world.[64] This is necessarily helped by the remoter locations that many indigenous people occupy.[65] The production of indigenous people as occupying the spaces similar to those represented in anthropological texts supports an interpretation of indigenous people, as a generic group, that is timeless and *a*historical.[66] In short, Aboriginal art is produced in an economic market for non-indigenous consumers.[67]

The fetishisation of 'traditional' Aboriginal art within the art market has had consequences for Aboriginal artists residing in cities and regional areas. The 1990s were characterised by the struggle for the recognition of the work of urban artists beyond the paradigm of 'tradition'.[68] Influenced by postmodernism, artists like Tracey Moffatt and Gordon Bennett remain concerned with questions of identity, hybridity and inter-cultural engagement.[69] As Bennett has explained:

> I didn't go to art college to graduate as an 'Aboriginal Artist'. I did want to explore my Aboriginality, however, and it is a subject of my work as much as colonialism and the narratives and language that frame it, and the language that has consistently framed me. Acutely aware of the frame, I graduated as a straight honours student . . . to find myself positioned and contained by the language of 'primitivism' as an 'Urban Aboriginal Artist'.[70]

These artists challenge colonial images and histories and their work often functions as clear postcolonial texts.[71] They bring into view the hierarchies that valued 'traditional' Aboriginal art, whilst also raising key questions about identity and the construction of Aboriginality.

It is these discussions prompted by 'non-traditional' Aboriginal artists that Shelley Wright draws upon to argue that discussions of Aboriginal art seldom engage in a discussion of the meaning of the term Aboriginal.[72] Wright's point is that there is a significant disjuncture between the concept of an Aboriginal person constructed for 'white Australian manufacture, and the reality of Indigenous peoples lives'.[73] This disjuncture results in an 'imaginary Aboriginality' that bares little resemblance to indigenous subjectivity, but powerfully supplies the market with its key symbols of value – tradition and cultural difference. Wright's concern is that the construction of the 'imaginary Aboriginal' within Australia affects how Australian indigenous people then relate, interrelate and maintain a level of management over their cultural traditions.[74] It narrows the conditions through which indigenous people can actively participate in the discourse.[75]

Wright identifies intellectual property law as the key legal mechanism in the production of a framework that creates and maintains a 'society which sees culture as the object of commodification, alienation and sale'.[76] This echoes the concerns of Martin Nakata about the ways in which the increasing discussions of indigenous knowledge remake this subject as 'a commodity, something of value, something that can be value added, something that can be exchanged, traded, appropriated, preserved, something that can be excavated and mined'.[77] In this context Nakata suggests that the indigenous knowledge enterprise, of which Aboriginal art is part, has everything and nothing to do with indigenous people.[78] Thus Wright and Nakata share a general concern regarding the ways in which indigenous subjectivity, and indigenous knowledges are produced and effectively managed, for instance through legal regimes of intellectual property. Wright takes this one step further in suggesting that the way in which indigenous subjectivity is constructed directly affects the way in which indigenous people see each other, both in regards to collective identity but also individual identity.

Wright is directly interested in the way in which the law further facilitates the construction of the 'imaginary Aboriginal'. By minimising indigenous experience, the law, presented with legal questions regarding 'infringement' and 'copyright' is able to respond because the concern is located and identified as within the capacity of the law. The commonality of indigenous experience is positioned within a market place of relations, and as an effect of exploitative market forces. But if the 'Aboriginal' positioned before the law is imaginary to begin with why is there surprise that the law is unable to accommodate indigenous difference except as 'imaginary Aboriginals'? Under such circumstances, the confining and redefining of Aboriginal culture and cultural products to fit within legal categories of identification is inevitable and predictable.

What is remarkable, and this will be illustrated presently through the case law, is that the law does seek to accommodate indigenous difference and it does this through looking at its points of inclusion. That this is tied to concepts of indigeneity that emphasises 'traditional' and 'authentic' culture where indigenous people reside in remote communities is a result of multiple factors, not least being the trouble that the Aboriginal artists in the copyright cases did reside in remote communities and emphasised the tradition embodied within the paintings in affidavits. The very facts of the case meant that the case law inevitably played right into the stereotypes that deny indigenous diversity. This reveals that the factors of influence at play here are far more complicated than are first thought. For whilst it may appear that the law is the primary agent consolidating the 'traditional' and timelessness of indigenous art and cultural traditions, certain institutional initiatives, picked up and advocated by Aboriginal people as much as the white bureaucrats, have also contributed to the reification of 'original' and 'authentic' Aboriginal culture, that is at once real as it is false. The character of governance is exposed wherein law both conforms to standards of identification and breaks these. This illustrates the tensions between agencies and the potential for action and change. It is to a greater understanding of these tensions that we will now move.

NOTES

1. This literature is extensive. See K. Maskus, *Intellectual Property Rights in the Global Economy*, Peterson Institute for International Economics: Washington DC, 2000.
2. *Donaldson v Becket* (1774) 4 Burr 2408, 98 Eng. Rep. 252.
3. See Chapter 3. B. Sherman and L. Bently, *The Making of Modern Intellectual Property: The British Experience 1760–1911*, Cambridge University Press: Cambridge, 1999 at 195.
4. F.W. Grosheide, 'When Ideas Take the Stage', (1994) 6 *European Intellectual Property Review* 219 at 219.
5. P. Drahos with J. Braithwaite *Information Feudalism: Who Owns the Knowledge Economy*?, Earthscan Publications Ltd: London, 2002 at 17.
6. See: A. Agrawal, 'Indigenous Knowledge and the Politics of Classification', (2002) 54 (173) *International Social Science Journal* 287.
7. These databases range from the local to the international, with support ranging from NGOs to international researchers and agencies such as the World Bank, UNCTAD, WIPO and UNESCO. The intention is 'to protect indigenous knowledge in the face of myriad pressures . . . [and] to collect and analyse the available information and identify specific features that can be generalised and applied more widely in the service of more effective development and environmental conservation.' Such efforts also position such knowledge in domains where it can be 'refined and privatized through the existing system of patents and intellectual property rights.' A. Agrawal, supra n.6. See also: P. Drahos, 'Indigenous Knowledge, Intellectual Property and Biopiracy: Is a Global Collecting Society the Answer?', (2000) 6 *European Intellectual Property Review* 245.
8. P. Drahos with J. Braithwaite, *Information Feudalism*, supra n.5 at 12.
9. See: C. May, *A Global Political Economy of Intellectual Property Rights: The New Enclosures?*, Routledge: London and New York, 2000; S. Sell, *Power and Ideas: North-South Politics of Intellectual Property and Antitrust*, State University of New York Press: New York, 1998; P.E. Geller, 'Must Copyright Be For Ever Caught between Marketplace and Authorship Norms?' in Sherman, B., and A. Strowel (eds), *Of Authors and Origins: Essays in Copyright Law*, Clarendon Press: London, 1994; R.V. Bettig and H.I. Shiller, *Copyrighting Culture: The Political Economy of Intellectual Property*, Westview Press: Boulder, Colorado, 1996; G. Smith and R. Parr, *Valuation of Intellectual Property and Intangible Assets*, John Wiley: New York, 1989.
10. E. Pashukanis, *A General Theory of Law and Marxism* (Arthur, C. (ed)), Ink Links: London, 1968.
11. B. Edelman, *Ownership of the Image: Elements for a Marxist Theory of Law* (transl. by Kingdom, E.), Routledge and Keegan Paul: London, 1979. For another discussion of

photography as 'difficult' subject matter see: K. Garnett, 'Copyright in Photographs', (2000) 5 *European Intellectual Property Review* 229.

12. See: P.Q. Hirst, 'Introduction' to B. Edelman, *Ownership of the Image: Elements for a Marxist Theory of Law*, Ibid. 1–18.
13. France has a different history in the emergence of intellectual property to that of Great Britain and consequently Australia. For an account of this differing history see: C. Hesse, 'Enlightenment Epistemology and the Laws of Authorship in Revolutionary France, 1777–1793', (1990) 30 *Representations* 109; C. Hesse, *Publishing and Cultural Politics in Revolutionary Paris, 1789–1810*, University of California Press: Berkeley, 1991. The *Berne Convention for the Protection of Literary and Artistic Works* (1886) standardised copyright protection at an international level. Original signatories included France, United Kingdom, Belgium, Germany, Haiti, Italy, Spain, Switzerland and Tunisia. Australia became a signatory in 1928. See: S. Ricketson, *The Berne Convention for the Protection of Literary and Artistic Works 1886–1986*, Kluwer: London, 1987.
14. B. Edelman, *Ownership of the Image: Elements for a Marxist Theory of Law* supra n.11 at 38.
15. Ibid., at 38.
16. Ibid., at 40.
17. Ibid., at 44. See also: K. Bowrey, 'Copyright, photography and computer works: the fiction of original expression' (1995) 18 (2) *UNSW Law Journal* 278.
18. M. Rose, 'The Author as Proprietor: *Donaldson v Becket* and the Genealogy of Modern Authorship' Sherman, B., and A. Strowel (eds), *Of Authors and Origins: Essays in Copyright Law*, Clarendon Press: London, 1994.
19. B. Edelman, *Ownership of the Image: Elements for a Marxist Theory of Law*, supra n.11 at 49.
20. Ibid., at 50.
21. Ibid., at 50.
22. Ibid., at 57.
23. Ibid., at 50.
24. M. Nakata, 'Indigenous Knowledge and the Cultural Interface: underlying issues at the intersection of knowledge and information systems' (2002) 28 *International Federation of Libraries Association Journal* 281 at 282. See also: C. Nicholls, *From Appreciation to Appropriation: Indigenous Influences and Images in Australian Visual Art Exhibition Catalogue*, March 2000.
25. C. Golvan, interview by author, 19 June 2002, tape recording, Owen Dixon Chambers, Melbourne. On file with author.
26. This will be explored further in relation to bureaucratic attention to Aboriginal art and the copyright cases.
27. E. Hettinger 'Justifying Intellectual Property' (1989) 18 (1) *Philosophy and Public Affairs* 31 at 38.
28. In Australia to date, there is no indigenous case law beyond art (artistic works).
29. B. Sherman and L. Bently, *The Making of Modern Intellectual Property: The British Experience 1760–1911* Cambridge University Press: Cambridge, 1999 at 194. Importantly, the displacement of mental labour and hence creativity was not an exclusion from intellectual property law. They both return to inform the identification of subject matter such as 'originality' discussed in Chapter Two, and novelty in the case of patents. In this way, creativity is repositioned within the law and exerts its influence in subtle forms.
30. Ibid., at 194.
31. Ibid., at 194–195.
32. Ibid., at 194. Sherman and Bently illustrate this point with reference to patents.
33. Ibid., at 195.
34. Ibid., at 195.
35. In another context see T. Mitchell, 'The Work of Economics: How a Discipline Makes its World', (2005) 45 (2) *European Journal of Sociology* 297.
36. S. Wright, 'Intellectual Property and the "Imaginary Aboriginal"' in Bird, G., G.

Martin and J. Neilsen (eds), *Majah: Indigenous Peoples and the Law*, The Federation Press: Sydney, 1996.

37. See: F. Myers, *Painting Culture: The Making of an Aboriginal High Art,* Duke University Press: Durham, 2002. For a striking illustration of this point see the recent submissions and hearings being undertaken for the Senate Standing Committee on Environment, Communication, Information, Technology and Arts Inquiry into Australia's Indigenous visual arts and crafts sector, 2007. [www.ahp.gov.au/hansard/senate/committee/ecita_ctte/indigenous_arts/hearings/index.htm].
38. Elizabeth Coleman has argued that 'Aboriginal art' is itself a western construction. By this she suggests that there may be variant ranges of ontological understandings of painting and art held by indigenous peoples in Australia – ranging from art produced for a market to art as part of traditional interpretative cultural practice. See E. Coleman, 'Aboriginal Painting: Identity and Authenticity', (2001) 59 (4) *The Journal of Aesthetics and Art Criticism* 385.
39. F. Myers, *Painting Culture: The Making of an Aboriginal High Art*, supra n.37.
40. Comments by Marcia Langton extend this observation: 'In sharp contrast to the "typical Australian" as the blue eyed surfie, popular images of Indigenous Australians tend to be negative, but also essentialised. These negative stereotypes are based on a belief that there are inelectable features of "Aboriginality" based on the tradition of "primitivism"'. M. Langton, *Valuing Cultures: Recognising Indigenous Cultures as a Valued Part of Australian Heritage* [prepared for the Council for Aboriginal Reconciliation] Australian Government Printing Service: Canberra, 1994 at 8.
41. The problem of what now to do with these collections is serious. See J. Anderson and K. Bowrey, 'The Imaginary Politics of Access to Knowledge: Whose Cultural Agendas are Being Advanced?', unpublished conference paper. On file with author.
42. N. Thomas, *Possessions: Indigenous Art/Colonial Culture*, Thames and Hudson: London, 1999 at 114.
43. Ibid., at 115.
44. Ibid., at 116.
45. This is Thomas' general argument in *Possessions: Indigenous Art/Colonial Culture*, supra n.42.
46. Ibid., at 121–123.
47. The complex positions that Albert Namatjira occupied within Australian society and his own community has been commented on elsewhere. See: J. Isaacs, *Spirit Country: Contemporary Australian Aboriginal Art*, Hardie Grant Books: Australia, 1999 at 23.
48. The 2003 retrospective of Namatjira's work at the National Gallery, *Seeing the Centre: The Art of Albert Namatjira (1902–1959)* curated by Alison French also illustrates this artistic status. Also see: M. Rimmer, 'Albert Namatjira: Copyright Estates and Traditional Knowledge' (2003) 24 *Incite* 6; and the discussion of this problem by Brenda L. Croft, 'Roundtable Discussion' AIATSIS Seminar Series, *Intellectual Property and Indigenous Knowledge: Access and Ownership of Indigenous Cultural Material* 16 June 2002.
49. The 1967 Referendum established Aboriginal and Torres Strait Islander people as citizens of Australia. For an insightful account of this process see: B. Attwood and A. Markus, 'Representation Matters: The 1967 Referendum and Citizenship' Peterson, N., and W. Sanders (eds), *Citizenship and Indigenous Australians: Changing Conceptions and Possibilities*, Cambridge University Press: Cambridge, 1998.
50. N. Thomas, *Possessions: Indigenous Art/Colonial Culture*, supra n.42 at 109.
51. The Albert Namatjira commemorative stamps released June 2002 highlight this juxtaposition, for they simultaneously establish the a sense of cultural identity through motifs but minimise the position of indigenous subjectivity: in this case the disturbing reality of Albert Namatjira's 'acceptance' and rejection within Australian settler society.
52. In 1966, with the introduction of decimal currency, the new one dollar note incorporated an Aboriginal theme in its design. The 'Aboriginal theme' was the work of the artist, David Malangi, however it had been assumed that the work was authorless. Malangi was presented with a fishing kit as compensation. The copyright case, *Yumbulul v*

Reserve Bank of Australia & Others (1991) 21 IPR 481 involved the unauthorised use of Yumbulul's 'Morning Star pole' on the bicentennial ten dollar note. See also: R. Sackville, 'Legal Protection of Indigenous Culture in Australia', (2003) 11 *Cardozo J. Int'l & Comp. L.* 711.

53. One of the artworks in the *carpets case*, George Milpurrurru's 'Goose Egg Hunt' was reproduced as stamps. 'As part of the program for the 1993 International Year for the World's Indigenous People, Goose Egg Hunt was adopted as the design for the 85 cent Australian stamp issued on 4 February 1993. A large number of these stamps were put into circulation, perhaps as many as two to three million' *Milpurrurru & Others v Indofurn Pty Ltd* 30 IPR 209 at 213. Also consider the following comments: 'The present array of Australian coins produced by the Australian Mint displays an interesting collection of icons which can be read, amongst other possible readings, as the colonial positioning of Aboriginal and Torres Strait Islander peoples as "primitives" and wildlife – a species of fauna along with the kangaroo and emu, the echidna, the lyrebird and the platypus. On all Australian coins, as would be expected, the "head" sign depicts the Queen, while on the "tail" side all the coins exhibit fauna. Except, that is, the two dollar coin, which carries a commemorative image of an Indigenous Australian male, which was intended to celebrate the bicentenary of Australia's "settlement".' M. Langton, *Valuing Cultures*, supra n.40 at 8.
54. M. Langton, 'Introduction: culture wars' in Grossman, M. (ed), *Blacklines: Contemporary Critical Writing by Indigenous Australians*, Melbourne University Press: Melbourne, 2003 at 81.
55. In particular, this art movement is contemporarily understood as beginning at Papunya, where in the 1960s the art teacher Geoffrey Bardon encouraged members of the Papunya community to depict their imagery and 'sand stories' on canvas using acrylic paints. The Papunya settlement was set up in 1959 and comprised of at least 6 different western desert communities that were governmentally 'moved' to the one location at Papunya. This was part of the broader assimilationist policy at the time. In 1972, the artists at Papunya formed a company, Papunya Tula Artists Pty Ltd. See: J. Isaacs, *Spirit Country: Contemporary Australian Aboriginal Art*, Hardie Grant Books: Australia, 1999 at 24–25.
56. The auction house Sotheby's annually holds an auction of Aboriginal art where recently artworks by the artists Kumuntjayi Tjapaltjarri and Rover Thomas have sold for over $400,000.
57. J. Clifford, *The Predicament of Culture: Twentieth Century Ethnography, Literature and Art*, Harvard University Press: Cambridge, MA, 1988.
58. Ibid., at 227.
59. W. Caruana, *Aboriginal Art*, Thames and Hudson: Singapore, 1993 at 7 [emphasis mine]. This book by Caruana is the most popular title in the Thames and Hudson catalogue and has been translated into six languages.
60. N. Thomas, *Possessions: Indigenous Art/Colonial Culture*, supra n.42 at 210.
61. See also: E. Michaels, 'Bad Aboriginal Art' (1988) 28 *Art and Text* 59. Also see Michaels's work published posthumously *Bad Aboriginal Art: Tradition, Media and Technological Horizons*, Allen and Unwin: Australia, 1994.
62. As Juan Davila has argued, the copying (or appropriation) of Aboriginal themes by non-Aboriginal artists assumes a connection to the 'primitive'. '[Tim] Johnson paints in the manner of an Aborigine, but feels the need to master . . . the cultures outside the dominant model . . . he relies on a rapport with an intuitive primitivism (naturalism?), an affinity with the "savage" mind.' J. Davila, 'Aboriginality: A Lugubrious Game?', (1987) 23 (4) *Art and Text* 53.
63. G. Marcus and F. Myers, *The Traffic in Culture: Refiguring Art and Anthropology*, University of California Press: Berkeley, 1995, at 20.
64. One notable demonstration in the value of the 'otherness' of indigenous art in the western discourse on art is found in the 1984 Museum of Modern Art in New York exhibition, *'Primitivism' in 20th Century Art: Affinity of the Tribal and the Modern.* In one of the many critiques written about the exhibition, Marianna Torgovnick explains that

the exhibition, 'proved that primitive objects exerted great power in the imagination of modern artists and that their forms, themes, and media coincided in interesting ways or were inspirational to one of the great flowerings of the visual arts in Western civilisation. The exhibition's demonstration of how modernism absorbed the primitive was broad, dramatic and stirring.' M. Torgovnick, *Gone Primitive: Savage Intellects Modern Lives*, The University of Chicago Press: Chicago, 1990 at 120.

65. 'According to Djon Mundine, the "spot the primitive" syndrome of some gallery owners and curators has led to their refusal to see classical indigenous art, such as bark paintings, sculpture and dot paintings, in a contemporary sense. Non classical, urban based contemporary art has not been accepted as true or authentic art.' M. Langton, *Valuing Cultures: Recognising Indigenous Cultures as a Valued Part of Australian Heritage*, supra n.40 at 14. See also a discussion on the estimated number of 'traditionally orientated' artists living on outstations or other communities as read from the 1991 census: D. Ellinson, 'Unauthorised Reproduction of Traditional Aboriginal Art', (1994) 17 (2) *UNSW Law Journal* 327.
66. J. Clifford, *The Predicament of Culture: Twentieth Century Ethnography, Literature and Art*, supra n.57 at 202.
67. S. Wright, 'Intellectual Property and the "Imaginary Aboriginal"', supra n.36 at 129.
68. See for instance: N. Thomas, 'Hierarchies: From Traditional to Contemporary', *Possessions: Indigenous Art/Colonial Culture*, supra n.42. See also: N. Thomas, 'Cold Fusion', (1996) 98 (1) *American Anthropologist* 9.
69. See: Tracey Moffatt's films *Night Cries – A Rural Tragedy* (1989) and *Nice Coloured Girls* (1987). See Gordon Bennett's work, *The Nine Ricochets (Fall Down Black Fella, Jump Up White Fella)* (1990) and *Myth of Western Man (White Man's Burden)* (1992).
70. G. Bennett, 'The Manifest Toe' McLean, I., and G. Bennett, *The Art of Gordon Bennett*, Craftsman House: Australia, 1996 at 58.
71. See: K. Neville, 'Art and Colonial Consciousness: Deconstructing the Colonial Imagination' (2000) 1 (2) *Balayi: Culture, Law and Colonialism* 39; D. Palmer and D. Groves, 'A Dialogue on Identity, Intersubjectivity and Ambivalence', (2000) 1 (2) *Balayi: Culture, Law and Colonialism* 19.
72. Similarly, Marcia Langton aptly illustrates the significant problematics of the term Aboriginal – see Introduction.
73. S. Wright, 'Intellectual Property and the "Imaginary Aboriginal"', supra n.36.
74. Ibid., at 133.
75. Consider the way many conferences convened on 'traditional knowledge and intellectual property' often don't have any indigenous speakers. While it is increasingly difficult to justify indigenous absence in Australia, in European contexts the politics of indigenous representation and the authority to speak remain peripheral issues.
76. S. Wright, 'Intellectual Property and the "Imaginary Aboriginal"', supra n.36 at 147.
77. M. Nakata, 'Indigenous Knowledge and the Cultural Interface: Underlying Issues at the Intersection of Knowledge and Information Systems', (2002) 28 *International Federation of Libraries Association Journal* 281 at 283.
78. Ibid., at 282. This concern was reiterated by the 2003 winner of the Twentieth National Aboriginal and Torres Strait Islander Art Award, Richard Bell. His artwork was entitled 'Aboriginal art. It's a white thing.'

5. Study of the bureaucratic agenda

With consideration of the way in which intellectual property law emerged as a unique cultural form, and the making of Aboriginal 'art', it is now time to explore the ways in which indigenous knowledge, within an Australian context, came into bureaucratic view as something that needed protection. To this end, I will look initially at the ways in which problems of protecting indigenous knowledge were raised and have subsequently been framed in Australia by governmental efforts in the form of bureaucratic response. What will become evident as I examine the 1981 *Report of the Working Party on the Protection of Aboriginal Folklore* and secondly the 1994 *Stopping the Rip Offs: Intellectual Property Protection for Aboriginal and Torres Strait Islander People*, is the profound difficulty of reconciling certain indigenous interests within a legal framework.

What follows is an extrapolation of how a dilemma of purpose characterises each governmental incentive, and this dilemma circulates around contested systems of value. In order to transcend such difficulties however, the Reports increasingly turn to the security and logic of the law to uphold and deal with issues that cannot be relegated solely to a legal domain. Enhancing both the legitimacy of the law, and positioning the problem of inappropriate use of indigenous knowledge as a legal problem, the Reports rely on traditionalised interpretations of Aboriginality, leaving contemporary and inter-cultural indigenous exchanges as peripheral 'problems'. Through the Reports an homogeneity of indigenous experience is reshaped which is, at best, imaginary. Participation by indigenous people demands that they identify with an impossible standard of authentic 'traditional' culture.[1] A consequent of this is that indigenous people are presented with 'enormous difficulties both in making claims and negotiating positions'.[2]

With attention to the ways by which knowledge is increasingly valued as a commodity in western society, governmental attention has been directed to the importance of developing frameworks that secure indigenous rights to knowledge, whilst also delivering surety to the legal discourse as the key agency dealing with knowledge management, access and distribution. What complicates the agenda of using the law to protect indigenous knowledge can be characterised as a certain dilemma of purpose: is the use of the law to further the economic interests of indigenous people, or to preserve indigenous knowledge as part of a valuable cultural artifact and an important part of constituting indigenous cultural identity, or both?

IDENTIFYING THE PROBLEM

The argument in Part One proposed that law reduces cultural difference but also relies upon it to understand the differing demands brought for legal interpretation. The point was that law rejects difference presented to it in a radical way: it accommodates difference when it is presented through the guise of its own categories and terms of reference. This is a reality of legal engagement with differentials, cultural or political, as it mediates a space that does not destablise its own narrative of internal cohesion. Remembering the comments of Noel Pearson, that legal frameworks can be adapted for purposeful strategies of recognition, voicing a concern for indigenous property within a legal framework of intellectual property, strategically works to alert the law to a concern to which it may otherwise have been blind. Because the challenge is set within the law's own terms of reference it must engage the challenge. Not to do so would undermine the narrative of 'universalism'. Thus the possibility of utilising the law depends upon a recognition of the emancipatory potential of property.

A key to understanding the inclusion of indigenous knowledge is in considering how the law treats the indigenous difference that is presented. The process of making indigenous knowledge as a category within intellectual property paradoxically seeks to sideline and cloak cultural difference within the category. Indigenous knowledge is instituted as part of the intellectual property narrative that minimises the specific historical conditions that has resulted in the law being faced with such problems – for example in Australia, colonisation. In addition the law is constructed as the mediator of indigenous difficulties, with little or no reflexivity of the actuality of law in facilitating the process of colonialism. While indigenous people do have a position in relation to the law, as Chapter Two suggested and later chapters will extend, the position is paradoxically exclusionary and inclusive, therefore making the location that indigenous people are expected to mediate extremely difficult. Thus solving the problems presented to intellectual property law is not about countering for the historical disadvantage or working towards establishing some form of indigenous sovereignty, where indigenous people choose how to regulate and manage their knowledge and images. Instead the framework establishes how copyright can incorporate this 'new' subject matter within its entrenched boundaries and in this way the law presumes to speak for indigenous people. As such, cultural differences are seen as 'incidental' rather than 'intrinsic' to the production of the category of indigenous intellectual property.

POLITICAL ENVIRONMENTS AND INDIVIDUAL INFLUENCE

By the late 1960s and throughout the 1970s in Australia, two distinct policy changes were evident in the way the government approached indigenous people. The first was a change from a policy of assimilation to one of self-determination and the second was in regards to land rights.[3] The policy shift to land rights was seen in the culmination of statutory land rights legislation in the Northern Territory and South Australia.[4]

The land rights movement consolidated a politics concerned with redressing the imbalance between western law and the interests of Aboriginal and Torres Strait Islander people. That these politics have undergone change and movement over the last thirty years is a testament to the dynamics of cultural production, political agendas, academic focus, and the sustained voice of indigenous people. In this way, the land rights movement presented a dialogic space where the interests of indigenous people were spoken, governmental objectives shaped, legal positions challenged and academic interests honed. While it should be emphasised that this space was never unilateral or bounded, the historical importance of the space enabled flows into various and multiple areas and generated, in particular, rethinking about the function of the law, with specific consideration of indigenous people as citizens, and therefore as legal subjects.[5] One example of this rethinking of indigenous people in relation to the law was the recognition that there was and had historically been a parallel body of law for many indigenous people even though the authority of these customary laws remained unacknowledged within the dominant legal system.[6]

Recognising indigenous legal rights and the importance of land rights legislation changed the face and direction of Australian legal history. My point here is to highlight the complex demands of political movements that shape the future direction and action of government and individuals. For on one level, the changes in governmental policy relating to indigenous people necessitated a re-conceptualisation in legal and political discourse of the relationship between many indigenous people, their spiritual connection to land and the importance of cultural imagery. The significance of the land claims was in 'introducing conceptions of land ownership that were not only collective but based on spiritual and social connections to place'.[7] In this way land rights and native title disrupt traditional jurisprudence on property ownership and rights, although such legislation is located and inseparable from such jurisprudence. The disruption highlights the discontinuity of the law and the possibility of developing new and productive legal narratives that incorporate the cultural differences presented by indigenous people as legal actors.

As a compliment to the increasing recognition of indigenous people as citizens, attention was also drawn to the different cultural practices and products of many indigenous people. As Wandjuk Marika, an artist from Yirrkala, Arnhem Land in northern Australia explained:

> We have found that within this culture, our art is appreciated and has material value. We have been very happy to sell our paintings and artifacts as this has enabled us to purchase the things that we now need so that our children can have enough to eat, go to school and learn to live as part of two cultures.[8]

Wandjuk Marika is significant in this story as he became the key spokesperson in advocating for equal treatment for Aboriginal artists before the law and within broader art spaces. His is an important example of the way in which individuals can influence and shape new areas of legal and bureaucratic concern. Through his direct and indirect lobbying of arts councils and government bureaucrats, in 1973 the first National Seminar on Aboriginal Arts was convened. The seminar prompted renewed calls for consideration of Aboriginal art as legitimate 'art' in a western sense. It also provided the initial context for the eye of bureaucracy to focus, thus leading to the creation of a governmental working group to discuss possibilities for the protection of Aboriginal art, which culminated in the 1981 *Report of the Working Party on the Protection of Aboriginal Folklore*.

Notably, the 1960s and 1970s were a period in Australia when the distinct 'otherness' represented by Aboriginal cultures began to rupture.[9] In this sense, the positioning of Aboriginal people at a point of exteriority to western 'cultures' was destabilised and aspects of indigenous cultures became part of the dominant western ethos. Aboriginal art, as 'art' was one such example. Despite the nascent primitivism and romanticism attached to indigenous people as a general category, certain indigenous spokespeople inevitably influenced the responsiveness of the government and the law in relation to these 'inappropriate' uses of indigenous imagery. For example, in 1976 and continuing his advocacy, Wandjuk Marika wrote in the *Aboriginal News* of his anguish at finding his art reproduced onto tea towels. Marika explained his position in the following way:

> Sometime ago, I happened to see a tea-towel with one of my paintings represented on it; this was one of the stories that my father had given me, and no-one else amongst my people would have painted it without my permission. But some unknown person copied my painting and had it reproduced in this way,

> without even first asking my permission. I was deeply upset and for some years was unable to paint.
>
> It was then that I realised that I and my fellow Aboriginal artists needed some form of protection. It is not that we object to people reproducing our work, but it is essential that we be consulted first, for only we know if a particular painting is of special sacred significance, to be seen only by certain members of a tribe, and only we can give permission for our works of art to be reproduced. It is hard to imagine the works of great Australian artists such as Sydney Nolan or Pro Hart being reproduced without their permission. We are only asking that we be granted the same recognition, that our works be respected and that we be acknowledged as the rightful owners of our own works of art.[10]

Marika was influential in prompting consideration of this issue, both within Federal Government and what was then called the Institute for Aboriginal Studies.[11] Marika's position on copyright was possibly informed by both the early confidential information case *Foster v Mountford & Rigby Ltd*[12] and even the land rights case, *Milpurrum v Nabalco Pty Ltd*[13], where the Yolngu people of Arnhem Land in northern Australia argued for land rights, presenting the now famous Bark Petition as evidence (and title) of knowledge, association and spirituality with the land.[14] Certainly because of the land rights cases, access to legal advice and legal advocates became somewhat easier in the Northern Territory. In a somewhat fluid political environment, indigenous issues of land rights, sovereignty and cultural control gained new points of leverage. It was thus also in this political environment that the Australian government turned attention to the protection of Aboriginal arts. Under these conditions, the 1981 *Report of the Working Party on the Protection of Aboriginal Folklore*[15] should be understood as operating within a context that: recognised the changing political environments which enabled new indigenous rights claims; was responsive to Marika and other Aboriginal artists' concerns about the use of cultural imagery; and realised the dangers and possibilities of the increasing market demand for indigenous artwork and design.

REPORT OF THE WORKING PARTY ON THE PROTECTION OF ABORIGINAL FOLKLORE

In December 1981 the *Report of the Working Party on the Protection of Aboriginal Folklore* was released.[16] In keeping with the international interest on 'folklore' at the time, the Report commenced debate in Australia on the adoption of a legislative approach to the protection of Aboriginal art.[17] The Report was initiated in 1973 following the first National Seminar on Aboriginal Arts where a key resolution to the newly formed Aboriginal Arts Board was that procedures should be developed 'which would enable each tribal body to protect its own particular designs and works and to strictly control the use of them by non-Aboriginals'.[18] The resolution was designed by the Copyright Committee of the Australia Council and, in turn, suggested that the government of the day should establish a committee to 'protect Aboriginal artists'.[19] As the Report notes;

> The first meeting of the Working Party was held on 28 October 1975. In 1979 it became clear that substantial issues beyond copyright were raised and the possibility of transferring the responsibility of the Working Party to the Minister for Aboriginal Affairs were canvassed. In the event it was considered more appropriate to transfer the Working Party to the Minister for Home Affairs and the Environment.[20]

The Report's primary recommendation concerned the introduction of special legislation in the form of an 'Aboriginal Folklore Act'. It was envisaged that the Act would protect Aboriginal folklore by providing for: prohibitions of using certain material; prohibitions on destructive uses of Aboriginal material; payments for the use of material in a commercial nature; the development of a system for clearing the use of works; an Aboriginal Folklore Board; and, a Commissioner for Aboriginal Folklore.[21]

The Report began with a preliminary discussion of the concerns regarding the 'use of Aboriginal designs taken from the original works by Aboriginal artists'.[22] The examples utilised focus exclusively on contexts where designs were used for commercial gain.[23] The Report highlights the 1976 case *Foster v Mountford & Rigby Ltd* where photographs of a secret/sacred nature were included in an anthropologist's publication.[24] The publication was restrained by a court injunction utilising the law of confidential information. The Report notes that 'this example highlights the difficulty which confronts non-Aboriginals proposing to use Aboriginal material, namely, that of finding an authority entitled to give permission for it to be used'.[25] It is important that from the outset, the Report espoused an inclusive nationalist objective. The purpose was not solely to consider means to protect indigenous imagery, but also mechanisms that allow non-indigenous peoples to access and use (predominately in a commercial context) indigenous imagery as well.

The Report was surprisingly candid regarding the problems that developed over the course of its writing and release, and these were openly incorporated into the body of the text. The first issue was terminology and consequently the inability to differentiate adequately Aboriginal 'folklore' from other Aboriginal material or knowledge. The Report was guided in using the term 'folklore' because of its usage within other international reports, but reinterpreted the term giving it 'local' subjectivity.[26] 'Folklore' was considered a sufficiently vague term to recognise the 'traditions, customs and beliefs that underlie forms of artistic expression'.[27] The key difficulties of the term (beyond that it was not technically legal) however, were acknowledged in the following way:

> We realise that the word 'folklore' in the proposed legislation could be subject to several misinterpretations. The word is not used narrowly to refer to oral literature only, as it is sometimes used. Nor do we mean to imply that Australian Aboriginals possess a rudimentary, unsophisticated artistic tradition; nor that Aboriginal traditions are static or even dead . . . [n]evertheless the word folklore has been adopted as a compromise meeting the conceptual and international *legal* requirements for such a term.[28]

From the first bureaucratic initiative, the legal discourse was instrumental in directing the way in which interests in indigenous knowledge (at this stage understood as folklore) were to be phrased. Whilst the term had no legal basis, its repetition in various international legal forums served to create a quasi precedent which then legitimised its use within the national context. The primary authority was legal and governmental not indigenous, and indigenous people were sidelined from participating in any discussion concerning the 'best' terminology for their knowledge structures and forms of expression. Indeed if they had been involved, arguably the pejorative meaning contained in the term 'folklore' and its sense of inferiority in relation to other cultural forms, which has been widely commented on by indigenous spokespeople, would have excluded it from becoming the key term used to identify forms of indigenous knowledge within legal frameworks.[29]

A further difficulty faced by the Working Party was in deciding on the purpose of the specific legislation. It was unclear whether the legislation was to preserve Aboriginal 'folklore' as part of a continuing tradition, 'allowing it to evolve within its *traditional context* unhampered by *external* influence'[30] or whether the aim of the legislation was to protect the economic interests of Aboriginal people.[31] While the two purposes were not necessarily mutually exclusive, the Working Party understood that the rationale underpinning each would take the policy objectives in different directions.[32] The key problem with the difficulty of purpose that characterised the Report was dually the use of the term 'folklore' which could not help but convey a perception of the past and the perception that culturally specific knowledge, positioned within a 'traditional' context, evolved 'unhampered by cultural influence'. Fundamental flaws in viewing indigenous people as only existing in 'traditional' contexts have been instrumental in producing the anxiety of positioning indigenous people both within modernity (with economic considerations) and simultaneously outside it, in traditional locales. In terms of fostering an anxiety that still characterises debate in this area, this Report instrumentally reinforced such myths regarding the location of indigenous people and the unchanging nature of tradition. This continues to influence current debates over who is legitimately entitled to claim 'ownership' of culturally specific knowledge. Despite its best intentions, the Report is part of a historical continuum where difficult negotiating positions are created for indigenous people who want to participate within the discourse.[33]

The disjuncture between economic interest and the preservation of cultural identity and integrity within the Report destabilised the expectation and function of intellectual property law with regard to indigenous knowledge as new subject matter. In this sense, while advocating the possibility of using laws of intellectual property, notably copyright, the Report strongly emphasised the limitations of these laws.[34] As Colin Golvan, the Barrister responsible for running all the Aboriginal art and copyright cases in the courts, observed, 'the Working Party concluded that the reliance on copyright was not appropriate in order to protect Aboriginal folklore'.[35] This was, in part, because 'folklore' was a vague descriptive term with no suitable legal equivalent. There also remained significant difficulties in determining ownership, originality and authorship as the very term excluded these kinds of categories. To this end, indigenous cultural expression remained unidentifiable for the requirements of copyright protection. As an alternative the Report recommended the establishment of 'special' legislation, developed in consideration with the differing requirements of Aboriginal people but also taking into account difficulties facing non-indigenous people with the use of indigenous cultural material. Here we find the first proposal for *sui-generis* legislation.[36] Whilst the Report ostensibly failed to envisage what form a law to protect the amorphous category of folklore would take, it did make an important contribution to the development of laws protecting certain aspects under the rubric of folklore, for instance tangible indigenous material such as sites and artifacts through the Heritage Acts.[37] However, the intangible and invisible dimensions of 'folklore' remained problematic, as the only kind of strategy available that protected rights in knowledge were laws of intellectual property.

The Report emphasises that legislation and bureaucracy are the only feasible and realistic outcomes for securing the use of Aboriginal arts, both by Aboriginal and Torres Strait Islander people but also non-indigenous people. In recommending that a Commissioner for Aboriginal Folklore should be appointed for the purpose of determining infringement, issuing clearance for use of works and negotiating payments, issues regarding how power in law is exercised come to the fore. The Commissioner would be a governmental representative and, by implication, non-indigenous –

another bureaucracy for the administration of indigenous affairs with little or no indigenous participation. Beyond assuming the inability of indigenous people to engage in such complex negotiations, the recommendation effectively removes indigenous involvement and denies indigenous interpretation and self-determination. The Report reshapes the issue as requiring legal authority and state intervention. This reshaping is significant as it reaffirms the legislative and administrative approach as the dominant way of considering any solution to Aboriginal issues – in this case the problem of protecting indigenous knowledge.[38]

Throughout the Report, indigenous people are defined as either 'customary users' and/or 'traditional owners'. Through this narrow view an homogeneity of Aboriginality is imposed. Whilst indigenous concerns are central, indigenous voice is absent.[39] This position of exteriority also creates a barrier for Aboriginal people to engage actively with its recommendations. Indigenous culture, in the singular, is romanticised and represented as a unitary phenomenon. Whilst this is a product of various kinds of historically informing discourses, it matters precisely because the romanticised vision of Aboriginal culture, and indeed cultural difference, is repeated and enhanced in each following governmental and legal initiative. It becomes harder and harder to account for Aboriginal experience that does not fit within the space of romantic Aboriginality. The legislative approach seeks to order specific cultural practices through assuming that these practices and how they relate to imagery are unified.[40] Normative assumptions regarding indigenous cultural practice overwhelmingly preclude the recognition of the diversity of indigenous practices and the multiplicity of positions and attitudes by indigenous peoples to the use of cultural imagery.

The *Report of the Working Party* establishes the precedent in regards to managing indigenous cultural material in Australia. The *Report of the Working Party* can be seen as a strategic way of making reality thinkable and practicable.[41] The Report is an attempt to make the problem of protecting Aboriginal 'folklore' open to remedy. It also functions to legitimate indigenous knowledge as a specific area of governmental and hence legislative and administrative attention. For our current purpose it illustrates how certain frameworks are developed that try to shape, mobilise and sculpt particular choices, needs and wants of indigenous and non-indigenous peoples to the subject indigenous intellectual property. The space through which the problem of misusing indigenous knowledge is to be understood is produced so as to be amenable to discrete projects and further programmes of management.

Consequently, the following Report, *Stopping the Rip Offs* shores up the legal and administrative boundaries and in doing so forecloses alternatives beyond law. Significantly through *Stopping the Rip Offs*, the distinct space of 'indigenous intellectual property' is consolidated, where the process of managing the problem of indigenous knowledge generates its own form of language, logic, rhetoric and possibility. The *Report of the Working Party* was an important precursor, but it is really *Stopping the Rip Offs* that secures the production of the legal category, fleshing out governmental ambition and marginalising questions about politics, indigenous rights and alternative indigenous subjectivities.

STOPPING THE RIP OFFS: INTELLECTUAL PROPERTY PROTECTION FOR ABORIGINAL AND TORRES STRAIT ISLANDER PEOPLES

In October 1994, the Federal Government released the Issues Paper *Stopping the Rip Offs: Intellectual Property Protection for Aboriginal and Torres Strait Islander Peoples*.[42] The intention of the paper was to improve the *legal* protection for Aboriginal and Torres Strait Islander 'arts and cultural expression'.[43] The release of the Issues Paper occurred prior to the final hearing and decision in the case *Milpurruru v Indofurn* (1994).[44] Such was the interest in the outcome of the case from legal, governmental agencies and individuals, that the Issues Paper appeared responsive to the increasing discussions about the possibility of legal protection for indigenous artistry. It was reactive, as evidenced in the title, and timely in relation to the case then before the Federal Court. It was clearly a product of a unique set of issues being played out in Australia.

Notably, *Stopping the Rip Offs* was developed after an increasing number of cases relating to the inappropriate use of Aboriginal art were appearing in the Australian courts.[45] Contrary to the opinion expressed in the *Report of the Working Party*, copyright was functioning as a viable tool for the protection of Aboriginal art. In this sense, concerns regarding legal limitations, (in terms of originality and individual authorship), were being addressed by the Court to the satisfaction of the indigenous litigants and counsel representing the indigenous artists. It was evident that it was both the disparity of economic return *and* the culturally inappropriate use of the Aboriginal artwork that formed the crux of these cases. Significantly the Issues Paper was also riding on the success of the *Mabo* decision that confirmed the possibility for law to be responsive to indigenous concerns in relation to land rights and questions associated with self-determination. This political environment reaffirmed the authority and primacy of the law to act 'on behalf' of indigenous people. Thus intellectual property law, as a legitimate vehicle for successful protection became the central theme for the Issues Paper.

In order for law to work effectively it cannot be seen to be anything other than 'fair' and 'neutral'. Jane Gaines notes that the legal discourse does not question its own categories as it depends on them for its perpetuation.[46] In the Issues Paper, the central characteristics of intellectual property law are utilised to position 'indigenous knowledge' as a natural subject of the law. To this end, the intangibility of the new 'indigenous knowledge' subject matter is made recognisable through established forms of classification. For instance, 'art', 'dance' and 'song', all culturally specific categories and established in copyright law are used to identify elements of indigenous knowledge. Through the deployment of these categories onto indigenous knowledge, a legal logic is imposed in both how indigenous knowledge is understood and how it can be dealt with. Nevertheless, the 'cultural' nature of indigenous knowledge continues to exert influence on these categories undermining its closure as a naturally occurring legal subject.

Two elements of the Issues Paper are fundamental for the future (re)production of indigenous knowledge within intellectual property law. Firstly, the position of indigenous people as a homogenous group residing within 'traditional communities' is reconfirmed. This facilitates the construction of indigenous knowledge as bounded and therefore 'different' from any other kind of knowledge that intellectual property has historically had to deal with. Secondly, by virtue of existing within 'traditional' communities and therefore 'naturally' not modern, vulnerability is presumed which reaffirms the need for (paternal) bureaucratic authority. 'In the same breath as admitting that communities are continually evolving, it [the Issues Paper] makes the seemingly contradictory statement that the focus is upon forms of artistic and cultural expression 'which are based on custom and tradition"'.[47] The danger is that in combination, these elements replicate constructions of indigenous people produced through colonial, anthropological and primitivist discourses. Indigenous people are denied access to contemporary practices of modernity, sovereignty and subjectivity. Like the art, Aboriginal people are produced as timeless, authentic communitarian and ahistorical.

Despite approximately three thousand copies of the Issues Paper being distributed to Aboriginal and Torres Strait Islander Commission (ATSIC) Regional Councils, Regional Offices, Aboriginal Legal Services, Land Councils, indigenous media associations, Aboriginal art centres, copyright interests and art interests, only eleven responses were received.[48] This illustrates starkly fundamental issues of access, for instance how the actual 'problem' as well as intellectual property law, was made intelligible to indigenous individuals and community representatives. The issue of access to the law continues to be a significant oversight in enabling (and encouraging) indigenous people to make decisions about the possibility of utilising and developing benefits from an intellectual property regime. Laws of intellectual property still remain exclusionary in practice, even though considerable effort has been made to locate indigenous knowledge within an intellectual property regime.[49]

Positioning itself comfortably within legal and bureaucratic authority, *Stopping the Rip Offs* effectively facilitates the extent to which the legal logic and language will be inscribed upon concepts of indigenous knowledge. In this way indigenous cultural expression becomes tied to the legal logic of intellectual property law, and most effectively appears as naturally given. Through the language and classifications of intellectual property law, indigenous knowledge is rendered thinkable and amenable to intervention. Legal discourse maintains its dominance by channelling discussions of the 'object' of concern through itself. For '[t]he law builds itself over time, by discarding possibilities for speech and thought as well as by making them; and what it discards for some person or people will be a living language, a living truth'.[50]

In using a dominant western regulatory mechanism of law, relations of power are exerted, for power is made possible through a 'plurality of relationships'.[51] One result of these relations is the production of knowledge, for example, what it is possible to know about intellectual property and indigenous knowledge. Importantly, processes of knowledge production highlight the variety of political movements that exist and are put into play in varying strategies. *Stopping the Rip Offs* indicates a paradox, namely that the terms of what is to be recognised and included are very vague, except when there is a commodity at stake. At that point the object of legal protection becomes surprisingly clear. For the differentiation is only sensitive and sensible in terms of securing the commodity. Aboriginal art is realised as the moment of capital. This gives intellectual property law its purpose and mode of identification. The issues of how the law treats difference are relatively benign within these Reports, that is, the bureaucratic agenda recognises difference, but fails to engage with it in any meaningful way. Treating cultural difference is left to the courts, where as we shall now consider, new and inventive ways of accommodating indigenous difference are imagined. The courts are left with no choice – they must deal with difference because indigenous people are present to express their voice and contextualise indigenous cultural identity through cultural and legal expression.

Following the two governmental reports, *Report of the Working Party* and *Stopping the Rip Offs*, indigenous knowledge was ultimately affirmed as a category in Australian intellectual property law, albeit one wrapped in difference. Significantly both reports consolidate the problem of the unauthorised use of Aboriginal art, design and knowledge as amenable to governable strategies of description, intervention and normalisation. Inevitably this has affected how remedial solutions have been developed and the way in which the law has sought to accommodate indigenous cultural differences. Both reports secured a very particular kind of governable space, replete with regimes of truth (for instance under what conditions indigenous knowledge is recognisable), including who is authorised to speak and under what circumstances.

As the position of indigenous people in the above mentioned Reports highlights the tendency is to locate indigenous culture as a unitary phenomenon, where there exists one voice and one perspective. Such a position is enhanced by the pervading emphasis on 'tradition' as a marker identifying cultural expression and cultural knowledge as 'indigenous'. This undermines the capacity for indigenous people actively to engage and utilise economic frameworks and thus generate legitimate forms of economic return either for themselves or their families and/or communities. The construct provided to indigenous people forecloses any real recognition of desires held by indigenous people to gain control of cultural knowledge for economic reasons. This is because the economic rationale disrupts the reliance on 'tradition' – the trope used to identify indigenous knowledge. The lack of any sustained negotiation and discussion, in governmental reports and legal initiatives, with the diversity of indigenous experience further exacerbates this concern and consequently places indigenous people in difficult negotiating positions.

That indigenous people have also expressed concern to protect cultural integrity through intellectual property highlights the complicated agendas that are presented to the law for remedy. There is a tendency in the governmental responses to focus on one of these elements at the expense of the other. There seems a reluctance to engage with the difficulties that these agenda generate, even though they have both been produced and phrased within the intellectual property discourse.[52] The contradictions and ambiguities remain concealed behind the face of bureaucracy.

In order to understand these difficulties more completely, and how they impact on the ways in which indigenous knowledges are identified within the law and how difference is understood beyond an abstract uniformity, it is imperative that we now explore these problems in the context of the case law.[53] What will now be considered is the way that in the specific cultural and political circumstances that generate instances of case law, indigenous individuals are provided with the capacity to push the limits of legal expectation. In this way challenging the law to accept fundamental differences inherent in indigenous subject matter also recognises existing degrees of similarity. Thus the key concern in how indigenous knowledge has been produced as a category in intellectual property law is the way that this new subject matter challenges precepts and concepts inherent within legal regimes of logic and the seepage between governance via bureaucracy. This influences the courts, thus effecting how the category is produced and legally secured.

NOTES

1. E. Povinelli, *The Cunning of Recognition: Indigenous Alterities and the Making of Australian Multiculturalism*, Duke University Press: Durham and London, 2002.
2. S. Wright, 'Intellectual Property and the "Imaginary Aboriginal"', in Bird, G., G. Martin and J. Neilson (eds), *Majah: Indigenous Peoples and the Law*, The Federation Press: Sydney, 1996 at 140.
3. Citizenship rights for Aboriginal people were established through the 1967 Referendum – however it took another decade for these to be fully recognised throughout the country.
4. See: *Aboriginal Land Rights (Northern Territory) Act 1976* (Cth) and the *Pitjantjatjarra Land Rights Act 1981* (South Australia).
5. See for example: A. Curthoys, 'Citizenship, Race and Gender' in Daley, C., and M. Nolan (eds), *Suffrage and Beyond*, Pluto Press: Sydney, 1994; A. McGrath, 'Citizenship, Rights and Aboriginal Women', (1993) 37 *Journal of Australian Studies* 99; and generally, N. Peterson and W. Sanders (eds), *Citizenship and Indigenous Australians: Changing Conceptions and Possibilities*, Cambridge University Press: Cambridge, 1988.
6. An attempt to understand indigenous customary law prompted the Australian Law Reform Commission Report, *The Recognition of Aboriginal Customary Laws* 1983. Between 2000 and 2006, the Law Reform Commission of Western Australia reinvestigated the role of customary law. The *Final Report: The Interaction of WA Law with Aboriginal Law and Culture*, 2006, made 131 recommendations for legislative and policy reform.
7. V. Strang, 'Not so Black and White' in Abramson, A. and D. Theodossopoulis (eds), *Land Law and Environment: Mythical Land, Legal Boundaries*, Pluto Press: London, 2000.
8. W. Marika, 'Copyright on Aboriginal Art', (1976) 3(1) *Aboriginal News* 7 at 7.
9. This rupture was also produced through an emergent black rights movement that adopted and reinterpreted strategies from the civil rights movement in the United States.
10. W. Marika, 'Copyright on Aboriginal Art', supra n.8 at 7.
11. The institution formerly known as Institute for Aboriginal Studies is currently known as the Australian Institute of Aboriginal and Torres Strait Islander Studies or AIATSIS.
12. *Foster v Mountford & Rigby Ltd* (1977) 14 ALR 71. In this case, the Pitjantjatjarra Land Council went to Court to stop the publication of the book *Nomads of the Desert* by Charles Mountford. The claim was that the book contained secret/sacred material and exposure to this material could fracture the social fabric of the Pitjantjatjarra people. The claim was successful and the book was withdrawn from publication until the material was removed.
13. *Milpirrum v Nabalco Pty Ltd* (1971) 17 FLR 141.
14. G. Yunupingu, 'From the Bark Petition to Native Title' in *Land Rights: Past Present and Future – Conference Papers,* Northern and Central Land Councils: Canberra, 1997. For an appreciation of the connection between art and land see: S. Cane, *Pila Nguru: The Spinifex People*, Fremantle Arts Centre Press: Fremantle, 2002.
15. Department of Home Affairs and the Environment, *Report of the Working Party on the Protection of Aboriginal Folklore,* Canberra, December 1981.
16. Ibid.

17. National attention to intangible cultural heritage was paralleled by international attention. The 1967 Stockholm Revision Conference of the Berne Convention discussed the inclusion of provisions relating to folklore – but considered the term 'folklore' too difficult to define. The UNESCO–WIPO *Tunis Model Law on Copyright for Developing Countries* 1976, discussed the way in which 'national folklore' should be protected. In July 1977 WIPO and UNESCO convened a 'Committee of Experts on the Legal Protection of Folklore'. In February 1980 and 1981 WIPO and UNESCO convened meetings of a 'Working Group on the Intellectual Property aspects of Folklore Protection'. The Report of the Working Group culminated in the UNESCO-WIPO *Model Provisions for National Laws on the Protection of Expressions of Folklore Against Illicit Exploitation and Other Prejudicial Actions* 1982. Concerns for the protection of moveable cultural property had been on the international agenda for several decades (although not necessarily in the context of indigenous rights) see *Convention for the Protection of Cultural Property in the Event of Armed Conflict* 1954 and *Convention on the Means of Prohibiting and Preventing the Illicit Import, Export and Transfer of Ownership of Cultural Property* 1970.
18. Department of Home Affairs and the Environment, *Report of the Working Party on the Protection of Aboriginal Folklore*, supra n.15 at 3.
19. Ibid., at 3.
20. Ibid., at 4.
21. Ibid., at 4.
22. Ibid., at 5.
23. This was also confirmed by the groups who were invited to comment. 'A summary of the report by the Department of Aboriginal Affairs was sent to interested parties. State and Territory governments, relevant Aboriginal organisations, interested non-Aboriginal groups and commercial users of Aboriginal folk art were all invited to comment.' R. Bell, 'Protection of Aboriginal Folklore: Or Do they Dust Reports?', (1985) 17 *Aboriginal Law Bulletin* 6.
24. *Foster v Mountford & Rigby Ltd* (1977) 14 ALR 71. See also *Pitjantjatjara Council Inc & Peter Nganingu v John Lowe & Lyn Bender* (1983) Victoria Supreme Court, unreported – noted in (1982) 4 *Aboriginal Law Bulletin* 11.
25. Department of Home Affairs and the Environment, *Report of the Working Party on the Protection of Aboriginal Folklore*, supra n.15 at 6.
26. Ibid., at 7. Despite repeated concerns about the pejorative connotations of the term, folklore continues to be used as an international standard. For a contemporary reference see: World Intellectual Property Organisation, *Intellectual Property Needs and Expectations of Traditional Knowledge Holders: WIPO Report on Fact Finding Missions on Intellectual Property and Traditional Knowledge (1998–1999)*, Geneva, Switzerland 2001; World Intellectual Property Organisation Secretariat, *Inter-Governmental Committee on Intellectual Property and Genetic Resources, Traditional Knowledge and Folklore*, Fourth Session, Geneva, 9–17 December 2002. For a discussion of the problem of folklore see: M. Blakeney, 'Protection of Traditional Knowledge under Intellectual Property Law', (2000) 22 (6) *European Intellectual Property Review* 251.
27. Ibid., at 7. Also: R. Bell, 'Use of the term "folklore" recognises that the traditions which underlie the Aboriginal arts are tightly integrated within the totality of Aboriginal culture. Expressions, in a variety of art forms, comprise the folklore traditions built up in a community.' R. Bell, 'Protection of Aboriginal Folklore: Or Do they Dust Reports?', supra n.23 at 6.
28. Ibid., at 7 [emphasis mine].
29. 'Although I do not agree with the term folklore to describe aspects of cultural heritage, I commend that Report for the initiatives it sought to encourage.' M. Dodson 'Indigenous peoples and intellectual property rights' *Ecopolitics IX – Conference Papers and Resolutions*, Northern Land Council: Sydney, 1996 at 35.
30. Department of Home Affairs and the Environment, *Report of the Working Party on the Protection of Aboriginal Folklore*, supra n.15 at 11 [emphasis mine].

31. 'The working party concluded that Aboriginal folklore is a national resource which should be protected in the interest of both Aborigines and the general public, but which should also be accessible to users. It identified two main areas where existing laws are inadequate: the use of traditional materials for commercial purposes without benefit to traditional owners.' R. Bell, 'Protection of Aboriginal Folklore: Or Do they Dust Reports?', supra n.23 at 6.
32. Department of Home Affairs and the Environment, *Report of the Working Party on the Protection of Aboriginal Folklore*, supra n.15 at 11.
33. This impossible position is also replicated in the Yorta Yorta native title case, *Members of the Yorta Yorta Community v State of Victoria* [2002] HCA 58 where the Yorta Yorta people were denied native title because their traditions and the community had changed over time. The key argument for the Government was that the Yorta Yorta people could not prove 'continuity' to their land (because of changes in tradition and community) therefore denying native title rights. See: L. Strelein, '*Members of the Yorta Yorta Aboriginal Community v Victoria* [2002] HCA 58 – Comment', (2003) 2 (21) *Land, Rights, Laws: Issues of Native Title* 1; R. Bartlett, 'The obsession with traditional laws and customs creates difficulties establishing native title claims in the South', (2003) 31 (1) *The University of Western Australia Law Review* 35.
34. Department of Home Affairs and the Environment, *Report of the Working Party on the Protection of Aboriginal Folklore*, supra n.15 at 13–17.
35. C. Golvan, 'Aboriginal Art and Copyright: The Case for Johnny Bulun Bulun' (1989) 10 *European Intellectual Property Review*, 346 at 347.
36. In international as well as national jurisdictions, sui-generis legislation constitutes the main option for accommodating intellectual property rights and indigenous interests. In Indonesia in 2007, for example, there are three sui-generis laws for the protection of traditional knowledge being drafted. For recommendations for one of these see: J. Anderson, L. Aragon, I. Haryanto, P. Jaszi, A. Nababan, H. Panjiatan, A. Sardjono, R. Siagian, R. Suryasaladin, *Traditional Arts: A Move Towards Protection in Indonesia* (forthcoming).
37. See generally Commonwealth legislation: *Aboriginal and Torres Strait Islander Heritage Protection Act 1984* (Cth); *Protection of Moveable Cultural Heritage Act 1987* (Cth). The State and Territory legislation focuses on different elements of Aboriginal and Torres Strait Islander Heritage. For example, the *National Parks and Wildlife Act 1974* (NSW) allows the Director-General of the National Parks and Wildlife services to create and control Aboriginal places, including those with Aboriginal remains. The *South Australian Aboriginal Heritage Act 1988* seeks to protect Aboriginal heritage in South Australia. The *Aboriginal Heritage Act 1972* (WA) protects places, sites and objects used by Aboriginal people.
38. For work that explores the significance of administrative intervention in the history of Australian colonial relations see: T. Rowse, *White Flour, White Power: From Rations to Citizenship in Central Australia*, Cambridge University Press: Cambridge, 1998; T. Rowse, *Remote Possibilities: The Aboriginal Domain and the Administrative Imagination*, Australian National University: Canberra, 1992; R. Folds, *Crossed Purposes: The Pintupi and Australia's Indigenous Policy*, University of New South Wales Press: Sydney, 2001; P. Batty, 'Private Politics, Public Strategies: White Advisors and their Aboriginal Subjects', (2005) 75 (33) *Oceania* 209.
39. Knowledge about Aboriginal people is provided through anthropological expertise – indigenous people are rendered as 'subjects' of the report.
40. Department of Home Affairs and the Environment, *Report of the Working Party on the Protection of Aboriginal Folklore*, supra n.15 at 19.
41. P. Miller, and N. Rose, 'Governing Economic Life', (1990) 19 (1) *Economy and Society* 1.
42. Attorney General's Department, *Stopping the Rip Offs: Intellectual Property Protection for Aboriginal and Torres Strait Islander Peoples,* Australian Government Publishing Service: Canberra 1994. In 1994, the Federal Government was a Labor government under the leadership of the Prime Minister Paul Keating.

43. Ibid., at ii.
44. *Milpurrurru & Others v Indofurn Pty Ltd*, (1994) 30 IPR 209.
45. From 1981 three cases appeared before the Courts and many others were settled. As Golvan explains, due to the number of cases at one point Lin Onus was instrumental in setting up the first arts management company 'to assist in managing these cases. I mean there were so many cases at one point that we needed a bit of a system.' C. Golvan, interview by author, 19 June 2002, tape recording, Owen Dixon Chambers, Melbourne. See also: V. Johnson, *Copyrites: Aboriginal Art in the Age of Reproductive Technologies*, Touring Exhibition Catalogue, 1996 as a historical record of these cases. Johnson's more contemporary work is the House of Aboriginality Project at www.mq.edu.au/house_of_aboriginality.
46. J. Gaines, *Contested Culture: The Image, the Voice and the Law*, The University of North Carolina Press: Chapel Hill, London, 1991 at 15.
47. S. Gray, 'Squatting in the Red Dust: Non-Aboriginal Law's Construction of the "Traditional" Aboriginal Artist', (1996) 14 (2) *Law in Context* 29 at 39.
48. C. Hawkins, 'Stopping the Rip-offs: Protecting Aboriginal and Torres Strait Islander Cultural Expression', (1995) 20 (1) *Alternative Law Bulletin* 7 at 10.
49. See: J. Anderson, *Indigenous Knowledge and Intellectual Property: Access, Ownership and Control of Cultural Materials – Final Report*, Australian Institute of Aboriginal and Torres Strait Islander Studies: Canberra (forthcoming).
50. J. Boyd White, *Justice as Translation: An Essay in Cultural and Legal Criticism*, University of Chicago Press: Chicago and London, 1990 at 262–263.
51. M. Foucault. 'Clarifications on the Question of Power', *Foucault Live: Collected Interviews, 1961–1984* (ed. Lotringer, S.) Semiotext(e): New York, 1989 at 260; M. Foucault, 'The Subject and Power' in Dreyfus, H. and P. Rabinow (eds), *Michel Foucault: Between Structuralism and Hermeneutics*, Harvester Press: Brighton, 1983; M. Foucault, 'Truth and Power' (Gordon, C. (ed)), *Power/Knowledge: Selected Interviews and Other Writings, 1972–1977*, Pantheon: New York, 1980.
52. See the work of Terri Janke. In particular, T. Janke, *Our Culture: Our Future. Report on Australian Indigenous Cultural and Intellectual Property Rights* (produced for Australian Institute of Aboriginal and Torres Strait Islander Studies [AIATSIS] and the Aboriginal and Torres Strait Islander Commission[ATSIC]), Michael Frankel and Company Solicitors: Surry Hills, 1998.
53. C. Helliwell and B. Hindess, 'The "Empire of Uniformity" and the Government of Subject Peoples', (2002) 6 (1&2) *Cultural Values* 139.

6. A tale of two cases

The previous chapter argued that governmental agendas, articulated through two key bureaucratic reports, have consolidated the extent that indigenous knowledge is positioned within legal discourse. This chapter will extend analysis of these dynamics by directly examining the importance of case law in facilitating the production of such categories. Furthermore the chapter will illustrate how judicial attempts at reconciling legal categories and legal language with indigenous knowledge are an inevitable and pragmatic response of governance.

Case law provides a space where the theoretical considerations highlighted in previous chapters can be considered through the practice of the law, constituting in its clearest form, legal action. Legal decisions are an event formative to the law itself.[1] In determining what the law says it becomes possible to recognise the limits and expectations of intellectual property law in relation to the indigenous knowledge category. This approach also inevitably reveals a hidden component that underpins copyright case law: the way in which the law seeks to determine (and even create) the essential core of the intangible matter that it seeks to protect.[2] However, the inevitably unstable nature of the intangible, and hence of intellectual property subject matter, means that determining the metaphysical nature of the intangible 'property' remains the key problematic for intellectual property law. Presented with 'indigenous knowledge' as the intangible subject matter and Aboriginal art as the tangible form, the law predominately determines the essential core of indigenous knowledge through tropes of 'tradition', 'Indigenous as Culture' and (cultural) difference. Significantly this solidifies the modern law by pointing out an external differentiation (rather than an inherent internal problem), but in doing so 'traditional'/indigenous knowledge remains unstable and therefore 'uncertain' legal subject matter. This alerts attention to where the disjuncture between recognising indigenous knowledge as a 'new' category occurs, and means that indigenous knowledge remains difficult to manage within an intellectual property discourse.

MILPURRURRU & OTHERS V INDOFURN PTY LTD

The two cases *Milpurrurru & Others v Indofurn Pty Ltd*[3] and *Bulun Bulun & Others v R & T Textiles*[4] have much in common in terms of the application of copyright law, however they also have distinctive differences that underpin their significance as case law. *Milpurrurru* (the *carpets case*) tested the extent to which intellectual property law could respond to and accommodate indigenous needs to secure forms of knowledge, especially with the increased infringement of Aboriginal art. The case informs the debate about the inclusion of indigenous difference in law. *Bulun Bulun* sought to extend the possibility for intellectual property law to encompass differing forms of ownership to that envisaged by the legislative scheme. In *Bulun Bulun* the cultural specificity of copyright was the key issue.[5] Both cases offer an opportunity to consider the practical response of law when managing both the category of indigenous knowledge and its product, namely Aboriginal art. The direction that law moved through these innovative cases was also facilitated because the same judge heard both cases: Justice von Doussa's voice has also been instructive in establishing a distinct indigenous narrative within intellectual property law.

The *carpets case* involved the unauthorised reproduction of the artwork of eight Aboriginal artists onto carpets. It was heard in the Federal Court of Australia, Northern Territory District Registry in 1994. There were four applicants. The first three were the Aboriginal artists George Milpurrurru,[6] Banduk Marika (both from Arnhem Land) and Tim Payunka Tjapangati (from Central Australia) and the fourth applicant was the public trustee for the Northern Territory representing the estates of five deceased Aboriginal artists. From the outset the judgment notes that all the artists have had their artwork exhibited in national and state galleries and that their artwork is 'recognised nationally and internationally as exceptional'.[7] This affirms both the status of the artists within the contemporary art world and the quality of the work infringed.

The respondents to the claim of copyright infringement were the company Indofurn Pty Ltd (formally Beechrow Pty Ltd) and its three directors: Brian Bethune, George King and Robert Rylands.

Predominately the case centred around two key elements. Firstly, the respondents were alleged to have infringed work under the Australian *Copyright Act 1968* (Cth) when they reproduced Aboriginal artworks onto carpets without the artists' consent and imported the works into Australia for commercial sale. Secondly, they were sued for false and misleading advertising in respect to the marketing of the carpets, thus breaching the *Trade Practices Act 1974* (Cth) for wrongful attribution.[8] In particular this part of the action related to the tags that were attached to the carpets stating that they were made by Aboriginal artists, and that the artists received royalties from each sale. Both statements were false.

The judicial interpretation offered in the case is significant and specifically relates to von Doussa's J response and mediation in terms of infringement and remedy. Infringement is a key issue in reading this case because in three of the works reproduced onto the carpets, the finding of infringement was debatable. Thus von Doussa J applied his own rationale and interpretation of the *Copyright Act 1968* (Cth) with regard to 'reproduction' in the context of the artwork. Determining infringement also provided a way to establish the originality of Aboriginal art, and thus confirm the legitimacy of its inclusion within the copyright framework.

In terms of remedy, von Doussa J awarded the damages communally to all the artists. In mediating the differences between the legal stipulations for individual damages and the indigenous claimants, His Honour recognised the disjuncture in awarding damages individually, owing to the claimants' differing perceptions of individual ownership. In addition, von Doussa J also awarded damages for 'cultural harm' herein acknowledging that the infringement had not only damaged the reputations or integrity of the artists in a western sense, but generated a 'cultural harm' that had no reference point in western law. This point was developed through the consideration that the infringement potentially had drastic repercussions for the artists within their community, where the responsibilities for safeguarding the use of the imagery differed significantly to those under western law. As von Doussa J observed within his judgment;

> This misuse of her (Banduk Marika) artwork has caused her great upset. If it had become widely known in her community at the time she believes that her family could have ordered her to stop producing any works of art; they might have outcast her, they may have sought recompense from her – nowadays in money terms . . . I note in passing the observation in the paper 'Aboriginal Designs and Copyright' . . . that punishment of the Aboriginal law breaker may to a large extent be determined by the success or failure of action in the Anglo-Australian Courts.[9]

Von Doussa J showed relative innovation in developing the law to accommodate indigenous differences. The recognition of a 'cultural harm' speaks to the special status provided to the Aboriginal artists within the law but also the importance of judicial decisions in building such a position. In addition, it highlights the capacity for liberal legal traditions to accommodate communal membership in certain instances. From a legal perspective, the damages represent an attempt to bridge a cultural gap, simultaneously reconciling and realising indigenous expectations about legal action and justice.

INFRINGEMENT

In all but three of the carpet reproductions direct infringement, as defined through the *Copyright Act 1968* (Cth), had taken place.[10] Direct infringement involves a determination of substantial similarity between the two works; in this case comparing the artworks with the carpets. As explained by McKeough et al, 'what amounts to a substantial part of a work must depend upon the nature of the work itself, and the characteristics or essential features which may *identify* the work'.[11] However in three works, substantial reproduction was a difficult question to be judicially determined. In the three of the eight paintings reproduced onto carpets direct infringement could not be made through a straightforward comparison. 'Wititj' by Paddy Dhatangu, 'Kangaroo and Shield People Dreaming' by Tim Payunka Tjapangati and 'Emu Dreaming' by Uta Uta Jangala presented more difficult questions with respect to identification and substantial reproduction and provide an apt example of how, faced with legal standards of identification, cultural factors come to be implicitly imbued within the judgment.

To what extent an infringement constitutes a substantial reproduction relies upon a distinction between the taking of the concept and the copying of the form of the expression, as ideas themselves are not protected by copyright.[12] Thus determining the issue of substantiality has both qualitative and quantitative elements where both the quality and quantity of the reproduction inform decisions regarding substantial infringement. However, such decisions are often made with 'an emphasis on the qualitative, rather than quantitative considerations'.[13] This is because greater weight is given to determining the copying of the concept itself rather than how much has been copied. With 'Wititj' and the corresponding Snake carpet, it was clear that there were discernable differences between the two works, namely Wititj involves four coils of one large python enclosing two smaller pythons, whereas the carpet consists of one large python as a border feature. These differences led the defendants, Indofurn Pty Ltd, to argue that the carpet was 'an adaptation' not an infringement.[14]

Von Doussa J rejected these claims. In interpreting the issue of substantiality he cited from *International Writing Institute Inc. v Rimila Pty Ltd* (1993):

> Reproduction in a material form of a substantial part of a work in which copyright exists is determined by applying the test of substantial use of the features of the applicants work in which copyright exists . . . Though it is permissible to look at the quantity of what the respondent is alleged to have taken from the applicant's work, the test of substantial reproduction is essentially to look to

the quality of what has been taken, although depending on the facts of the case, the two will often overlap.[15]

For von Doussa's J purpose, the application of the precedent informs the process of determining the key principles to consider in deciding whether there had been any copying, and secondly whether the copying had been substantial. With Wititj and the Snake carpet he found it clear that copying occurred in the following elements: the shape and construction of the python; the similar position in the placement of the larger python on the carpet; the white border line; and, the detail within the body of the python (a style named as rarrk by both the artists and expert witnesses).[16] However, as is evident from comparing the artwork to the carpet, the copying is not necessarily substantial.

In considering the question of substantiality, von Doussa J applied a qualitative judgment, deciding that 'there are striking visual similarities on a comparison of the artwork and the carpet'.[17] In this decision the quality of the copying rather than the quantity taken provided the means of identification, affirming that 'quality is more important than quantity'.[18] His Honour identified the depiction of the tail with rarrk as 'original and distinctive' thereby rejecting the respondent's argument 'that the particular depiction of the Wititj on the carpet is common to many Aboriginal artworks and involves no originality'.[19] (This argument is only possible in an environment that already has the discursive markers of 'timeless tradition' that automatically precludes originality.)

The judgment of substantiality rests on an analysis of the plaintiff's work alone rather than looking at the defendant's to see what had been added to make it distinct from the original. Earlier I explained how in the nineteenth century, the law shifted its form, so that determining substantial copying effectively became a means to identify the originality of the applicant's work. Originality in turn helps determine and identify to some extent, the process of individuating an idea and expressing it in a work. Thus by only looking at the applicant's work, sensitive questions regarding the status of Aboriginal art as 'original' are curiously resolved.

Similar issues to those above were involved in determining whether the Green centre carpet was a substantial reproduction of 'Kangaroo and Shield People Dreaming'. Again there are striking differences between the artwork and the carpet, the carpet being a significantly simpler interpretation of the artwork. However, in terms of quality being the most important factor of identification, this simplicity is irrelevant. Initially von Doussa identifies the prominent shade of green both in the artwork and central to the carpet. He then sets about determining the extent to which the border feature of the carpet has been extracted from part of the original artwork and thus not 'simply a repetition of an elementary or common design pattern'.[20] Importantly His Honour notes that the copy comprises only five–ten per cent of the artwork, which has been repeated and modified. The judgment then incorporates the 'expert' evidence of Vivien Johnson who verified the uniqueness of the pattern; that it was not used by any other Aboriginal artist and that the design 'adopts *common western desert symbols* as part of the design but that does not prevent the result having a *high degree of originality*'.[21] It is significant that Johnson phrases her expertise in the language of copyright and normalizes the description of Aboriginal art as original.[22] In turn, this assists von Doussa's J decision that the carpet significantly copies the artwork, for the carpet replicates the work's most 'striking feature'.[23] In this regard, while the quantity reproduced may have only amounted to a proportion of five–ten per cent of the original work, nevertheless on a judgment of the quality of the copying, substantial reproduction was determined. Therefore copyright infringement (and originality) was affirmed.

In the case of Emu Dreaming and the Waterholes carpet, the above principles were also applied. When considered concurrently, the Waterholes carpet is again a simpler modification of the artwork, yet reproducing the most significant feature of the original work. Thus von Doussa J also held that the 'waterholes carpet is a copy of a significant part of the original work'.[24]

In arriving at his decision with respect to these three artworks and the infringing carpets, von Doussa's J judgment drew upon both academic (anthropological) expertise in the appreciation of Aboriginal art and the flexibility inherent in the application of legal principles concerning infringement. Yet under similar circumstances, a different judge could have found that there wasn't an infringement in the case of these three artworks. This is precisely because such a judgment requires judicial interpretation, both in applying findings of quality, and understanding the cultural content of the original artworks.[25] This is the space where cultural and social influences are incorporated into law.

One element demonstrating the cultural considerations imbued within von Doussa's J determination is the extent to which his judgment refers to the actual content of the artwork: what it depicts in terms of 'tracks', 'dreamings' and 'sites'.

> The original artwork is a very complex painting which incorporates numerous important sites, represented by concentric circles, joined by dreaming or journey tracks in a multi-coloured dot-painting style, characteristic of some of the leading artists of the Pintupi tribe in the 1970s and 1980s. The detailed pattern represents, as it were, a topographical map, recording many important sites and events that impacted upon the life of the artist.[26]

Von Doussa takes the disruption of these stories, owing to their significance to the artists and the artists' families and communities, as one of the significant elements in determining the quality of the copy. Thus cultural factors, seemingly sensitive to an indigenous reading of the works, are fundamental to determining the infringement.

The cultural sensitivity shown by the Judge was commented on by Colin Golvan, the Barrister who ran the case.[27] Golvan suggested that von Doussa's analysis was influenced by his 'cultural appreciation . . . of the artworks being reproduced'.[28] Golvan explains that where the Judge utilised legal reasoning, to some extent he also 'took some trouble to understand the content aspects and appreciate that what might appear to be simple artistry was more complicated. For example the parts that were copied included the idea of cross hatching which was part of the totemic imagery, and he wanted to deal with that'.[29]

The cultural considerations imbued in the judicial reasoning reveal an instance of how the law treats cultural difference. While moderated through the legal categories, judicial discretion allows for cultural difference to be accepted and incorporated into categories of identification. Even though liberal law seeks to avoid 'cultural judgments', with this case it must strategically engage with these. Thus (indigenous) 'culture' functions as an important means for understanding the infringement and also legitimising the subject matter. Embedding cultural considerations within the law also neutralises the implications. By this I mean that indigenous knowledge can be targeted effectively for techniques of management as it fits within the legal schema. Importantly the effort on behalf of von Doussa J to appreciate indigenous cultural difference is indicative of the judgment as a whole. This is further highlighted in the way in which von Doussa J developed the type and form of remedy to be awarded from the finding of substantial infringement.

REMEDY

With the finding of the original 'quality' of the Aboriginal artworks and copyright infringement of these elements, it then became necessary to determine the damages to be awarded.[30] It is at this point that cultural considerations are perhaps most explicitly engaged even though it is contained within a framework of legal delivery such as 'remedy'. Significantly, damages were awarded communally to the artists, rather than on a pro rata basis to the number of carpets made. In reflecting his concern with cultural differences and demonstrating a willingness to imagine ways of incorporating these within intellectual property law, von Doussa J had informed himself about the previous copyright cases involving Aboriginal art. His Honour was aware that following the 1989 case *Bulun Bulun v Nejlam Pty Ltd* counsel for the applicants, Colin Golvan and Martin Hardie had held a meeting with the artists involved in the case in order to determine how they wanted the compensation monies to be divided.[31] The artists decided that such a division was to be done in such a way where no one artist or family received more than any other.[32]

Awarding 'communal' damages recognised this as a form of remedy in the law for the first time. To this end, specific cultural differences distinguished through the awarding of damages communally function to codify these particular differences within the law. Indeed, this is a key example in the shoring up of the relationship between the indigenous and the communal. The codification of difference sets it out in spheres that can be managed – the field becomes knowable and contained: the direction of the narrative consistent.

Colin Golvan succinctly observes that von Doussa J 'was very concerned that the case was being put at a cultural level'.[33] This 'cultural level' thus becomes a key characteristic of the case, and confirms the capacity of the law to adapt to changing social circumstance. The judicial officer is thus the mediator between techniques managing the inclusion and identification of 'new' subject matter, and also pointing the law in directions where it could adequately treat cultural differences without explicitly being seen to do so.

The way in which the judgment appreciates cultural differences and then incorporates these into the current law, is striking. Thus law treats difference through absorbing it into already existing processes of identification and classification. While recognising the cultural differences presented to him in this case, von Doussa J also strategically limits how they can be interpreted through the law: the Court interprets the *Copyright Act 1968* (Cth) 'in a sensitive but basically orthodox manner'.[34] As the mediator, von Doussa, J reconciles indigenous knowledge 'to' *not* 'with' the law. As a consequence the story of indigenous intellectual property becomes part of the broader intellectual property narrative, but only as a sub-set: it is one of many incidences that constitute the grand intellectual property law narrative. The 'specialness' of indigenous concerns are absorbed into the intellectual property framework, where the production of the category of indigenous knowledge speaks more to the agenda of accommodating new intangible subject matter than accepting and appreciating the cultural circumstances and dynamics that result in the misuse of indigenous knowledge. Indigenous difference is not seen as particularly insurmountable – and it certainly does not challenge the legitimacy of the categories that identify copyright subject matter. This observation helps an appreciation of the manifold ways in which efforts are directed at managing copyright categories of identification.

In order to expand upon this point it is illustrative to consider the development of an additional form of damages based on the notion of 'cultural harm'. What the development of this point shows is that in establishing a new reasoning for remedies in relation to the copyright infringement of Aboriginal art the issue of 'culture' was directly engaged and the 'specialness' of the category addressed.

Instrumental in positioning 'culture' within the law's eye, counsel for the artists, Colin Golvan, ran the argument that the harm sustained to the artists from the infringement of their work on carpets was more profound than could possibly be understood and recognised in western law. This was because the harm extended beyond the individual to the community. As the artists' affidavits explained, the damage caused by the infringement also affected the community where it potentially and significantly displaced the continuity and significance of the role and function of the artist.[35] Upon reflection Golvan explained this argument in the following way:

> To describe . . . the harm, was that it was harm to the integrity of the image and was kind of quasi religious, so they were worried that ceremonies that surrounded the making of the particular artworks would be impeded, and also that their custodial functions were not being honoured, so that they might be seen by others in the clan group as not being proper custodians; that they can't manage. There is competition over these things, as the custodial rights brought with them status and all those things were terribly important.[36]

Von Doussa J was sympathetic to these diverging perceptions of harm and community. He developed his notion of 'cultural harm' because he considered that the other remedial avenues offered through the law were inadequate. For instance, on one level, the economic mode of measurement was not how the artists were measuring the harm. This is particularly clear where he states:

> The applicants contend that the unauthorised use of the artwork was in effect the pirating of cultural heritage. That is so, but under copyright law damages can only be awarded insofar as the 'pirating' causes a *loss* to the copyright owner resulting from infringement of copyright. Nevertheless, in the *cultural environment of the artists* the infringement of those rights has, or is likely to have, far reaching effects on the copyright owner. Anger and distress suffered by those around the copyright owner constitute part of that person's injury and suffering.[37]

To this end, von Doussa established a new form of damages and in doing so established precedent for the law to consider the cultural specificity of the harm caused to the artists and by extension, their families and communities.[38] In short, he extends the measurement of loss beyond the economic to the cultural. In finding a place for community, liberal expectations of justice are realised. However the specificity of the context, that the case derives from particular and unique locales of Arnhem Land and Central Australia, is overshadowed by the reliance and emphasis on the 'cultural'. The cultural becomes a universal explanatory tool for difference, curiously thin in detail about the unique and specific circumstances of the case at hand. For von Doussa reflected that the extent of damage constituted by the infringement to the communities to which the artists belonged was implicitly related to 'cultural environment' and cultural differences. Justifying these specific damages he referred to s115(4) (b) of the *Copyright Act 1968* (Cth), where remedies are to have 'regard to all their relevant matters'. Thus von Doussa J states that 'it is upon this consideration that the cultural issues which are so important to the artists and their communities, assume great importance'.[39] In short cultural issues are positioned as 'relevant matters'. Here 'culture' is called on to be present, but not to challenge the legitimacy of the framework. It is an explanatory mechanism but not a destabilising element.

The precedent created by von Doussa J for the notion of 'cultural harm' is significant. That he justifies this not only through the specific section of the Copyright Act with regard to all 'relevant matters' but also through a comparison to personal injury is worth noting. Referring to the personal injury case, *Williams v Settle* (1960)[40] von Doussa J cites the trial judge who observed in that particular case that the degree of injury was so flagrant that '[i]t was an intrusion into his life, deeper and graver than an intrusion into a man's property'.[41] Through this reasoning von Doussa J is able to juxtapose damage of a cultural nature to the harm experienced through personal injury whilst also extending cultural harm beyond property damage. The purpose to juxtapose otherwise differing associations between an individual and a community, is actually to stress the similarity. Understanding the cultural dimensions of harm for Aboriginal artists through the lens of personal injury presents a case where the law is able to accommodate difference through its own forms of rationalisation. Such rationalisation is contingent on the already existing construct, in this case personal injury, so that law can develop the notion of cultural harm. The positioning of cultural harm is dependent on the constructions around which it circulates wherein cultural harm is produced as akin to personal injury therefore circulating in a field of considerable case law and juridical consideration. It becomes a codified standard of identification.

The case reveals the practical possibility of law living up to expectations about its capacity to be inclusive and to an extent sympathetic to the differences posed by indigenous knowledge. The flexibility in the judgment for cultural difference endorses these appreciations of law. Importantly, bringing indigenous subject matter to the law demonstrates the adaptability of the law: the law is inclusive, 'universal' and capable. Thus the indigenous category circulates within the broader narrative structure promoting the coherence and legitimacy of intellectual property law, whilst also highlighting the diversity and complexity of indigenous knowledge as copyright subject matter. Even remedies that recognise legal limitations are only valid when exercised within the law. They dually provide a way to recognise difference, but also to manage and contain it within a regulatory framework. The irony is that while recognising Aboriginal art as an original work imbued with cultural considerations, the law also recognises that the work is not just a commodity.

BEYOND ABORIGINAL ART AS TANGIBLE GOOD

The recognition and inclusion of indigenous knowledge within intellectual property law is due to the value of Aboriginal art as a commodity. Importantly the judgment in the *carpets case* implicitly emphasises and relies upon the value of Aboriginal art within a western art space, to the extent that this also underpins the case. The historical emergence of Aboriginal art into a global art market has meant that copyright law has logically been utilised to protect the art from infringement, again reaffirming continuity in how to treat 'new' subject matter. The circulation of Aboriginal art within an economic realm of value has contributed significantly to the impetus to use intellectual property law to protect indigenous art forms. It is the similarity of form that at first instance allows for Aboriginal art to be considered copyright subject matter at all. In this way, 'legal practice supports a culture of commodification'.[42] This is also where the politics of law become more transparent; a key point to be developed in the following chapter.

For the two Aboriginal communities represented in the *carpets case,* their art is understood as integral to the transference and reaffirmation of specific indigenous knowledges, traditions and heritage.[43] This nexus between art, land, heritage and spirituality serves to contextualise the practice and creation of Aboriginal art. Again art sits inside and astride the economic discourse because of its spiritual qualities, and clearly more so when identifiably 'traditional'.[44] However as cultural context is irrelevant to copyright law and not a factor for consideration, the fundamental differential for considering the methods of creativity between Aboriginal art and copyright material is relegated to the margins of the law. Aboriginal art remains incorporated because it is viewed through the same prism of western art – it is understood through the copyright criteria of property, value, art, authenticity and the individual artist. The commonality of economic incentive overrides the 'specialness' of the category: the economic becomes the normalising element.

The Australian legislation requires no consideration of artistic merit – Aboriginal art qualifies for protection whether or not it has artistic merit; protection, as for any other subject matter, is contingent on the definitions supplied through the *Copyright Act 1968* (Cth). An artistic work defined in s10(1) is;

> (a) a painting, sculpture, drawing engraving or photograph, *whether the work is of artistic quality or not*;
> (b) a building or model of a building, whether the building or model is of artistic quality or not; or
> (c) a work of artistic craftsmanship to which neither of the last two preceding paragraphs applies; but does not include a circuit layout within the meaning of the *Circuit Layouts Act* 1989. [Emphasis mine]

Further, as McKeough et al point out, 'works of artistic craftsmanship are treated as "artistic" only if they have aesthetic appeal, whereas works encompassed within paragraphs (a) and (b) have only to exhibit the originality and substance generally required in order for copyright to exist'.[45] Hence issues that I considered in depth earlier regarding markers that identify copyright subject matter, (the markers being originality and authorship), return to inform not only the inclusion of indigenous subject matter but also its production (and subsequent regulation) as a specific legal category. However, the greatest irony of the *carpets case* is that while all these elements are functioning, the judgment recognises through remedy, specifically 'cultural harm', that Aboriginal art is not just a tangible good. It is both cultural commodity and cultural product. The possibility for allowing a greater recognition of cultural difference and for the economic value of creating and using indigenous cultural products was precisely what the following case *Bulun Bulun & Others v R & T Textiles Pty Ltd* explored.

BULUN BULUN & OTHERS V R & T TEXTILES PTY LTD

While the *carpets case* (1994) confirmed the practical extent to which the law could respond to the infringement of Aboriginal art, *Bulun Bulun & Others v R & T Textiles Pty Ltd* (1998) sought to extend the way in which communal ownership was recognised within the law. At first instance, proceedings were initiated by the artist Mr John Bulun Bulun, and also Mr

George Milpurrurru, acting on behalf of his and Bulun Bulun's community, the Ganalbingu people. *Bulun Bulun & Others v R & T Textiles Pty Ltd* can be seen as a kind of test case, which was only possible through the expectations of legal response generated through the earlier *carpets case*.[46]

In similar circumstances to the *carpets case,* the *Bulun Bulun & Others v R & T Textiles Pty Ltd* case arose after fabric printed in Indonesia was imported into Australia.[47] The fabric infringed the copyright of John Bulun Bulun's work 'Magpie Geese and Water Lilies at the Waterhole'. This particular work of Bulun Bulun's had been sold to a public museum in the Northern Territory and also reproduced, with the artist's consent, in a significant book on Aboriginal art.[48] It was also the painting that was at the centre of the earlier 1989 case *Bulun Bulun v Nejlam Pty Ltd.*[49]

Initially the proceedings issued by Mr Bulun Bulun and Mr Milpurrurru were against R & T Textiles and its three directors. However, soon after proceedings were issued the fabric company went into administration. An amended statement of claim was filed and the respondent company consented to final declarations and orders in relation to Bulun Bulun's claim. Copyright infringement was admitted before proceedings began with arrangements made between the parties for damages.[50]

With the approach of the date that had been set for the trial, it became apparent that no-one would be appearing on the respondent's behalf. Under such circumstances, the applicants brought the proceedings to the attention of the Minister for Aboriginal and Torres Strait Islander Affairs.[51] Consequently the Federal Government was granted leave to intervene against the applicant's claims.[52] In addition, the Attorney General for the Northern Territory was granted leave to make a submission, as *amicus curiae.*[53] Specifically this was with respect to the 'power of the Court to make a determination as to the existence of native title rights'.[54] The submission by the Attorney General was in response to the claim, advanced by counsel on behalf of Milpurrurru, that communal ownership of the painting arose by incidence of native title rights in the land that the painting represented. As is recorded in the judgment,

> The Minister and the Attorney General were concerned with the pleadings claimed that: 1) the intellectual property rights in the artistic work were an incidence of native title; 2) being an incidence of native title the intellectual property rights constituted an interest in land; and 3) the Ganalbingu people were entitled to a determination in these proceedings that they were the native title holders of the Ganalbingu country. The outline of submissions presented by the applicants at the start of the trial appeared to support this interpretation of their claim.[55]

In general terms the intervention by the Government meant that the case could proceed. The intervention came about because the Government was concerned specifically about the potential associations that could be drawn between intellectual property rights in the artistic works as arising out of native title. In this regard, the Government sought to limit such arguments, in itself indicating the unease felt owing to the possibly that, considering the leeway provided in the *carpets case* for cultural difference, such arguments could be accepted.[56] Moreover this unease highlights a tension between, on the one hand, recognising the rights of indigenous people and the difficulty of the law acquiescing to such rights, while on the other, that the recognition of such rights potentially could destabilise the coherence and stability of both bodies of law (intellectual property law and native title). In this sense, with the coherence of the law threatened, there was a pressing obligation to limit and curtail such possibility. The central argument made by the Government relied upon s213 (1) of the *Native Title Act 1993* (Cth) wherein states:

> If for the purpose of any matter or proceeding before the Federal Court, it is necessary to make a determination of native title, *that determination must be made in accordance with the procedures in this Act*. [Emphasis mine]

The argument here was that no determination of native title could be made outside the *Native Title Act 1993* (Cth). Locating the problem as one within the statute secured the closure of each body of law, assisting to reify the object of focus and maintain the distinction between 'real' property and species of intangible property. Such a position was endorsed by von Doussa J where he stated that native title could only be determined through the *Native Title Act 1993* (Cth) alone, not the *Copyright Act 1968* (Cth). 'This Court has no jurisdiction to make a determination in respect of the claimed native title rights'.[57] This reaffirmed that the judiciary does not make changes in the law: judges merely apply the law rather than creating it.[58] Further, judges do not explicitly respond to politics. Citing Brennan J in *Mabo* [No.2] von Doussa J continued his justification for excluding consideration of native title rights arising out of copyright in the artistic work, where;

> [i]n order to be successful, the applicants' foreshadowed argument that a right of ownership arises in artistic works and copyright attaching to them as an aspect of native title would appear to require that the Court accept that the insepara-ble nature of ownership in land and ownership in artistic works by Aboriginal people is recognised by the common law. The principle that ownership of land and ownership of [sic] artistic works are separate statutory and common law institutions is a fundamental principle of the Australian legal system which may well be characterised as 'skeletal' and stand in the road of acceptance of the foreshadowed argument.[59]

Thus von Doussa J was able to uphold the governmental concerns through the justification of judicial interpretation that stressed the importance of separate categories of law and the impossibility of crossing these boundaries owing to a (mythical) division between law and politics. Governmental intervention sought to have the distinct legal boundary between intellectual property law and native title law upheld. This speaks to the relationship between the law and governmental rationality, whereby such arguments displace the context and politics and are pared back to the basic principles of law; asserting legal power and control through perpetuating an effective narrative of the law where each body of law functions separately and independently. Through von Doussa's reasoning the law retreats to a position of coherence and stability rather than addressing the fuzziness in the margins, which is precisely where the indigenous claim was directed, where the law is not clear and definitive. Further debate around this issue of margins and separate legal jurisdictions was limited as counsel for the applicants chose not to pursue this claim vigorously. Instead they attempted a different tactic, testing the limits of the law in another way.

As already stated, George Milpurrurru pursued his claim on behalf of himself and in his capacity as a representative of the Ganalbingu people. Through his affidavit, he claimed that as the traditional Aboriginal inhabitants of a specific part of Arnhem Land, the Ganalbingu people have an equitable ownership of copyright in Bulun Bulun's painting and that the artist owed a fiduciary duty to the Ganalbingu people in relation to the copyright.[60] In essence, what was argued was that the ownership of the imagery depicted by Bulun Bulun was not 'owned' in the western sense solely (or individually) by Bulun Bulun, but that it was held in trust for all the members of the Ganalbingu people. In such circumstances as an infringement arose, the Ganalbingu people could claim copyright in the work if the artist failed to act. The argument was one where the court was directed to how the copyright infringements affected interests beyond that of the copyright owner. This directly flowed from the acknowledgement in the *carpets case* that the community had a legitimate position in relation to the infringement of an artwork. The Court was asked to recognise the rights of the Ganalbingu people in the artwork – disrupting the notion of individual authorship and ownership – owing to the effects upon the community caused by the infringement.[61]

The case presented an opportunity for the presiding Judge to expand upon his previous judicial reasoning where the damage to the community was reflected through the notion of 'cultural harm'. Von Doussa J was encouraged to consider a more sustained recognition of communal rights as a category that helped identify indigenous rights in intellectual property. Thus in this case, the significant element for intellectual property law circled back to the issue of 'culture', in particular the cultural differences extant within the Ganalbingu community and the reproduction of cultural imagery and how this presented a 'special' case for law to absorb.

The shape that the case took determining the copyright infringement became a secondary element of the case: for this was already admitted and Bulun Bulun was no longer a party.[62] Instead the case focused on the way that copyright law conceived of an owner and importantly the different constructions of ownership that could arise from the different cultural positions held by indigenous people, represented by Milpurrurru and the Ganalbingu people. Thus the case essentially revolved around the issue of determining the extent to which cultural difference could be absorbed into the schema of copyright law by pushing the classification of 'joint-ownership' to incorporate 'community-ownership'.

JOINT OWNERSHIP AND COMMUNAL OWNERSHIP

As part of the case, and in an effort to come to terms with the different notions of ownership proffered by the applicants, von Doussa J heard extensive evidence about the importance of Ganalbingu law and custom and included a site visit in the hearing.[63] These aspects suggest that von Doussa J was concerned to provide a space within the case and by association within the law, for the hearing and speaking of different cultural positions. The potentially troubling legal questions regarding the admissibility of oral evidence were resolved early by von Doussa J through direction to precedent in other Australian cases, specifically native title, but also the Canadian case *Delgamuukw*.[64] His Honour decided that evidence of customary laws was a crucial element for determining damages and appreciating the manifold cultural effects of infringement. However customary laws could not disrupt the linearity of legal determinations, or the objects that constitute such judgments.

The Court was unable to entertain the possibility of communal title existing within the Copyright Act. Von Doussa J noted that,

> Whilst it is superficially attractive to postulate that the common law should recognise communal title, it would be contrary to established legal principle for the common law to do so.[65]

Specifically he explained that while there may have been scope for continued recognition of 'indigenous intellectual property' law from the time of European occupation of Australia in 1788 until at least the codification of copyright law in the *Copyright Act 1912* (Cth), copyright is now entirely a creature of statute.[66] In this sense then, '[t]he exclusive domain of the

Copyright Act 1968 (Cth) in Australia is expressed in section 8 . . . namely that "copyright does not subsist otherwise than virtue of this Act".'[67] At this point mainstream jurisprudential arguments about copyright law return to inform von Doussa's decision. By relying on the authority of the common law jurisprudence, the possibility of accepting an alternative appreciation of title was foreclosed. Kathy Bowrey has argued that the reference to copyright being a creature of statute 'affirms the sovereignty of the Commonwealth Parliament and the authority of positive law over common law and customary law'.[68] Bowrey continues by noting that,

> Our positivised copyright law is presented as rational and coherent, (potentially) culturally inclusive, open and impartial. In this sense copyright is not just a body of law dealing with the intellectual property rights of authors, artists and alike. Copyright is also constructed as symbolic of all liberal law.[69]

The possibility for indigenous rights to be addressed is foreclosed. Indeed, the reluctance of the law to recognise the capacity to endorse indigenous rights highlights precisely what a major shift would be required and that quite possibly, the security and stability of the law would be undermined. This illustrates how the push for recognition of communal ownership not only destabilised traditional jurisprudence, but also the liberal traditions of governance.

Insofar as the current *Copyright Act 1968* (Cth) is concerned, s35(2) states that what subsists by virtue of that Act is that the *author* of an artistic work is the *owner* of the copyright – the two are imbricated in each other. It follows that a work of 'joint-authorship' is where a work has been produced by the collaboration of two or more authors where 'the contribution of each author is not separate from the contribution of the other author or the contributions of the other authors'.[70] Citing the case *Kenrick v Lawrence*[71] where 'a person who supplies an artistic idea to an artist who then executes the work is not, on that ground alone, a joint author with the artist'[72] von Doussa J explained that therefore the *Copyright Act 1968* (Cth) effectively precluded any notion of group ownership in a work unless it was within the meaning of joint-ownership as defined in the Act. Herein the Copyright Act, as an arm of government, regulates the inclusion of new meanings: the responsibility of judicial discretion and its effects are hidden behind the seamless regulation of the Act.

Hence, the difference and subsequent difficulty of applying intellectual property laws to indigenous knowledge is realised. For while it is generally assumed in intellectual property law, that the material form is the idea expressed and that the idea has come from a space or domain where ideas freely flow, within Yolngu and more specifically, Ganalbingu community cultural practice, the realm where the idea has come from is strictly controlled by customary law. Bulun Bulun explains this complex relationship in his affidavit,

> Barnda not only created the place we call Djulibinuyamurr but it populated the country as well. Barnda gave the place its name, created the people who follow him and named those people. Barnda gave us our language and our law. Barnda gave to my ancestors the country and the ceremony and paintings associated with the country. My ancestors had a responsibility given to them by Barnda to perform the ceremony and to do the paintings that were granted to them. This is part of the continuing responsibility of the traditional Aboriginal owners handed down from generation to generation . . . The continuity of our traditions and ways including our traditional Aboriginal ownership depends upon us respecting and honouring the things entrusted to us by Barnda.[73]

The art at the centre of the *Bulun Bulun* case is not just art, and therefore the same judicial principles have difficulty in application and transference. Primary legal assumptions are shown to be culturally contingent. For example in the context of Yolngu cultural practice, there can not be assumed to be an 'intellectual commons' where ideas are freely chosen and then expressed.[74] Instead, and this highlights the different elements that are taken to be indigenous property in cultural expression, the intangible produced into tangible form comes from a space that is strictly patrolled and regulated according to community and familial traditions and status. For example only John Bulun Bulun could paint 'At the waterhole' even though the imagery existed for the whole community:

> [t]he creation of artworks such as 'At the waterhole' is part of my responsibility in fulfilling the obligations I have as a traditional Aboriginal owner of Djulibinyamurr. I am permitted by my law to create this artwork, but it is also my duty and responsibility to create such works, as part of my traditional Aboriginal land obligation.[75]

The argument for communal ownership derived from the distinct cultural position held by the Ganalbingu people – that the community had group ownership in the work precisely because Bulun Bulun was permitted through customary law and obligation to reproduce the imagery to a material form. In dismissing these claims it is evident that the capacity of the law to include such significant differences must initially begin by destabilising the fundamental premise upon which intellectual property law functions – that intangible subject matter is freely available and only requires one's labour to make it into a thing of property. Thus the indigenous position put through the *Bulun Bulun* case is an untenable position for the law not least because, as has been illustrated in other areas,[76] it is quite disinterested in (re)addressing cultural bias. The mythologising process of the law is perpetuated through a refusal to acknowledge the culturally contingent nature of categories and premises. Under such circumstances, the law retreats to a position of uniformity.

Thus the difficulty and applicability of definitions from the Copyright Act regarding joint authorship under these conditions is exposed. It is the construction of Bulun Bulun as the 'author' in the copyright sense that gives rise to these problems. For if Bulun Bulun painted the work and is the 'executor' of the work, it is his contribution in the 'action' of painting that makes him the author. To be a contributor to the work, in any way besides an action of painting, precludes the possibility of ownership. The stringent controls and regulations in the Ganalbingu community intrinsically affect the action of the painting: painting is only possible through the direct sanction of the community. It is precisely this perspective of ownership that provides the difficulty in reconciling the form of ownership directed by the Copyright Act. However in the circumstances of the case, and recognising these considerable and insurmountable issues of difference, counsel attempted to weave another way around the obstacle presented by definitions of joint-ownership in the Copyright Act. The subsequent position presented was that the Ganalbingu community had an equitable interest arising out of Bulun Bulun's copyright. In this sense, the challenge was phrased in the law's own language.

EQUITABLE INTEREST

To this end, the central concern in the case then moved to the claim for equitable interest in Bulun Bulun's copyright where equitable interest was argued to arise incidentally to the Ganalbingu people's traditional use and occupation of the land. Specifically the equitable claim pursued was that an artist comes under a fiduciary obligation to the community or its senior members when an artist reduces part of its ritual knowledge to a material form. As such the property that is created as soon as the ritual knowledge is expressed in material form is not solely the responsibility of the person who made it into that form, but rather the whole community. As von Doussa J explains, '[t]hat the claim was ultimately confined to one for recognition of an equitable interest in the legal copyright of Mr Bulun Bulun is an acknowledgement that no other possible avenue had emerged from the researches of counsel'.[77] With the argument pushed to equity no rupture in the coherence of intellectual property's positivist narrative occurred: the centrality of notions of ownership and authorship, and importantly 'labour' remained intact and 'stable'.

In order to consider whether the Ganalbingu people had an equitable interest in Bulun Bulun's copyright, von Doussa J first considered whether an express trust could be found and secondly whether Bulun Bulun held the copyright as a fiduciary. Bulun Bulun's claim is positioned centrally within legalese. An express trust is an express obligation in legal terms evidenced by an agreement in writing or by practice dealing with economic proceeds.[78] The existence of an express trust depends upon the intention of the creator and this functions in certain circumstances, for instance when the work is a commodity. An obligation is made in contractual or economic terms and linked to western notions of property. Consequently von Doussa J found that there was no express trust because '[n]otions of copyright ownership have not developed under Ganalbingu law'.[79] This explicitly illustrates a position of incommensurability – for the legal standard cannot be applied. In addition, von Doussa J points to the different ways in which the work could be used in an economic sense without community approval thus excluding the possibility of an express trust, for:

> [t]here is no usual or customary practice whereby artworks are held in trust for the Ganalbingu people. In the present case neither Mr Bulun Bulun's djungaye or Mr Milpurrurru suggest that the commercial sale of the artwork by Mr Bulun Bulun was contrary to customary law, or to the terms of the permission which was given to him to produce the artwork. In these circumstances that fact of the sale and the retention of the proceeds for his own use is inconsistent with their being an intention on the part of Mr Bulun Bulun to create an express trust. Further the fact that the artwork was sold commercially, and has been the subject of reproduction with the apparent permission of those who control its reproduction, in *Arts of the Dreaming: Australian Living Heritage* forecloses any possibility of arguing that the imagery in the artwork is of a secret or sacred nature that it could be inferred that the artist must have had the intention in accordance with customary law to hold the artwork for the benefit of the Ganalbingu people.[80]

Subsequently, His Honour considered the existence of a fiduciary relationship arising from the nature of the ownership of artistic works among the Ganalbingu people.[81] In doing so he explained 'the factors and relationships giving rise to a fiduciary relationship are nowhere exhaustively defined'.[82] Owing to the lack of definitional security, the 'indigenous' circumstance is offered a new kind of space. His Honour, citing Mason J in *Hospital Products*[83] and Toohey J in *Mabo*[84] set the parameters for how his interpretation of a fiduciary duty within the specifics of the case could be understood. Toohey J in *Mabo* notes:

> Underlying such relationships is the scope for one party to exercise a discretion which is capable of affecting the legal position of the other. One party has a special opportunity to abuse the interests of the other. The discretion will be an incident of the first party's office or position.[85]

Within such parameters, von Doussa J explains that the complexity of the relationship arises out of Bulun Bulun's use of a corpus of ritual knowledge. He states:

> The relationship between Mr Bulun Bulun as the *author* and *legal title holder* of the artistic work and the Ganalbingu people is unique. The 'transaction' between them out of which a fiduciary relationship is said to arise is the use with permission by Mr Bulun Bulun of ritual knowledge of the Ganalbingu people, and the embodiment of that knowledge within the artistic work. That use has been permitted in accordance with the law and customs of the Ganalbingu people.[86]

In this instance, it is clear that von Doussa J reflects upon the customary evidence provided where 'customary evidence may be used as a foundation of rights, interests and obligations'.[87] Therefore His Honour finds that a fiduciary relationship between Bulun Bulun and the Ganalbingu people existed whereby:

> the artist is required to act in relation to the artwork in the interests of the Ganalbingu people to preserve the integrity of their culture and ritual knowledge. However this fiduciary relationship does not vest any equitable interest in the copyright in the Ganalbingu people. Rather their right, in the event of a breach of obligation by the fiduciary is a right in personam to bring action against the fiduciary to enforce the obligation.[88]

Directing further attention to precedent in relevant case law and an African decision concerning tribal property,[89] His Honour found other members of the group may be able to initiate proceedings to preserve the property where the head of the group fails to act.

Importantly, the turn to the legal conception of constructive trust maintains the coherence of intellectual property law as a whole. The concern for developing a solution is shifted away from intellectual property law to trust. Constructive trust is a body of law developed to have more fluidity so as to provide remedial relief in the interest of mitigating against the 'harsh' outcomes of property transactions.[90] That other legal jurisdictions have used trust to reconcile indigenous people interests recognises a more general failing in formal law for the recognition of indigenous rights. Such problems stimulate law to take action and in this regard equity is a body of law that can provide some solace and in doing so save face, legally and politically, as law is seen as responsive rather than inactive. In this way law recognises the problem and produces the solutions. This is achieved through the governable space that directs attention and intervention making the challenge legally knowable and workable. Thus the solutions are articulated at the legal level, because the problem has already been composed as legal in scope. What remains unclear however is whether law created the problem through the categorising of issues itself. The governable space allows for a displacement of the responsibility of the law in general instead positing a consideration for how the individual categories include and characterise indigenous issues. Paradoxically, everyone and no-one is to blame in law for the problem, and the solution of 'constructive trust' shifts the view to the productive action of the law to develop a solution – the effectivity of the law through the function and action of governmental programmes to garner solutions to complicated cultural issues is affirmed.

Consequently, von Doussa J found that an artist's fiduciary obligation existed and it had two features. Firstly there was an obligation not to exploit the work contrary to Ganalbingu law and custom. Secondly, where a third party infringes Ganalbingu law, the fiduciary must take action to restrain and remedy any infringement. As already stated, this does not grant the community any direct equitable interest in the copyright, rather the community's primary remedy is to force the fiduciary to act. However von Doussa J noted the following where he recognised that in some cases the artist may not be able to act:

> In other circumstances if . . . an artistic work which embodies ritual knowledge of an Aboriginal clan is being used inappropriately, and the copyright owner fails or refuses to take appropriate action to enforce the copyright, the Australian legal system will permit remediation through the courts by the clan.[91]

Von Doussa J leaves open what such circumstances may include for the community to act.

JUDICIAL DISCRETION AND LEGAL BOUNDARIES

The *Bulun Bulun* case demonstrates the extent to which the power and authority to maintain the legal boundaries of copyright remain within the limits of judicial discretion. Thus the cultural specificity of copyright can be contained to the sphere where it speaks to itself rather than recognising the significance of indigenous claims in broader areas of law. Certainly von Doussa J was sensitive to the cultural differences to which he was exposed, but ultimately he only viewed these through the prism of copyright law. In doing so von Doussa J was active in maintaining consistency in the borders of copyright law. While he recognised cultural difference, for instance in the form of fiduciary duty of the copyright owner, he foreclosed the discussions that would have extended the recognition of the cultural specificity of copyright law. Instead he moved the discussion to other areas of law such as equity and constructive trust, effectively maintaining the coherence of intellectual property law, for its core categories remained unchallenged.[92]

That said, it is worth being mindful of the way in which, through this case copyright does, to an extent, take on board the reality of Aboriginal art as greater than a commodity. This however only functions at the margins of the law. The fuzziness at the margins provides for the possibility of both accepting and dismissing elements of cultural difference, and this is determined both by degree and judicial discretion. For example, von Doussa recognises that the material expression of ritual knowledge and the responsibility of the community is beyond the jurisdiction of copyright.[93] Thus he understands the art as more than a commodity but limits how this can be understood in the law, primarily because the law minimises issues of cultural difference when these potentially expose the contingency of its own categories and processes of identification. This is similarly the case when von Doussa J observes that:

> customary Aboriginal laws relating to ownership of artistic works survived the introduction of the common law of England in 1788. The Aboriginal people did not cease to observe their *sui generis* system of rights and obligations upon the acquisition of sovereignty of Australia by the Crown. The question however is whether those Aboriginal laws can create binding obligations on persons outside the relevant Aboriginal community, either by recognition of those laws by the common law, or by their capacity to found equitable rights in *rem*.[94]

The possible existence and continued function of a system of indigenous collective ownership of artistic works remains an abstract problem to be considered through the common law. However, and it is here that such recognition is relegated to the margins of copyright law, the statute governing the Copyright Act precludes such possibility – 'If the common law had not been amended in the meantime by statute an interesting question would arise as to whether Aboriginal customs and laws could be incorporated into the common law'.[95] Thus the reality of Aboriginal responsibility in art is acknowledged but cannot be formally recognised through copyright. The creature that is 'statute' effectively consolidates and confirms the limits of the law and the legal values that identify intangible subject matter.

So it is in the margins that the law grapples with appreciating cultural differences. However these are brought into the judgment as 'background' rather than 'facts' of the case. This provides a way of managing what is centrally within the purview of the law. In the same way that, 'law and facts are not separate because what counts as a fact is made so by the law'[96] what is made background material is similarly relegated so by the law. However, categories that function to identify and classify indigenous subject matter maintain their purpose and the questions that remain are ones about the metaphysical dimensions of property. This is precisely where the politics of law become more transparent.

NOTES

1. M. Davies, *Delimiting the Law: Postmodernism and the Politics of the Law*, Pluto Press: Chicago and London, 1996 at 94.
2. See discussion in Chapter 2.
3. *Milpurrurru & Others v Indofurn Pty Ltd* (1994) 30 IPR 209.
4. *Bulun Bulun & Others v R & T Textiles Pty Ltd* (1998) 41 IPR 513.
5. K. Bowrey, 'The Outer Limits of Copyright Law – Where Law meets Philosophy and Culture', (2001) 12 *Law and Critique* 75 at 79.
6. George Milpurrurru has since died and for this reason the case is also known as *Deceased Applicant v Indofurn*.
7. *Milpurrurru & Others v Indofurn Pty Ltd* (1994) 30 IPR 209 at 212.
8. ss.52, 53(c) and (d) and 55.
9. *Milpurrurru & Others v Indofurn Pty Ltd* (1994) 30 IPR 209 at 215.
10. Infringement of copyright may be direct as described in ss.13 (2), 36 (1), 101 (1) *Copyright Act 1968* (Cth) or indirect as described in ss.37, 38, 39 (1), 102, 103.
11. J. McKeough, K. Bowrey and P. Griffith, *Intellectual Property: Commentary and Material* (third edition), The Lawbook Company: Sydney, 2002, at 169 [emphasis mine].
12. Ibid., at 168.
13. S. Ricketson, *Intellectual Property: Cases, Materials and Commentary*, Butterworths: Australia, 1994, at 185.
14. *Milpurrurru & Others v Indofurn Pty Ltd* (1994) 30 IPR 209 at 227.
15. *Milpurrurru & Others v Indofurn Pty Ltd* (1994) 30 IPR 209 at 227–228.
16. *Milpurrurru & Others v Indofurn Pty Ltd* (1994) 30 IPR 209 at 226.
17. *Milpurrurru & Others v Indofurn Pty Ltd* (1994) 30 IPR 209 at 226.
18. *Milpurrurru & Others v Indofurn Pty Ltd* (1994) 30 IPR 209 at 228 citing *Ravenscroft v Herbert and New English Library* (1998) RPC 193 at 203.
19. *Milpurrurru & Others v Indofurn Pty Ltd* (1994) 30 IPR 209 at 226.
20. *Milpurrurru & Others v Indofurn Pty Ltd* (1994) 30 IPR 209 at 230.
21. *Milpurrurru & Others v Indofurn Pty Ltd* (1994) 30 IPR 209 at 230. Law demands that participants conform to particular frameworks. 'Expert' evidence is one example. Expert evidence often functions to confirm the legitimacy and authority of legal modes of identification, for instance – originality. There are additional questions here about the production of the 'expert' that the court recognises in the first place. It is notable that indigenous people are not produced as 'experts' for the court. For readings on the importance of expertise in liberalism see: T. Mitchell, *Rule of Experts: Egypt, Technopolitics, Modernity*, University of California Press: Berkeley, 2002; N. Rose, 'Government, authority and expertise in advanced liberalism' (1993) 22(3) *Economy and Society* 283; P. O'Malley, 'Uncertain subjects: risks, liberalism and contract' (2000) 29(4) *Economy and Society* 460.
22. Affidavits provide an authoritative 'truth'. The creation of affidavits is a highly structured activity that ultimately produces an additional (truth) narrative to the court.
23. *Milpurrurru & Others v Indofurn Pty Ltd* (1994) 30 IPR 209 at 230.
24. *Milpurrurru & Others v Indofurn Pty Ltd* (1994) 30 IPR 209 at 231.
25. Remembering my discussion of the cultural conditions of law in Chapter 1.
26. *Milpurrurru & Others v Indofurn Pty Ltd* (1994) at 30 IPR 209 at 229. See also at 230–231 for a similar reading of the Waterholes carpet.
27. It is significant that the same Barrister, Colin Golvan ran all the copyright cases in the 1980s and 1990s.
28. C. Golvan, interview by author, 19 June 2002, tape recording, Owen Dixon Chambers, Melbourne. On file with author.
29. Ibid.
30. Whilst this case is also important because of the substantial damages that were awarded ($188,000), this was arguably purely procedural in the sense that it was well known that

the defendants had no money and declared bankruptcy soon after this judgment was handed down. No monies were ever paid to the artists.

31. C. Golvan, interview by author, 19 June 2002 supra n.28.
32. Ibid.
33. Ibid.
34. G. Bird, 'Koori Cultural Heritage: Reclaiming the Past?' in Bird, G., G. Martin and J. Neilsen (eds), *Majah: Indigenous Peoples and the Law*, The Federation Press: Sydney, 1996, at 119.
35. See the affidavits of Banduk Marika and Tim Payunka Tjapangati incorporated into *Milpurrurru & Others v Indofurn Pty Ltd* (1994) 30 IPR 209 at 215 and 230. Also see Banduk Marika's comments in C. Eatock and K. Mordaunt, *Copyrites*, Australian Film Finance Corporation Limited, 1997.
36. C. Golvan, interview by author, 19 June 2002 supra n. 28.
37. *Milpurrurru & Others v Indofurn Pty Ltd* (1994) 30 IPR 209 at 244 [emphasis mine].
38. Remembering the arguments in the making of intellectual property law about how to measure the loss of this unique form of property. Part One, Chapter 2.
39. *Milpurrurru & Others v Indofurn Pty Ltd* (1994) 30 IPR 209 at 246.
40. *Milpurrurru & Others v Indofurn Pty Ltd* (1994) 30 IPR 209 at 244–245.
41. *Milpurrurru & Others v Indofurn Pty Ltd* (1994) 30 IPR 209 at 245 citing *Williams v Settle* [1960] 1 WLR 1072 at 1082.
42. K. Bowrey, 'The Outer Limits of Copyright Law – Where Law Meets Philosophy and Culture', supra n.5 at 97.
43. See for instance Marika's comments in C. Eatock and K. Mordaunt, *Copyrites* Australian Film Finance Corporation Limited, 1997. Also F. Myers, *Painting Culture: The Making of an Aboriginal High Art*, Duke University Press: Durham and London, 2002; J. Isaacs, *Spirit Country: Contemporary Australian Aboriginal Art*, Hardie Grant Books: Australia, 1999.
44. That is untainted by 'commercial' exposure or interference. This way of reading 'traditional' art is repeated in many scholars' work. In particular see K. Puri's 'Is traditional or cultural knowledge a form of intellectual property?' (2000) *Oxford Electronic Journal of Intellectual Property Rights* at www.oiprcox.ac.uk/EJWP0100.pdf. As Puri states, 'traditional means untouched, untainted and pure. Traditional is entwined with primitive people who lacked materialism and were unimpressed by commodities and conveniences European societies had to offer.' Many writers in this area consistently evoke an impossible dichotomy between indigenous (primitive) people and the western individual. At best this is naïve, at worst it creates impossible positions for indigenous people to negotiate and claim legitimate recognition.
45. J. McKeough, K. Bowrey, and P. Griffith, *Intellectual Property: Commentary and Materials*, supra n.11 at 100.
46. The legal argument is progressed because of the participation of several key artists involved in the earlier cases.
47. The case could only proceed because the material had been imported into Australia. Australian copyright law has no jurisdiction outside of Australia – so for instance, the claim could not be heard in the country where the material was manufactured.
48. J. Isaacs, *Arts of the Dreaming: Australia's Living Heritage*, Lansdowne Press: Sydney, 1994.
49. *Bulun Bulun v Nejlam Pty Ltd*, (1989) Federal Court, unreported.
50. *Bulun Bulun & Others v R & T Textiles Pty Ltd* (1998) 41 IPR 513 at 516.
51. J. McKeough, K. Bowrey, and P. Griffith, *Intellectual Property: Commentary and Materials*, supra n.11 at 132.
52. Political changes that occurred within Australia are highly significant. The change of government in 1998 to the conservative Liberal Party disrupted the previously progressive attitude to Aboriginal rights, to land claims, and consequently in intellectual property. The political fear of the potential linkage between native title and intellectual property also needs to be understood in the context of the politics of native title, where, as an example, there was a flurry of government attention, and the introduction in 1998

of an amendment to the *Native Title Act* (1993) that significantly wound back the rights that could be claimed, and increased the conditions through which Aboriginal people could be identified as legitimate claimants.

53. *Amicus curae* means friend of the court and allows a party to make a submission on one point that is raised by the applicant. *Amicus curae* can only be granted by the presiding judge.
54. *Bulun Bulun & Others v R & T Textiles Pty Ltd* (1998) 41 IPR 513 at 522.
55. *Bulun Bulun & Others v R & T Textiles Pty Ltd* (1998) 41 IPR 513 at 523. In their final form, the applicants' submissions did not seek to have the Court declare that the Ganalbingu people had native title in their land.
56. This case was a site that mobilised political over-determination of indigenous rights more generally.
57. *Bulun Bulun & Others v R & T Textiles Pty Ltd* (1998) 41 IPR 513 at 523. For a critique of this approach see: K. Howden, 'Indigenous Traditional Knowledge and Native Title', (2001) 24 (1) *UNSW Law Journal* 60; S. Gray, 'Peeking into Pandora's Box: Common Law Recognition of Native Title to Aboriginal Art', (2000) 9 (2) *Griffith Law Review* 227. For an interesting reversal of this argument, see the discussion of 'cultural knowledge' in the native title High Court decision *State of Western Australia v Ward* [2002] HCA 28 (8 August 2002).
58. See: M. Davies, *Delimiting the Law: Postmodernism and the Politics of the Law* supra n.1. Creating a new form of remedy (for example 'cultural' harm in the *carpets case*) was entirely different to a process of challenging and changing the statute.
59. *Bulun Bulun & Others v R & T Textiles Pty Ltd* (1998) 41 IPR 513 at 524.
60. These legal categories and legal language functioned as a strategic way of framing Milpurrurru's claims. It is unlikely that Milpurrurru spoke in such terms. As Colin Golvan readily accepts, 'the process of drafting affidavits is tricky because it is a classic case of the reduction of knowledge.' See C. Golvan, interview by author, 19 June 2002, tape recording, Owen Dixon Chambers, Melbourne. Milpurrurru's claims were translated into legalese and thus the law's own parameters of logic.
61. *Bulun Bulun & Others v R & T Textiles Pty Ltd* (1998) 41 IPR 513 at 516.
62. *Bulun Bulun & Others v R & T Textiles Pty Ltd* (1998) 41 IPR 513 at 516.
63. *Bulun Bulun & Others v R & T Textiles Pty Ltd* (1998) 41 IPR 513 at 521.
64. The Canadian case cited is *Delgamuukw v British Columbia* (1997) 153 DLR (4th) 193. The Australian cases cited include: *Mabo v Queensland* [No.2] (1992) 175 CLR 1; *Walker v New South Wales* (1994) 182 CLR 45; *Coe v Commonwealth of Australia* (1993) 118 ALR 193; *Wik Peoples v State of Queensland* (1996) 187 CLR 1. His Honour concludes that 'Australian Courts cannot treat as irrelevant the rights, interests and obligations of Aboriginal people embodied within customary law. Evidence of customary law may be used as a basis for the foundation of the rights recognised within the Australian legal system. Native title is a clear example.' *Bulun Bulun & Others v R & T Textiles Pty Ltd* (1998) 41 IPR 513 at 517.
65. *Bulun Bulun & Others v R & T Textiles Pty Ltd* (1998) 41 IPR 513 at 524.
66. *Bulun Bulun & Others v R & T Textiles Pty Ltd* (1998) 41 IPR 513, at 525, citing J. McKeough and A. Stewart, *Intellectual Property in Australia*, Butterworths: Sydney, 1991 at [504].
67. *Bulun Bulun & Others v R & T Textiles Pty Ltd* (1998) 41 IPR 513 at 524.
68. K. Bowrey, 'The Outer Limits of Copyright Law – Where Law Meets Philosophy and Culture', supra n.5 at 83.
69. Ibid., at 83.
70. *Bulun Bulun & Others v R & T Textiles Pty Ltd* (1998) 41 IPR 513 at 525.
71. *Kenrick v Lawrence* (1890) 25 QBD 99.
72. *Bulun Bulun & Others v R & T Textiles Pty Ltd* (1998) 41 IPR 513 at 525.
73. *Bulun Bulun & Others v R & T Textiles Pty Ltd* (1998) 41 IPR 513 at 518.
74. This is not only restricted to expressions of knowledge in art but also in music and dance. Matthew Rimmer has explored these inter-relations in the context of the Bangarra Dance Company and Manyarrun Clan. Bangarra Dance Company is based

on the artistic collaboration of David and Stephen Page and the Manyarrun Clan. As he explains, 'Bangarra Dance Theatre must be faithful to the particular experiences of Indigenous peoples, and yet at the same time reach a universal audience. It seeks to avoid the twin traps of being trapped in the ghetto, and being totally absorbed into an international commodity culture. Bangarra Dance Theatre has a prodigious task in educating people about Indigenous heritage, about retaining the languages, the stories and the lands.' M. Rimmer, *The Pirates' Bizarre* PhD Dissertation UNSW, 2001 unpublished at 296. See also: M. Rimmer, 'Bangarra Dance Theatre: Copyright Law and Indigenous Culture', (2000) 9 (2) *Griffith Law Review* 275.

75. J. Bulun Bulun, affidavit evidence presented in the case and reprinted in the judgment, *Bulun Bulun & Others v R & T Textiles Pty Ltd* (1998) 41 IPR 513 at 518–520.
76. The most obvious example being the legal fiction of *terra nullius* that still underpins Australian law in regards to assertions of indigenous sovereignty.
77. *Bulun Bulun & Others v R & T Textiles Pty Ltd* (1998) 41 IPR 513 at 524.
78. The existence of an express trust depends upon the intentions of the creator. *Registrar, Accident Compensation Tribunal v FCT* (1993) 178 CLR 145 at 166. See also: J. Gibson, 'Justice of Precedent, Justness of Equity: Equitable Protection and Remedies for Indigenous Intellectual Property', (2001) 6 (1) *Australian Indigenous Law Reporter* 1.
79. *Bulun Bulun & Others v R & T Textiles Pty Ltd* (1998) 41 IPR 513 at 527.
80. *Bulun Bulun & Others v R & T Textiles Pty Ltd* (1998) 41 IPR 513 at 527.
81. *Bulun Bulun & Others v R & T Textiles Pty Ltd* (1998) 41 IPR 513 at 527–530.
82. *Bulun Bulun & Others v R & T Textiles Pty Ltd* (1998) 41 IPR 513 at 528.
83. *Hospital Products v United States Surgical Corporation* (1984) 156 CLR 41.
84. *Mabo v Queensland* [No.2] (1992) 175 CLR 1.
85. *Bulun Bulun & Others v R & T Textiles Pty Ltd* (1998) 41 IPR 513 at 528 citing Toohey J in *Mabo v Queensland* [No.2] (1992) 175 CLR 1 at 200.
86. *Bulun Bulun & Others v R & T Textiles Pty Ltd* (1998) 41 IPR 513 at 530 [emphasis mine].
87. *Bulun Bulun & Others v R & T Textiles Pty Ltd* (1998) 41 IPR 513 at 529.
88. *Bulun Bulun & Others v R & T Textiles Pty Ltd* (1998) 41 IPR 513 at 530.
89. The case concerning tribal property was from Ghana, *Kwan v Nyieni* (1959) 1 GLR 67, 'where the Court of Appeal of Ghana held that members of the tribal group were entitled to initiate proceedings for the purpose of preserving family property in the event of the failure of the head of the tribal group to do so'. *Bulun Bulun & Others v R & T Textiles Pty Ltd* (1998) 41 IPR 513 at 529.
90. See: *Muschinki v Dodds* (1985) 160 CLR 583 at 614 (per Dean J). See also: M. Cope, *Constructive Trusts,* The Law Book Company: Sydney, 1992; J. Dodds, 'The New Constructive Trust: An Analysis of its Nature and Scope', (1988) 16 *Melbourne University Law Review* 482; P. O'Connor, 'Happy Partners or Strange Bedfellows: The Blending of Remedial and Institutional Features in the Evolving Constructive Trust', (1996) 30 *Melbourne University Law Review* 735; D. Wright, *The Remedial Constructive Trust*, Butterworths: Chatswood, 1998.
91. *Bulun Bulun & Others v R & T Textiles Pty Ltd* (1998) 41 IPR 513 at 532.
92. It is worth noting that von Doussa J may have done this to protect his 'innovations', securing them from the probability of appeal – if not in this case, perhaps in a later one.
93. *Bulun Bulun & Others v R & T Textiles Pty Ltd* (1998) 41 IPR 513 at 524.
94. *Bulun Bulun & Others v R & T Textiles Pty Ltd* (1998) 41 IPR 513 at 524.
95. *Bulun Bulun & Others v R & T Textiles Pty Ltd* (1998) 41 IPR 513 at 525.
96. M. Davies, *Delimiting the Law: Postmodernism and the Politics of the Law*, supra n.1 at 45.

7. The politics of law

In the previous chapters I argued that the importance of undertaking a reading of case law is that it provides an instance of legal action: it becomes possible to recognise certain limits and expectations of law. This is because legal decisions are formative to the law itself. Considering the identification and inclusion of Aboriginal art as copyright subject matter through the judicial interpretation provided by Justice von Doussa, the cases can be seen as representative of assumptions made in copyright law.

Both the *carpets case* and *Bulun Bulun v R & T Textiles* are important cases in the landscape of copyright law as they spur debate about the terms of inclusion – for instance how authorship and ownership of indigenous works are to be identified. The judicial interpretation offered illustrates the cultural life of copyright law. It also highlights how values of liberal jurisprudence and legal positivism exert pressure: from trying to identify types of knowledge to securing the closure of copyright law wherein limitations of inclusion are explained in reference to the legislation rather than matters of judicial interpretation. The point is that politics, philosophy and cultural values underpin case law, and these factors duly exert influence in how new categories are incorporated and the extent to which cultural difference is treated. Legal instrumentality seeks to play down the 'specialness' of indigenous difference. This is in order to maintain management over the identification of markers that constitute a property right in Aboriginal art ensuring that they are in keeping with the principles and categories of copyright law. Simultaneously, however, the law is constantly evoking the indigenous difference in order to deflect attention away from its disorderly internal mechanics. In this sense, it is the new subject, indigenous knowledge, which creates the problem (which law is actively seeking to solve) not the consistent and more general issue of granting property rights in knowledge *per se*.

Justice von Doussa was certainly aware of the cultural dimensions presented in each case. To some extent, von Doussa J was positioned as a direct interpreter of indigenous culture.[1] The *carpets case* required an appreciation of difference within the law in terms of including Aboriginal art as a product that satisfied the categories and markers of property and exclusive possession. In *Bulun Bulun* the cultural specificity of the law was directly in question. This was in terms of authorship and ownership, where both the traditional western concept of authorship and the philosophical valuation of the 'indigenous' relied upon possessive individualism. Importantly, as an interpreter of indigenous culture, von Doussa's J position necessarily became one of translator. Von Doussa's commitment to upholding the integrity of copyright law meant that indigenous cultural values were interpreted within the paradigm of copyright law. In this way, as Bowrey explains, the '*Bulun Bulun* decision can be confidently claimed as representative of copyright law in general. It is not just a "special" case where the law has to manage the consequences of the invasion'.[2]

In hearing extensive evidence from John Bulun Bulun regarding the creation of the artwork, and incorporating his affidavit within the body of the judgment, the unstable nature of the intangible that intellectual property law is set to identify and then mediate, is perhaps most explicitly revealed. In this sense, the artwork 'Magpie Geese at the Waterhole' is not just the product of an expression of ritual knowledge, it is ritual knowledge, and therefore Bulun Bulun cannot only be seen as the individual author or creator of the work. Von Doussa J however, perhaps makes a tenuous parallel between Bulun Bulun as the custodian of the work (in the context of trust law), and Bulun Bulun as the executor and 'owner' of the work (as per copyright law). This is a clear instance of the role of the judge in translating indigenous conceptions into the legal framework and policing those legal boundaries. In doing so difference is subsumed within the broader intellectual property narrative, but the real point of the translation displaces the unstable nature of (any) knowledge itself.

The two key ways in which the volatility of the subject matter is displaced are in the construction of identifiable artists, and the emphasising of the value of Aboriginal art as a cultural product. In both instances judicial interpretation is integral in establishing and normalising authorship and also endorsing the culture of commodification. Both elements draw attention away from the intangible subject matter, and more to the familiar features of engagement as 'art' in tangible form. Arguably it is the cultural differences in knowledge management and ownership unique to the Ganalbingu people that really threaten to reveal the erratic nature of copyright subject matter as a whole. The law retreats to a position where judicial interpretation consolidates and confirms the legitimacy of property rights in intangible subject matter, and normalises such modes of identification and classification. Copyright law naturalises various forms of social discrimination through endorsing a culture of commodification. How the law treats difference is on its own terms. Presented with complications in identifying intangible subject matter, for instance in the disruption of the category of authorship, the law is pressed to determine the essence of the metaphysical property. In the case of Aboriginal art, this is achieved through the paradigm/prism of 'tradition' which reads 'indigenous as culture'.

TREATING CULTURAL DIFFERENCE

Extensive evidence reflecting the importance of Aboriginal art to indigenous people is incorporated into both judgments. The judicial interpretation offered in the *carpets case* shifts between recognising the value of the art in a western sense, through the western art spaces it occupies, to the statements by the artists about the importance not only of the art at the centre of the case, but more broadly the importance of the art as a 'traditional' form of expression tied to the identity and existence of the particular Aboriginal community. Yet, concerns for the commodity form that the art takes are centrally engaged whereas accounting for the manifold ways in which ownership, control and access to knowledge have historically been managed are temporal issues engaged at the margins. The space provided for translating cultural differences facilitates a means for authorising that knowledge through the legal discourse. This is due, in part, to the way in which the artist's claims have initially been framed, both in affidavits and expert evidence, which support the methods of classification utilised within the law.

Arguably however, judicial decisions function both as a strategy for governing difference, and providing a portal – a means for opening space for appreciating difference. By this I mean that whilst law, presented with difference, minimises this through applying certain frameworks of classification, nevertheless the account of difference remains. To the extent that Bulun Bulun's statement regarding the association with his community, land and responsibility is incorporated into the judgment, it remains a record of a different way of viewing Aboriginal art, community and management of knowledge. Although attempts were made to make Bulun Bulun's account knowable and functional within a legal sense, it maintains and conveys a differing cultural heritage and intellectual tradition.

> 'At the Waterhole' is the number one item of Madayin (corpus of ritual knowledge) for Djulibinyamurr – it is number one Madayin for Ganalbingu – Gurrumba Gurrumba people. It has all the inside meaning of our ceremony, law and custom encoded in it. 'At the Waterhole' has inside meaning encoded in it. Only an initiate knows that meaning and how to produce the artwork. It is produced in an outside form with encoded meaning inside. It must be produced according to the specific laws of the Ganalbingu people . . . Paintings, for example, are a manifestation of our ancestral past. They were first made, in my case by Barnda. Barnda handed the painting to my human ancestors. They have been handed from generation to generation ever since.[3]

Bulun Bulun's statement invites an appreciation of its power within this legal text. Here it is clear that cultural difference remains fundamental to the law, and informs how other identifications are to be made and assumed. Thus Bulun Bulun's statement exerts a dynamic whereby it fulfils a role in identifying how the metaphyisical dimensions of the intangible property are determined as 'traditional', but also a recognition of the differential cultural values engaged within the law.

It is significant that the cases exist as a response to infringement within the art market and that this context has provided leverage for social justice issues to be (re)framed. The cases arise from problems within the market. The remedy in the *carpets case* reflects the problem of marketplace origins, as does the additional award of 'cultural harm'. The problem here is not that the indigenous artists are outside the market, only to be incorporated in cases of infringement. They are intrinsically engaged with the market, by providing consumers with cultural products, and also in their engagement with each other. What is lacking in the case law, and how it is discussed in the subsequently extensive literature, is recognition of this reality and the intrinsic power that this position holds. Amongst other elements, Fred Myers has considered the competition for art sales from the western desert region.

> With so many communities turning to the popular medium of dot paintings, there is a competitive struggle as the objects take on the formal properties of commodities: 'Everybody's trying to promote their community and get a little bit ahead, you know. Come up with an idea that is going to get a slightly higher profile for their community, to promote those artists . . . I don't think that the market is so big that it can cope with such a huge number of players in it'.[4]

This highlights some of the growing issues, including competitiveness and the danger of saturating the market that characterises contemporary engagement in the art market by artists, communities and consumers with implications at both local and international levels. There is reluctance by commentators, legal academics, and policy makers to deal with these complications. The complex realities that produced the cases in the first place are sidelined in favour of a minimalist narrative privileging the responsive (and redemptive) scope of law.

In *Bulun Bulun* von Doussa J states:

> The artistic work was painted by Mr Bulun Bulun in 1978 with permission of senior members of the Ganalbingu people. He sold it to the Maningrida Arts and Craft Centre. At that time Mr Peter Cooke was the arts advisor at the Centre. Mr Cooke then arranged the sale of the artistic work to the Northern Territory Museum of Arts and Sciences. It was reproduced with Mr Bulun Bulun's consent in the book 'Arts of the Dreaming – Australia's Living Heritage' by Jennifer Isaacs at page 198.[5]

Here von Doussa emphasises both the cultural origins and the commercial transaction associated with how the artworks circulated within the market and as such are transferred into commodities to be bought or sold. The 'aesthetic' value of the work produces it as an artistic activity that is always-already a product in the market and a category of law. Indeed it is the 'aesthetic' quality of the work that is strongly evoked through von Doussa's J description of the spaces that the art occupies in the *carpets case*. For example:

> The first four artists are from Central Arnhem Land. The artworks in question are bark paintings. The first three paintings are presently owned by the Australian National Gallery, ('the NGA'). In 1993 in recognition of the International Year for the World's Indigenous People, the NGA held the first solo exhibition of the works of an Aboriginal artist. The exhibition was a retrospective look at the works of Mr Milpurrurru, and included the art work 'Goose Egg Hunt' and was also featured in the publication 'The Art of George Milpurrurru' which was published by the NGA at the same time.[6]

These comments, as well as others within the judgment, confirm both the recognition of the creative endeavor implicit in the work and establish that a measure of the value of the artworks as works of art is that they appear or have appeared in the National Gallery of Australia and other important national and international cultural institutions. Their value is thereby justified through the western art spaces that they occupy and the abstraction of the subject from the cultural context facilitates the economic worth. This provides a context for the rearticulation of Bernard Edleman's observations where 'the aesthetic is subordinated to commerce'.[7] This then demands an appreciation of the power of the abstract aesthetic to generate value. In this sense, the market demand for the aesthetic value of Aboriginal art means that it necessarily functions as a commodity, the cultural context is repositioned as a marker of value and the subject of the law is abstracted. Tradition becomes central to the art's worth in the market but only for its transactional value, and is consequently generated as the essential core that determines the philosophical dimensions of metaphysical property. Indeed it is the market that helps develop ways that the identification of indigenous knowledge can be made.

In endorsing the 'works', von Doussa J also generates consequences through privileging good and worthy artwork for protection. With the shift from the aesthetic to the economic a further justice expectation is created. This is because the beneficiaries of the 'good' and 'worthy' artworks are not necessarily the artists themselves. The argument for resale royalties (*droit de suite*) sought to illustrate the extent that indigenous people are still disadvantaged in the art market.[8] Whilst such arguments have recently been silenced, the proposed change in copyright law sought to remedy the disparity of economic return where Aboriginal works that sold for paltry amounts thirty, twenty, even ten years ago now command prices in the hundreds of thousands of dollars.[9] That the artists tend to receive little financial benefit illustrates the inequity within the market and thus fuels the debate for the introduction of resale royalties and indeed indigenous property rights.[10] The significant amount of money being paid for the artwork is a direct effect of the exponential growth and success of the Aboriginal art industry. However, as one indigenous commentator, who prominently critiqued the industry in an award winning painting stated, 'Aboriginal art is a white thing': the statement suggesting that the real beneficiaries of Aboriginal art industry are not indigenous.[11] Bell provides a highly political and challenging critique of the Aboriginal art industry. Yet it is at the expense of recognising there are real beneficiaries.[12] It is these real beneficiaries, Aboriginal artists and communities, that do raise justice claims for the equitable distribution of economic benefits – a claim that is not beyond the scope of intellectual property law.

Here the challenge for the law is set within its own framework. For instance, to remedy the economic balance to some degree, it is not a new law that is required, but instead a yet to be established intellectual property category. There is potential for this category because it exists elsewhere within intellectual property regimes.[13] Resale royalties are picked up as a real possibility because Aboriginal concerns compliment the greater intellectual property narrative. This is because the law is already intrinsically engaged in managing the economic capital generated by the Aboriginal art market.

Von Doussa J is motivated to put a positive spin on the consequences of the Aboriginal art market and thereby to make the most of that for indigenous owners. However, his efforts feed back into and support that dynamic whereby copyright and intellectual property law facilitates and legitimises further appropriation and commodification. Von Doussa J presents his task as simply dealing with the end of commodification and rectifying injustices related to that – but at the same time his stance is reinvigorating and re-legitimising the 'indigenous' capital threatened by 'offensive misappropriation and insensitive commodification'.

The cases present law with the challenge of recognising indigenous rights deriving from differences in cultural knowledge but also require a recognition of the relations of power that have historically positioned indigenous people's claims for recognition of full rights of sovereignty and self-determination at the margins of the law. In this sense, the cases can be read as directly managing the 'excesses' of colonial dispossession. Pressed with this difficulty von Doussa J resorts to an engagement with standard jurisprudential concerns central to copyright. He understands that he has pushed the law as far as it can go, and he is sympathetic to indigenous claims, but in his position these can only be reconciled within the limits of the Copyright Act. He does not want, nor cannot necessarily engage in broader philosophical concerns about protecting cultural identity, power imbalances nor effects of Empire. The danger in doing so would be that such recognition would require intellectual property law to acknowledge its own cultural specificity. As Bowrey explains:

> Von Doussa's acknowledgement that the law has limitations in reckoning with significant cultural differences was potentially radical. It could have led the judge to expressly formulate the values of copyright law in cultural terms. Once these values were articulated, they could have been more broadly examined and their contemporary relevance debated. However this path was precluded by the jurisprudential choices he made. Von Doussa hints at the cultural particularity of the law but fails to address the privileged cultural values at stake . . . Ultimately he prevents the hearing of a debate that could lead to a challenge to the presumed neutrality, generality and universality of copyright law.[14]

In this way, the arguments that test the limits of copyright law also appear in the broader intellectual property discourse because they raise an awareness of the cultural contingency of laws categories of identification. These limits are political as they are set up and informed by a specific system of power.[15] Certainly there is recognition of indigenous cultural difference, but such considerations do not challenge the coherence of the body of law to deal with indigenous knowledges. Rather the cases consolidate the position of indigenous knowledge within an intellectual property discourse: a point consolidated through the debate for resale royalties and even moral rights legislation which will be explored in the final part of this book. These points of inclusion reaffirm the power of the law to sustain itself and perpetuate its abstracted categories. The problem is thus phrased as one that indigenous people have with copyright law, not the problem that copyright law has with the intangibility of indigenous knowledge. The onus is on indigenous people to accommodate the difficulties of the law. It is their responsibility. These decisions provide an instance of producing an account of the interaction between the cultural specificity of copyright and an understanding that difference can be managed through legally informing parameters. In providing an account of this interaction, a position for indigenous knowledge within the law is produced that is as complete as it is temporary and partial.

In reading case law it is possible to discern the many social and cultural elements that duly influence the way in which copyright law engages with new subject matter. It also reveals the manifold ways in which indigenous differences are treated within the law. On one hand, indigenous perceptions of ownership, communal or custodial, are reduced to standard interpretations – there is a uniformity of approach that maintains the consistency and cohesion of classifications and categories. However below the surface of mainstream jurisprudential concerns, indigenous difference is left to speak for itself and in so doing exerts an influence that helps the law come to terms with a key problem: the determination of the dimensions of the property right in this new subject matter.

Case law is an important instance for facilitating the production of categories that influence and identify exclusive possession within a commodity discourse. Legal decisions provide an account of legal action, they help us understand what happens in the practice of the law: where the limitations are, and how expectations are generated. It is nevertheless ironic that these instances of legal practice also reveal the instability of copyright categories, (re)exposing contingencies that have remained relatively hidden. In de-emphasising the 'special' case of indigenous art, the law unwittingly exposes the inconsistency of its modes of identification. For if the law had admitted the 'special' status of indigenous subject matter, it would have been able to shift the problem from the inability to secure the closure of the subject matter to the 'specialness' of the indigenous demands within the case. Instead, in disavowing any particular problem with the indigenous category, the issue of the unstable intangible is revealed as still operating as the fundamental element of intellectual property as a whole. Thus the politics of law are rendered visible.

NOTES

1. K. Bowrey, 'The Outer Limits of Copyright Law – Where Law meets Philosophy and Culture', (2001) 12 *Law and Critique* 75 at 79.
2. Ibid., at 79.
3. *Bulun Bulun & Others v R & T Textiles Pty Ltd* (1998) 41 IPR 513 at 518.
4. F. Myers, *Painting Culture: The Making of an Aboriginal High Art Market*, Duke University Press: Durham and London, 2002 at 217. Quoting from an interview with Christine Lennard from Warlukurlangu Arts at Yuendumu.
5. *Bulun Bulun & Others v R & T Textiles Pty Ltd* (1998) 41 IPR 513 at 520.
6. *Milpurrurru & Others v Indofurn Pty Ltd* (1994) 30 IPR 209 at 212–213.
7. B. Edelman, *Ownership of the Image: Elements for a Marxist Theory of Law* (transl. Kingdom. E.), Routledge and Keegan Paul: London, 1979 at 57.
8. *Droit de suite* or resale royalties provides that visual artists or their estates receive the royalties on the resale of the artworks. The royalty is usually between 3% and 5% of the price of the artwork.
9. There are too many examples to cite here. Nevertheless see: 'Aboriginal artwork bought for $20 sells at $120,000', *The Advertiser*, 1 August 2003; 'Royalties for art's sake' *Sydney Morning Herald*, 6 September 2002.
10. See: Australian Copyright Council, *The Art of Resale Royalty and its Implications for*

Australia, February 1989; *Fourth National Aboriginal and Torres Strait Islander Visual Arts Conference: Conference Report*, March 2002 at 32.

11. See Richard Bell's manifesto: *Bell's Theorem – Aboriginal Art: It's a White Thing,* at www.kooriweb.org/foley/news/bell.html.
12. Bell himself being one – walking away with $40,000 prize money for his artwork in the 2003 Twentieth National Aboriginal and Torres Strait Islander Art Award.
13. It was raised in the *Berne Convention on the Protection of Literary and Artistic Works* (1886) and remained voluntary. It was adopted in France in the 1920s and the European Union now has the *EU Resale Royalty Directive* which harmonises legislation in the various EU states. The discussion over the introduction of Resale Royalties in Australia has been ongoing. In 2006 the Australian government decided that it would not introduce resale royalties and instead would commit six million dollars over four years, to the arts sector. Attorney–General the Hon Philip Ruddock MP and Minister for Arts and Sport Senator the Hon Rod Kemp, *Press Release* 9 May 2006.
14. K. Bowrey, 'The Outer Limits of Copyright Law – Where Law meets Philosophy and Culture', supra n.1 at 82.
15. M. Davies, *Delimiting the Law: Postmodernism and the Politics of the Law*, Pluto Press: Chicago and London, 1996 at 94.

PART III

Culture

Introduction

> Question: My name is Marie Samuel. I am with the NGO Yachy Wasi, based in Peru and New York. I am not indigenous but our constituency is. I am glad to see WIPO is there, but at the same time I have a question. As you know the Permanent Forum on Indigenous Issues has been adopted. I assume that one of the questions that they will deal with is traditional knowledge. Now I see that there is a panel of scholars, but you do not have an indigenous representative speaking from their point of view . . .
> Professor Hugh Hansen: May I ask you a question? From which indigenous group should we have had a representative?
> Questioner: It could have been any indigenous group.
> Professor Hugh Hansen: What would they have said that was not said today or that you did not say?
> Questioner: Well it is like speaking about a dead body or something. The person is not there to speak. Apparently none of you are indigenous. It would have been good to have an indigenous point of view. That is my point.
> Professor Hugh Hansen: Okay. I might say we did put out a word to invite some NGOs to speak and, for whatever reason it never happened. But there was an invitation.[1]

So far this book has focused on the social, economic, political and individual influences that have produced the category of indigenous knowledge in Australian intellectual property law. In particular it has considered the way in which national-specific governmental initiatives and case law progressed and developed the making of the category. However, the problem of protecting indigenous knowledge and the attention to intellectual property law for remedy whilst a relatively new issue, is not only confined to Australia. It is also a pressing international matter that peak global bodies, indigenous alliances and national governments are fervently discussing.[2]

This final part will illustrate how the issues already explored within a national context are re-inscribed and developed in parallel within the international domain. For the process of generating the category of indigenous knowledge within an intellectual property regime is also a product of multidimensional networks of power crossing transnational borders and incorporating varying levels of political interpretation, agency and imagination.

The first chapter of this final part begins with a consideration of the global politics of intellectual property. This is necessary for understanding the way in which indigenous knowledge is positioned as a particularly pressing, yet differential 'global issue' of international legal concern. It will illustrate how many of the problems that are present in the national discourse on the protection of indigenous knowledge also thrive in and underpin international efforts and debate. However, these are moderated through differing political agendas engaged at the international level.

The point is to expose the 'interpenetration' of national and international objectives governing how the category of indigenous knowledge is created and managed. Thus, this chapter will highlight the overlapping strategies for identifying indigenous subject matter, and demonstrate the extent to which cultural difference and the problems of 'culture' and community are re-arranged in global initiatives. This is in order to illuminate the concomitant elements engaging with the intangible subject matter of indigenous knowledge and how a combination of these help construe the category as legally given and therefore open to techniques of legal ordering.

The second chapter will directly engage with the problem of 'culture' as it remains at the heart of both global and national discourses on indigenous intellectual property. My primary concern is how 'culture' has become positioned within the intellectual property discourse with a specific reference to indigenous interests. Part of the problem, and this affects legislative and policy developments nationally and internationally, is that in intellectual property law 'culture' has re-emerged as a generalised and essentialised concept, a peculiar indigenous trait and thus an explanatory tool for indigenous difference within law. Culture is read out of any other kind of intellectual property activity and read into indigenous issues exclusively. This helps reaffirm the indigenous claim as the problem, rather than it being one internal to law and its modern manifestation. The challenge for intellectual property law remains with the intangibility and invisibility of knowledge *per se*, not indigenous knowledge alone.

As a consequence of this dependence upon the 'culture' trope to understand indigenous needs, the strategies that are discussed and developed remain relatively limited. This is because they are unable to account for fluidity in indigenous experience and expectations of law, and importantly local demands in terms of action and remedy. Efforts at cultural inclusion within law need to be mindful of the extent of situations where indigenous needs overlap with those common to the aims of intellectual property law. These are most particularly felt in relation to the market, to the development of new kinds of audiences, to the recording and documentation of knowledge as well as controlling and protecting access to certain kinds of information.

The concluding chapter will take the deployment of 'culture' in intellectual property law as the point of departure for considering two recent Australian initiatives within this field: The Labels of Authenticity and the draft Communal Moral Rights legislation. Whilst these developments seek to target directly indigenous differentiation, and importantly, to address specific concerns raised by indigenous people (namely the concern for communal over individual ownership rights), they nevertheless create new tensions in terms of understanding the complex negotiations between individuals, families and clans that are intrinsic to any notion of community. For law, the applicability of abstract categories (like 'community' for instance) to complicated social realities remains a significant challenge. Whilst these new initiatives are again specific to Australia, their guiding principles regarding the recognition of community ownership and the positioning of 'culture', are increasingly being found and incorporated into national jurisdictions beyond Australia. Given the interpenetration of strategies and Australia's role in influencing and authorising the global construction of the indigenous knowledge category, the conclusions that will be drawn have implications beyond this context.

In general, this final part of the book will reflect upon and encourage further critique about how international and national discourses on intellectual property rights are formed, socialised and distributed. To this end, it is important to bring into question key assumptions upon which the current discourse rests. Such interrogation may make new interpretations possible and facilitate the development of clearer and less rhetorical perspectives on the dynamics that continue to marginalise indigenous interests by treating them as exceptional to the broader intellectual property dialectic. Before advocating for more intellectual property protectionism, there should be more reflection upon the effects of law, and indeed the new kinds of communities, authorities and cultures that new laws inevitably generate.

NOTES

1. 'Global Intellectual Property Rights: Boundaries of Access and Enforcement. Panel II: The Law and Policy of Protecting Folklore, Traditional Knowledge and Genetic Resources' (2002) 11(3) *Fordham Intellectual Property, Media and Entertainment Law Journal* 753 at 793.
2. See the World Intellectual Property Organisation – Intergovernmental Committee on Traditional Knowledge, Genetic Resources and Traditional Cultural Expressions www.wipo.org. The eleventh meeting was held in July 2007 and incorporated a range of statements produced from smaller regional meetings.

8. Globalising indigenous rights in intellectual property

A summary of the World Intellectual Property Organisation (WIPO) and its history of engagement with colonial/postcolonial relations establishes the initial discussion for this chapter. This is in order to contextualise the current politics involving the position of indigenous people and indigenous knowledge in international regimes of intellectual property. It will illustrate that the fluidity of issues within the international domain are related to both the decolonisation period following the Second World War and the increased globalisation of markets and trade that dominated the world economic stage for the last quarter of the twentieth century.

As already stated in Part One, prior to the establishment of WIPO in 1967, there existed a series of international conventions that regulated intellectual property frameworks and shaped intellectual property norms.[1] Theorists have highlighted how these conventions, in particular the *Paris Convention for the Protection of Industrial Property* (1883) and the *Berne Convention on the Protection of Literary and Artistic Works* (1886), were established through political, social and cultural indices. For example, Saunders argues that the signing of the Berne Convention 'was the outcome of unforeseeable interactions between a variety of geopolitical interests, legal traditions, cultural politics, commercial calculations, literary and artistic professional pressures and governmental concern with trade economics, foreign policy priorities and national cultural distinction'.[2] Bently and Sherman take this argument as a point of departure in their analysis and conclude that, 'Berne emerged out of a complex matrix of pre-existing international and colonial relations'.[3] What is important in Bently and Sherman's reading of this history is the distinct presence of a colonial politics that informed the production of international standards for intellectual property protection. For instance, Britain was reluctant to enter a multilateral treaty owing to concerns regarding the negative impact such a treaty might have on Britain's relationship with its many colonies.[4] As Grosheide observes, '. . . for the domain of early intellectual property law, the relationship between law and culture is basically determined by the power structure within countries and between countries'.[5] Colonial (and later post-colonial) politics have always been formative to the law in this area.

The Convention establishing WIPO occurred in 1967. It replaced the numerous treaties and conventions relating to intellectual property and WIPO thus assumed a governing and administrative role in setting international standards and norms.[6] With the 1974 agreement to join the United Nations system, WIPO functions as the international government organisation (IGO) most central to the international intellectual property regime.[7] This is despite significant challenges from a turbulent and changing political environment that has marked the period. For instance, WIPO has faced encroachment by the World Trade Organisation (WTO) that sponsored the multilateral negotiations resulting in the TRIPs agreement, 'challenging its own position as the forum for making international intellectual property law'.[8]

The transition of WIPO to a United Nations international governmental organisation effectively tipped the balance of power in decision-making matters towards the decolonising and developing countries dominant in the new global polity.[9] 'For the first time since the industrial revolution [there was] a shift from the developed to the underdeveloped world.'[10] As Ryan notes, 'the postcolonial enlargement of the United Nations in the 1960s and 1970s offered the best institutional setting to become a universal organization with the goal of promoting the "protection of intellectual property throughout the world"'.[11] However, with the 'one vote, one nation' system, the international intellectual property framework developed with weak rules and limited enforcement capabilities.[12]

The 'one nation one vote' decision-making at WIPO gave developing countries control over the WIPO agenda.[13] This disrupted the ambitions of other wealthier states (aptly demonstrated in the Group of 77) that asserted 'state rights to rationalize foreign enterprises, create commodity cartels and regulate multinational organizations'.[14] WIPO provided a forum where advocates from developing countries were provided with a platform to suggest the lowering of intellectual property standards.[15] Drahos aptly captures the tension:

> As the number of developing countries joining WIPO grew, the task of the WIPO secretariat in managing conflict grew increasingly difficult . . . But there was little hope of achieving consensus between the numerous states of the South, which were intellectual property importers, and a few wealthy states that were intellectual property exporters, especially in the 1970s and 1980s when developing countries were claiming that much technological knowledge was in fact the heritage of mankind. Moreover since Western intellectual property systems did not recognize the intellectual property of indigenous people, the states of the South were participating in a regime that by definition made them part of the intellectual property poor.[16]

Beginning in the 1980s, intellectual property industries based predominately in the United States and governmental representatives began turning away from WIPO in order to consider alternative and more effective ways of establishing and enforcing standards of international intellectual property protection.[17] Attention turned to the General Agreement on Tariffs and Trade (GATT) multilateral trade negotiations to secure such global ambitions. GATT, later the World Trade Organisation (WTO),[18] provided institutional support for developing and enforcing the agendas of states with intellectual property rich industries because it directly tied intellectual property protection and enforcement to trade. The most effective tool in securing this aim has been the Agreement on Trade Related Aspects of Intellectual Property (TRIPs).[19] 'TRIPs for the first time covers all areas of ip [intellectual property] law and for the first time ever determines substantive minimum standards for the protection of iprs [intellectual property rights] . . . it really introduces global norms rather than being once more an instrument resting on a diversity of common rules.'[20]

With such changes the WTO has had a significant impact on the organisational responsibilities of WIPO.[21] Whilst WIPO has struggled to remain relevant, both the WTO and WIPO have redefined their respective roles and cooperate where their roles intersect, for example in the implementation of TRIPs; the creation of new norms; and, intellectual property dispute settlement.[22] WIPO has also remained relevant by taking charge of discrete research interests that have arisen in relation to the increased promulgation of intellectual property regimes throughout the world. It is in this way that discussions regarding the possible protection of indigenous knowledge, in these forums known predominately through the analogues 'traditional knowledge, folklore and genetic resources', have fallen under the auspices of WIPO. The immense literature now produced by WIPO on traditional knowledge matters signals both the elevated status of the issue within the international domain as well as its discursive and political limits. One obvious limit emanates from unresolved tensions between member states and their indigenous populations. Whilst the stated ambitions of indigenous people in relation to intellectual property often conflict with those of member states, in the WIPO forums, they are afforded co-existence. However, any decision-making that might need to be made remains a privilege of those same member states owing to their recognition within the UN system.[23] The inevitable dilemma that this creates has established a certain kind of circularity within the debate, which in turn limits the development of resolutions that might change intellectual property agendas so that they benefit indigenous people. Whilst this has not escaped the attention of sympathetic WIPO bureaucrats, representatives from indigenous alliances or even member states with majority indigenous populations, it remains a substantial stumbling block for the development of an international consensus (and a binding treaty) on traditional knowledge issues. Nevertheless and despite such core problems, the international concern for indigenous/local/traditional knowledge matters is certainly more visible than it has historically been and this does affect the extent that indigenous advocacy can even be voiced and documented within these contexts. Certainly how 'traditional knowledge' gained the attention of WIPO as a 'special' intellectual property concern is also directly related to colonial/postcolonial politics and the emergence of indigenous people as subjects within international law.[24]

Indigenous people and indigenous interests have slowly been recognised in the international arena.[25] The 1957 International Labor Organisation (ILO) Convention 107 was instrumental in positioning the initial claims for the recognition of indigenous rights.[26] However, as Martin Nakata suggests, the 'specific concerns relating to indigenous populations had not been on the agenda at all prior to 1969'.[27] The study on indigenous people in 1970 'directly led to the establishment of the UN Working Group on Indigenous Populations in 1982'.[28] Coupled with special reports on discrimination and racism as part of a human rights agenda,[29] the concerns of indigenous people are currently dispersed across several United Nations forums.[30] In 2002 the General Assembly endorsed the establishment of a Permanent Forum on Indigenous Issues. The Forum now meets annually and conducts specialist expert meetings throughout the year on issues considered critical to the advancement of indigenous rights.[31] Yet the recent difficulties in passing the draft Declaration on the Rights of Indigenous Peoples highlights the continued reluctance to endorse fully indigenous participation within the international domain.[32] The power dynamics between indigenous people and state frameworks remain relatively intact even though postcolonial politics has informed the indigenous rights platform. As the opening quote to this part of the book demonstrates, the question of indigenous representation remains a significant challenge. Both the moderator and the interlocutor face the same anxiety. Yet the problem of 'who to ask' is only one of a series of unresolved issues relating to indigenous inclusion, participation and procedural concerns within the international domain.

During the last seven years, WIPO has reinvigorated fresh research to the area of traditional knowledge.[33] This was initially achieved by targeted 'fact-finding missions' and led to the development of a special inter-governmental committee within WIPO that now meets annually to discuss recent developments as well as working towards some kind of joint resolution.[34] This attention must also be understood as part of the WIPO continuum, and in the light of my earlier comments about WIPO – given that trade issues were being decided elsewhere, to remain relevant WIPO has taken on issues of 'culture' and other fringe concerns.[35] However, now that trade is also in 'culture', new strategies for controlling and protecting traditional/indigenous knowledge are being hotly debated in both national and international political and policy contexts.

Yet complicated political elements integral to indigenous interests in intellectual property remain peripheral concerns within the international domain. For instance, critical questions of sovereignty, entrenched racism and the equitable participation of indigenous people within nation states, are repetitively raised, but not addressed in any substantial manner by member states: WIPO's authority not extending to such issues. The reluctance of member states to engage with such complex concerns results in a continual relegation of these to the periphery. The dominant discourse remains one of member state choosing: of intellectual property rights and its classificatory frameworks. Indeed, because of the difficulty of incorporating the diversity of indigenous contexts and expectations of law, there remains a sense of 'pan' indigeneity at the heart of global theorising of indigenous concerns.

I will return to the dangers of pan-indigeneity and expand it in terms of considering the future expectations of indigenous people in relation to intellectual property in the concluding chapter. At this point I want to continue with an exploration of how the international debates summarily exclude politics and context. This is inevitably related to the effects of recent globalisation trends in intellectual property promulgation, which directly impacts the way indigenous knowledge is imagined as an intellectual property category in a global regime. What happens with this new global category, is that through the exclusion of politics and context, the culture trope comes to occupy a new reified space – but only in relation to indigenous issues.

GLOBALISING INTELLECTUAL PROPERTY

Recent literature has highlighted the significance of globalisation (and the counter effects of regionalism) on intellectual property protection.[36] As globalisation has generated an increased intersection of markets and stakeholders, new economic rights have been produced.[37] Concern for the effects of protecting these new rights at both an international and institutional level have left many commentators wary of the corresponding development of global standards for intellectual property frameworks.[38] As Drahos notes, '[t]he dangers of central command and loss of liberty flow from the relentless global expansion of intellectual property *systems* rather than individual possession of an intellectual property right'.[39]

To demonstrate and hence examine the effects of the global expanse of intellectual property systems focus has been directed to the multilateral TRIPs agreement.[40] TRIPs provides an example of how intellectual property harmonisation can profoundly alter strategies of global governance. For TRIPs makes explicit the direct relationship between trade, economics and intellectual property. It has effectively consolidated a power dynamic privileging countries that are already key players in international markets of information and industrial technology.[41] Thus the TRIPs agreement has fundamentally shifted the way individual countries engage with intellectual property rights, the market and other nation states. As Ryan explains,

> TRIPs is potentially the most important legal advance for the world trading system since the establishment of the General Agreement on Tariffs and Trade (GATT) in 1947. Postwar diplomats conducted an 'industrial diplomacy' . . . Now post-cold war diplomats are conducting a knowledge diplomacy that is institutionalising trade in products of invention and expression, offering innovators the incentive to make their products for the global market.[42]

The implementation of the TRIPs agreement is significant in determining what options for global reform of intellectual property to protect indigenous knowledge can be considered for the future. Yet there remain considerable political tensions within and between states that the TRIPs agreement has ignored and these have come to characterise the debates regarding the inherent inequities codified through the agreement and the sense that it presents deeply perspectival positions.

Work that investigates the new global politics of intellectual property has been slow to develop.[43] Indeed it was predominately non-legal scholars who drew attention to the wider political issues that surround concerns for intellectual property protection and the social effects generated by such rights. Christopher May has emphasised the need for discussion of intellectual property law to be set within broader political contexts.[44] As he states:

> . . . much of the current legal discussion misses important global political issues related to the general balance between the private right to reward and the construction or fostering of a public realm of 'free knowledge' . . . While legal scholars have much to offer these debates they also need to think about the global context of these issues and address the issues that stem from the mismatch of the (national) justifications and (global) society.[45]

One primary problem is how inequitable relations of power are disguised under the rubric of 'equitable' international standards. There is a presumption of equality in the global politic that belies the multiple social and economic inequalities that characterise relations between (and within) countries and nation states.[46] 'We are currently in a transitory period, where the global governance regime of IPRs has been established but the political community on which the justification of intellectual property itself depends is far from globalised.'[47] Here May makes a pertinent point, namely the danger of assuming a generality of purpose from international discussions about intellectual property to the particular social and political contexts governing their adoption and utilisation. As Aoki also notes, '[o]ne of the biggest mistakes one can make when considering the globalisation of intellectual property law is to assume away the increasingly contentious politics of the phenomenon'.[48]

Differing national concerns and contexts destabilise the universality approach in setting global intellectual property standards. Attention to the increased globalisation in knowledge management frameworks of intellectual property and the attempts at harmonisation of standards and procedural rules misunderstands the underlying disparity in social and economic wants of individual countries and stakeholders. As Ryan has observed, '[k]nowledge diplomacy is being conducted with participation from nearly all the world's states. But state's interests and goals differ widely because of variations in levels of wealth, economic structure, technological capability, governmental form and cultural tradition'.[49] This makes for contested politics informing both national and international domains. Yet circularity characterises the tension between the national and the international development of intellectual property standards because 'each depends on the other for integrity'.[50]

It is crucial to note that within each nation state multiple subjectivities exist that also respond, engage and interact within the circularity of local and global engagement. The presumption that power is vested in nation states misunderstands the dynamics internal to these same states and that individual subjectivity is intrinsic to the complicated relays, dispersions and resistances of power. As Sarat and Simon have noted, '[r]ealist legal studies almost always operate within a political body, usually the nations, although this body is not often itself an object of realist analysis. The boundaries and exclusions wrapped up in this national frame are made up not just of its political borders, but also of its racial, cultural and linguistic embodiments'.[51]

It is the interwoven strategies of the global and the local that makes the dichotomy between the two unworkable. This runs against the popular argument that the 'global entails homogenization and undifferentiated identity whereas the local preserves heterogeneity and difference'.[52] Whilst there lies an homogenisation of indigenous interests (a pan-indigeneity) at an international level, this is an observation about the lack of politics and subjectivity informing the construction of the 'indigenous knowledge' category.

For instance, the diversity of indigenous political interests within a state like Australia remain relatively undisclosed. Politics and particularity can be missed in both national and international contexts: this allows the imaginary Aboriginal/indigenous to be stretched across transnational borders.

The global and the local are intermeshed with the production of the local context informing the interest in the global spaces. Hardt and Negri suggest that this process requires reflection upon the 'production of locality, that is, the social machines that create and recreate the identities and differences that are understood as the local'.[53] Thus the governing strategies are understood as mutually engaged but produce 'different networks of flows and obstacles in which the local moment or perspective gives priority to the reterritorialising of barriers and boundaries and the global moment privileges the mobility of deterritorialising flows'.[54] What Hardt and Negri suggest here is that mobile and modulating networks of power produce problems of differentiation.

Whilst political elements may underpin (and contest) the classification of other intellectual property subject matter, indigenous knowledge presents special difficulties for the law owing to its now highly politicised character. Broader political claims (like those for sovereignty and/or self-determination) and diverse indigenous contexts and expectations are flattened, with attention to indigenous differences deflected by the primacy of the established modern/tradition polarity within the intellectual property framework. Any incongruity is identified as cultural in nature. Increasingly, it is through indigenous claims that the culture trope is implicitly brought within a legal discourse.

The turn to culture within legal study more generally indicates a conscious sensitivity to these issues. The law has been forced to consider the world beyond its boundaries through the specific moments where claims of legal expectation also incorporate arguments regarding cultural integrity and identity. As examined in Part One, the implications such claims have for law point to the need for legal studies to engage more fully cultural critiques.[55] The position of cultural issues within law significantly indicates a shift in how culture has become a nexus for governing. As Sarat and Simon explain, '[w]hether we like it or not, the practices of governance help set the agenda for legal scholarship'.[56]

To some extent political and cultural contexts are rendered explicit in the identification of indigenous subject matter in intellectual property frameworks. However, rather than finding a stable legal object, the recognition of the cultural elements also influence perceptions of the incompatibility of the subject matter. This is not a problem for those comfortable with post-structuralist deconstruction and cultural approaches to the law. However with indigenous knowledge the interest in the 'indigenous' exceeds that particular discursive legal framework. For the more traditional legal scholar, such as the legal realist, the lack of solidity and universality in the legal object creates an unhappy tension. Under such circumstances, cultural politics within the 'indigenous' category are underplayed so that attempts to manage the legitimacy of the broader negotiation of cultural inclusion, within the law's established terms, can be effected. It is this interplay between acknowledging the cultural politics and reducing it that characterises the position of indigenous knowledge within both Australian and global systems of intellectual property.

MAKING A 'GLOBAL' INDIGENOUS KNOWLEDGE CATEGORY

Since 1967 discussion about how to protect indigenous knowledge adequately has featured in international forums, and since that time there has been contest over the identification and even the instrumentality of the law in this area.[57] For instance, as mentioned above, attention to secure indigenous knowledge as subject matter in intellectual property discourse was made difficult by the ambiguity of term 'folklore'. National reports like the Australian 1981 *Report of the Working Party on the Protection of Aboriginal Folklore*[58] and the discussion stimulated internationally following the 1967 Tunis Model Law, indicated the varying difficulties in developing a representational consensus about the nature of 'folklore' and how an identification of folklore might be achieved.

The sustained international struggle to describe indigenous knowledge was illustrated in the Introduction through a quote from a key WIPO Report.[59] To date the exact position of indigenous knowledge within the intellectual property discourse remains uncertain. What is certain however, is that in any literature that discusses indigenous knowledge and intellectual property, culture or cultural will be deployed as an explanatory tool for indigenous differentiation. The following example, taken from a public academic forum dedicated to the subject of indigenous rights in intellectual property (of which there are now many) aptly illustrates the point.

> We are going to discuss two issues: a *cultural* one which is loosely referred to as 'folklore' and a *scientific* one, which is referred to as 'traditional knowledge and genetic resources' – traditional knowledge being those remedies which indigenous people usually have developed over time.[60]

In the last few years, in an attempt to understand and manage the amorphous character of indigenous knowledge, new kinds of categorisation that separate parts of indigenous knowledge to accord with the international intellectual property framework have occurred. In this instance, traditional knowledge is deployed in a limited sense – it refers only to a medicinal and hence scientific discursive form which in intellectual property law tends to map easily onto the already existing operational system of patents not copyright. Through such separation, a troubling binary is replayed where folklore equates to 'culture' whilst traditional knowledge becomes scientifically identifiable and consequently set apart from the 'cultural'. To this end 'culture' becomes representative of difference whereas 'traditional knowledge' is made identifiably familiar through its association with science. In similar circumstances to those analysed in reference to the 1981 *Report of the Working Party on the Protection of Aboriginal Folklore*, the problem of identifying the substance of folklore is remade as ambiguous and anthropological. Indigenous 'cultural' expression remains unidentifiable to the law except in the circumstances of knowledge pertaining to 'remedies' classified through a scientific lens. The very presumption of such a division reproduces the artificial divide assumed between indigenous and scientific knowledge. Echoing similar concerns but in a different context, Long has also observed that 'culture and intellectual property appear to have gotten a divorce'.[61] Culture remains a term that is utilised to indicate (irreconcilable) difference rather than recognised as intrinsic to the emergence and function of intellectual property law.[62] This is because, as Geller reiterates, 'the categorical terms of the law do not easily translate into the terms of the constantly mutating cultural discourse'.[63]

It is somewhat troubling then, that these international divisions and false segmentations are being adopted and becoming normalised through their incorporation into state jurisdiction. For example, in Indonesia, there are three new laws currently being drafted by different Indonesian government ministries.[64] One law specifically addresses traditional knowledge (and replicates current Indonesian patent law: traditional knowledge will need to be registered in order for it to be protected), the second addresses genetic resources (and follows guidelines being established through the convention on biological diversity) and the third law focuses on cultural expressions in art (and hence resembles a reinvigorated highly protective copyright approach to be administered through the creation of a new bureaucracy and the Indonesian state). From an abstracted perspective, this developing categorisation and segmentation appeals to both international and national governmental ambition to solve the problems through new forms of regulation. However, from the perspective of local and traditional communities across the Indonesian archipelago, it is a false distinction that threatens to undermine belief systems, functioning social structures as well as creating substantial burdens and conflicts between people.[65] It raises serious questions as to whom these new intellectual property laws will really benefit.

The extent of interest in developing an intellectual property remedy for indigenous knowledge furthers the production of the category within global frameworks. In addition, globalisation trends also inform the identification and hence the construction of the category. Correspondingly, effects of globalisation that result in increased markets for cultural commodities means that expressions of indigenous cultures are remade into commodities of high value within national contexts and also across international borders – 'culture' is big business.[66] But as Appadurai explains, 'The new global cultural economy has to be understood as a complex, overlapping disjunctive order, which can no longer be understood in terms of centre-periphery models'.[67] Like other evolving and lucrative industries, indigenous knowledge has been subject to new strategies for identification in order to streamline and better regulate these new markets. This is because the 'complexity of the current global economy has to do with certain fundamental disjunctures between economy, culture and politics'.[68]

The resulting international attention to indigenous knowledge subject matter has established the broader significance of the category 'indigenous knowledge'. Yet the preferred analogue 'traditional knowledge' or more often the acronym TK circulates as a global term that is relatively featureless. Arguably the category of 'traditional knowledge' functions as a viable standard that can cut across national and international borders, and contested political and cultural environments. The postcolonial politics in which the international arena is engaged means that terms have to be inclusive of the diverse political environments that characterise the world order. But, 'in a world composed of diverse cultures, histories, and political, economic and legal realities, a universal standard is not only incapable of achievement but also poses the risk of being an externally imposed standard'.[69]

This observation also has direct relevance in regard to the opening quote to this part of the book – where in certain forums it is enough that the 'traditional knowledge' issue is on the agenda, but it is not engaged with any real sensitivity or particularity. As inferred from the quote, the respondent appears to suggest that cultural particularity or specificity would be disruptive and pose problems of legitimacy. With such potential challenges, it is far safer (and easier) to avoid the problem by abstraction, objectification and exclusion. The very politics of indigenous knowledge remain absent from discussions of its (potential) intellectual property protection. Local identities might be privileged in making the category legitimate in terms of international discussion, but these identities are displaced when they actually threaten to reveal the explicit cultural politics (and prejudices) at play within the global polity.

Arguably the cultural particularity is deemed a subject more worthy of consideration by each nation state. In this sense, the nation state is posited as more qualified to address the issue in view of the distinct colonial and postcolonial experiences of governing indigenous people. This also presents the quandary where the international forums seek to set the terms of the debate and authorise discussions set in those terms, but ignore quite fundamental questions about the limitations of the debate. Cultural particularity is relegated to a position that does not disrupt the dominant circulation and proliferation of preferred classificatory indices.

While indigenous people may increasingly be recognised as an international group commanding attention, they remain situated in incredibly difficult subject positions that must be mediated. Especially in forums (academic and otherwise) where indigenous issues are addressed, but indigenous people themselves are absent, it is easy to perpetuate romantic assumptions about indigenaity and disavow the ongoing political battles of which intellectual property is just one. The communicative practices that affect the expression of indigenous subjectivities in global law have significant consequences for indigenous agency. Appadurai aptly captures this paradox of representation wherein he states: 'The critical point is that both sides of the coin of global cultural processes today are products of the infinitely varied mutual contest of sameness and difference on a stage characterized by radical disjunctures between different sorts of global flows and the uncertain landscapes created in and through these disjunctures'.[70]

The international arena is integral in setting the key terms of the debate and sidelines discussion that may compromise the adoption of those terms within national contexts. This way of shaping the categories and hence the terms of the debate has direct correlation with processes of harmonisation. In this context, harmonisation means the adoption of very broad abstract statements that imply an intention to 'do better' in relation to a particular concern. It suggests agreement upon the various cultural aspects embedded within the construction of the categories and the subsequent relation to economics and obligations for the enforcement of private property rights. At the same time it deflects attention from claims that do not fit that particular formula of rights. Whilst critiques of harmonisation point to the inequitable frameworks of intellectual property that are imposed as regulatory standards, the very construction of the category of 'traditional knowledge' imposes its own regulatory standards. In this context, the term most utilised to establish the standard is the trope of 'culture'. It is the prevailing emphasis on culture to explain why indigenous claims are different to any other that intellectual property law has had to deal with in its long history that I will now explore.

NOTES

1. Arup suggests that through these conventions, intellectual property provided one of the earliest occasions for multilateral agreement. C. Arup, *The New World Trade Agreements: Globalizing Law Through Services and Intellectual Property*, Cambridge University Press: Cambridge, 2000 at 65.
2. D. Saunders quoted in L. Bently and B. Sherman, 'Great Britain and the Signing of the Berne Convention in 1886', (2001) 48 (3) *Journal of the Copyright Society of the USA* 311 at 312. See: D. Saunders, *Authorship and Copyright* Routledge: London and New York, 1992. See also: S. Ricketson, *The Berne Convention for the Protection of Literary and Artistic Works: 1886–1996* Centre for Commercial Law Studies, Queen Mary College: London, 1987. This text is limited to a discussion of politics as primarily a product of the nation state – which is not my interest here.
3. Ibid., at 339.
4. Ibid., at 318.
5. F.W. Grosheide, 'General introduction' in Grosheide, F.W., and J.J. Brinkoff (eds), *Intellectual Property Law 2002: The Legal Protection of Cultural Expressions and Indigenous Knowledge*, Intersentia Publishers: Antwerp, Oxford, New York, 2002 at 7.
6. M. Ryan, *Knowledge Diplomacy: Global Competition and the Politics of Intellectual Property*, Brookings Institution Press: Washington D.C. 1998 at 94–101.
7. Ibid., at 125.
8. Ibid., at 125. See also: C. Arup, *The New World Trade Agreements: Globalizing Law Through Services and Intellectual Property*, supra n.1 at 40 for an account of the norms and processes of the WTO.
9. Grosheide comments, 'As a consequence of decolonization the geopolitical and demographic map changed dramatically. In Asia the amount of internationally recognized states multiplied by a factor of five. Whereas Africa in 1939 knew of only one such state, after the war this amounted to about fifty. Even in South and Central America, some twelve states were formed.' F.W. Grosheide, 'General Introduction', supra n.5 at 13.
10. Ibid., at 13. It is important to note that the distinction between 'developed' and 'underdeveloped' nations is not clear. Moreover the terms of description are unsatisfactory in that they convey negative associations. For a good consideration of this problem see: D.E. Long, '"Globalisation": A Future Trend or a Satisfying Mirage?', (2001) 49 (1) *Journal of the Copyright Society of USA* 313 at ft.11 at 317.
11. M. Ryan, *Knowledge Diplomacy: Global Competition and the Politics of Intellectual Property*, supra n.6 at 127.
12. Drahos (with Braithwaite) argues that 'WIPO's deepest failure from the US perspective lay in the arena of enforcement. The general view in the US private sector was that even if they could get a treaty through WIPO there was little point if the treaty standards were not enforceable.' P. Drahos with J. Braithwaite, *Information Feudalism: Who Owns the Knowledge Economy?*, Earthscan: London, 2002 at 111.
13. M. Ryan, *Knowledge Diplomacy: Global Competition and the Politics of Intellectual Property*, supra n.6 at 91.
14. Ibid., at 127.
15. P. Drahos with J. Braithwaite, *Information Feudalism: Who Owns the Knowledge Economy?*, supra n.12 at 195.
16. Ibid., at 112.
17. M. Ryan, *Knowledge Diplomacy: Global Competition and the Politics of Intellectual Property*, supra n.6 at 132. See also: P. Drahos with J. Braithwaite, *Information Feudalism: Who Owns the Knowledge Economy?*, supra n.12 at 110.
18. The WTO was established at the end of the 1994 Uruguay Round and replaced GATT. See: C. Arup, *The New World Trade Agreements: Globalizing Law Through Services and Intellectual Property*, supra n.1 at 45–48.
19. For a considered study of the political, bureaucratic, cultural and individual influences that led to the TRIPs agreement see generally: P. Drahos with J. Braithwaite,

Information Feudalism: Who Owns the knowledge Economy?, supra n.12. Also see: M. Blakeney, *Trade Related Aspects of Intellectual Property Rights: A Concise Guide to the TRIPs Agreement*, Sweet and Maxwell: London, 1996.

20. F.W. Grosheide, 'General Introduction', supra n.5 at 17. Arup also notes that the 'agreement cuts across provisions made in other international organisations but in some instances defer to or actively support them.' But the question remains whether the WTO is serious about this project of complementarity. C. Arup, *The New World Trade Agreements: Globalizing Law Through Services and Intellectual Property*, supra n.1 at 42.
21. 'WIPO was rather taken by surprise by the TRIPs agenda.' C. Arup, *The New World Trade Agreements: Globalizing Law Through Services and Intellectual Property*, supra n.1 at 182.
22. M. Ryan, *Knowledge Diplomacy: Global Competition and the Politics of Intellectual Property*, supra n.6 at 132.
23. See: www.un.org/aboutun/.
24. See: R.L. Barsh, 'Indigenous Peoples: An Emerging Object of International Law', (1986) 80 *The American Journal of International Law* 369.
25. See: S. Pritchard, 'The United Nations and the Making of a Declaration on Indigenous Rights', (1997) 3 (89) *Aboriginal Law Bulletin* 4; and generally, S. Pritchard (ed), *Indigenous Peoples, the United Nations and Human Rights,* Zed Books: London, 1997; P. Thornberry, *International Law and the Rights of Minorities*, Clarendon Press: Oxford, 1991.
26. International Labor Organisation, *Convention 107 concerning Indigenous and Tribal Population* (1957). See also: the International Labor Organisation, *Convention 169 concerning Indigenous and Tribal peoples in Independent Countries,* 76th Session, Geneva Switzerland, 1989.
27. M. Nakata, 'The United Nations and Indigenous People' in Nakata, M. (ed), *Indigenous Peoples, Racism and the United Nations*, Common Ground: Sydney, 2001 at 18.
28. Ibid., at 18.
29. In 1970 the Sub-Commission on Prevention of Discrimination and Protection of Minorities recommended that a complete and thorough study of the problem of discrimination against indigenous people be undertaken. See: J. Martinez Cobo, *Study of the Problem of Discrimination against Indigenous Populations*, U.N Sub-Commission on Prevention of Discrimination and Protection of Minorities E/CN.4/Sub.2/1986/7/Add.4(1986); and E.I. Daes, *Discrimination against Indigenous Peoples: Protection of the Heritage of Indigenous Peoples*, Final report of the Special Rapporteur, Mrs. Erica-Irene Daes in conformity with Sub-Commission resolution 1993/44 and decision 1994/105 of the Commission on Human Rights, Geneva, 47th Session, E/CN.4/Sub.2/1995/26.
30. For example: UNESCO; the UN Development Program; and WIPO.
31. See [www.un.org/esa/socdev/unpfii/] See also: P. Havermann, 'The Participation Deficit: Globalisation, Governance and Indigenous Peoples', (2001) 3 *Balayi: Culture: Law and Colonialism* 9 at 24.
32. Australia, Canada and the United States repeatedly vote against the draft. The Declaration on the Rights of Indigenous Peoples was adopted in a majority vote (143–4) by the UN General Assembly on 14 September 2007.
33. As Nakata notes, 'In 1998, WIPO was mandated to identify and explore the issues with intellectual property aspects of traditional knowledge and folklore protection.' M. Nakata, 'The United Nations and Indigenous People', supra n.27 at 18.
34. The interest was initially in folklore. See: M. Blakeney, 'Protection of Traditional Knowledge under Intellectual Property Law', (2000) 22 (6) *European Intellectual Property Review* 251. E.I. Daes, *Discrimination against Indigenous Peoples: Study on the Protection of the Cultural and Intellectual Property of Indigenous People,* presented by Erica-Irene Daes, Special Rapporteur of the Sub-Commission on Prevention of Discrimination and Protection of Minorities and President of the Working Group on Indigenous Populations, Geneva, 45th Session, E/CN.4/Sub.2/1993/28. See: *The Mataatua Declaration on Cultural and Intellectual Property Rights of Indigenous Peoples.*

Written and adopted at the First International Conference on Cultural and Intellectual Property Rights of Indigenous Peoples, Whakatane, New Zealand, 12–13 June 1993.

35. Grosheide argues that it was UNESCO that 'started introducing treaties, organizing conferences and setting up projects in order to stimulate a process of world wide reflection as to how cultural policies could be integrated into development strategies.' F.W. Grosheide, 'General Introduction', supra n.5 at 21.
36. See for instance: D.E. Long, 'The Impact of Foreign Investment on Indigenous Culture: An Intellectual Property Perspective', (1998) 23 *N.C.J. Int'l L. & Com. Reg.* 229; D.E. Long, 'Democratising "Globalisation": Practicing the Politics of Cultural Inclusion' (2002) 10 *Cardozo Journal of International and Comparative Law* 218; C. Arup, *The New World Trade Agreements: Globalizing Law Through Services and Intellectual Property*, supra n.1. See also the following collection of essays: P. Drahos and R. Mayne (eds), *Global Intellectual Property Rights: Knowledge, Access and Development*, Palgrave Macmillan: Hampshire, 2002.
37. P.E. Geller, 'Copyright History and the Future: What's culture got to do with it?', (2000) 48 *Journal of the Copyright Society of the USA* 210 at 251. See also: P. Hirst and G. Thompson, 'Globalisation and the History of the International Economy' in Held, D., and A. McGrew (eds), *The Global Transformations Reader: An Introduction to the Globalisation Debate*, Polity Press: Cambridge, 2000; and, J. Perraton, D. Goldblatt, D. Held and A. McGrew, 'Economic Activity in a Globalising World' in Held, D., and A. McGrew (eds), *The Global Transformations Reader: An Introduction to the Globalisation Debate*, Polity Press: Cambridge, 2000.
38. R. Gana, 'Has Creativity Died in the Third World? Some Implications of the Internationalisation of Intellectual Property', (1995) 24 *Denv. J. Int'l L. & Pol'y* 109; R. Oekdiji, 'The International Relations of Intellectual Property: Narratives of Developing Country Participation in the Global Intellectual Property System', (2003) 7 *Singapore Journal of International and Comparative Law* 315; and, K. Aoki, 'Considering Multiple and Overlapping Sovereignties: Liberalism, Libertarianism, National Sovereignty, 'Global' Intellectual Property and the Internet', (1998) 5 *Ind. J. Global Leg. Studies* 443.
39. P. Drahos with J. Braithwaite, *Information Feudalism: Who Owns the Knowledge Economy?*, supra n.12 at 5 (emphasis in text).
40. For a selection in the otherwise extensive literature see: S. Sell, *Power and Ideas: North-South Politics of Intellectual Property and Antitrust*, State University of New York Press: New York, 1998; S. Sell, 'Industry Strategy for Intellectual Property and Trade: The Quest for TRIPs and post-TRIPs Strategies', (2002) 10 *Cardozo Journal of International and Comparative Law* 79; P. Drahos and R. Mayne (eds), *Global Intellectual Property Rights: Knowledge, Access and Development*, supra n.36; P. Drahos and J. Braithwaite, *Information Feudalism: Who Owns the Knowledge Economy?*, supra n.12; C. Correa, 'Harmonisation of Intellectual Property Rights in Latin America: Is There Still Room for Differentiation?', (1997) *N.Y.U. J. Int'l L. & Pol'y*. 109.
41. K. Aoki, 'Neocolonialism, Anticommons Property and Biopiracy in the (Not-So-Brave) New World Order of International Intellectual Property Protection', (1998) 6 *Ind. J. Global Leg. Stud.* 11.
42. M. Ryan, *Knowledge Diplomacy: Global Competition and the Politics of Intellectual Property*, supra n.6 at 1. See also: P. Drahos with J. Braithwaite, *Information Feudalism: Who Owns the Knowledge Economy?*, supra n.12.
43. C. May, 'Why IPRs are a Global Political Issue', (2003) 1 *European Intellectual Property Review* 1.
44. Ibid., at 1.
45. Ibid., at 5.
46. May understands the most obvious economic divide to be between 'developed' and developing countries (despite the inherent problems in making such a neat division). See also: C. May, *A Global Political Economy of Intellectual Property Rights: The New Enclosure?*, Routledge: London and New York, 2000; S. Sell, *Power and Ideas: North South Politics of Intellectual Property and Antitrust*, supra n.40; P. Drahos, 'BITs and

BIPs: Bilateralism in Intellectual Property', (2001) 4 (6) *The Journal of World Intellectual Property* 791.
47. Ibid., at 4.
48. K. Aoki, 'Neocolonialism, Anticommons Property and Biopiracy in the (Not-So-Brave) New World Order of International Intellectual Property Protection', supra n.41 at 11.
49. M. Ryan, *Knowledge Diplomacy Global Competition and the Politics of Intellectual Property*, supra n.6 at 191.
50. K. Aoki, 'Considering Multiple and Overlapping Sovereignties: Liberalism, Libertarianism, National Sovereignty, 'Global' Intellectual Property and the Internet', supra n.38 at 469.
51. A. Sarat and J. Simon, 'Beyond Legal Realism?: Cultural Analysis, Cultural Studies, and the Situation of Legal Scholarship', (2001) 13 (35) *Yale Journal of the Humanities* 1 at 7.
52. M. Hardt and A. Negri, *Empire*, Harvard University Press: Cambridge MA and London, 2000 at 45.
53. Ibid., at 45.
54. Ibid., at 45.
55. See the collection of essays in: A. Sarat and J. Simon (eds), *Cultural Analysis, Cultural Studies and the Law: Moving Beyond Legal Realism*, Duke University Press: Durham and London, 2003.
56. A. Sarat and J. Simon, 'Beyond Legal Realism?: Cultural Analysis, Cultural Studies, and the Situation of Legal Scholarship', supra n.51 at 6. See also: N. Mezey, 'Approaches to the Cultural study of Law: Law as Culture', (2001) 13 (35) *Yale Journal of Law and the Humanities* 35.
57. See: M. Blakeney, 'The Protection of Traditional Knowledge under Intellectual Property Law', supra n.34.
58. Department of Home Affairs and the Environment *Report of the Working Party on the Protection of Aboriginal Folklore* Canberra, December 1981.
59. World Intellectual Property Organisation, *Intellectual Property Needs and Expectations of Traditional Knowledge Holders: WIPO Report on Fact-finding Missions on Intellectual Property and Traditional Knowledge (1998–1999)*, Geneva, Switzerland, 2001. See Introduction.
60. 'Global Intellectual Property Rights: Boundaries of Access and Enforcement. Panel II: The Law and Policy of Protecting Folklore, Traditional Knowledge and Genetic Resources', (2002) 11 (3) *Fordham Intellectual Property, Media and Entertainment Law Journal* 753 at 754 [emphasis mine].
61. D.E. Long, 'Democratising "Globalisation": Practicing the Politics of Cultural Inclusion', supra n.36 at 217.
62. The cultural production of intellectual property law was considered in Part One.
63. P.E. Geller, 'Copyright History and the Future: What's culture got to do with it?', supra n.37 at 261.
64. J. Anderson, L. Aragon, I. Haryanto, P. Jaszi, A. Nababan, H. Panjiatan, A. Sardjono, R. Siagian, R. Suryasaladin, *Traditional Arts: A Move Towards Protection in Indonesia* (forthcoming).
65. Ibid. See also: J. Anderson, 'The Politics of Indigenous Knowledge: Australia's Communal Moral Rights Bill,' (2004) 27 (3) *University of New South Wales Law Journal* 85.
66. D.E. Long, 'The Impact of Foreign Investment on Indigenous Culture: An Intellectual Property Perspective', supra n.36 at 229–231.
67. A. Appadurai, 'Disjuncture and Difference in the Global Cultural Economy' in Held, D., and A. McGrew (eds), *The Global Transformations Reader: An Introduction to the Globalisation Debate*, Polity Press: Cambridge, 2000 at 231.
68. Ibid., at 231.
69. D.E. Long, 'Democratising "Globalisation": Practicing the Politics of Cultural Inclusion', supra n.36 at 225.
70. A. Appadurai, 'Disjuncture and Difference in the Global Cultural Economy', supra n.67 at 237.

9. The culture concept

In the twenty-first century, culture is a deeply compromised idea.[1]

In *Who Owns Native Culture?* Michael Brown makes the following observation:

> If we turn culture into property, its uses will be defined and directed by law, the instrument by which states impose order on an untidy world. Culture stands to become the focus of litigation, legislation and other forms of bureaucratic control.[2]

Here Brown makes a very important point. The danger of making culture property is in the unpredictable ways in which it will then become subject to classification, codification, legislation and legal intervention. This will effect how 'culture' can be understood, including the parameters set for inclusions and exclusions. It also impacts upon the extent that law becomes a central mechanism for reproducing functionalist frameworks for the interpretation of 'culture' and cultural products.

Whilst sympathetic to Brown's concerns, the presumption that 'making culture property' will be something 'new' that law does, misunderstands law and its cultural practices. Law is inherently cultural: it has been working on 'culture' (and vice versa) for some time. As discussed earlier in the book, the two are imbricated in each other in ways that are not always easy to discern. Perhaps it is because the terms of the debate have never been as explicit, or put so simply, that this function of law has escaped more considered attention. There is an acute need to be wary of assuming that this new kind of legalism is also something novel for indigenous people: indigenous people and 'ways of being' have been documented, classified, typologised, defined and directed by laws relating to personhood, location, sovereignty, citizenry, sociality and cultural objects (to name a few) for quite some time and as a direct result of various modalities of colonialisms and post-colonialisms, as well as national and international legal strategies of governing.

Certainly the translation of explicit claims for the ownership of culture into a context of intellectual property has generated particular demands on this body of law. In particular, indigenous claims have raised additional concerns and primarily these have manifested themselves through issues of ownership.[3] Yet the limited attention to the framing of the question of ownership has narrowed the ways in which law is understood as operating. Altering the direction of the interrogation, however, results in an appreciation of the complex and often contested (social) negotiations occurring around law, knowledge, culture and property. Further, it prompts reflection on the new kinds of languages, paradigms and exclusions that are *always* produced through laws specifically designed to regulate and protect certain kinds of knowledge.

How indigenous 'culture' has come to be understood as 'owned' cannot be seen outside a contested history of empire, imperialism, colonialism, post-colonialism as well as legal and bureaucratic influence and determinacy. Nor can it be understood as existing outside early philosophical traditions of Enlightenment and Romanticism, notions of civilisation and progress, and the liberal democratic polity. The knowledge hunting and gathering about indigenous people and cultures has a particular history. Conversely, so do the current claims for restitution and control of these collections.[4] When claims to culture are made, they are also framed by these same historical relationships of power. Nevertheless, the current claims to the ownership of culture, as a particular kind of ownable object, have evoked problematic interpretations of culture, and in particular of indigenous cultures. This is part and parcel of the inherent volatility and indeterminacy of the term 'culture' itself. One clear problem is that in many interpretations of indigenous 'culture', most especially those found in intellectual property law, there is a (naïve) insistence upon homogeneity in the (global) category of the indigenous. In the making of Indigenous as Culture, binaries between indigenous and western cultures as bounded cultural entities, are perpetuated. These continue to feed interpretations of indigenous epistemology and existence, and consequently the governing strategies that are developed to target, for instance, indigenous interests in intellectual property. These are carried blindly from the legacy of earlier historical frameworks of knowledge interpretation. They thus continue to present considerable problems for action.

In much of the literature dedicated to addressing indigenous interests in intellectual property, a reading of the term 'indigenous intellectual property' assumes a distinct cultural derivation. Yet conceptualising relations between and through something named as 'culture' has, at least in the latter part of the twentieth century, become more attenuated to the fluidity and dynamism that often defies description in theory or in practice.[5] As an outcome of this growing understanding certain disciplines, namely anthropology, cultural studies and sociology, have responded by articulating the many ways in which the location of culture is disparate and moveable, being nowhere and everywhere.[6] Culture remains a deeply compromised idea.[7]

THE CULTURE CONCEPT

Raymond Williams has done much to foster understanding of the complexities and fluidities of the concept of 'culture', especially in tracing the trajectories of the term.[8] Utilised as a plural in the eighteenth century, the term 'culture' came to relate to the 'specific and variable cultures of different nations and periods, but also the specific and variable cultures of social and economic groups within a nation'.[9] The transition of the term also speaks to the change in conceptualising 'culture', where the term, as it was posited by Matthew Arnold in the nineteenth century, came to refer exclusively to intellectual and artistic expression.[10] Notably, in contexts such as indigenous interests in intellectual property, this perception of culture has shifted but has not totally disappeared from contemporary ways of appreciating 'other' cultures. Arnold's conception still resonates within our current situation. It returns in a modified way in reference to indigenous art and artistic expression, where in particular, the intellectual and artistic expression of Aboriginal and Torres Strait Islander people signifies and confirms the sense of indigenous 'culture'. A further complexity has emerged however, because this notion has come to be treated as if it were unified, bounded and singular both in law, politics and popular culture.

Williams sketched the social definition of culture, where:

> culture is a description of a *particular* way of life, which expresses certain meanings and values, not only in art and learning, but also in institutions and ordinary behaviour. The analysis of culture, from such a definition, is the clarification of the meaning and values implicit and explicit in a *particular* way of life, a *particular* culture.[11]

This description has had a significant impact on a range of disciplines and influenced how many theorists conceptualise relations of culture in theory and practice as being a 'whole way of life'. The particularity pointed to by Williams also infers a singularly expressed spatiality and temporality.

Critiques of Williams, particularly for what Ian Hunter refers to as his evocation of Romantic aesthetics,[12] have generated alternative ways of talking about culture that include consideration of how culture is not just the 'whole way of life' of any given group, but also the way in which experience is shaped, mapped and interpreted. The very problem of the term is its inability to securely capture experience.[13] The (im)possibility of naming and claiming what a culture is, depends significantly on demarcations and identifications of what a culture is not.

The rethinking of categories of class, gender, race and ethnicity as being constitutive of culture has produced a shift in the way specific social groupings have been studied and understood. This shift has destabilised the assumption that the notion of culture is 'shared' by all members of a given society. Postcolonial politics as well as substantial philosophical reflection suggest that through hierarchies of knowledge gathering, accumulation and classification, the parameters for 'sharing' have not always been experienced as equal flows.[14] Sharing between people, groups and communities depends significantly upon the power-relations operating within any locale.[15]

Conceptually, cultures are elusive and complex and defy simple definitions. Further, the differences within cultures and the multiple actors that structure and position themselves between and through different cultural spaces necessitates recognition of the fluidity and permeability of cultural exchange. The reality of the translocation of culture sits uncomfortably with definitions of cultures that emphasise the wholeness of groups. Cultures are also imagined, but it is as an imaginary, and an organisational conceptual tool that inevitably also lends power to the deployment of the term.[16]

As powerful factors – political, social and economic – produce images of culture as a heterogeneous unit, it is advantageous to think of culture as a theory, rather than a given category that describes the spatial parameters of social relations. Indeed it could be argued that culture is a political project of interpretation and reinterpretation, where no one meaning can fully maintain a grasp on the proliferation of the term.[17] 'Culture' as theory provides a lens through which the use of the term can signify the engagement of relations of power – for example, where distinct groups effectively emphasise their own cultural uniqueness. Such evocations invariably function in response to various fluctuations within society at any given period and are inextricably tied to renegotiating specific relations of power.

The point at which the consideration of 'culture' informs intellectual property law derives from a tension. This tension is between the fluid and the fixed concepts of 'culture'. While theories of culture and cultural production (that pay attention to the fluidity and dynamism of culture) circulate and proliferate, these are countered by an increasing number of social groups (and their advocates) demanding recognition of their cultural distinctiveness that is bounded by a distinctive and unitary 'culture' and inseparable from a unique cultural identity. As Michael Brown observes, 'the ongoing struggle for political and cultural sovereignty often leads indigenous activists to talk about culture as if it were a fixed and corporeal thing'.[18] With legal commentators and indigenous activists basing their arguments on an abstract notion of culture there is an ironic synthesis of perspective.

The concept of cultural appropriation deftly illustrates the tension. Some have argued (and been summarily publicly rebuked) that cultural appropriation is no more than an exercise of cultural hybridity.[19] The counter argument is that cultural appropriation presumes an act of 'theft' whereby the dominant 'culture' adopts something 'belonging' to the 'minority' culture.[20] The conditions that lead observers to name cultural appropriation derive from multiple histories of colonisation, domination and subjugation.[21] Most importantly, inequitable relations of power often underpin claims of cultural appropriation. However, it is dangerous to assert that the process of cultural appropriation is as clear as the 'taking' by one culture of what is 'owned' by another.[22] Binaries between cultures can never be neat, and such a perception of cultural appropriation insists on a process of hegemony and subjugation that leaves little room for resistance and agency. Nothing is achieved in pitting colonisers against colonised; as Ann Stoler notes the perpetuation of such binaries speaks more to 'political agendas than to ambiguous colonial realities'.[23]

Cultural appropriation can also occur within spaces named as 'cultures' as there exist considerable differences between the conditions of inclusion, and 'sharing' within the same spatiality. For cultural appropriation is not solely a characteristic of a 'dominant' culture: it is a more complex process. The danger is in reducing the issue to the tension between two distinct groups, vying for control of what is seen as uniquely owned by another one 'whole' culture. For in missing the fluidity between and through cultures, phantoms of romanticism in the reliance on 'tradition' and ahistoricity are constructed, whereby cultural practices are rendered functional in a timeless vacuum, impervious to historical, cultural, political and individual adaptation and influence. The effects of such imaginings include the relegation of particular groups of people to positions 'outside' modern and contemporary practice. Attention to calls to stop cultural appropriation must be mindful of these dangers and the layering of influences that makes legal solutions difficult to determine because the reality of cultural exchange is infinitely polyvalent.

Power is fundamentally engaged within claims of cultural appropriation and claims to 'culture' – both in attempts to address historical imbalances, such as past histories of dispossession and colonisation and also in the renegotiation of contemporary positions within societies and nations for differing cultural and social groupings. Indeed there is no 'right' way of looking at culture, but rather a variety of ways that can illuminate the making of certain kinds of relationships as well as how these produce quite specific responses. This lends strength to an appreciation of culture as a theory that indicates multiple interests and projects of interpretation, including how relations of power are intrinsically imbued within evocations of cultural dominance. In this sense then, arguments regarding cultural appropriation can be understood as particular (and strategic) responses to historical and cultural factors. The naming of the process of cultural appropriation reveals a struggle between relations of power.

Meaghan Morris recognises that the term has been positioned within a framework that denotes a 'marauding' element of all forms of cultural exchange.[24] In this sense Morris has articulated 'appropriation' as a 'lexical mini-myth of power'.[25] By this she means that appropriation is a term that can be used strategically to evoke relations of dominance and that these disrupt familiar relations of property. However, the extent to which appropriation is, or could be, post-colonial resistance falls sharply from view when cultural appropriation is only seen through the lens of exploitation.

The language and framework of intellectual property law have been employed firstly by 'experts' and latterly by indigenous people to counter the notion of cultural appropriation and as a response to perceptions of loss of control over intangible cultural property.[26] Here there is a neat morphing of intangible cultural property into culture perhaps because the properties of both are difficult to identify and name, both in their capturing and their loss.[27] This context utilises a language of 'theft' and 'ownership', and extends the underlying assumptions to a broader evocation of culture as 'property'.[28]

But the positioning of a problem such as cultural appropriation within a *legal* framework is of profound importance. As Pat O'Malley has observed:

> The identification of a social problem as a legal need rather than some other sort of problem altogether is dependent on the place that the law occupies in the society concerned, and especially the extent to which legalism permeates social consciousness. To identify a problem as a legal need is to make a particular judgment about appropriate solutions to that problem and then to recast the conception of the problem to accord with the nature of the proposed solution.[29]

Whilst the complexity of issues are not only legal in nature, law provides a space where political and ethical judgments echo an assumption that a wrong is being committed, enhancing the possibility (and indeed necessity) of the solution remaining within the domain of law. The gaze is turned away from any detailed consideration of the broader global political context of intellectual property law, and the subjugation of indigenous persons throughout its history. Instead law becomes almost self-congratulatory in its capacity to respond to a 'new' indigenous subject by making it an area of specialisation. This is instead of recognising that indigenous relations have always been imbricated in the laws.

As a response to the cultural appropriation of intangible subject matter, intellectual property law has positioned itself as the viable point for possible solutions. Here law is set a tough challenge: it must mediate discrete indigenous (cultural) differences whilst also countenancing for the commonality of indigenous needs and interests, for example in demands for controls over knowledge circulation and use. Inevitably this has led to revelations of incommensurability between indigenous and legal value systems.[30] Yet the ambiguity of cultural appropriation effects how political influences can realistically engage in workable legal strategies that manage such a problem. As a result of an ill-defined context, the argument for intellectual property protection frustrates itself because it fails to clarify the purpose of employing intellectual property law. This creates a conflict for intellectual property law that arises for two reasons: firstly there is a mixed narrative of what realistically intellectual property is for and can achieve; and, secondly there is an expectation that it should be modified to accommodate the different interests of indigenous actors.[31] Thus intellectual property is imagined as a necessary mechanism that has the scope to respond to historical power imbalances in colonial relations, even though it doesn't even acknowledge its role within that very history.

Part of the tension between historical exclusion and later inclusion of indigenous interests within law specifically, comes from the (re)figuring of culture.[32] In Australia, like elsewhere, projects of Empire set culturally specific ways for understanding indigenous peoples.[33] Indigenous people were brought into the predominately European gaze through those early endeavours. Key philosophical traditions also helped shape what was being seen, and what was being understood about those peoples.[34] For example, romanticism helped make the noble savage, and it is significant for our current situation that subjectivity and practice were aligned more naturally with nature, than with 'culture'. Indigenous people were valued because of perceived associations with nature, but devalued within other contexts such science, progress and human improvement. Indigenous art wasn't even understood as 'art' until late in the twentieth century. Whilst knowledge that was garnered from indigenous people was incorporated into the scientific vision of the world, indigenous experiences remained 'other' to that vision.

The reality, of course, is that indigenous people were not 'fully' excluded from earlier colonial projects. But inclusion did have very specific parameters, and these included the frameworks for participation and recognition, as well as a very limited sense of freedom, subjectivity, choice and citizenry. So from our initial point of departure for projects that now 'include' indigenous needs within the intellectual property framework we are not working with very clear demarcations of the exclusion/inclusion of the indigenous subject. However, the early problem with aligning indigenous people with nature makes the current reliance and reification of indigenous 'culture', all the more difficult to deal with.

As has already been discussed at earlier points of this work, law doesn't address the exclusion, and latterly inclusion of indigenous interest by considering its own role in colonial projects. This prompts the question: how does the indigenous get recognised as a subject deserving inclusion at all?

In part, indigenous issues are firstly rendered visible by expert knowledges, much more than through their own agency and articulation.[35] But the making of such visibility draws again from the same early colonial knowledge in order to justify the inclusion, whilst also emphasising a newly respected difference. Here the reification of (indigenous as) culture is of another order. For it is so tightly bound to conceptions of difference. The romantic appeal to natural, original existence also helps feed law's current fixation with indigenous culture's apparent static 'boundedness'. As already discussed, even WIPO for example, deals with 'culture' by isolating it as a peculiar indigenous trait.

Endless new categories and subsets are being created in order to accurately capture the difference. Yet in the constantly mutating categories, indigenous knowledge and indigenous people remain tied to a distinct, if not also unitary, heritage. Indigenous people as 'traditional knowledge holders' are imagined as existing somewhere outside modernity as they 'create, originate, develop and practice traditional knowledge in a traditional setting and context'.[36] This invariably plays into perceptions of indigenous identity – from both indigenous and non-indigenous perspectives.

Tying indigenous experience with concerns for culture, tradition and the value of nature and land (and the sacred) permits a very limited consideration of economics and indigenous interests in new audiences and new markets. However, the very real fluidity and dynamism of any culture means that the ascribed classification will always be shown to be arbitrary and partial. One way that this problem is managed by bodies such as the WIPO is by framing the primary mandate over indigenous inclusion as one of collection of 'facts'. Here the facts superficially suggest their own authority and capacity to represent a more complex reality.[37] The functionalism of law, that is, the imperative of the legal inquiry itself, is the very reason why indigenous culture is created as a 'special' problem with its own category and subsets.

Further, commentators on the nature of indigenous knowledge always emphasise its collective character thus leading to the assertion that in an indigenous context, intellectual property rights must accommodate group rights.[38] The presentation is one of a zero/sum game. 'A particular deficiency of the existing copyright regime . . . has been the refusal of copyright courts to allow indigenous communities to enforce communal intellectual property rights in those cultural expressions'.[39] The lack of clarity in how to respond to differences between individual ownership and communal ownership (and the murky inbetween) has forced law to consider a world beyond its cultural borders. This has been enhanced by academic writing as well as the litigants themselves who insist on these issues being addressed.[40]

However, these representations of indigenous interests have also become synonymous with legal accommodation of communal rights. This familiar supposition warrants a little attention precisely because it has also generated troubling effects. For instance, Marilyn Strathern notes that group rights have become interpreted as cultural rights. She observes that,

> [w]hile fully cognisant of difficulties of assigning rights, advocates of IPR for indigenous peoples in resting their case on traditional knowledge rest it on collective possession. By conserving their cultural base, it is argued, people will have a core around which they will adapt for the future.[41]

But there is a circular argument here, communal rights are required to protect culture and culture becomes tantamount to the articulation of a communal identity, a whole way of life, provided through property rights. Where there is a neat fit with social circumstances there is no problem, but where communal identity has been fragmented through invasion, dispossession and the passage of time, a stable indigenous subject seems to fade from legal view. In order to develop flexible legal remedies, quite complicated cultural and social politics must be engaged. Is law equipped to do this?

Inescapably, in discussions about intellectual property and indigenous knowledge, 'culture' has come to occupy a central political position.[42] Concern for collective ownership, as a key characteristic of indigenous knowledge and hence representative of problems of protecting this subject matter, also functions as an identifier of difference. For collective ownership helps establish limits between what is understood to be indigenous knowledge and what isn't, what is understood to be indigenous culture and what isn't, what is within the competence of intellectual property law and what isn't.

Inevitably, discussions of collective ownership rely heavily upon a construction of 'community' and this raises corresponding concerns. As Frances Peters-Little explains,

> [t]he concept of community invokes notions of an idealized unity of purpose and action among social groups who are perceived to share a common culture. To some extent, 'community' and 'culture' are treated as synonymous, rather than principles operating at different levels of social realities. Indigenous culture is therefore seen to define Indigenous community. This, of course, is not so.[43]

One of the most obvious problems for the culture/community relationship is that community becomes the target of legal intervention. The institution of community (one not only experienced as peculiarly indigenous – other liberal strategies of governing target the 'community') as Nikolas Rose has persuasively argued, becomes 'a sector brought into existence whose vectors and forces can be mobilised, enrolled, deployed in novel programmes and techniques which encourage and harness active practices of self-management and identity construction, of personal ethics and collective allegiances'.[44] 'Government through community' means that a range of new techniques of understanding indigenous interests, and morphing them into a special category named as 'indigenous' is possible. But this is at the expense of appreciating indigenous subjectivity and expectations of intellectual property law, and of course provides little room for those indigenous people who do not identify directly with a 'community'.[45] Moreover, as community is not a stable concept, it also becomes a very difficult conceptual base upon which legal remedies are to be developed. This observation will be expanded in the following chapter, when discussion will turn to the latest Australian government endeavour to deal with collective indigenous interests in copyright law – *communal* moral rights.

Political differences experienced at a local, regional or even at a national level are seldom articulated within the Australian discourse on intellectual property. For instance, what might be a workable strategy in one community or region of Australia is often inappropriate for another.[46] This can be due to differing social, cultural and/or economic circumstances, infrastructure, alternative interpretations of the issue and challenges in terms of representation. Whilst national legislation cannot necessarily be attuned to site and locale differences, it is nevertheless ironic that it is precisely these differences, which in themselves are highly political, that will undermine the affectivity of legislative strategies relating to indigenous people. As I shall discuss presently, the 'Labels of Authenticity' and the introduction of specific communal moral rights legislation explicitly illustrate how these problems of political differentiation, if noticed at all, are enhanced by the pervading emphasis on indigenous sameness in developing solutions within intellectual property law. It is therefore not surprising that these problems of differentiation and the contextual politics that they generate remain noticeably absent from the international discourse as well.

THE PROBLEM WITH 'CULTURE'

The problem with 'culture', as it is used in reference to indigenous people and their interests in intellectual property law, is that it becomes an explanatory tool for difference. Through the emergence of claims to culture, as a discrete kind of object, the very concept has changed. As Benhabib explains:

> Culture has become. . . an identity marker and differentiator. Of course, culture has always been the mark of social distinction. What is novel is that groups now forming around such identity markers demand legal recognition and resource allocations from the state and its agencies to preserve their cultural specificities.[47]

In this sense, much contemporary politics today is an odd mixture of an anthropological view of the democratic equality of all cultural forms of expression, and the Romantic, Herderian emphasis on each forms irreducible uniqueness. Whether in politics or in policy, in courts or the media, one assumes that each human group 'has' some kind of 'culture' and that the boundaries between these groups and the contours of their cultures are specifiable and relatively easy to depict.[48]

From the specific moment of identifying an indigenous subject within intellectual property, complete with unique needs and expectations, indigenous people's cultures are reified as wholly separate entities. Overemphasising the boundedness and distinctiveness of all indigenous peoples risks omission of the internal heterogeneity of cultures, to the detriment of differences experienced within and between indigenous people and their communities. For law's interpretation of indigenous people in particular, culture and community become synonymous rather than concepts operating at different levels of social reality.[49] As Baxter emphasises: 'In placing a definition on what an Indigenous culture is' (and this is done from the UN, picked up throughout the international network and fed into more localised contexts) 'communities are forced to maintain a static entity containing the necessary attributes to retain the rights bestowed upon them as Indigenous'.[50] Irreducible uniqueness ironically enhances the contradictions of inclusion/exclusion within the indigenous knowledge category. For many, the constraining nature of this newly fashioned category of identity is too restrictive. It means that individuals and their work become classified in ways that engender specific meanings – that it is 'indigenous'. As discussed earlier in relation to the Aboriginal art marketplace of relations, Tracey Moffat is one Australian artist who seeks to transcend such restrictive elements in being labelled as only an 'indigenous artist'. Gordon Bennett is another.[51]

Interpretation of indigenous knowledge in intellectual property law is dependent upon a specific construction of 'indigenous as culture'. This is in relation to how indigenous knowledge is conceived but, importantly, also differentiated within a legal discourse. In Australia, like elsewhere, there has been a tendency to imagine indigenous 'culture' in its singularity despite the myriad of experiences integral to knowledge and cultural production.[52] This means that indigenous issues relating to intellectual property are conceived as being relatively the same – that is different from standard intellectual property issues but the same in their identification as 'indigenous'. There is little space for differentiation within the 'indigenous' category. As Helliwell and Hindess have observed:

> concepts denoting unities that are both ideational and systematic serve the dual role of inscribing ideational *sameness* within a population, and *difference* between one population and another . . . [however] a stress on sameness or homogeneity is at the expense of the recognition of the disorder that can also be observed within a society or culture, and of the ideational diversity pertaining between its members.[53]

Whilst the community versus individual binary may appear to establish a starting point in considering the inclusion of indigenous interests within the intellectual property discourse, it actually diverts attention away from the inherent social and cultural complications informing the law. When the problem becomes presented as one of clear sociological and ontological otherness, inevitably there is a failure to account for those indigenous people who do not necessarily identify with distinct communities. There is a failure to consider the internal politics that confounds identification of the spatial unit that could be named as a 'community'. The focus on community versus individual ownership as the loci of the intellectual property and indigenous knowledge problematic relegates the diverse dynamics and relationships of control and ownership over knowledge within indigenous social and political contexts to the margins. It excludes recognition of indigenous people as 'individual' owners and at the same time it removes interrogation of the laws' own processes of categorisation, identification and marginalisation.

As a primary site where the reductionist sociology of culture makes a significant impact on what indigenous interests are considered to be, and how they are expected to be addressed, intellectual property law has, so far, provided little room to move and gives little ground. New possibilities for regulatory frameworks need more considered attention, not only to what they comprise but also the effects of new kinds of codifications, classifications and legislation. Law is not benign. It exerts a range of effects upon how we relate in the world, what kind of frameworks are privileged over others as well as how identities are shaped and experienced. As the ground upon which intellectual property seeks to tread is actually a fault line of significant proportions that involves colonial conflict, politics, power, economics and histories of human relationships, all of which are minimised or omitted from laws' account of itself, to what extent can this body of law offer emancipatory potential for indigenous interests?

NOTES

1. J. Clifford, *The Predicament of Culture: Twentieth Century Ethnography, Literature and Art,* Harvard, University Press: Cambridge MA, 1988.
2. M. Brown, *Who Owns Native Culture?*, Harvard University Press: Cambridge MA, 2004 at 8.
3. 'A first cause of the differences in treatment of intellectual property is that forms of property ownership in these societies are different. Many indigenous societies are not organized around individuals as such but around a clan or other extended unit.' R. Gana, 'Has Creativity Died in the Third World? Some Implications for the Internationalization of Intellectual Property', (1995) 24 (1) *Denv. J. Int'l. L. & Pol'y* 109 at 132.
4. J. Anderson, 'Access and Control of Indigenous Knowledge in Libraries and Archives: Ownership and Future Use', American Library Association and The MacArthur Foundation, Columbia University, New York, May 5–7, 2005.
5. See for example: R. Williams, *The Long Revolution*, Penguin Books: Harmondsworth, London, 1965; R. Williams, *Keywords: A Vocabulary of Culture and Society*, Fontana/Croom Helm: London, 1976; E. Said, *Orientalism*, Penguin Books: London, 1985; T. Bennett, *Culture: A Reformer's Science*, Allen and Unwin: Sydney, 1998; N. Dirks, G. Eley and S. Ortner (eds), *Culture/Power/History: A Reader in Contemporary Social Theory*, Princeton University Press: Princeton, New Jersey, 1994.
6. See: H. Bhabha, *The Location of Culture*, Routledge: London and New York, 2004.
7. J. Clifford, *The Predicament of Culture: Twentieth Century Ethnography, Literature and Art*, supra n.1 at 10.
8. See: R. Williams key works: *Culture and Society 1780–1950*, Penguin Books: Harmondsworth, London, 1963; *The Long Revolution*, Penguin Books: Harmondsworth, London, 1965; *Politics and Letters*, New Left Books: London, 1979; *The Politics of Modernism: Against the New Conformists*, Verso: London, 1989.
9. R. Williams, *Keywords: A Vocabulary of Culture and Society*, supra n.5 at 87.
10. See in M. Arnold, *Culture and Anarchy: An Essay in Social and Political Criticism*, Bobbs-Merrill: Indianapolis and New York, 1971. See also: E. Gellner, *Culture, Identity and Politics*, Cambridge University Press: Cambridge, 1987.
11. R. Williams, *The Long Revolution*, supra n.5 at 41.
12. I. Hunter, 'Aesthetics and Cultural Studies' in Grossberg, L., C. Nelson, P. Treichler (eds), *Cultural Studies*, Routledge: New York and London, 1992.
13. For a good discussion see: T. Bennett *Culture: A Reformer's Science*, Allen and Unwin: Sydney, 1998.
14. See for instance: B. Cohn, *Colonialism and its Forms of Knowledge: The British in India*, Princetown University Press: New Jersey, 1996; E. Said, *Orientalism*, Penguin Books: London, 1985; N. Dirks, *Castes of Mind: Colonialism and the Making of Modern India*, Princeton University Press: Princeton, 2001 and; M. Heidegger, *Being and Time*, Basil Blackwell: Oxford, 1962; H. Arendt, *The Human Condition*, University of Chicago Press: Chicago and London, 1958. J.L. Nancy, *The Experience of Freedom*, Stanford University Press: Stanford, 1993; J. Derrida, *Writing and Difference*, Routledge: London, 1993.
15. H. Caygill, 'Philosophy, Violence, Freedom' in *On Jean-Luc Nancy: The Sense of Philosophy*, Sheppard, D., S. Sparks and C. Thomas (eds), Routledge: London and New York, 1997; H. Arendt, *The Human Condition*, ibid. at 205.
16. B. Anderson, *Imagined Communities: Reflections on the Origins and Spread of Nationalism*, Verso Publishing: London, 1983. With critical attention to the term 'culture', more recently 'community' has come to circulate similar characteristics previously associated

with 'culture': that is 'community' has come to represent homogenous spatial structures. Arun Agrawal and Clark Gibson have drawn attention to the growing body of work that emphasises the 'wholeness' of communities. Agrawal and Gibson argue that it is essential for initiatives involving communities to recognise the multiple interests and actors within communities and how 'these actors influence decision making and the internal and external institutions that shape the decision making process.' A. Agrawal and C.C. Gibson, 'The Role of Community in Natural Resource Conservation', Gibson, C., M. McKean, E. Ostrom (eds), *People and Forests: Communities, Institutions and Governance*, Massachusetts Institute of Technology: Massachusetts, 2000 at 2.

17. As Ziff and Rao have suggested, 'the term culture is as indeterminate as any within the social sciences. It therefore cannot be relied upon to set clear limits'. B. Ziff and P. Rao, 'Introduction to Cultural Appropriation' in Ziff, B., and P.V. Rao (eds), *Borrowed Power: Essays on Cultural Appropriation,* Rutgers University Press: New Jersey, 1997 at 2.
18. M. Brown, 'Can Culture be Copyrighted?', (1998) 39 (2) *Current Anthropology* 193 at 197.
19. In Australia, three cases illustrate the difficulty in determining what is, and what is not, cultural appropriation. These also hint at the complexity of regulating representations of Aboriginality in fiction and art. See for instance: Marlo Morgan's book (*Mutant Message Down Under,* Harper Collins: New York, 1995) where she records a meeting with the last (and lost) Aboriginal tribe and is initiated into the tribe revealing tribal 'secrets' of the Dreamtime in the (fiction) book; Elizabeth Durack painting as an Aboriginal man named Eddie Burrup and winning the prestigious Telstra Indigenous Art Award, ('Male Aboriginal artist turns out to be woman with Irish descent' *Australian Associated Press*, 7 March 1997); and Satchi Amyettere arguing Arrente cultural identity and painting a church in 'Aboriginal' styles and adopting an Aboriginal name. These instances were widely reported in the Australian media. Stephen Gray considers these three cases in more detail in his article, 'Black, White or Beyond the Pale: The Authenticity Debate and Protection for Aboriginal Culture', (2001) 15 *The Australian Feminist Law Journal* 105. See also: Fred Myers, *Painting Culture: The Making of an Aboriginal High Art*, Duke University Press: Durham and New York 2003 at 330–336.
20. See a consideration in: L. Lippard, *Mixed Blessings: New Art in Multicultural America*, Pantheon Books, New York, 1990; C. Nicholls, *From Appreciation to Appropriation: Indigenous Influences and Images in Australian Visual Art Exhibition Catalogue*, March 2000. See also: H. Fourmile, 'Some Background to Issues Concerning the Appropriation of Aboriginal Imagery', in Cramer, S. (ed), *Postmodernism: A Consideration of the Appropriation of Aboriginal Imagery: Forum Papers*, Institute of Modern Art, Brisbane, 1989; H. Fourmile, 'The Aboriginal Art Market and the Repatriation of Aboriginal Cultural Property', (1989) 8 (1) *Social Alternatives* 19; H. Fourmile, 'Cultural Survival v Cultural Prostitution', Paper presented at the Cultural Tourism Awareness Workshop, Cairns, Queensland, 1993; L. Behrendt, 'In Your Dreams: Cultural Appropriation, Popular Culture and Colonialism', (1998) 4 (1) *Law, Text, Culture* 256.
21. See generally: S. Cramer (ed), *Postmodernism: A Consideration of the Appropriation of Aboriginal Imagery: Forum Papers, Institute of Modern Art*, Brisbane, 1989.
22. For another discussions of the tensions between cultural appropriation and law see: S.E. Merry, Tenth Anniversary Symposium: New Direction: 'Law Culture and Cultural Appropriation', (1998) 10 *Yale Journal of Law and the Humanities* 575.
23. A. Stoler, *Race and the Education of Desire: Foucault's* History of Sexuality *and the Colonial Order of Things*, Duke University Press: Durham and London, 1995 at 199.
24. M. Morris, 'Tooth and Claw: Tales of Survival and *Crocodile Dundee*', (1987) 25 *Art and Text* 267.
25. Ibid., at 267.
26. There are a range of intersections between debates on tangible cultural property and intangible cultural property. For instance, the making of the problem and then its articulation in law and through international bureaucracies is just one similarity. The production of the tangible cultural property discourse could be unpacked in the same

way as this undertaking on the intangible. At the moment, this remains another project, and is not engaged in this discussion.

27. Remembering the importance of loss and its measurement, both in early intellectual property law (Part One, Chapter 2) and in the Aboriginal art and copyright cases (Part Two, Chapter 3).
28. See for example: T. Janke, *Our Culture, Our Future: Report on Australian Indigenous Cultural and Intellectual Property Rights* (prepared for Australian Institute of Aboriginal and Torres Strait Islander Studies [AIATSIS] and Aboriginal and Torres Strait Islander Commission [ATSIC]), Michael Frankel and Company Solicitors: Surry Hills, Sydney, 1998.
29. P. O'Malley, *Law, Capitalism and Democracy*, Allen and Unwin: Sydney, 1983 at 104.
30. See: J. McKeough and A. Stewart, 'Intellectual Property and the Dreaming' in Johnstone, E., M. Hinton and D. Rigney (eds), *Indigenous Australians and the Law*, Cavendish: Sydney, 1996; M. Blakeney, 'Protecting the cultural Expressions of Indigenous Peoples under Intellectual Property Law – the Australian Experience', in Grosheide, F.W., and J.J. Brinkhof (eds), *Intellectual Property Law 2002: The Legal Protection of Cultural Expressions and Indigenous Knowledge*, Intersentia Publishers: Antwerp, Oxford, New York, 2002; T. Davies, 'Aboriginal Cultural Property?', (1996) 14 (2) *Law in Context* 1; K. Bowrey, 'The Outer Limits of Copyright Law – Where Law Meets Philosophy and Culture', (2001) 12 *Law and Critique* 75.
31. There is an assumption that indigenous people require a 'wholly different' structure of the law. This misunderstands the divergent histories and experiences of indigenous peoples within Australia and throughout the world.
32. The following discussion draws from J. Anderson and K. Bowrey, 'The Imaginary Politics of Access to Knowledge: Whose Cultural Agendas are Being Advanced?', *Con/Texts of Invention: Creative Production in Legal and Cultural Perspective*, Case Western Reserve University, Ohio, 20–23 April 2006.
33. See: T. Bennett, *Pasts Beyond Memory: Evolution, Museums, Colonialism*, Routledge: London and New York, 2004; T. Bennett, 'Exhibition, difference and the logic of culture' in I. Karp and C. Kratz (eds) *Museum Frictions: Public Cultures/Global Transformations*, Duke University Press: Durham, North Carolina, 2006; T. Mitchell, *Colonizing Egypt*, University of California Press: Berkeley, 1988.
34. Silvia Sebastiani considers the manifold ways in which race and gender were considered by key thinkers of the Scottish Enlightenment. See: S. Sebastiani, ''Race', Women and Progress in the Scottish Enlightenment' in Knott, S. and B. Taylor (eds) *Women, Gender and the Enlightenment*, Palgrave Macmillan: London, 2005.
35. In the Aboriginal art and copyright cases in Australia, expert evidence was fundamental to explaining indigenous artistry to the Court. Indigenous perspectives were incorporated, but these were treated as 'background' material rather than 'facts' which were supplied through 'experts'.
36. World Intellectual Property Organisation, *Intellectual Property Needs and Expectations of Traditional Knowledge Holders: WIPO Report on Fact Finding Missions on Intellectual Property and Traditional Knowledge, 1998–1999,* Geneva, 2001 at 26.
37. M. Poovey, *A History of the Modern Fact: Problems of Knowledge in the Sciences of Wealth and Society*, Chicago University Press: Chicago, 1998.
38. As Silke von Lewinski explains: 'In general the main obstacles to copyright protection of folklore are grounded in the fact that copyright protection is based on an individualistic concept as opposed to a collective one.' S. von Lewinski, 'The Protection of Folklore', (2003) 11 *Cardozo Journal of International and Comparative Law* 747 at 757.
39. M. Blakeney, 'Protecting the Cultural Expressions of Indigenous Peoples under Intellectual Property Law – The Australian Experience' above n.30 at 152.
40. In particular see comments by G. Gumana, Y. Wunungmura and B. Marika in Eatock, C. and K. Mordaunt, *Copyrites*, Australian Film Finance Corporation Limited, 1997.
41. M. Strathern, *Property, Substance and Effect: Anthropological Essays in Persons and Things*, The Athlone Press: London, 1999 at 168.
42. For instance see: M. Sunder, 'Intellectual Property and Identity Politics: Playing with

Fire', (2000) 4 (1) *Journal of Gender, Race and Justice* 69; M. Brown, *Who Owns Native Culture?*, Harvard University Press: Cambridge MA, 2003; M. Brown, 'Can Culture be Copyrighted?', (1998) 39 (2) *Current Anthropology* 193; S. Greene, 'Indigenous People Incorporated? Culture as Politics, Culture as Property in Pharmaceutical Bioprospecting', (2004) 45 (2) *Cultural Anthropology* 211.

43. F. Peters-Little, 'The Community Game: Aboriginal Self Definition at a Local Level', (1998) 10 *AIATSIS Research Discussion Paper* 1 at 4.
44. N. Rose, *Powers of Freedom: Reframing Political Thought*, Cambridge University Press: Cambridge, 1999, at 176.
45. Indeed the contests that can arise around who is and who isn't a member of a community are often conveniently ignored – the contests are not understood as an inevitable effect of the category but as an altogether separate issue.
46. Debates about the best way of managing alcohol consumption in Aboriginal communities illustrates the multiple strategies that must be engaged – and that a 'one fix' solution is inappropriate.
47. S. Benhabib, *The Claims of Culture: Equality and Diversity in the Global Era*, Princeton University Press: Princeton, 2002 at 1.
48. Ibid., at 4.
49. F. Peters-Little, 'The Community Game: Aboriginal Self Definition at a Local Level', supra n.43.
50. J.E. Baxter, 'Commentary on "Fear, Hope and Longing for the Future of Authorship and Revitalized Public Domain in Global Regimes of Intellectual Property"', (2003) 52 *DePaul Law Review* 1235 at 1237.
51. As Gordon Bennett has explained: 'I didn't go to art college to graduate as an "Aboriginal Artist". I did want to explore my Aboriginality, however, and it is a subject of my work as much as colonialism and the narratives and language that frame it, and the language that has consistently framed me. Acutely aware of the frame, I graduated as a straight honours student . . . to find myself positioned and contained by the language of "primitivism" as an "Urban Aboriginal Artist".' G. Bennett, 'The Manifest Toe' in McLean, I., and G. Bennett, *The Art of Gordon Bennett*, Craftsman House: Australia, 1996 at 58.
52. See also: Wright, S., 'Intellectual Property and the "Imaginary Aboriginal"' in Bird, G., G. Martin and J. Neilson (eds), *Majah: Indigenous Peoples and the Law*, The Federation Press: Sydney, 1996; J. R. Bowen, 'Should We Have a Universal Concept of "Indigenous Peoples' Rights"? Ethnicity and Essentialism in the Twenty First Century', (2000) 16 (4) *Anthropology Today* 12.
53. C. Helliwell and B. Hindess, '"Culture", "Society" and the Figure of Man', (1999) 12 (4) *History of the Human Sciences*, 1 at 2.

10. Community and culture/community claims

In Australia, two initiatives have been developed in order to work towards accommodating indigenous interests in intellectual property. They are the Labels of Authenticity and more recently the (draft) Communal Moral Rights legislation. Both potentially position Australia at the forefront internationally in terms of developing alternatives in response to indigenous requests for legal action. Importantly, they seek to enhance existing parts of current law: trademark law to help with relations with the art market, and moral rights as commensurate (in an odd way) with community rights within a derived work (communal moral rights).

The goodwill behind these initiatives can be taken at face value. There is a legitimate effort on behalf of policy makers and legislative drafters to address indigenous concerns. These are also governmental responses to broader social pressures that demand that indigenous issues be addressed – for instance, I have never come across any literature, academic or otherwise that argues *against* indigenous interests in intellectual property. These attempts should be seen as innovative: they really do try and tackle a difficult problem and provide remedy through the law. But certain difficult legacies remain, and these are implicitly contained within each initiative. They are evidenced in the very naming of the initiatives 'authenticity marks', 'communal moral rights', through to the inevitable effects of certain kinds of legal codification (the presumption of community as a stable legal object for example) and their accessibility and applicability to indigenous circumstance.

THE LABELS OF AUTHENTICITY

There are a variety of models of authenticity that circulate contemporary debate. However, in the context of Aboriginal art, authenticity is tightly tied to both originality and tradition (and primitivism).[1] In general terms this means that an Aboriginal artwork is not considered to be authentic if it is not an original work derived from an Aboriginal tradition. Unlike the dependency between originality and authorship, which is also upheld in copyright statutes, an original and authentic Aboriginal artwork is dependent upon a marker of tradition before it is dependent upon the author.[2] As Stephen Gray has noted, '[n]on-Aboriginal law's fixation upon "traditionality" as the condition for determining which Aboriginal laws are capable of recognition is merely one symptom of a wider societal fixation upon the "traditional" or "authentic" Aboriginal person'.[3] Indeed, the pervasive emphasis on the 'authentic' elements of indigenous art and culture has functioned to the detriment of much contemporary indigenous art practice.

Given the entwined relationships between tradition, originality and authenticity within the context of Aboriginal art, it is thus curious that the key innovative idea developed to protect indigenous artistry within the market, the Labels of Authenticity[4], were not exposed to a more nuanced critique in regards to what kind of art they were, in fact, authenticating. Moreover, there was an assumption, at least on behalf of the bureaucrats behind the Labels, that all Aboriginal artists would embrace this national labelling system (and thus render it effective). Initial success gave way to a range of destablising issues that seemed somehow inevitable. What happened to the Labels remains an important lesson in assuming pan-Aboriginality: the presumed singularity of Aboriginal culture breaks apart in the reality of distinct contextual artistic practice. It also points to the complicated political aims and ambitions of indigenous organisations based in capital cities vis-à-vis the needs of indigenous communities based in more regional and remote areas.

The Labels of Authenticity were suggested as a legislative response in regards to the growing level of copying of Aboriginal style motifs and designs and the notable increase in reproductions of Aboriginal art circulating in tourist shops and markets, popularly described as the x-ray koala trade.[5] As a differential to copyright, which is more concerned with issues of production, the Labels of Authenticity were suggested as certification marks utilising trademark law. Trademark law is the marketing end of intellectual property law and consists of a sign or logo which is used to distinguish the commercial 'origin' of goods and services.

The Labels of Authenticity were specifically suggested as a labelling system 'to promote and market the *origin* and *authorship* of indigenous cultural products'.[6] As the Report *Our Culture: Our Future* explains,[7]

> A proposal raised in the early 1980s was to develop a national Indigenous 'authenticity trademark'. The idea is that an authentication mark would be reproduced on labels attached to *authentically produced Indigenous arts and cultural products*. The labels would help consumers identify genuine Indigenous arts and cultural products. This would hopefully encourage retailers to stock the products which have the labels, which would in turn benefit Indigenous artists.[8]

In Australian law trademarks require registration. A consequent to registration is that there is also clarity about the meanings of words certifying the purpose of the marks. The problem of legal definition comes back to haunt in very important ways. In this case, the primary word requiring definitional certainty was 'authentic': there needed to be a clear sense of what an 'authentic' Aboriginal cultural product was, and how it could be identified. This subsequently led to the National Indigenous Arts Advocacy Association (NIAAA) conducting research into how to define and identify such products.[9] Research conducted by Kathryn Wells suggested that for indigenous people in communities, 'authenticity' related to indigenous identity, belonging, knowledge, respect and responsibility.[10] It did not necessarily correspond with legal interpretations, namely individual authorship. Nor did it necessarily correspond with how the market had come to understand an authentic Aboriginal product: which was in reference to the 'truthfulness' of its origination in tradition.

The key problems with the Labels of Authenticity that ultimately contributed to their demise as an idea and a practical tool, relate to three areas. Firstly, the term 'authentic' resonated with a past romanticism utilised to identify indigenous people. In defining authenticity, it was difficult to escape historically informing categorisation and constructions of 'Aboriginality' that remained as remnant markers in the art world. This was most evident in the way that many Aboriginal artists, often utilising non-traditional styles and mediums, refused to be part of a national Aboriginal labelling system. Secondly, the Labels offered an overarching umbrella term that would refer to indigenous peoples' cultural products nation wide. As a consequence there was little room for an appreciation of indigenous individual, family, clan or community and/or cultural diversity within the Labels. There was legitimate perception that the Labels further homogenised indigenous cultural identity into a position of sameness for bureaucratic ease. As Brenda Croft, a foremost curator of Aboriginal art at the National Gallery of Australia, explained:

> With the greatest respect for NIAAA's intentions, I feel that an aspect of the Label of Authenticity is reminiscent of the old 'Dog Tag' system . . . As it currently stands, NIAAA's position on the Label is that the entire Indigenous visual arts/cultural industry requires a blanket approach.[11]

Additionally, certain indigenous communities already had their own identification marks, indicating the regional specificity and regional identity of the cultural products. These communities, for instance those on both Melville and Bathurst Islands (the Tiwi Islands), and the Ngaantjatjara, Pitjantjatjara, Yankantjatjara Women's Cooperative in Central Australia, already had their own unique style of labelling that associated the label with the place of origin of the work. Within communities themselves, there was concern that the Labels were being imposed by bureaucrats in the eastern cities, without involvement or input from the diverse northern Australian indigenous communities.

The third problem was practical – who was to certify, distribute, regulate and police the Labels?

In an article explaining the purpose of the Labels, Leanne Wiseman identified the implicit complexities that remained as serious hurdles to overcome;

> The attempt to define authenticity with respect to Indigenous goods and services raises a number of complex issues. One issue that arises is how the notion of authenticity will relate to 'traditional' Indigenous art. Here the concern is that there is a tendency to see Aboriginal art that employs traditional techniques, materials and imagery, such as well known dot paintings, as if it alone were authentically Aboriginal. To see Aboriginal art in these terms does many artists a disservice and also reinforces public misconceptions about Aboriginal art. For urban and non-traditional artists, the way authenticity is defined raises the problem that they may be stigmatised for not being 'real' or 'authentic' Aboriginal artists.[12]

Certainly the labels represent a pragmatic approach and there remains a need for the market to differentiate genuine Aboriginal products from the fakes. Consumers themselves are demanding this. Nevertheless, the complexities that Wiseman identifies were always going to undermine the capacity for success and practical engagement with the Labels as a pan-Aboriginal strategy promoting 'authenticity'.

It is possible that ultimately the complexity and fluidity of indigenous subjectivity was a key element that undermined the success of the Labels – as they are no longer in operation.[13] At one level, the Labels endorsed a particular and partial version of Aboriginality that complimented the market and the styles of Aboriginal art that dominated the market – for instance more traditionally recognised raark bark paintings from Arnhem Land and 'dot' style art from Central Australia. However, many Aboriginal artists had nothing to gain by using the Labels, as they predominately sat astride the 'traditionalised' and marketable constructions feeding the demand for Aboriginal art. Questions were also raised about 'quality control': for example who was judging and overseeing the quality of the art (and the Aboriginality of the artists) being granted Labels. An additional bureaucratic problem, which signalled the demise of the Labels practically, was that the body designed to oversee their administration, the National Indigenous Arts Advocacy Association (NIAAA), was stripped of funding by both the Department of Communication, Information Technology and the Arts and the then Aboriginal and Torres Strait Islander Commission (ATSIC) because of allegations relating to significant misappropriated funds.

On reflection it is always easier to point to the shortcomings of the Labels. But the current localised success of community labelling perhaps points to a way forward. Cultural identity, respect and responsibility, the key elements that Wells identified as what certain communities interpreted authenticity to be, can be delivered when each community is given certain tools to choose for themselves how the artists within the community are to be represented to the market. For many artists within communities, it is the association with familial relationships as well as the community itself that is fundamental to identity, respect and responsibility. Shifting these to an amorphous category named 'Aboriginal' was never going to work where people have (to say the least) pride and responsibility to the familial networks, clan relations, the broader community and importantly the land. As these localised systems of labelling remain in operation, it may be useful to give these re-invigorated support and to watch carefully to see how they are negotiated and developed, and how they are working for the artists, families and communities involved, as well as for consumers. Not having an overarching Label makes for a headache in policing and administrative terms, but there are legitimate questions as to how effective this would have been anyway. Instead, it is worth recognising that locally developed labels already have forms of regulation, and these conform to regulatory standards in operation within the communities themselves. Invigorating local decision-making capacity and determination around locally developed artistic practice should be a priority. After all, the artists, the representatives in art centres and members of local governing councils often have a comprehensive grasp of what is occurring in relation to artistic practice within their own context. With the increasing use of digital technology – they are also in a much better position to identify and locate instances of appropriation of styles or stories. Art centres and artistic communities need support when they identify instances of appropriation. Such support at a local level sends a clear message about who is listening to whom. This approach has the capacity to demonstrate that an individuated community does have a legitimate voice and as such can exercise control over the production and circulation of its cultural knowledge products.

Certainly the Labels of Authenticity provided a further means for the law to be seen as capable and responsive. It is interesting however, that the ultimate demise of the Labels is not really seen as a failure of the law – it is more a cultural and funding problem. Indigenous difference, in this instance within and between communities, clans, families and individuals, emerges as the feature characterising the failure of the Labels: an ironic twist given that the effort to provide practical legal mechanisms rendered silent the diversity of indigenous interests and positions. Whilst the intention is to be applauded, the failure of the tactic should also be understood for what it is, and that these same problems, unless approached differently, will inhibit future attempts to find lateral solutions in law by using the fuzzy margins.

COMMUNAL MORAL RIGHTS

With these concerns in relation to the Labels in mind, it is time to move onto a consideration of a more recent development in Australia – that of the draft *Copyright Amendment (Indigenous Communal Moral Rights) Bill* 2003. The Bill presents an opportunity to explore the disjuncture between broader discourses of indigenous intellectual property rights and the local political context where aspirations of reform circulate.

Specifically, the draft Bill has been posited as a solution to the issue of community ownership.[14] However, drawing from the Australian context, the emphasis on 'community' and communal ownership presents considerable difficulties for the utility of this approach. Simply put, the differing needs, articulations, political representations and definitions of Aboriginal 'communities' within Australia seriously compromises a singular legislative solution to the issue of community rights. Indeed this raises important questions about how indigenous peoples' needs have been constructed and are represented, and how these influence national and international attention to developing strategic approaches for protecting indigenous knowledge through intellectual property law.

Earlier in Part Two, it was argued that whilst there was some accommodation made for communal rights within the case law (the Bulun Bulun case) these were not really within the purview of copyright law.[15] For instance, the community's interest was only recognised via equity, thus skirting around the issue of ownership and the economic and other rights enjoyed by copyright owners. As Kathy Bowrey notes:

> Here equity was used to ameliorate the harshness of the current definition of joint-ownership. Justice can be seen to be done, although given the circuitous mechanism provided for binding third parties, its practical application might be quite limited. The redress to equity for justice relegates the issue of indigenous intellectual property claims to the category of unexpected personal problems, at least until there is appropriate legislative action. That equity can offer some solace reinforces the assumption that no major reform of copyright law is necessary.[16]

In her analysis, Bowrey makes note of how the case illustrated the cultural politics of law and how law justifies its own competence to manage the field. I would add to this by suggesting that the case set the parameters for the localisation of difference, isolating the 'indigenous' interest in terms of the one indigenous group – the Ganalbingu people. That the issue has been extended from one indigenous community to all illustrates the presumption of indigenous sameness, and conversely, difference in relation to intellectual property law. To this end the case has had a significant impact in consolidating what was understood as a key expectation of intellectual property law held by indigenous people: the ownership rights of the community. But it is the presumption of the *stability* of 'community' that presents the fundamental problem for developing any legislative strategy addressing communal ownership.

Towards the end of the 1999 parliamentary debate on Australia's introduction of a Moral Rights Bill, as an amendment of the Copyright Act, Senator Aden Ridgeway introduced the proposal that indigenous communities should be provided with special communal moral rights within the legislation. Whilst this proposition was rejected (explained as bad timing – the Parliament not having sufficient time to consider and debate the proposal), the Government did signal (and continues to reiterate) its commitment to developing a (regulatory) framework that would recognise the communal rights of indigenous people within law.[17]

In 2001, the Government's pre-election arts policy *Arts for All* this commitment was reiterated:

> The Coalition will take steps to protect the unique cultural interests of Indigenous communities and the cultural works that draw upon communal knowledge in conjunction with relevant Indigenous arts groups and ATSIC. Amendments to the moral rights regime will give Indigenous communities a means to prevent unauthorised and derogatory treatment of works that embody community images or knowledge.[18]

In a joint media release of May 2003 it was further stated that:

> Indigenous communities will be able to take legal action to protect against inappropriate, derogatory or culturally insensitive use of copyright material under new legislation proposed by the Government. Amendments to the Copyright Act, to be introduced into Parliament later this year (2003) will give Indigenous communities legal standing to safeguard the integrity of creative works embodying community knowledge and wisdom.[19]

In mid December 2003 copies of the draft *Copyright Amendment (Indigenous Communal Moral Rights) Bill* 2003 were distributed to several organisations and one nominated individual for comment.[20] Australia again showed itself as a key player in developing innovative provisions for the incorporation of indigenous rights within the frameworks provided by intellectual property. The Attorney-General, Philip Ruddock, explained how copyright law extended beyond purely economic considerations, in that it could play a vital role in fostering and protecting 'our' indigenous and cultural heritage: significantly, 'the protection of Indigenous culture depends upon strong and effective copyright laws'.[21]

It should be acknowledged at the outset that moral rights do not provide ownership rights *per se*. Nor do they provide economic rights. In Australian law they involve: the right of attribution of authorship;[22] the right not to have authorship of a work falsely attributed;[23] and, the right of integrity of authorship in a work attributed.[24] However, a general precondition is that 'only individuals have moral rights'.[25] The draft bill directly sought to expand the precondition of individual rights to include communal rights.

Unlike the automatic nature of moral rights for individual authors and creators, the draft Bill had five formal requirements that must be met before a community could claim an 'indigenous communal moral right'. Firstly (as per the existing moral rights legislation) there must be copyright subject matter – literary, dramatic, musical or artistic works and cinematograph films (sound recordings are excluded). Secondly, the work must draw on the particular body of traditions, observances, customs or beliefs held in common by the indigenous community. Thirdly, an agreement must be entered into between an indigenous community and the creator of the work (the copyright holder). This is a voluntary agreement, which could be oral in nature. The presumption here is that at the time of executing a work the individual artist would first attend to their legal affairs and formally consider the question of communal moral rights management, presumably in anticipation of commercial potential in the reproduction of the work. Since indigenous communal rights cannot exist without this agreement, the emphasis is on indigenous people and communities to initiate contact and negotiation with those interested parties. There is an implicit presumption that the community will know or will find out, possibly through the benevolence of the owner/creator, that the work is being created that draws upon that community's 'traditions, customs or practices'. Fourthly, there must be an acknowledgement of the indigenous community's association on or with the work. Finally, interested parties in the work need to have consented to the rights arising. There is no clarification of who constitutes an interest holder – and this consent must be provided through written notice. All of these requirements must be met before the first dealing (or first sale) of the work otherwise no rights arise.

CULT(URE) OF THE COMMUNAL OR A SOLUTION?

Besides it now being 2007 and there being reiterated statements by the Government that the Bill will be before Parliament this year, there is a peculiar politics at play here. It is worth exploring this a little before continuing into the discussion of the Bill itself. Aboriginal and Torres Strait Islander people as well as those who work in Aboriginal political contexts and Aboriginal organisations in Australia have over the last six years, experienced new kinds of racism from the current Australian government's approach to the administration of Aboriginal and Torres Strait Islander affairs. The effects have been profound and will continue for sometime.[26] When the draft Bill was initially circulated in December 2003, the key indigenous body for advising the Government on indigenous affairs, the Aboriginal and Torres Strait Islander Commission (ATSIC) still existed. In March of 2005 this body's twenty-year function was revoked.[27] This matters because ATSIC functioned as the central agency through which consultation about the development of new laws and policies that would affect indigenous people occurred. There is a ten member, government selected council as replacement.[28] What this means is that indigenous people are effectively excluded from participating in decisions about the appropriateness or otherwise of legislation that will directly target and affect social relationships. These are matters of political importance, but they create a vacuum in terms of indigenous people participating in their own governance. The limited discussion around problems that indigenous people might be directly qualified to identify (for instance difficulties in relation to accessing legal advice and brokering agreements with external parties) inevitably suggests that matters of practicality have been displaced in favour of abstracted legal functionalism.

The draft Bill is illustrative of the persisting conflict between modern social theory and positivist legal approaches to particular problems. There is a tendency in law-making communities to assume that the most important issues revolve around what the law says, rather than the effects of the law.[29] This is contrary to how academics and academic lawyers understand law and legal processes as significantly impacting upon people, societies and cultural production – and often reflecting quite specific agendas. For instance, the draft Bill represents its key terms, such as 'community', as unproblematic. This is despite the wide body of academic work that is engaged in analysing such concepts and importantly the broader implications of codifying such terms.[30] The draft Bill sits astride contemporary research on the ambiguity and metamorphosis of the notion of community – thus also remaining unconcerned with the inevitable social and cultural impact of legally imagined conditions of identification.

For critical legal scholars it is not easy to divorce the creation of a specific law from the application and practical utilisation of that law by those whom it is purportedly for. Thus practical questions must be raised, directed primarily at how this law would be used, who could access it and through what means. These are crucial questions that are integral to the development of solutions that are amenable to all stakeholders. Unfortunately the answers to these questions remain far from clear.

The Australian Institute of Aboriginal and Torres Strait Islander Studies provided substantive and technical comments on the draft Bill.[31] Recognising the potential impact on communities and those working in the Aboriginal arts sector alike, in the short period for responding (three weeks), the draft Bill was sent to as many regional Indigenous organisations and Land Councils as was possible in order to garner perspectives. There were limited responses because of the time period, and the lack of explanatory counsel. For those who did respond it was clear that there was confusion. Whilst many supported the basic idea behind the Bill, it was seriously compromised by the conditions under which a communal moral right would be recognised. For instance, it was unlikely that an indigenous community would be able to meet all the conditions necessary for the right to be recognised.

From 2004, there was an ironic secrecy about the new draft, with even fewer people being privy to its contents and revisions.[32] At a copyright symposium in Sydney in late 2006, the Attorney General again reiterated that the Bill would be presented to Parliament in 2007.[33] Junior legal officers are now in charge of the drafting and, through open conversations, appear very uncomfortable about the Bill. For not only have they never been in an Aboriginal community which therefore produces serious limitations in thinking about function and purpose of this new legislation, but they also appeared unsure about what the effects of the Bill would be. The imaginary Aboriginal community is everywhere apparent – particularly in bureaucracies. Unfortunately, the gulf between governmental imagination and reality is substantial. With few comments from Aboriginal and Torres Strait Islander people and/or communities and agencies being garnered, the utility and effectivity of the Bill appears somewhat compromised.

So besides questions of utility, what are the problems with the Bill? What is the matter with making Aboriginal community a legal object? Why is making a new law to remedy a complex social, cultural and economic problem never that simple? Why is it necessary to think about the effects of laws before we make them?

From a practical perspective, the presumption of action implicit in the draft Bill is that communities will enter formal agreements. This forgets difficulties of language access, legal translation and legal mediation. As the *Yumbulul* case (1991) aptly demonstrates, acknowledging and understanding contractual obligations can be a cause of substantial conflict between parties.[34] In this case, the key tension was between the Aboriginal artist, and the agency representing him. The artist claimed that he wasn't informed, and therefore didn't consent to the use of his artwork in the context of a new $10 note. The Aboriginal Agency argued that he had been informed several times and had consented on each occasion. It turned into a dispute about legal translation not copyright infringement, which the second party to the case, the Reserve Bank of Australia settled out of Court. With difficulties in simple service delivery for remote and rural communities, it is important to recognise the extent that accessing legal advice on copyright matters remains a substantial challenge for the communities that are the target of the draft Bill. There is no overarching framework to help in this process, and very few people working in communities and regional organisations who understand the intricacies of intellectual property in general or copyright in particular.

Broader critical questions concern presumptions made in the draft Bill that a 'community' – so defined – will follow the direction of the law. In presuming rational legal actors, law also presumes to know how communities will behave as legal subjects: for instance that the community will follow the directions set out in the communal moral rights bill. But with language issues, questions of translatability and legal mediation, the presumption of community behaviour seems to be at odds with the reality of legal subjectivity. Why would communities behave in rational and predictable ways before the law when individuals themselves do not? Moreover, this presumption of legal direction is problematic given the requirements that the community must reach – for instance the voluntary agreements.

This returns us to discussions about the intersections between law and culture – or, more specifically, the implications of cultural production in the shape that the law takes. The inevitable engagement of law with practical cultural functions or challenges is, in part, due to the difficulty of people as legal subjects who do not necessarily behave in a predictable manner for law or governance. Thus one of the difficulties for law is that it must constantly be dealing with the complexity of individuals and how they perform as legal subjects. For it is almost impossible to speculate upon the specificity of action undertaken by individuals as legal subjects. In short, there is no certainty in how individuals relate to the law, and this makes for complex legal subjects. These observations also hold when talking about indigenous communities, which are made up of individuals that the law enacts influence upon. But each community will act differently before the law – and also challenge law in terms of legal subjectivity, not only community subjectivity but also individual. As Peters-Little reflects 'Aboriginal people are individuals and need to be respected as such and not pressured into thinking that they are speaking on behalf of a race, community, organisation and doctrine, which I usually find is a relief for many'.[35]

Beyond these practical problems with the draft Bill, there are larger more substantial questions with legislating community rights. On one level these are obviously related to difficulties with definition and the inherent instability of 'community' as a legal object. On another level they concern the increasing tendency to deal with indigenous differences before the law, especially intellectual property law, in terms of community relief.[36] The rationale behind the draft Bill presumes there is no substantial problem in making 'community' a legal object. This is despite other areas of law being overrun by disputes about what constitutes a 'community'.

For instance in the native title Yorta Yorta case,[37] a fundamental tension revolved around whether the Yorta Yorta people were the *same* 'community' of people who had demonstrated continuity with customs and traditions that had survived British sovereignty.[38] In the case, which ran for ten years, native title and ownership of land was eventually denied to the Yorta Yorta claimants. The rationale for denying the Yorta Yorta people rights to their country was based heavily on the records of an early colonist. Because indigenous accounts of their own history and experience did not fit the framework established for justifying claims to land ownership, Yorta Yorta people were caught in a legal contest that, from the outset, privileged certain kinds of information, descriptions of community and sociality and historical narrative over others.[39]

Indeed native title law in Australia (itself an instance of *sui-generis* law) provides an excellent illustration of the difficulties in the codification of community – this is not only in relation to problems of legal definition and identification, but also the effects that these legal processes of codification have on communities, individuals and the resulting social and political relations.[40] Alternatively, the cases regarding the construction of the Hindmarsh Island Bridge demonstrate the divisions that can exist within a community and the politics of representation over who can speak and to whom as well as who is entitled to know about certain types of knowledge.[41] With such recent examples, surely intellectual property law cannot be naïve about the reality of difficult and often political intersections that inform communities? Moreover, it is also worth reflecting upon the role that legislation and governmental policy has had in formulating concepts of Aboriginal 'communities' and their contemporary social organisation, geographical boundaries and cultural identities. This also requires consideration of the way that 'Aboriginal people have actively played the community game to their own advantage'.[42]

The politics of community arise precisely because communities are not static or bounded, but instead dynamic and changeable. Communities come together for different purposes, in different contexts and split, coalesce or develop over time. The issue here is that there is no clear consensus about the markers to be used in identifying a community or membership of a community. The intense politics around the term makes its very use open to contest and dispute. Communities are notoriously difficult to define – as the abstract identification is likely to bare little resemblance to the practical sociality at a given space and time. The key point being that the category of 'community' is anything but stable and thus a difficult notion to rest legislative remedies upon.

Despite its persuasive name, the draft Bill does not actually offer realistic protection for knowledge held communally. But the power of the title *Copyright Amendment (Indigenous Communal Moral Rights) Bill* is that unless one actually reads the draft Bill (and there are only a few that have been distributed) it would superficially appear to break new ground in the field of indigenous interests in intellectual property. In its general appearance, the draft Bill suggests that the Government is responsive to indigenous rights. Yet it presents considerable, and possibly overwhelming, practical difficulties. Indigenous communities would be in no better situation than they were before the draft Bill. Besides being practically difficult to access – interpretation will need to be mediated by legal experts, the legislation ostensibly reduced to a 'lawyer's playground'.[43] Further, the requirements to be met before the rights can be granted mean that infringements are unlikely and remedy almost impossible.

That infringements would be unlikely is one of the more insidious implications of the draft Bill. For once the law is passed it will be very difficult to amend. This is because without litigation highlighting the difficulties there will be no examples showing the shortcomings of the law.

As mythical images of indigenous people and communities are constructed in national and international intellectual property forums, so too are their needs and expectations. In many cases these are set against the current intellectual property framework. This is most noticeable in the insistence of communal ownership versus individual ownership arguments.[44] The search for a differential creates a binary that masks the fluidity between these categories. The unity and agreement assumed of community is problematic given the extent that, in Australia at least, communities are far from neat linear models, but exist as contested spaces with dynamics that expose multiple positions and levels of agency and action. Thus it is important to encourage reflective critique of the range of interests and actors within communities and a consideration that these shape decision-making processes.[45]

CONCLUSION

Indigenous people are invited participants when they affirm the legitimacy of the discourse to account for what indigenous people want and how they expect the law to function. In this sense the authority of the law is maintained in intellectual property forums and indigenous perspectives are incorporated when they confirm the authorised conception of the problem and correspondingly, the nature of the proposed solution. The dynamics of these relations of power mean that indigenous participants are included when they comply with particular assumptions about the legal nature of the problem (indigenous culture) and the legal discourse governing future solutions.

It is important to highlight the internal national politics imbued within the development of a communal moral rights bill – and to bring to the fore of international discussions particular localised contexts where meaning, expectation and anticipation remain fluid and contested. In certain other national jurisdictions, for instance, a communal moral rights bill might be usefully developed. In the context of Australia, and with regard to the particular history and politics, it is dangerous – dangerous in what law takes an indigenous community to be, and how identifications of that legal community are played out. Without attention to these elements there remains a risk of replicating ineffective remedies that appear influential and pander to the rhetoric at international levels, but are practically unusable because they remain based on imagined communities that bear little resemblance to their practical articulation and continual metamorphosis. Thus a central challenge for intellectual property law remains grasping the changing dynamics of indigenous differentiation and adequately accounting for the moments of locality.

A very real possibility that would be advantageous to government and community alike would be to develop some kind of sound road-test for the Bill before it became legislation. This is possible, and given the complex terrain that it is seeking to navigate perhaps advisable. It might be that given time and the space for direct negotiation over expectations and needs for protection, other avenues may be uncovered. Given my reservations about new laws, and their effects on conceptions of identity, group definition and membership, the new kinds of authorities that are established, the problems of service delivery and the very real capacity to act as well as the complexity of the situation from community to community, there needs to be the possibility of there being something useful beyond law. Practicing the politics of cultural inclusion in intellectual property necessitates the recognition of the social and cultural contexts in which people make claims, identify needs, and generate expectations.

NOTES

1. Marcia Langton has written extensively about the inter-dependencies of these terms. See: M. Langton, 'Dreaming Art' in N. Paprastergiadis (ed) *Complex Entanglements: art, globalization and cultural difference*, Rivers Oram: London 2003; M. Langton,

'Aboriginal Art and Film: the politics of representation' in Grossman, M. (ed) *Blacklines: Contemporary critical writing by Indigenous Australians*, Melbourne University Press: Victoria, 2003.

2. It is only recently that debates around authorship – individual authorship in particular – have been developed in relation to Aboriginal art. These have developed from instances where non-indigenous people have tried to 'pass-off' their work as Aboriginal, and controversy that works by famous Aboriginal artists have not actually been executed by that individual artist. On the former problem see: S. Gray, 'Going Native: Disguise, forgery, imagination and the European Aboriginal', (2003) 170 *Overland* 34. On the latter see: C. Adler, 'The Aboriginal Art Market: Challenges to Authenticity' *Aboriginal Art Online*, www.aboriginalartonline.com/forum/articles6.php.
3. S. Gray, 'Squatting in the Red Dust: Non-Aboriginal Law's Construction of the "Traditional" Aboriginal Artist', (1996) 14 (2) *Law in Context* 29.
4. Established under the *Trade Marks Act 1995* (Cth).
5. See: M. Langton, C. Anderson, J. Sutherland, A. Garnett, N. Theiberger, S. Titchen, *Valuing Cultures: Recognising Indigenous cultures as a valued part of Australian heritage*, Australian Government Publishing Services: Canberra, 1994; S. Gray, 'Wheeling, Dealing and Deconstruction: Aboriginal Art and the Land', (1993) 3 (63) *Aboriginal Law Bulletin* 6. Also see comments by B. Bancroft and T. Janke in the documentary by C. Eatock and K. Mordaunt, *Copyrites*, Australian Film Finance Corporation Limited, 1997.
6. M. Annas, 'The Label of Authenticity: A Certification Trade Mark for Goods and Services of Indigenous Origin', (1997) 3 (90) *Aboriginal Law Bulletin* 4 at 6 [emphasis mine]. The plan was for two labels: one for indigenous artists and another for works produced collaboratively. See: L. Wiseman, 'The Labels of Authenticity: An Overview', (2000) 1 *Media and Culture Review* 3.
7. It is significant that in this report, culture is articulated in its singularity.
8. T. Janke, *Our Culture: Our Future. Report on Australian Indigenous Cultural and Intellectual Property Rights* [produced for the Australian Institute of Aboriginal and Torres Strait Islander Studies and the Aboriginal and Torres Strait Islander Commission], Michael Frankel and Company Solicitors: Surry Hills, 1998 at 197 [emphasis mine].
9. See: K. Wells, 'Authenticity-Promotion and Protection of Aboriginal and Torres Strait Islander Art' Paper on Research and Development – preliminary advice to NIAAA, 15 June 1995; K. Wells, *Draft Discussion Paper on the Proposed Authenticity Trade Mark*, NIAAA, October 1996. Also see: K. Wells, 'The Cosmic Irony of Intellectual Property and Indigenous Authenticity', (1996) 7 (3) *Culture and Policy* 45.
10. M. Annas, 'The Label of Authenticity: A Certification Trade Mark for Goods and Services of Indigenous Origin', supra n.6 at 5. Also see: T. Janke, *Our Culture: Our Future. Report on Australian Indigenous Cultural and Intellectual Property Rights*, supra n.8 at 202.
11. B. Croft, cited in D. Mellor and T. Janke, *Valuing Art, Respecting Culture: Protocols for Working with the Australian Indigenous Visual Arts and Crafts Sector*, National Association for the Visual Arts: Sydney, 2001 at 46. The 'dog tag' system to which Croft refers, functioned between 1943–1964 in NSW. Aboriginal people who were deemed to be 'deserving and superior' by the Aborigine Welfare Board were awarded exception certificates, otherwise known as 'dog tags' – which ostensibly afforded these select Aboriginal people similar citizenship rights to that of other Australians. Mark McKenna has described this as 'yet another bureaucratic devise aimed at exerting control over the behaviour of Aboriginal people and depriving those who failed to meet the Welfare Board's standards of their basic human rights. In the eyes of the government, Aboriginal people could only be accepted as equal citizens if they shed their culture.' M. McKenna, *Looking for Blackfella's Point: An Australian History of Place*, University of New South Wales Press: Sydney, 2002 at 168.
12. L. Wiseman, 'The Protection of Indigenous Art and Culture in Australia: The Labels of Authenticity' (2001) 23 (1) *European Intellectual Property Review* 14 at 20.
13. See: D. Jopson, 'Aboriginal seal of approval loses its seal of approval', *Sydney Morning Herald*, 14–15 June, 2002.

14. As Justice French lamented in *Yumbulul v Reserve Bank of Australia* (1991) 2 IPR 490 'Australia's copyright law does not provide adequate recognition of Aboriginal community claims to regulate the reproduction and use of works that are essentially communal in origin.' See also: G. Singh Nijar, 'Community Intellectual Rights Protect Indigenous Knowledge', (1998) 36 *Biotechnology and Development Monitor* 11.
15. See Part Two Chapter 3.
16. K. Bowrey, 'The Outer Limits of Copyright Law – Where Law Meets Philosophy and Culture', (2001) 12 *Law and Critique* 75.
17. I. McDonald, 'Indigenous communal moral rights back on the agenda', (2003) 16 (4) *Australian Intellectual Property Law Bulletin* 47.
18. Australian Federal Government, *Arts for All*, Australian Government Publishing Services: Canberra, 2001.
19. Department of Communication Information and Technology, Department of the Attorney General and Department of Immigration and Indigenous Affairs, *Indigenous Communities to Get New Protection*, Joint Press Release 19 May 2003.
20. Introductory letter for the Draft Bill (on file with author).
21. P. Ruddock, 'The Government's Copyright Policy Agenda', Conference Paper delivered at *The Eleventh Biennial Copyright Law and Practice Symposium*, Darling Harbour, Sydney, November 2003.
22. Section 193 *Copyright Act 1968* (Cth).
23. Section 195AC *Copyright Act 1968* (Cth).
24. Section 195AI *Copyright Act 1968* (Cth).
25. Section 190 *Copyright Act 1968* (Cth).
26. This politics cannot be understated. For those not familiar, see the submissions to the parliamentary inquiry into the administration of Aboriginal affairs at www.aph.gov.au/Senate/committee/indigenousaffairs_ctte/submissions/sublist.htm. This site provides perspectives about the effects of eliminating the Aboriginal and Torres Strait Islander Commission – the central agency for the management of Indigenous affairs with an elected Aboriginal Council. In rendering ATSIC defunct, the Australian government effectively silenced the representative voice for Aboriginal and Torres Strait Islander people, and with it the capacity to make comments on policy and legislation that directly affects Aboriginal and Torres Strait Islander people.
27. ATSIC was formally abolished at midnight on March 24, 2005. Both major parties and both houses of Parliament supported the legislation.
28. The National Indigenous Council is now responsible for advising the Australian Government on Indigenous Issues. See www.atsia.gov.au/NIC/default.aspx.
29. For an articulate exploration of this shift see: K. Bowrey, *Law and Internet Cultures*, Cambridge University Press: Cambridge, 2004.
30. For recent work see: P. Sullivan, 'Searching for the Inter-cultural, Searching for the Culture', 2005 75 (2) *Oceania*; A. Agrawal, and C.C. Gibson, 'The Role of Community in Natural Resource Conservation' in Gibson, C., M. McKean, E. Ostrom (eds), *People and Forests: communities, institutions and governance*, Massachusetts Institute of Technology: Massachusetts 2000; A. Agrawal, 'The Regulatory Community: Decentralisation and the Environment in the Van Panchayats (Forest Councils) of Kumaon, India', (2001) 21 (3) *Mountain Research and Development* 208.
31. 'Copyright Act Amendment (Communal Moral Rights) Bill 2003', Submission to Attorney General's Department on behalf of Australian Institute of Aboriginal and Torres Strait Islander Studies, 2004.
32. It is an ironic twist that the Australian government is using secrecy as a tool against indigenous interests, when secrecy still functions as an important part of certain indigenous cultural practices.
33. *Twelfth Biennial Copyright Law and Practice Symposium*, Australian Copyright Council, Darling Harbour, Sydney, 18 November 2006.
34. See: *Yumbulul v Reserve Bank of Australia & Others* (1991) 21 IPR 481. While the case was initially about the use of Yumbulul's Morning Star Pole design by the Reserve Bank on the bicentennial $10 dollar note, it predominately was revealed as a dispute over

contractual authority and the rights that Yumbulul believed he still retained in his work as opposed to those he had assigned.

35. F. Peters-Little, 'The Community Game: Aboriginal Self Definition at a Local Level', (1998) AIATSIS *Research Discussion Paper 10*, at 3.
36. This is also reflected in *sui generis* proposals.
37. *Members of the Yorta Yorta Community v State of Victoria* [1998] FCA 1606; *Members of the Yorta Yorta Community v State of Victoria* [2001] FCA 45 and *Members of the Yorta Yorta Community v State of Victoria* [2002] HCA 58.
38. See the High Court judgment: *Members of the Yorta Yorta Community v State of Victoria* [2002] HCA 58.
39. V. Kerriush and C. Perrin, 'Awash in Colonialism', (1999) 24 (1) *Alternative Law Journal*, 3; S. Young, 'The Trouble with "Tradition": Native Title and the *Yorta Yorta* Decision' (2001) 30(1) *The University of Western Australia Law Review* 28; J. Weiner, 'Diaspora, Materialism, Tradition: Anthropological Issues in the Recent High Court Appeal of the Yorta Yorta', (2002) 2 (18) *Land, Rights, Laws: Issues of Native Title* 1; R. Bartlett, 'The Obsession with Traditional Laws and Customs Creates Difficulties Establishing Native Title Claims in the South', (2003) 31 (1) *The University of Western Australia Law Review* 35.
40. See also: E. Povinelli, *The Cunning of Recognition: Indigenous Alterities and the Making of Australian Multiculturalism*, Duke University Press: Durham, 2002.
41. For a summary of the cases and the political challenges see the judgment by von Doussa J: *Chapman v Luminis Pty Ltd and Others* [2001] FCA 1106. For further discussion about the politics of knowledge within a community see: J. Weiner, 'Culture in a sealed envelope: the concealment of Australian Aboriginal heritage and tradition in the Hindmarsh Island Bridge Affair', (1999) 5 (2) *The Journal of the Royal Anthropological Institute* 193. D. Bell, *Ngarrindjeri Wurrurarrin: A World That Is, Was and Will Be*, Spinifex Press: Melbourne, 1998.
42. F. Peters-Little, 'The Community Game: Aboriginal Self Definition at a Local Level', above n.35 at 4.
43. I. Eagles, 'New Zealand Moral Rights Law: Did Something Get Lost in Translation?', (2002) 8 *New Zealand Business Law Quarterly* 26 at 27.
44. See for instance: M. Blakeney, 'Communal Intellectual Property Rights of Indigenous Peoples in Cultural Expressions', (1998) 1 (6) *Journal of World Intellectual Property* 985; R. Grad, 'Indigenous Rights and Intellectual Property Law: A Comparison of the United States and Australia', (2003) *Duke J. Comp. & Int'l. L.* 203.
45. A. Agrawal and C.C. Gibson, 'The Role of Community in Natural Resource Conservation', in Gibson, C., M. McKean, E. Ostrom (eds), *People and Forests: Communities, Institutions and Governance*, Massachusetts Institute of Technology: Massachusetts, 2000.

Conclusion

This book began with the premise that in all the writing dedicated to discussing indigenous knowledge and intellectual property law, none had looked at the production of this category in law, and what the effects of this position were. Curiously little investigation in this area has been directed to the way in which law grants property rights in intangibles, nor how this has been justified through particular categories and forms of classification.

This work has provided an account of the complicated emergence of indigenous knowledge, as a discrete category, in intellectual property law. Whilst the work has primarily been restricted to an Australian context, similar examination could be extended into other national sites. This would further illuminate the multiple ways in which indigenous knowledge has been produced within legal discourse, and the regimes of truth about its inclusion and properties that have subsequently been generated. Significantly this work has looked to the internal mechanisms of the law to explain problems of accommodating indigenous difference. This investigation has revealed that the hidden dilemma of providing protection for indigenous knowledge resonate with tensions that characterise intellectual property as a whole: namely how it is possible to justify property rights in *any* intangible subject matter.

Intellectual property is always being presented with 'new' knowledges as subject matter and thus it is always in a position of managing difference. Owing to its adaptability in the face of new developments, and we may consider digital technology and biotechnology as two examples that demonstrate the range and variability of new kinds of subject matter, questions remain as to why indigenous knowledge generates particular contests about its inclusion and what form these take. Much critical literature has focused on the incommensurability between indigenous knowledge systems and western intellectual property frameworks. Such analyses provide wide-ranging critiques of the culturally contingent nature of the law. Yet even within these positions, there remains little examination of the complex ways in which knowledge is understood as property in both indigenous and non-indigenous contexts, and how the law is deeply imbued with managing this process of identification.

The term 'indigenous intellectual property' invites a misplaced perception that this subject is a naturally occurring body of law. Rather than assume the naturalness, this work has examined the politics of its construction precisely as a 'special' category. In examining its production, I have sought to highlight the manifold ways in which the category has been produced by social, political, governmental, legal and individual agents and influences. Through the interplay of such diverse elements, the extent of legal power becomes more transparent and this helps in understanding both the production of the category and also the capacity for future directions.

It was the copyright cases in the 1980s involving Aboriginal art that provided the first solid catalyst for the inclusion of indigenous knowledge in intellectual property law in Australia. Prior to this, indigenous knowledge was predominately translated through anthropological and ethnographic discourses. The copyright cases are important because they were indicative of various fluctuations in the utility and interpretation of a body of knowledge termed 'indigenous knowledge'. This was in regards to the increased value that was attached to the knowledge, in research, scientific, indigenous and artistic domains. In various forms, an international and national industry circulating around and dependent upon indigenous knowledges, has been generated. In Australia at least, the industry has fostered and supported valuable infrastructure within indigenous communities. Significantly with this industry has come an inevitable push for ways of compensating for the value of the knowledge and measures to restrict and control the circulation in certain circumstances. In many ways a corollary can be drawn between the indigenous knowledge industry and new technologies, where the increased circulation means greater access from differing communities, which also correspondingly leads to misuse and inappropriate applications of this knowledge. What constitutes inappropriate behaviour changes from context to context, and this challenges the competency of the law: for such struggles inevitably arise from relations of power.

There is little surprise that the indigenous knowledge enterprise has turned to intellectual property law for remedy to readdress issues of control and modes of circulation by the 'owners' and custodians of indigenous knowledge. In a globalising and interconnected world, knowledge itself has been naturalised as generating property rights, even though the historical justification of this remains unclear. The increased circulation of rights in intellectual property provides an interpretative framework that normalises the concept of a property right in information and relies upon narratives of its emergence, logic and rationale. This is helped by the generality of discussions that intellectual property and copyright have produced when detached from specific practical negotiations. 'Copyright law questions can make delightful cocktail party small talk, but copyright law answers tend to make eyes glaze over everywhere.'[1]

Competing interests vie for control of the intellectual property language: what is an infringement, what is property, how to determine originality and so forth. Indigenous people also have the power to effect such changes as the term 'indigenous intellectual and cultural property' illustrates. Yet the legal framework remains pivotal and influences how discussions about knowledge use and information exchange are made. Intellectual property is not a neutral form but is also open to influence from a range of interested parties and competing interests, something that can be seen from any considered look at its history. Yet the challenge remains that of exposing contingencies that have (ironically) historically remained hidden.

Jessica Litman has argued, that faced with pressures in terms of what intellectual property can include and whether the copyright statute can adjust, two familiar lines of debate are engaged. One side claims an incommensurability with the current regime and calls into question the 'assumptions upon which our copyright laws are based'.[2] The other camp insists that copyright is always faced with the issue of change in subject matter and as a consequence continues to manage the orbit of its categories with relative success thus not requiring any substantial change.[3] Litman's comments are useful and worth considering in a more complicated matrix. For one argument that points to the problems of assumptions about copyright law can also recognise the relative success in how the categories have been historically employed. With these positions in mind, this work has sought a middle road, arguing that the issues faced here are part of an intellectual property continuum in managing differing sorts of knowledge.

The point is that the success in mediating categories and the difficulties of including new subject matter are part of one and the same concern: how to justify property in something that has no clear boundaries of marks of identification. Any claim to property in knowledge faces this same problematic, whether property rights are argued to be invested in 'culture' and 'heritage' or in some form of 'labour' exerted to compile a telephone book. To avoid sustained challenge on what would otherwise be a destabilising element, the law has come to rely on the tangible product to invest property. But in certain cases, like indigenous knowledge, this reliance is revealed as being culturally contingent on certain standards of identification. A key irony is that in positioning indigenous knowledge within an intellectual property regime, the law produces a subject that is difficult to manage, and this exposes the instability of the law's own metaphysical categories.

A more complicated question remains: given intellectual property is limited and perhaps inappropriate in catering for the diversity of indigenous epistemologies and ontologies, both in its remedy and forms of justification, why hasn't it then been abandoned as a political cause? Whilst there is no clear answer, it is apparent that in the circumstances where the legal potential resides and involves the market, and law is the carrier of important entitlements, an abandonment of the language and framework of intellectual property could potentially discriminate against indigenous interests that intersect the market. There also needs to be a realistic awareness of the extent that indigenous people use the tools that are available. This also means recognising the moments of agency, both in its possibilities and in its compromises. Further, it is necessary to recognise the diversity of agency across and within indigenous contexts – for clearly not all indigenous people reside in traditional communities and remote communities, or relate directly to notions of community. We cannot afford to continue talking as though all indigenous people are the same, have the same problem with intellectual property, or would want to be part of a unique indigenous *sui generis* system. We need to start arguing in the particular, rather than the general. This is because the general does specific, and at times dangerous work in abstracting and decontextualising indigenous experience in ways that are curiously similar to the critiques levelled at the biases with intellectual property law.

Indigenous needs can and do differ. This helps us understand why the intellectual property framework has not been abandoned: it provides a means of leverage for indigenous self-determination claims in that it allows the exercise of control over uses and circulations of information. These are legitimate claims that engage international and national discourses of human rights and demand recognition of the troubling pasts that inform indigenous circumstance within many nations. But at the same time, we have to be realistic about what can be gained through an intellectual property regime: legal frameworks of themselves cannot ever adequately provide a stand-in-grid for issues that require social and cultural reflection and reconciliation.

The objective of this project has been to highlight the complicated relations of power implicit in producing indigenous knowledge within intellectual property law. It has revealed the concomitant political, social and cultural mechanisms within the struggles for inclusion and recognition, and that it is these intersections that influence legal possibility and direct the potential capabilities for future practical engagement. Yet this work contains within its frame directions for future research: specifically projects focused on understanding the diverse ways in which indigenous people come to and appreciate certain kinds of knowledge as property and the varied ways in which intellectual property can be employed effectively.[4] Only a sustained examination of the particular can begin to generate some useful and workable strategies. In this sense 'the particular' means working *with* indigenous people and indigenous communities on problems that are being experienced now. It is time for critical engagement on problems that are already manifest – and this means reinterpreting this issue beyond that of a quaint intellectual property problem that can be addressed by academics from their offices.

NOTES

1. J. Litman, *Digital Copyright*, Prometheus Books: New York, 2001 at 13.
2. Ibid., at 35.
3. Ibid., at 35.
4. For example see the following projects: Australian Institute of Aboriginal and Torres Strait Islander Studies and the Intellectual Property Research Institute of Australia, *Intellectual Property and Indigenous Knowledge: Access, Ownership and Control of Cultural Materials*, 2002–2004; Ford Foundation, Social Science Research Council and Lembaga Studi Pers dan Pambangunan (LSPP), *The Propertisation of Traditional Arts in Indonesia*, 2005–2007; Department of Cultural Development, Sport and Tourism, Northern Territory and Jumbunna Indigenous House of Learning, University of Technology, *Evaluation of the Northern Territory's Library and Knowledge Centre Models*, 2005.

Bibliography

Aboriginal and Torres Strait Islander Social Justice Commissioner (1994), *First Report,* Canberra: Australian Government Publishing Service: Canberra.

Aboriginal and Torres Strait Islander Social Justice Commissioner (1997), *Fifth Report,* Sydney: Human Rights and Equal Opportunity Commission.

Aboriginal and Torres Strait Islander Social Justice Commissioner (2000), *Social Justice Report,* Sydney: Superfine Printing.

Aboriginal and Torres Strait Islander Social Justice Commissioner (2001), *Social Justice Report,* Sydney: J.S. McMillan Publishing.

Aboriginal and Torres Strait Islander Social Justice Commissioner (2002), *Social Justice Report,* Sydney: J.S. McMillan Publishing.

Adler, Christine (1999), 'The Aboriginal Art Market: Challenges to Authenticity' *Aboriginal Art Online* at www.aboriginalartonline.com/forum/articles6.php (last accessed 17 September 2007).

Agrawal, Arun (1995), 'Dismantling the Divide Between Indigenous and Scientific Knowledge', *Development and Change,* 26, 413–439.

Agrawal, Arun and Clark C. Gibson (2000), 'The Role of Community in Natural Resource Conservation' in Arun Agrawal and Clark C. Gibson (eds), *Communities and Nature*, Piscataway, NJ: Rutgers University Press, pp. 1–31.

Agrawal, Arun (2001), 'The Regulatory Community: Decentralisation and the Environment in the Van Panchayats (Forest Councils) of Kumaon, India', *Mountain Research and Development,* 21 (3), 208–211.

Agrawal, Arun (2002), 'Indigenous Knowledge and the Politics of Classification', *International Social Science Journal,* 54 (173), 287–297.

Almog, Shulamit (2002), 'From Sterne and Borges to Lost Storytellers: Cyberspace, Narrative and Law', *Fordham Intellectual Property, Media and Entertainment Law Journal,* 13 (1), 1–34.

Anderson, Benedict (1983), *Imagined Communities: Reflections on the Origins and Spread of Nationalism,* London UK: Verso Publishing.

Anderson, Jane (2003) 'Chapter Nine – Globalising Indigenous Rights in Intellectual Property' in *The Production of Indigenous Knowledge in Intellectual Property Law*, PhD Dissertation, Law Faculty, University of New South Wales.

Anderson, Jane (2004), 'The Politics of Indigenous Knowledge: Australia's Proposed Communal Moral Rights Bill', *University of New South Wales Law Journal,* 23 (4), 585–604.

Anderson, Jane (2005), 'Access and Control of Indigenous Knowledge in Libraries and Archives: Ownership and Future Use', American Library Association and The MacArthur Foundation, Columbia University, New York, May 5–7.

Anderson Jane and Kathy Bowrey (2006), 'The Imaginary Politics of Access to Knowledge: Whose Cultural Agendas are Being Advanced?', *Con/Texts of Invention Conference*, Case Western Reserve University, 20–22 April.

Anderson, Jane (2007), *Intellectual Property and Indigenous Knowledge: Access, Ownership and Control of Cultural Materials – Final Report*, AIATSIS, Australia.

Anderson, Jane, Lorraine Aragon, Ignatius Haryanto, Peter Jaszi, Abdon Nababan, Hinca Panjiatan, Agus Sardjono, Rizaldi Siagian, R. Suryasaladin, (forthcoming), *Traditional Arts: A Move Towards Protection in Indonesia.*

Annas, Marianna (1997), 'The Label of Authenticity: A Certification Trade Mark for Goods and Services of Indigenous Origin', *Aboriginal Law Bulletin,* 3 (90), 4–8.

Aoki, Keith (1998), 'Neocolonialism, Anticommons Property and Biopiracy in the (Not-So-Brave) New World Order of International Intellectual Property Protection', *Indiana Journal of Global Legal Studies*, 6 (1), 11–58.

Aoki, Keith (1998), 'Considering Multiple and Overlapping Sovereignties: Liberalism, Libertarianism, National Sovereignty, "Global" Intellectual Property and the Internet', *Indiana Journal of Global Legal Studies,* 5 (2), 443–474.

Appadurai, Arjun (2000), 'Disjuncture and Difference in the Global Cultural Economy' in David Held and Anthony McGrew (eds), *The Global Transformations Reader: An Introduction to the Globalisation Debate,* Cambridge UK: Polity Press, pp. 230–238.

Arendt, Hannah (1958), *The Human Condition,* Chicago USA and London UK: University of Chicago Press.

Arnold, Matthew (1868) *Culture and Anarchy: An Essay in Social and Political Criticism,* reprinted in J. Dover Wilson (ed) (1960) Cambridge UK: Cambridge University Press.

Arup, Christopher (2000), *The New World Trade Agreements: Globalizing Law Through Services and Intellectual Property,* Cambridge UK: Cambridge University Press.

Ashcraft, Richard (1991), *John Locke: Critical Assessments,* London UK: Routledge.

Attwood, Bain and Andrew Markus (1998), 'Representation Matters: The 1967 Referendum and Citizenship' in Nicolas Peterson and Will Sanders (eds), *Citizenship and Indigenous Australians: Changing Conceptions and Possibilities*, Cambridge UK: Cambridge University Press, pp. 118–140.

Austin, John (1832), *The Province of Jurisprudence Determined*, reprinted in Wilfrid E. Rumble (ed) (1995), Cambridge UK: Cambridge University Press.

Australian Broadcasting Commission (2002), *Cultural Protocol.*

Australian Copyright Council (1989), *The Art of Resale Royalty and its Implications for Australia.*

Australian Copyright Council (1998), *Protecting Indigenous Intellectual Property: A Discussion Paper*.

Australian Copyright Council (1999), *Indigenous Arts and Copyright*.

Australian Federal Government (2001), *Arts for All*, Canberra: Australian Government Publishing Services.

Australian Institute of Aboriginal and Torres Strait Islander Studies (2002), *Guidelines for Ethical Research in Indigenous Studies*, Canberra: Aboriginal Studies Press.

Barcham, Manuhuia (2000), '(De)Constructing the Politics of Indigeneity' in Duncan Ivison, Paul Patton and Will Sanders (eds), *Political Theory and the Rights of Indigenous Peoples*, Cambridge UK: Cambridge University Press, pp. 137–151.

Barron, Anne (1998), 'No Other Law? Author-ity, Property and Aboriginal Art' in Lionel Bently and Spyros Maniatis (eds), *Perspectives on Intellectual Property Volume 4: Intellectual Property and Ethics,* London UK: Sweet and Maxwell, pp. 37–88.

Barsh, Russell L. (1988), 'Indigenous Peoples and the Right to Self-determination in International Law' in Barbara Hocking (ed) *International Law and Aboriginal Human Rights*, Sydney: The Law Book Company, pp. 68–82.

Barsh, Russell L. (1986), 'Indigenous Peoples: An Emerging Object of International Law', *The American Journal of International Law,* 80 (2), 369–385.

Bartlett, Richard (2003), 'The Obsession with Traditional Laws and Customs Creates Difficulties Establishing Native Title Claims in the South', *The University of Western Australia Law Review,* 31 (1), 35–46.

Batty, Philip (2005), 'Private Politics, Public Strategies: White Advisors and their Aboriginal Subjects', *Oceania,* 75 (33), 209–221.

Baxter, Jane (2003), 'Commentary on "Fear, Hope and Longing for the Future of Authorship and Revitalized Public Domain in Global Regimes of Intellectual Property"', *DePaul Law Review*, 52 (4), 1235–1240.

Beckett, Jeremy (ed) (1988), *Past and Present: The Construction of Aboriginality,* Canberra: Aboriginal Studies Press.

Behrendt, Larissa (1998), 'In Your Dreams: Cultural Appropriation, Popular Culture and Colonialism', *Law/Text/Culture,* 4 (1), 257–279.

Bell, Diane (1998), *Ngarrindjeri Wurrurarrin: A World that Is, Was and Will Be,* Melbourne: Spinifex Press.

Bell, Robin (1985), 'Protection of Aboriginal Folklore: or Do they Dust Reports', *Aboriginal Law Bulletin,* 17 (5), 17–19.

Benhabib, Seyla (2002), *The Claims of Culture: Equality and Diversity in the Global Era,* Princeton USA: Princeton University Press.

Bengwayan, Michael (2003), *Intellectual and Cultural Property Rights of Indigenous and Tribal Peoples in Asia,* London UK: Minority Rights Group International.

Bennett, David (1996), 'Native Title and Intellectual Property', *Land, Rights, Laws: Issues of Native Title*, 10, 2–11.

Bennett, Gordon (1996), 'The Manifest Toe' in Ian McLean and Gordon Bennett (eds), *The Art of Gordon Bennett*, Sydney: Craftsman House, pp. 9–62.

Bennett, Tony (1998), *Culture: A Reformer's Science,* Sydney: Allen and Unwin.

Bennett, Tony (2004), *Pasts Beyond Memory: Evolution, Museums, Colonialism*, London UK and New York USA: Routledge University Press.

Bennett, Tony (2006), 'Exhibition, Difference and the Logic of Culture' in Ivan Karp and Corrine Kratz (eds), *Museum Frictions: Public Cultures/ Global Transformations,* Durham, North Carolina: Duke University Press, pp. 46–69.

Bentham, Jeremy (1789), *The Theory of Legislation,* reprinted in C.K. Ogden (ed) (1931), London UK: Keagan Paul Publishers.

Bentham, Jeremy (1789) (1978), 'Chapter VIII – Of Property' reprinted in Crawford Brough Macpherson (ed), *Property: Mainstream and Critical Positions*, Toronto: University of Toronto Press, pp. 51–52.

Bently, Lionel and Brad Sherman (2001), 'Great Britain and the Signing of the Berne Convention in 1886', *Journal of the Copyright Society of the USA*, 48 (3), 311–340.

Bently, Lionel, (2004), 'Copyright and the Victorian Internet: Telegraphic Property Laws in Colonial Australia', *Loyola Los Angeles Law Review*, 38, 71–176.

Bettig, Ronald (1997), *Copyrighting Culture: The Political Economy of Intellectual Property*, Boulder, Colorado: Westview Press.

Bhabha, Homi (1994), *The Location of Culture*, London UK, New York USA: Routledge.

Bird, Greta (1987),'The Civilising Mission: Race and the Construction of Crime', *Contemporary Legal Issues No.4*, Monash University.

Bird, Greta (1996), 'Koori Cultural Heritage: Reclaiming the Past?' in Greta Bird, Gary Martin and Jennifer Nielsen (eds), *Majah: Indigenous Peoples and the Law*, Sydney: The Federation Press.

Bird, Greta and Gary Martin and Jennifer Nielson (eds) (1996), *Majah: Indigenous Peoples and the Law*, Sydney: The Federation Press.

Blackstone, William (1765–1769), *Commentaries on the Laws of England*, facsimile of the first edition (1979), Chicago: University Press.

Blakeney, Michael (1995), '*Milpurrurru & Ors v Indofurn Pty Ltd & Ors* – Protecting Expressions of Aboriginal Folklore Under Copyright Law', *elaw: Murdoch Electronic Law Journal* at www.murdoch.edu.au/elaw/issues/v2n1/blakeney.txt.

Blakeney, Michael (1996), *Trade Related Aspects of Intellectual Property Rights: A Concise Guide to the TRIPs Agreement*, London UK: Sweet and Maxwell.

Blakeney, Michael (1997), 'Bioprospecting and the Protection of Traditional Medicinal Knowledge of Indigenous Peoples: An Australian Perspective', *European Intellectual Property Review*, 19 (6), 298–303.

Blakeney, Michael (1998), 'Communal Intellectual Property Rights of Indigenous Peoples in Cultural Expressions', *Journal of World Intellectual Property*, 1 (6) 985–992.

Blakeney, Michael (2000), 'Protection of Traditional Knowledge under Intellectual Property Law', *European Intellectual Property Review*, 22 (6), 251–258.

Blakeney, Michael (2002), 'Protecting the Cultural Expressions of Indigenous Peoples under Intellectual Property Law – the Australian Experience' in F. Willem Grosheide and and Johannes J. Brinkhof (eds), *Intellectual Property Law 2002: The Legal Protection of Cultural Expressions and Indigenous Knowledge*, Antwerp, Oxford UK, New York USA: Intersentia Publishers, pp. 151–180.

Bonham-Carter, Victor (1978), *Authors by Profession, Volume One and Two*, London UK: The Society of Authors.

Bottomley, Stephen and Stephen Parker (eds) (1997), *Law in Context* (second edition) Sydney: The Federation Press.

Bowen, John (2000), 'Should we have a Universal Concept of "Indigenous Peoples' Rights"? Ethnicity and Essentialism in the Twenty First Century', *Anthropology Today*, 16 (4), 12–16.

Bowrey, Kathy (1994), *Don't Fence Me In: The Many Histories of Copyright*, Doctor of Juridical Studies, University of Sydney, Australia.

Bowrey, Kathy (1995), 'Copyright, Photography and Computer Works: the Fiction of Original Expression', *University of New South Wales Law Journal*, 18 (2), 278–99.

Bowrey, Kathy (1996), 'Who's Writing Copyright's History?', *European Intellectual Property Review*, 18 (6), 322–329.

Bowrey, Kathy (2001), 'The Outer Limits of Copyright Law – Where Law meets Philosophy and Culture', *Law and Critique*, 12 (1), 1–24.

Bowrey, Kathy (2001), 'Originality in Copyright: How Low can you Go?', University of New South Wales Seminar Paper, September 11, 2001.

Bowrey, Kathy (2004), *Law and Internet Cultures,* London UK: Cambridge University Press.

Bowrey, Kathy and Matthew Rimmer (2002), 'Rip, Mix, Burn: The Politics of Peer to Peer and Copyright Law', *First Monday*, 7 (8), at http://firstmonday.org/issues/issue7_8/bowrey/index.html.

Boyd White, James (1985), *Heracles' Bow: Essays on the Rhetoric and Poetics of the Law*, Wisconsin: University of Wisconsin Press.

Boyle, James (1996), *Shamans, Software and Spleens: Law and the Construction of the Information Society*, Cambridge MA USA: Harvard University Press.

Brosius, Peter (1999), 'Analyses and Interventions: Anthropological Engagements with Environmentalism', *Current Anthropology*, 40 (3), 277–309.

Brosius, Peter (1999), 'Green Dots, Pink Hearts: Displacing Politics from the Malaysian Rain Forest', *American Anthropologist,* 101 (1), 36–57.

Brown, Michael (1998), 'Can Culture be Copyrighted?', *Current Anthropology*, 39 (2), 193.

Brown, Michael (2004), *Who Owns Native Culture?*, Cambridge MA USA: Harvard University Press.

Brush, Stephen (1996), 'Whose Knowledge, Whose Genes, Whose Rights?' in Stephen Brush and Doreen Stabinsky (eds), *Valuing Local Knowledge: Indigenous Peoples and Intellectual Property Rights*, Washington DC: Island Press, pp. 1–24.

Bryan, Bradley (2000), 'Property as Ontology: On Aboriginal and English Understandings of Ownership', *Canadian Journal of Law and Jurisprudence*, 13, 3–32.

Bunting, Susan (2000), 'Limitations of Australian Copyright Law in the Protection of Indigenous Music and Culture', *Context: Journal of Music Research*, 18, 15–23.

Butler, Judith (1990), *Gender Trouble: Feminism and the Subversion of Identity,* New York USA: Routledge.

Cane, Scott (2002), *Pila Nguru: The Spinifex People,* Fremantle: Fremantle Arts Centre Press.

Caruana, Wally (1993), *Aboriginal Art,* Singapore: Thames and Hudson.

Caygill, Howard (1997), 'The Shared World: Philosophy, Violence, Freedom' in Darren Sheppard, Simon Sparks and Colin Thomas (eds), *On Jean-Luc Nancy: The Sense of Philosophy*, London and New York: Routledge, pp. 19–31.

Chambers David Wade and Richard Gillespie (2000), 'Locality in the History of Science: Colonial Science, Technoscience and Indigenous Knowledge', *Osiris*, 15, 221–240.

Chander, Anupam and Madhavi Sunder (2004), 'The Romance of the Public Domain', *California Law Review*, 92, 1331–1374.

Christie, Jean (1998), 'Enclosing the Biodiversity Commons: Bioprospecting or Biopiracy?' in Richard Hindmarsh, Geoffrey Lawrence, Janet Norton (eds), *Altered Genes: Reconstructing Nature – the Debate*, Sydney: Allen and Unwin.

Clarke, Jennifer (1997), 'Law and Race: The Position of Indigenous people' in Stephen Bottomley and Stephen Parker (eds), *Law and Context* (second edition), Sydney: The Federation Press.

Clifford, James (1988), *The Predicament of Culture: Twentieth Century Ethnography, Literature and Art*, Cambridge MA USA: Harvard University Press.

Cohn, Bernard (1996), *Colonialism and its Forms of Knowledge: The British in India*, New Jersey: Princeton University.

Coleman, Elizabeth (2001), 'Aboriginal Painting: Identity and Authenticity', *The Journal of Aesthetics and Art Criticism*, 59 (4), 385–402.

Coleman, Elizabeth Burns (2005), *Aboriginal Art, Identity and Appropriation*, Aldershot UK: Ashgate Publishing.

Commission on Intellectual Property Rights (2002), *Integrating Intellectual Property Rights and Development Policy*, London UK.

Coombe, Rosemary (1993), 'The Properties of Culture and the Politics of Possessing Identity: Native Claims in the Cultural Appropriation Controversy', *Canadian Journal of Law and Jurisprudence*, 6 (2), 249–285.

Coombe, Rosemary (1997), 'The Properties of Culture and the Possession of Identity: Postcolonial Struggle and the Legal Imagination' in Bruce Ziff and Pratima V. Rao (eds), *Borrowed Power: Essays on Cultural Appropriation,* New Jersey USA: Rutgers University Press, pp. 74–96.

Coombe, Rosemary (1998), *The Cultural Life of Intellectual Properties: Authorship, Appropriation and the Law,* Durham USA: Duke University Press.

Coombe, Rosemary (1998), 'Intellectual Property, Human Rights and Sovereignty: New Dilemmas in International Law Posed by the Recognition of Indigenous Knowledge and the Conservation of Biodiversity', *Indiana Journal of Global Legal Studies*, 6, 59–115.

Coombe, Rosemary (2001), 'The Recognition of Indigenous People's and Community Traditional Knowledge in International Law', *St Thomas Law Review*, 14, 275–285.

Coombe, Rosemary (2003), 'Fear, Hope and Longing for the Future of Authorship and a Revitalized Public Domain in Global Regimes of Intellectual Property', *De Paul Law Review*, 52, 1171–1191.

Cope, Malcolm (1992), *Constructive Trusts,* Sydney: The Law Book Company.

Cornell, Drusilla (1991), *The Philosophy of the Limit*, New York USA: Routledge.

Correa, Carlos (1997), 'Harmonisation of Intellectual Property Rights in Latin America: Is there still room for differentiation?', *New York University Journal of Law and Policy,* 109–134.

Cotterrell, Roger (1989), *The Politics of Jurisprudence*, London UK: Butterworths.

Cotterrell, Roger (1995), *Law's Community: Legal Theory in Sociological Perspective*, Oxford UK: Clarendon Press.

Cramer, Sue (ed) (1989), *Postmodernism: A Consideration of the Appropriation of Aboriginal Imagery,* Brisbane: Institute of Modern Art.

Croft, Brenda (2002), 'Roundtable Discussion' at *Intellectual Property and Indigenous Knowledge: Access and Ownership of Indigenous Cultural Material,* (AIATSIS Seminar Series). Paper on file with author.

Cuneen, Chris (1992), 'Judicial Racism', *Aboriginal Law Bulletin,* 2 (58), 9–11.

Cuneen, Chris (2001), *Conflicts, Politics and Crime,* Sydney: Allen and Unwin.

Cuneen, Chris and Terri Libesman (1995), *Indigenous People and the Law in Australia,* Sydney: Butterworths.

Cuneen, Chris and Julia Grix (2004), 'The Limitations of Litigation in Stolen Generation Cases', *Australian Institute of Aborignal and Torres Strait Islander Studies Research Discussion Paper*, 15.

Curthoys, Ann (1994), 'Citizenship, Race and Gender: the Debates in Australia over Equal Rights and Special Rights for Women and Indigenous People', in Melanie Nolan (ed), *Suffrage and Beyond*, Sydney: Pluto Press, pp. 89–106.

Daes, Erica Irene (1993), *Discrimination against Indigenous Peoples: Study on the Protection of the Cultural and Intellectual Property of Indigenous Peoples*, E/CN.4/Sub.2/1993/28, July 28.

Daes, Erica Irene (1994), *Discrimination against Indigenous Peoples: Protection of the Heritage of Indigenous Peoples*, E/CN.4/Sub.2/1995/26.

Daes, Erica Irene (1995), *Note on the Concept of Indigenous People*, E/CN.4/Sub.2/AC.4/1995/3, July.

Daes, Erica Irene (2000), 'Striving for Self-determination for Indigenous People' in Y.N. Kly, and D. Kly (eds), *In Pursuit of the Right to Self-determination*, Collected Papers and Proceedings of the First International Conference in the Right to Self-determination as the United Nations, Geneva: Clarity Press.

Dahl, Tove Stang (1987), *Women's Law: An Introduction to Feminist Jurisprudence*, Oxford UK: Oxford University Press.

Davies, Margaret (1996), *Delimiting the Law: Postmodernism and the Politics of Law*, London UK and Chicago USA: Pluto Press.

Davies, Tony (1996), 'Aboriginal Cultural Property?', *Law in Context*, 14 (2), 1–23.

Davila, Juan (1987), 'Aboriginality: A Lugubrious Game?, *Art and Text*, 23 (4), 53–59.

Davis, Michael (1996–7), 'Indigenous Peoples and Intellectual Property Rights', *Parliamentary Library Research Paper*, 20, 1–45.

Davis, Michael (1997), 'Indigenous Intellectual Property Protection Consultations with Aboriginal and Torres Strait Islander Peoples', *Aboriginal Law Bulletin*, 3 (90), 22–23.

Dawson, Freya (1996), 'The Importance of Property Rights for Biodiversity Conservation in the Northern Territory', *The Australian Journal of Natural Resources Law and Policy*, 3 (2), 179–195.

Dean, Mitchell (1999), *Governmentality: Power and Rule in Modern Society*, London UK: Sage Publications.

Deazley, Ronan (2003), 'Re-reading Donaldson (1774) in the Twenty First Century and Why It Matters', *European Intellectual Property Review*, 25 (6), 270–279.

Deazley, Ronan (2004), *On the Origin of the Right to Copy: Charting the Movement of Copyright Law in Eighteenth Century Britain (1695–1775)*, Oxford UK and Portland USA: Hart Publishing.

de Certeau, Michel (1984), *The Practice of Everyday Life*, Los Angeles: University of California Press.

Delueze, Gilles (1994), *Difference and Repetition*, New York USA: Columbia University Press.

Department of Home Affairs and the Environment (1981), *Report of the Working Party on the Protection of Aboriginal Folklore*, Canberra: Australian Government Printing Service.

Derrida, Jacques (1990), 'Force of Law: The Mystical Foundation of Authority', *Cardozo Law Review*, 11, 919–1047.

Derrida, Jacques (1993), *Writing and Difference*, London UK: Routledge.

Dirks, Nicholas (2001), *Castes of Mind: Colonialism and the Making of Modern India*, Princeton NJ: Princeton University Press.

Dirks, Nicholas, Geoffrey Eley and Sherry Ortner (eds) (1994), *Culture/Power/History: a Reader in Contemporary Social Theory*, Princeton NJ: Princeton University Press.

Dodds, John (1988), 'The New Constructive Trust: An Analysis of its Nature and Scope', *Melbourne University Law Review*, 16, 482–502.

Dodson, Michael (1994), 'The End in the Beginning: Re(de)finding Aboriginality', *Australian Aboriginal Studies*, 1, 2–13.

Dodson, Michael (1996), 'Indigenous Peoples and Intellectual Property Rights' in *Ecopolitics IX: Conference Papers and Resolutions*, Casuarina: Northern Land Council, pp. 30–36.

Dodson, Patrick (1991), *Royal Commission into Aboriginal Deaths in Custody: Regional Report of the Inquiry into Underlying Issues in Western Australia*, Canberra: Australian Government Printing Service.

Dodson, Patrick (2000), *The Wentworth Lecture 2000 – Beyond the Mourning Gate: Dealing with Unfinished Business*, Canberra: Australian Institute of Aboriginal and Torres Strait Islander Studies.

Drahos, Peter (1996), *A Philosophy of Intellectual Property*, Sydney: Dartmouth Press.

Drahos, Peter (2000), 'Indigenous Knowledge, Intellectual Property and Biopiracy: Is a Global Collecting Society the Answer?', *European Intellectual Property Review*, 6, 245–250.

Drahos, Peter (2001), 'BITs and BIPs: Bilateralims in Intellectual Property', *The Journal of World Intellectual Property,* 4 (6), 791–808.

Drahos, Peter (2003), 'Capitalism, Efficiency and Self-Ownership', *Australian Journal of Legal Philosophy*, 28, 215–220.

Drahos, Peter with John Braithwaite (2002), *Information Feudalism: Who Owns the Knowledge Economy?*, London UK: Earthscan Publications.

Drahos, Peter and Ruth Mayne (eds) (2002), *Global Intellectual Property Rights: Knowledge, Access and Development*, Hampshire UK: Palgrave Macmillan.

Drayton, Richard (2000), *Nature's Government: Science, Imperial Britain and the Improvement of the World*, New Haven USA and London UK: Yale University Press.

Dunn, John (1969), *The Political Thought of John Locke*, Cambridge UK: Cambridge University Press.

Dworkin, Ronald, *Law's Empire*, London UK: Fontana Press.

Eagles, Ian (2002), 'New Zealand Moral Rights Law: Did Something Get Lost in Translation?', *New Zealand Business Law Quarterly*, 8, 26–74.

Eatock, Cathy and Kim Mordaunt (1997), *Copyrites*, Australian Film Finance Corporation Limited.

Edelman, Bernard (1979), *Ownership of the Image: Elements for a Marxist Theory of Law*, London UK: Routledge and Keegan Paul.

Edmond, Gary (2004), 'Thick Decisions: Expertise, Advocacy and Reasonableness in the Federal Court of Australia', *Oceania*, 74 (3), 190–230.

Eisenstein, Elizabeth (1983), *The Printing Revolution in Early Modern Europe*, Cambridge UK: Cambridge University Press.

Ellinson, Dean (1994), 'Unauthorised Reproduction of Traditional Aboriginal Art', *University of New South Wales Law Journal*, 17 (2), 327–344.

Elyachar, Julia (2005), *Markets of Dispossession: NGOs, Economic Development and the State in Cairo*, Durham: Duke University Press.

Feather, John (1985), *The Provincial Book Trade in Eighteenth Century England*, Cambridge UK: Cambridge University Press.

Fitzpatrick, Peter (1991), 'Racism and the Innocence of Law' in Peter Fitzpatrick and Alan Hunt (eds), *Critical Legal Studies*, Basil Blackwell: Oxford.

Fitzpatrick, Peter (1992), *The Mythology of Modern Law*, London UK and New York USA: Routledge Press.

Fitzpatrick, Peter (2001), *Modernism and the Grounds of Law*, Cambridge UK: Cambridge University Press.

Flessas, Tatiana (2005), 'Aphorisms, Objects and Culture' in Peter Goodrich and Mariana Valverde (eds), *Nietzsche and Legal Theory: Half-Written Laws*, New York USA: Routledge Press, pp. 105–124.

Folds, Ralph (2001), *Crossed Purposes: The Pintupi and Australia's Indigenous Policy*, Sydney: University of New South Wales Press.

Foucault, Michel (1980), 'Truth and Power' in Colin Gordon (ed), *Power/Knowledge: Selected Interviews and Other Writings, 1972–1977*, New York USA: Pantheon Press, pp. 109–133.

Foucault, Michel (1980), 'Two Lectures' in Colin Gordon (ed), *Power/Knowledge: Selected Interviews and Other Writings, 1972–1977*, New York USA: Pantheon Press, pp. 78–108.

Foucault, Michel (1983), 'The Subject and Power' in Hubert Dreyfus and Paul Rabinow (eds), *Michel Foucault: Between Structuralism and Hermeneutics*, Brighton: Harvester Press, pp. 208–228.

Foucault, Michel (1984), 'What is an Author?' in Paul Rabinow (ed), *The Foucault Reader: an Introduction to Foucault's Thought*, London UK: Penguin Books, pp. 101–120.

Foucault, Michel (1989), 'Clarifications on the Question of Power' in Sylvere Lotringer (ed), *Foucault Live: Collected Interviews, 1961–1984*, New York: Semiotext(e).

Foucault, Michel (1991), 'Governmentality' in Graeme Burchell, Colin Gordon and Peter Miller (eds), *The Foucault Effect: Studies in Governmentality*, Chicago: The University of Chicago Press, pp. 87–104.

Fourmile, Henrietta (1989), 'Some Background to Issues Concerning the Appropriation of Aboriginal Imagery' in Sue Cramer (ed), *Postmodernism: a Consideration of the Appropriation of Aboriginal Imagery: Forum Papers*, Brisbane: Institute of Modern Art.

Fourmile, Henrietta (1989), 'The Aboriginal Art Market and the Repatriation of Aboriginal Cultural Property', *Social Alternatives*, 8 (1), 19–22.

Fourmile, Henrietta (1993), 'Cultural Survival v Cultural Prostitution' in *Cultural Tourism Awareness Workshop*, Cairns, Queensland, pp. 46–52.

Fourmile, Henrietta (1996), 'Protecting Indigenous Intellectual Property Rights in Biodiversity' in *Ecopolitics IX: Conference Papers and Resolutions*, Casuarina: Northern Land Council, pp. 37–42.

Fox, Christopher (1988), *Locke and the Scriblerians: Identity and Consciousness in Early Eighteenth Century Britain*, Berkeley: University of California Press.

Gaines, Jane (1991), *Contested Culture: The Image, the Voice and the Law*, Chapel Hill: The University of North Carolina Press.

Gana, Ruth (1995), 'Has Creativity Died in the Third World? Some Implications of the Internationalization of Intellectual Property', *Denver Journal of International Law & Policy*, 24 (1), 109–144.

Garnett, Kevin (2000), 'Copyright in Photographs', *European Intellectual Property Review*, 5, 229–231.

'Global Intellectual Property Rights: Boundaries of Access and Enforcement. Panel II: The Law and Policy of Protecting Folklore, Traditional Knowledge and Genetic Resources' (2002), *Fordham Intellectual Property, Media and Entertainment Law Journal*, 11 (3), 753–803.

Geismar, Haidy (2005), 'Copyright in Context: Carvings, Carvers and Commodities in Vanuatu', *American Ethnologist*, 32 (3), 437–459.

Geller, Paul Edward (1994), 'Must Copyright Be For Ever Caught between Marketplace and Authorship Norms?' in Brad Sherman and Alain Strowel (eds), *Of Authors and Origins: Essays on Copyright Law*, London UK: Clarendon Press, pp. 159–184.

Geller, Paul Edward (2000), 'Copyright History and the Future: What's Culture Got to Do With It?', *Journal of the Copyright Society of the U.S.A.*, 48 (1), 209–264.

Gellner, Ernest (1987), *Culture, Identity and Politics*, Cambridge UK: Cambridge University Press.

Gibson, Johanna (2001), 'Justice of Precedent, Justness of Equity: Equitable Protection and Remedies for Indigenous Intellectual Property', *Australian Indigenous Law Reporter*, 6 (1), 1–21.

Gibson, Johanna (2005), *Community Resources: Intellectual Property, International Trade and the Protection of Traditional Knowledge*, Aldershot UK: Ashgate Publishing.

Ginsburg, Jane (1990), 'Creation and Commercial Value: Copyright Protection of Works of Information', *Columbia Law Review*, 90, 1865–1938.

Golvan, Colin (1989), 'Aboriginal Art and Copyright: The Case for Johnny Bulun Bulun', *European Intellectual Property Review*, 10, 346–351.

Golvan, Colin (1992), 'Aboriginal Art and the Protection of Indigenous Cultural Rights', *European Intellectual Property Review*, 7, 227–232.

Golvan, Colin (1995), 'Court Provides Strong Protection for Aboriginal Artwork', *Australian Intellectual Property Law Bulletin*, 8 (1), 6–15.

Golvan, Colin (1996), 'Aboriginal art and copyright infringement' in Luke Taylor and Jon Altman (eds), *Marketing Aboriginal Art in the 1990s*, Canberra: Aboriginal Studies Press, pp. 73–75.

Golvan, Colin, (2001), 'Copyright in Aboriginal Art: An Overview', Paper delivered at the Australasian Intellectual Property Teachers Conference, University of Melbourne.

Golvan, Colin (2002), interview by author, 19 June, Owen Dixon Chambers, Melbourne.

Gordon, Colin (1991), 'Governmental rationality: an introduction' in Graeme Burchell, Colin Gordon and Peter Miller (eds), *The Foucault Effect: Studies in Governmentality*, Chicago: The University of Chicago Press, pp. 1–52.

Grad, Rachel (2003), 'Indigenous Rights and Intellectual Property Law: A Comparison of the United States and Australia', *Duke Journal of Comparative and International Law*, 13, 203–222.

Graeber, David (2001), *Toward an Anthropological Theory of Value: The False Coin of Our Own Dreams*, New York USA: Palgrave Press.

Gray, Kevin (1991), 'Property in Thin Air', *Cambridge Law Journal*, 50, 252–307.

Gray, Stephen (1993), 'Wheeling, Dealing and Deconstruction: Aboriginal Art and the Land, *Aboriginal Law Bulletin*, 3 (63), 10–12.

Gray, Stephen (1996), 'Squatting in the Red Dust: Non-Aboriginal Law's Construction of the "Traditional" Aboriginal Artist', *Law in Context*, 14 (2), 29–41.

Gray, Stephen (1997), 'Vampires around the Campfire', *Alternative Law Journal*, 22 (2), 60–63.

Gray, Stephen (2000), 'Peeking into Pandora's Box: Common Law Recognition of Native Title to Aboriginal Art', *Griffith Law Review*, 9 (2), 227–247.

Gray, Stephen (2001), 'Black, White or Beyond the Pale: The Authenticity Debate and Protection for Aboriginal Culture', *The Australian Feminist Law Journal*, 15, 105–116.

Gray, Stephen (2003), 'Going Native: Disguise, Forgery, Imagination and the European Aboriginal', *Overland*, 170, 34–42.

Greene, Shane (2004), 'Indigenous People Incorporated? Culture as Politics, Culture as Property in Pharmaceutical Bio-prospecting', *Cultural Anthropology*, 45 (2), 211–237.

Grosheide, F. Willem (2002), 'General Introduction' in Willem F. Grosheide, and Johannes. J. Brinkoff (eds), *Intellectual Property Law 2002: The Legal Protection of Cultural Expressions and Indigenous Knowledge*, Antwerp, Oxford UK, New York USA: Intersentia Publishers, 1–24.

Grosheide, F. Willem (1994), 'When Ideas Take the Stage', *European Intellectual Property Review*, 6, 219–222.

Guha, Ranajit (1988), 'The Prose of Counter Insurgency' in Ranajit Guha and Gayatri Spivak (eds), *Selected Subaltern Studies*, New York: Oxford University Press, pp. 45–86.

Haebich, Anna (2000), *Broken Circles: Fragmenting Indigenous Families 1800–2000*, Fremantle: Fremantle Arts Centre Press.

Hanks, Peter and Bryan Keon-Cohen (1984), *Aborigines and the Law*, Sydney: Allen and Unwin.

Hardt, Michael and Antonio Negri (2000), *Empire,* Massachusetts USA: Harvard University Press.

Harris, Cheryl (1993), 'Whiteness as Property', *Harvard Law Review*, 106 (8), 1707–1791.

Harrison, Simon (1992), 'Ritual as Intellectual Property', *Man*, 27, 225–244.

Harrison, Simon (2002), 'The Politics of Resemblance: Ethnicity, Trademarks: Head-Hunting', *Journal of the Royal Anthropological Institute*, 8, 211–232.

Hart, Herbert L.A. (1961), *The Concept of Law*, Oxford UK: Clarendon Press.

Hayden, Cori (2003), *When Nature Goes Public: The Making and Unmaking of Bioprospecting in Mexico*, Princeton: Princeton University Press.

Havemann, Paul (2001), 'The Participation Deficit: Globalisation, Governance and Indigenous Peoples', *Balayi: Culture: Law and Colonialism*, 3, 9–17.

Hawkins, Catherine (1995), 'Stopping the Rip-offs: Protecting Aboriginal and Torres Strait Islander Cultural Expression', *Alternative Law Bulletin*, 20 (1), 7–9.

Heidegger, Martin (1962), *Being and Time*, Oxford UK: Basil Blackwell.

Helliwell, Christine and Barry Hindess (1999), '"Culture", "Society" and the Figure of Man', *History of the Human Sciences*, 12 (4), 1–20.

Helliwell, Christine and Barry Hindess (2002), 'The "Empire of Uniformity" and the Government of Subject Peoples', 6 (1&2) *Cultural Values*, 139–152.

Hesse, Carla (1990), 'Enlightenment Epistemology and the Laws of Authorship in Revolutionary France, 1777–1793', *Representations*, 30, 109–137.

Hesse, Carla (1991), *Publishing and Cultural Politics in Revolutionary Paris, 1789–1810*, Berkeley USA: University of California Press.

Hettinger, Edwin (1989), 'Justifying Intellectual Property', *Philosophy and Public Affairs*, 18 (1), 31–52.

Hirsch, Eric (2002), 'Malinowski's Intellectual Property', *Anthropology Today*, 18 (2), 1–2.

Hirst, Paul and Graham Thompson (2000), 'The Limits to Economic Globalisation' in David Held and Andrew McGrew (eds), *The Global Transformations Reader:*

An Introduction to the Globalisation Debate, Cambridge UK: Polity Press, pp. 335–348.

Hobsbawm Eric and Terence Ranger (eds) (1992), *The Invention of Tradition*, Cambridge UK: Cambridge University Press.

Hohfeld, Wesley (1913), 'Some Fundamental Legal Conceptions as Applied in Juridical Reasoning', *Yale Law Journal*, 23, 16–59.

Howden, Kristen (2001), 'Indigenous Traditional Knowledge and Native Title', *University of New South Wales Law Journal*, 24 (1), 60–84.

Hughes, Justin (1988), 'The Philosophy of Intellectual Property', *The Georgetown Law Journal*, 77, 28–330.

Hunter, Ian (1992), 'Aesthetics and Cultural Studies' in Larry Grossberg, Carla Nelson, Paul Treichler (eds), *Cultural Studies*, New York and London: Routledge, pp. 347–372.

International Labor Organisation (1957), *Convention 107 concerning Indigenous and Tribal Populations*.

International Labor Organisation (1989), *Convention 169 concerning Indigenous and Tribal peoples in Independent Countries*.

Isaacs, Jennifer (1999), *Spirit Country: Contemporary Australian Aboriginal Art*, Australia: Hardie Grant Books.

Isaacs, Jennifer (1999), *Arts of the Dreaming: Australia's Living Heritage*, Sydney: Lansdowne Press.

Ivison, Duncan, Paul Patton and Will Sanders (eds) (2000), *Political Theory and the Rights of Indigenous Peoples*, Cambridge UK: Cambridge University Press.

Janke, Terri (1995), 'Copyright: the Carpets Case', *Aboriginal Law Bulletin/ Alternative Law Journal*, (Joint Issue) 3 (72), 36–39.

Janke, Terri (1998), *Our Culture: Our Future. Report on Australian Indigenous Cultural and Intellectual Property Rights* (produced for Australian Institute of Aboriginal and Torres Strait Islander Studies [AIATSIS] and the Aboriginal and Torres Strait Islander Commission [ATSIC]), Sydney: Michael Frankel and Company Solicitors.

Johnson, Elliot, Martin Hinton and Daryl Rigney (eds) (1997), *Indigenous Australians and the Law*, Sydney: Cavendish Publishing.

Johnson, Vivian (1988), 'A Whiter Shade of Paleolithic: Aboriginal Art and Appropriation', *Aboriginal Law Bulletin*, 34, 8–11.

Johnson, Vivian (1996), *Copyrites: Aboriginal Art in the Age of Reproductive Technologies*, Sydney: National Indigenous Arts Advocacy Association and Macquarie University.

Kaplan, Benjamin (1967), *An Unhurried View of Copyright*, New York: Columbia University Press.

Kerriush, Valerie and Colin Perrin (1999), 'Awash in Colonialism', *Alternative Law Journal*, 24 (1), 3–8.

Kerruish, Valerie (2001), 'Reconciliation, Property and Rights' in Christodoulidis, Emilios and Stuart Veitch (eds), *Lethe's Law: Justice Law and Ethics in Reconciliation*, Oxford University: Hart Publishing, pp. 191–205.

Kinnane, Stephen (2004), *Shadow Lines*, Fremantle: Fremantle Press.

Kirsch, Stuart (2001), 'Environmental Disaster, "Culture Loss" and the Law', *Current Anthropology*, 42 (2), 167–198.

Langton, Marcia (1991), *Too Much Sorry Business: the Report of the Aboriginal Issues Unit of the Northern Territory*, Canberra: Australian Government Printing Services.

Langton, Marcia (1993), *'Well I Heard it on the Radio and Saw it on the Television...': An Essay for the Australian Film Commission on the Politics and Aesthetics of Filmmaking By and About Aboriginal People and Things*, Sydney: The Australian Film Commission.

Langton, Marcia (1994), *Valuing Cultures: Recognising Indigenous Cultures as a Valued Part of Australian Heritage* (prepared for the Council for Aboriginal Reconciliation), Canberra: Australian Government Printing Service.

Langton, Marcia (2000), 'Dumb Politics Wins the Day', *Land Rights Queensland*, 11.

Langton, Marcia (2003), 'Introduction: Culture Wars', in Michel Grossman (ed), *Blacklines: Contemporary Critical Writing by Indigenous Australians*, Melbourne: Melbourne University Press, pp. 81–91.

Langton, Marcia (2003), 'Dreaming Art' in Nikos Paprastergiadis (ed), *Complex Entanglements: Art, Globalization and Cultural Difference*, London UK: Rivers Oram, pp. 42–56.

Langton, Marcia (2005), 'Aboriginal Art and Film: The Politics of Representation', *Rouge*, 6.

Leiberman, David (2002), *The Province of Legislature Determined: Legal Theory in Eighteenth Century Britain*, Cambridge UK: Cambridge University Press.

Lessig, Lawrence (2001), *The Future of Ideas: The Fate of the Commons in an Interconnected World*, New York USA: Random House.

Li, Tania Murray (2000), 'Articulating Indigenous Identity in Indonesia: Resource Politics and the Tribal Slot', *Comparative Studies in Society and History*, 42 (1), 149–79.

Lippard, Lucy (1990), *Mixed Blessings: New Art in Multicultural America*, New York USA: Pantheon Books.

Litman, Jessica (1990), 'The Public Domain', *Emory Law Journal*, 39 (4), 965–1023.

Litman, Jessica (2001), *Digital Copyright*, New York USA: Prometheus Books.

Locke, John (1689), *Two Treatises of Government*, reprinted in Peter Laslett (ed) (1990), London UK: J.M. Dent & Sons.

Lofgren, Neil (1995), 'Common Law Aboriginal knowledge', *Aboriginal Law Bulletin*, 3 (77), 10–13.

Long, Doris Estelle (1998) 'The Impact of Foreign Investment on Indigenous Culture: An Intellectual Property Perspective', *North Carolina Journal of Comparative Law and Competition Regulation*, 23, 229–243.

Long, Doris Estelle (2002), '"Democratising Globalisation": Practicing the Policies of Cultural Inclusion', *Cardozo Journal of International and Comparative Law*, 10, 218–268.

Long, Doris Estelle (2001), '"Globalization": A Future Trend or a Satisfying Mirage?', *Journal of the Copyright Society of the USA*, 49 (1), 313–343.

Loos, Noel and Edward Koiki Mabo (1996), *Edward Koiki Mabo: his life and struggle for land rights*, St Lucia: Queensland University Press.

Lury, Celia (1993), *Cultural Rights: Technology, Legality and Personality*, New York USA: Routledge.

McKenna, Mark (2002), *Looking for Blackfella's Point: An Australian History of Place*, Sydney: University of New South Wales Press.

MacKinnon, Catharine (1987), *Feminism Unmodified: Discourses on Life and Law*, Massachusetts USA: Harvard University Press.

Macpherson, Crawford Brough (1962), *The Political Theory of Possessive Individualism: Hobbes to Locke*, Oxford UK: Clarendon Press.

Maddock, Kenneth (1988), 'Copyright and Traditional Designs: An Aboriginal Dilemma', *Aboriginal Law Bulletin*, 34, 8–10.

Mansell, Michael (1997), 'Barricading Our Last Frontier – Aboriginal Cultural and Intellectual Property Rights', *Land Rights: Past Present and Future – Conference Papers*, Canberra: Northern and Central Land Councils, pp. 195–209.

Marcus, George and Fred Myers (1995), *The Traffic in Culture: Refiguring Art and Anthropology*, Berkeley: University of California Press.

Marden, Emily (1999), 'The Neem Tree Patent: International Conflict over the Commodification of Life' (1999), *Boston College International and Comparative Law Review*, 22, 279–296.

Marika, Wandjuk (1976), 'Copyright on Aboriginal Art', *Aboriginal News*, 3 (1), 7–8.

Marika, Wandjuk (1976), 'Aboriginal Copyright', *Art and Australia*, 13 (3), 242–244.

Martinez Cobo, Jose (1986), *Study of the Problem of Discrimination against Indigenous Populations*, UN Sub-Commission on Prevention of Discrimination and Protection of Minorities E/CN.4/Sub.2/1986/7/Add.4.

Maskus, Keith (2000), *Intellectual Property Rights in the Global Economy*, Washington DC: Peterson Institute for International Economics.

May, Christopher (2000), *A Global Political Economy of Intellectual Property Rights: The New Enclosures?*, London UK: Routledge.

May, Christopher (2003), 'Why IPRs are a Global Political Issue', *European Intellectual Property Review*, 1, 1–6.

May, Christopher and Susan Sell (2005), *Intellectual Property Rights: A Critical History*, London UK: Lynne Rienner Publishers.

McDonald, Ian (2003), 'Indigenous Communal Moral Rights Back on the Agenda', *Australian Intellectual Property Law Bulletin*, 16 (4), 47–50.

McGrath, Ann (1993), 'Beneath the Skin: Australian Citizenship, Rights and Aboriginal Women' *Journal of Australian Studies*, 37, 99–122.

McKeough, Jill and Andrew Stewart (1996), 'Intellectual Property and the Dreaming', in Elliot Johnstone, Martin Hinton and Dary Rigney (eds), *Indigenous Australians and the Law*, Sydney: Cavendish.

McKeough, Jill, Kathy Bowrey and Philip Griffith (2002), *Intellectual Property: Commentary and Materials* (third edition), Sydney: The Lawbook Company.

McMahon, Michael (1997), 'Indigenous Cultures, Copyright and the Digital Age', *Aboriginal Law Bulletin*, 3 (90), 14–16.

McMahon, Michael (1997), 'The Intellectual Property Regime and the Protection of Indigenous Cultures' in *Land Rights: Past Present and Future – Conference Papers*, Canberra: Northern and Central Land Councils.

Mellor, Doreen and Terri Janke (2001), *Valuing Art, Respecting Culture: Protocols for Working with the Australian Indigenous Visual Arts and Crafts Sector*, Sydney: National Association for the Visual Arts.

Merry, Sally Engel (1998), 'Law Culture and Cultural Appropriation', *Yale Journal of Law and the Humanities*, 10, 101–129.

Mezey, Naomi (2001), 'Approaches to the Cultural Study of Law: Law as Culture', *Yale Journal of Law and the Humanities*, 13, 35–67.

Michaels, Eric (1988), 'Bad Aboriginal Art', *Art and Text*, 28, 59–73.

Michaels, Eric (1994), *Bad Aboriginal Art: Tradition, Media and Technological Horizons,* Sydney: Allen and Unwin.

Miller, Peter and Nikolas Rose (1990), 'Governing Economic Life', *Economy and Society*, 19 (1), 1–31.

Mitchell, Timothy (1988), *Colonizing Egypt*, Berkeley, USA: University of California Press.

Mitchell, Timothy (2002), *Rule of Experts: Egypt, Technopolitics, Modernity*, Berkeley, USA: University of California Press.

Mitchell, Timothy (2004), 'The Properties of Markets: Informal Housing and Capitalism's Mystery', Cultural Political Economy Working Paper Series, Institute for Advanced Studies in Social and Management Sciences, University of Lancaster.

Mitchell, Timothy (2005), 'The Work of Economics: How a Discipline Makes its World', *European Journal of Sociology*, 45 (2), 297–320.

Morgan, Marlo (1995), *Mutant Message Down Under,* Harper Collins: New York.

Morris, Meaghan (1987), 'Tooth and Claw: Tales of Survival, and *Crocodile Dundee*', *Art and Text*, 25, 36–69.

Mundy, Martha and Alain Pottage (2004), *Law, Anthropology and the Social,* Cambridge UK: Cambridge University Press.

Munger, Frank (1998), 'Mapping Law and Society' in Austin Sarat, Marianne Constable, David Engel, Valerie Hans and Susan Lawrence (eds), *Crossing Boundaries: Traditions and Transformations in Law and Society Research*, Chicago: Northwestern University Press, pp. 21–88.

Myers, Fred (2002), *Painting Culture: The Making of an Aboriginal High Art Market*, Durham USA: Duke University Press.

Nadasdy, Paul (2003), *Hunters and Bureaucrats: Power, Knowledge and Aboriginal State Relations in the Southwest Yukon*, Vancouver and Toronto: University of British Columbia Press.

Nader, Laura (ed) (1969), *Law in Culture and Society*, Illinois: Aldine Publishing Company.

Nakata, Martin (ed) (2001), *Indigenous Peoples, Racism and the United Nations*, Sydney: Common Ground.

Nakata, Martin (2002), 'Indigenous Knowledge and the Cultural Interface: Underlying Issues at the Intersection of Knowledge and Information Systems', *International Federation of Libraries Association Journal*, 28, 281–286.

Nakata Martin and Marcia Langton (2005), *Australian Indigenous Knowledge and Libraries*, Canberra: Australian Academic and Research Libraries.

Nancy, Jean-Luc (1993), *The Experience of Freedom*, Stanford USA: Stanford University Press.

Neville, Kathryn (2000), 'Art and Colonial Consciousness: Deconstructing the Colonial Imagination', *Balayi: Culture, Law and Colonialism*, 1 (2), 39–51.

Nicholas George and Kelly Bannister (2004), 'Copyrighting the Past?', *Cultural Anthropology*, 45 (4), 327–350.

Nicholls, Christine (2000), *From Appreciation to Appropriation: Indigenous Influences and Images in Australian Visual Art Exhibition Catalogue*, Sydney.

O'Connor, Paul (1996), 'Happy Partners or Strange Bedfellows: The Blending of Remedial and Institutional Features in the Evolving Constructive Trust', *Melbourne University Law Review*, 30, 735–759.

O'Faircheallaigh, Cairan (2000), 'Negotiating Major Agreements: The "Cape York Model"', Australian Institute of Aboriginal and Torres Strait Islander Studies Discussion Research Paper No. 11, Canberra.

O'Malley, Pat (1983), *Law Capitalism and Democracy*, Sydney: Allen and Unwin.

O'Malley, Pat (1998), 'Indigenous governance' in Barry Hindess and Mitchell Dean (eds), *Governing Australia: Studies in contemporary rationalities of government*, Sydney: Cambridge University Press, pp. 156–172.

O'Malley, Pat (2000), 'Uncertain Subjects: Risks, Liberalism and Contract', *Economy and Society*, 29 (4), 460–484.

Okediji, Ruth Gana (1995), 'Has Creativity Died in the Third World? Some Implications of the Internationalization of Intellectual Property', *Denver Journal of International Law and Policy*, 24 (1), 109–132.

Okediji, Ruth Gana (2003), 'The International Relations of Intellectual Property: Narratives of Developing Country Participation in the Global Intellectual Property System', *Singapore Journal of International & Comparative Law*, 7, 315–356.

Osborne, Thomas (1999), 'The Ordinariness of the Archive', *History of Human Sciences*, 12 (2), 51–64.

Otto, Dianne (1999), 'Subalterity and International Law: The Problems of Global Community and the Incommensurabilty of Difference' in Eve Darian-Smith and Peter Fitzpatrick (eds), *Laws of the Postcolonial*, Michigan USA: University of Michigan, pp. 145–180.

Palmer, David and Denise Groves (2000), 'A Dialogue on Identity, Intersubjectivity and Ambivalence', *Balayi: Culture, Law and Colonialism*, 1 (2), 19–31.

Pashukanis, Evgeny (1924), *Law and Marxism*, Chris Arthur (ed) (1978), London UK: Ink Links.

Patterson, Lyman Ray (1968), *Copyright in Historical Perspective*, Nashville USA: Vanderbilt University Press.

Patton, Paul (2000), 'The Translation of Indigenous Land into Property: the Mere Analogy of English Jurisprudence…', *parallax*, 6 (1), 25–38.

Pearson, Noel (1994) 'Aboriginal Law and Colonial Law since Mabo' in Christine Fletcher (ed), *Aboriginal Self-determination in Australia*, Canberra: Aboriginal Studies Press, pp. 23–27.

Penner, James E. (1996), 'The Bundle of Rights Picture of Property', *University of California Los Angeles Law Review*, 43, 711–820.

Perraton, Jonathon, David Goldblatt, David Held and Anthony McGrew (2000), 'Economic Activity in a Globalising World' in David Held and Anthony McGrew (eds), *The Global Transformations Reader: An Introduction to the Globalisation Debate*, Cambridge: Polity Press, pp. 287–299.

Perrin, Colin (1999), 'Approaching Anxiety: The Insistence of the Postcolonial in the Declaration of the Rights of Indigenous People' in Eve Darian-Smith and Peter Fitzpatrick (eds), *Laws of the Postcolonial*, Michigan USA: University of Michigan, pp. 19–38.

Peters-Little, Frances (1998), 'The Community Game: Aboriginal Self Definition at a Local Level', *Australian Instiute of Aboriginal and Torres Strait Islander Research Discussion Paper*, 10, 1–34.

Peterson, Noel and Will Sanders (eds) (1998), *Citizenship and Indigenous Australians: Changing Conceptions and Possibilities*, Cambridge UK: Cambridge University Press.

Poovey, Mary (1998), *A History of the Modern Fact: Problems of Knowledge in the Sciences of Wealth and Society*, Chicago USA: Chicago University Press.

Posey, Darrell (1996), 'Indigenous Peoples and Traditional Resource Rights: A Basis for Equitable Relationships', in *Ecopolitics IX: Conference Papers and Resolutions*, Casuarina: Northern Land Council.

Posey, Darrell. and Graham Dutfield (1996), *Beyond Intellectual Property*, Ottowa: International Development Research Centre.

Posner, Richard (1990), *The Problems of Jurisprudence*, Cambridge, Massachusetts: Harvard University Press.

Povinelli, Elizabeth (2002), *The Cunning of Recognition: Indigenous Alterities and the Making of Australian Multiculturalism*, Durham USA: Duke University Press.

Pritchard, Sarah (1997), 'The United Nations and the making of a Declaration on Indigenous Rights', *Aboriginal Law Bulletin*, 3 (89), 4–9.

Pritchard, Sarah (ed) (1997), *Indigenous Peoples, the United Nations and Human Rights*, London UK: Zed Books.

Purdy, Jeannine (1996), 'British Common Law and Colonised Peoples: Studies in Trinidad and Western Australia' in Greta Bird, Gary Martin and Jennifer Nielson (eds), *Majah: Indigenous Peoples and the Law*, Sydney: The Federation Press, pp. 23–36.

Purdy, Jeannine (1999), 'Postcolonialism: The Emperor's New Clothes?' in Eve Darian-Smith and Peter Fitzpatrick (eds), *Laws of the Postcolonial*, Michigan USA: University of Michigan, pp. 203–232.

Puri, Kamal (1993), 'Copyright Protection for Australian Aborigines in the Light of Mabo' in Margaret Ann Stephenson and Suri Ratnapala (eds), *Mabo: A Judicial Revolution*, St Lucia, Queensland: The University of Queensland Press, pp. 132–164.

Puri, Kamal (1995), 'Cultural Ownership and Intellectual Property Rights Post-Mabo: Putting Ideas into Action', *Intellectual Property Journal*, 9 (3), 293–347.

Puri, Kamal (2000), 'Is traditional or cultural knowledge a form of intellectual property?', *Oxford Electronic Journal of Intellectual Property Rights* at www.oiprcox.ac.uk/EJWP0100.pdf.

Radin, Margaret Jane (1993), *Reinterpreting Property*, Chicago USA: University of Chicago Press.

Rappaport, Joanne (2005), *Intercultural Utopias: Public Intellectuals, Cultural Experimentation, and Ethnic Pluralism in Columbia*, Durham USA: Duke University Press.

Reich, Charles (1964), 'The New Property', *Yale Law Journal*, 73, 733–787.

Ricketson, Sam (1987), *The Berne Convention for the Protection of Literary and Artistic Works 1886–1986*, London UK: Centre for Commercial Law Studies, Queen Mary College.

Ricketson, Sam (1994), *Intellectual Property: Cases, Materials and Commentary*, Sydney: Butterworths.

Rimmer, Matthew (2000), 'Bangarra Dance Theatre: Copyright Law and Indigenous Culture', *Griffith Law Review*, 9 (2), 275–302.

Rimmer, Matthew (2001), *The Pirates' Bizarre*, PhD Dissertation, University of New South Wales, Sydney, Australia.

Rimmer, Matthew (2003), 'Albert Namatjira: Copyright Estates and Traditional Knowledge', *Incite*, 24, 6–8.

Rose, Mark (1993), *Authors and Owners: The Invention of Copyright*, Cambridge MA USA: Harvard University Press.

Rose, Mark (1994), 'The Author as Proprietor: *Donaldson v. Becket* and the Genealogy of Modern Authorship' in Brad Sherman and Alain Strowel (eds), *Of Authors and Origins: Essays on Copyright Law*, Oxford UK: Clarendon Press, pp. 23–55.

Rose, Nikolas (1993), 'Government, Authority and Expertise in Advanced Liberalism', *Economy and Society*, 22 (3), 273–299.

Rose, Nikolas (1999), *Powers of Freedom: Reframing Political Thought*, London UK: Cambridge University Press.

Rose, Nikolas and Peter Miller (1992), 'Political Power Beyond the State: Problematics of Government', *British Journal of Sociology*, 43 (2), 173–205.

Rowse, Tim (1992), 'The Royal Commission, ATSIC and Self-determination: A Review of the Royal Commission into Aboriginal Deaths in Custody', *Australian Journal of Social Issues*, 27 (3), 153–172.

Rowse, Tim (1992), *Remote Possibilities: The Aboriginal Domain and the Administrative Imagination*, Casuarina NT: Australian National University.

Rowse, Tim (1998), *White Flour, White Power: From Rations to Citizenship in Central Australia*, Cambridge UK: Cambridge University Press.

Royal Commission into Aboriginal Deaths in Custody – Interim Report (1988), Canberra: Australian Government Publishing Service.

Royal Commission into Aboriginal Deaths in Custody – National Report (1991), Canberra: Australian Government Publishing Service.

Ruddock, Phillip (2003), 'The Government's Copyright Policy Agenda' Conference Paper delivered at *The Eleventh Biennial Copyright Law and Practice Symposium*, Darling Harbour, Sydney, November.

Ryan, Michael (1998), *Knowledge Diplomacy: Global Competition and the Politics of Intellectual Property Future*, Washington, DC: Brookings Institution Press.

Sackville, Ronald (2003), 'Legal Protection of Indigenous Culture in Australia', *Cardozo Journal of International and Comparative Law*, 11, 711–746.

Said, Edward (1985), *Orientalism*, London UK: Penguin Books.

Sandel, Michael (ed) (1984), *Liberalism and its Critics*, New York USA: New York University Press.

Sarat, Austin and Thomas Kearns (eds) (1999), *History, Memory and the Law*, Ann Arbor USA: University of Michigan Press.

Sarat, Austin and Jonathan Simon (2001), 'Beyond Legal Realism?: Cultural Analysis, Cultural Studies and the Situation of Legal Scholarship', *Yale Journal of Law and the Humanities*, 13 (1), 1–35.

Sarat, Austin and Jonathon Simon (eds) (2003), *Cultural Analysis, Cultural Studies and the Law: Moving Beyond Legal Realism*, Durham USA: Duke University Press.

Saunders, David (1992), *Authorship and Copyright*, London UK and New York USA: Routledge.

Sebastiani, Silvia (2005), '"Race", Women and Progress in the Scottish Enlightenment' in Sarah Knott and Barbara Taylor (eds), *Women, Gender and the Enlightenment*, London UK: Palgrave Macmillan, pp. 75–96.

Seeger, Anthony (1997), 'Ethnomusicology and Music Law' in Bruce Ziff and Pratima Rao (eds), *Borrowed Power: Essays on Cultural Appropriation*, New Jersey USA: Rutgers University Press, pp. 52–70.

Sell, Susan (1998), *Power and Ideas: North-South Politics of Intellectual Property and Antitrust*, New York USA: State University of New York Press.

Sell, Susan (2002), 'Industry Strategy for Intellectual Property and Trade: The Quest for TRIPs and post-TRIPs Strategies', *Cardozo Journal of International and Comparative Law*, 10, 79–108.

Sherman, Brad (1994), 'From the Non-original to the Ab-original' in Brad Sherman and Alain Strowel (eds), *Of Authors and Origins: Essays on Copyright Law*, Oxford UK: Clarendon Press, pp. 111–131.

Sherman, Brad and Alain Strowel (eds) (1994), *Of Authors and Origins: Essays on Copyright Law*, Oxford UK: Clarendon Press.

Sherman, Brad and Lionel Bently (1999), *The Making of Modern Intellectual Property: The British Experience 1760–1911*, Cambridge UK: Cambridge University Press.

Sherwin, Richard (2000), *When Law Goes Pop: The Vanishing Line Between Law and Popular Culture*, Chicago USA: The University of Chicago Press.

Shiva, Vandana (1993), *Monocultures of the Mind: Perspective on Biodiversity and Biotechnology*, India: Zed Books.

Shiva, Vandana (2001), *Protect or Plunder? Understanding Intellectual Property Rights*, India: Zed Books.

Shulman, Seth (1999), *Owning the Future*, Boulder Colorado: Houghton and Mifflin.

Singh Nijar, Gurdial, (1998), 'Community Intellectual Rights Protect Indigenous Knowledge', *Biotechnology and Development Monitor*, 36, 11–12.

Smart, Carol (1989), *Feminism and the Power of Law*, London UK: Routledge.

Smith, Gordon and Russell Parr (1989), *Valuation of Intellectual Property and Intangible Assets*, New York USA: John Wiley.

Stacey, Helen (1996), 'Legal Discourse and the Feminist Political Economy: Moving Beyond Sameness/Difference', *The Australian Feminist Law Journal*, 6, 115–129.

Stevenson, Nina (1985), 'Case Note: Infringement in Copyright in Aboriginal Artworks', *Aboriginal Law Bulletin*, 17, 5–6.

Stoler, Ann Laura (1995), *Race and the Education of Desire: Foucault's* History of Sexuality *and the Colonial Order of Things*, Durham USA: Duke University Press.

Stoler, Ann Laura (2002), 'Colonial Archives and the Arts of Governance', *Archival Science*, 2(1–2), 87–109.

Strang, Veronica (2000), 'Not so Black and White: The Effects of Aboriginal Law on Australian Legislation' in Allen Abramson and Dimitrios Theodossopoulis (eds), *Land, Law and Environment: Mythical Land, Legal Boundaries*, London UK: Pluto Press, pp. 93–115.

Strathern, Marilyn (1996), 'Potential Property: Intellectual Rights and Property in Persons', *Social Anthropology*, 4 (1), 17–32.

Strathern, Marilyn (1999), *Property, Substance and Effect: Anthropological Essays on Persons and Things*, London UK: Athlone Press.

Strathern, Marilyn (2005), *Kinship, Law and the Unexpected: Relatives are Always a Surprise*, Cambridge UK: University of Cambridge Press.

Strelein, Lisa (2003), 'Members of the Yorta Yorta Aboriginal Community v Victoria *[2002] HCA 58* – Comment', *Land, Rights, Laws: Issues of Native Title*, 2 (21), 1–12.

Strelein, Lisa, Jane Anderson and Stuart Bradfield (2004), *Submission to the Senate Select Committee on the Administration of Indigenous Affairs by the Australian Institute of Aboriginal and Torres Strait Islander Studies.*

Sullivan, Patrick (2005), 'Searching for the Inter-cultural, Searching for the Culture', *Oceania*, 75 (2), 183–194.

Sunder, Madhavi (2000), 'Intellectual Property and Identity Politics: Playing with Fire', *Journal of Gender, Race and Justice*, 4 (1), 69–91.

Sunder, Madhavi (2007), 'The Invention of Traditional Knowledge', *Duke Journal of Law and Contemporary Problems*, 17 (2), 97–124.

The Attorney General's Department (1994), *Stopping the Rip Offs: Intellectual Property Protection for Indigenous Arts and Cultural Expression*, Canberra: Australian Government Publishing Services.

The Mataatua Declaration on Cultural and Intellectual Property Rights of Indigenous Peoples (1993), Written and adopted at the First International Conference on Cultural and Intellectual Property Rights of Indigenous Peoples, Whakatane, New-Zealand, 12–13 June.

Thomas, Nicholas (1996), 'Cold Fusion', *American Anthropologist*, 98 (1), 9–16.

Thomas, Nicholas (1999), *Possessions: Indigenous Art/Colonial Culture*, London UK: Thames and Hudson.

Thornberry, Paul (1991), *International Law and the Rights of Minorities*, Oxford, UK: Clarendon Press.

Thornton, Margaret (1991), 'Portia Lost in the Grove of Academe Wondering What to Do About Legal Education', Inaugural Lecture, La Trobe University Legal Studies, 3 June.

Thornton, Margaret (1991), *The Liberal Promise: Anti-Discrimination Legislation in Australia*, Melbourne: Oxford University Press.

Torgovnick, Marianna (1990), *Gone Primitive: Savage Intellects Modern Lives*, Chicago USA: The University of Chicago Press.

Trioli, Virginia (1994), 'Record Damages for Illegal Aboriginal Images', *The Age*, Melbourne, Australia, 14 December.

Tully, James (1980), *A Discourse on Property: John Locke and his adversaries*, Cambridge USA: Cambridge University Press.

Tushnet, Mark (1991), 'Critical Legal Studies: A Political History', *The Yale Law Journal*, 100, 1515–1544.

Unger, Roberto (1976), *Law in Modern Society: Toward a Criticism of Social Theory*, London UK and New York USA: The Free Press, McMillan Publishers.

Unger, Roberto (1986), *The Critical Legal Studies Movement*, Cambridge MA USA: Harvard University Press.

Vaidhyanathan, Siva (2001), *Copyrights and Copywrongs: The Rise of Intellectual Property and How it Threatens Creativity*, New York USA: New York University Press.

von Lewinski, Silkie (2003), 'The Protection of Folklore', *Cardozo Journal of International and Comparative Law*, 11 (2), 747–768.

Vandervelde, Kenneth (1980), 'The New Property of the Nineteenth Century: The Development of the Modern Concept of Property', *Buffalo Law Review*, 29, 325–352.

Walker, John and David McDonald (1995), 'The Over Representation of Indigenous Peoples in Custody in Australia', *Trends and Issues in Crime and Criminal Justice*, 47, 1–6.

Watson, Irene (1997), '"Indigenous Peoples" Law-Ways: Survival against the Colonial State', *Australian Feminist Law Journal*, 8, 39–58.

Watson, Irene (2000), 'There is No Possibility of Rights Without Law: So Until Then Don't Thumb Print or Sign Anything!', *Indigenous Law Bulletin*, 5, 4–7.

Watson, Irene (2002), 'Buried Alive', *Law and Critique*, 13 (3), 253–269.

Weiner, Annette (1992), *Inalienable Possessions: The Paradox of Keeping While Giving*, California USA: University of California Press.

Weiner, James (1987) 'Protection of folklore: A political and legal challenge', *International Review of Industrial Property and Copyright Law*, 18 (1), 56–92.

Weiner, James (1999), 'Culture in a sealed envelope: the concealment of Australian Aboriginal heritage and tradition in the Hindmarsh Island Bridge Affair', *The Journal of the Royal Anthropological Institute*, 5 (2), 193–210.

Weiner, James (2002), 'Diaspora, Materialism, Tradition: Anthropological Issues in the Recent High Court Appeal of the Yorta Yorta', *Land, Rights, Laws: Issues of Native Title*, 2 (18), 1–12.

Wells, Kathryn (1995), 'Authenticity – Promotion and Protection of Aboriginal and Torres Strait Islander Art', Paper on Research and Development – Preliminary advice to National Indigenous Arts Advocacy Association Australia, 15 June.

Wells, Kathryn (1996), *Draft Discussion Paper on the Proposed Authenticity Trade Mark*, National Indigenous Arts Advocacy Association, Australia.

Wells, Kathryn (1996), 'The Cosmic Irony of Intellectual Property and Indigenous Authenticity', *Culture and Policy*, 7 (3), 45–63.

White, James Boyd (1990), *Justice as Translation: An Essay in Cultural and Legal Criticism*, Chicago USA and London UK: University of Chicago Press.

Williams, Brett (ed) (1991), *The Politics of Culture*, Washington DC: The Smithsonian Institution.

Williams, Patricia (1991), *The Alchemy of Race and Rights*, Cambridge MA USA: Harvard University Press.

Williams, Raymond (1963), *Culture and Society 1780–1950*, London UK: Penguin Books.

Williams, Raymond (1965), *The Long Revolution*, London UK: Penguin Books.

Williams, Raymond (1976), *Keywords: A Vocabulary of Culture and Society*, London UK: Fontana/Croom Helm.

Williams, Raymond (1979), *Politics and Letters*, London UK: New Left Books.

Williams, Raymond (1989), *The Politics of Modernism: Against the New Conformists*, London: Verso.

Windshuttle, Keith (2002), *The Fabrication of Australian History*, Sydney: Macleay Press.

Wiseman, Leanne (2000), 'The Labels of Authenticity: An Overview', *Media and Culture Review*, 1, 3–8.

Wiseman, Leanne (2001), 'The Protection of Indigenous Art and Culture in Australia: The Labels of Authenticity', *European Intellectual Property Review*, 23 (1), 14–25.

Woodmansee, Martha (1984), 'The Genius and the Copyright: Economic and Legal Conditions of the Emergence of the Author', *Eighteenth Century Studies*, 17, 425–448.

Woodmansee, Martha and Peter Jaszi (eds) (1994), *The Construction of Authorship: Textual Appropriation in Law and Literature*, Durham USA: Duke University Press.

Wootten, Hal (1992), 'Deaths in Custody', Paper delivered at the Coronial Inquest Seminar, Sydney University Law School, Australia.

World Intellectual Property Organisation (2001), *Intellectual Property Needs and Expectations of Traditional Knowledge Holders: WIPO Report on Fact Finding Missions on Intellectual Property and Traditional Knowledge (1998–1999)*, Geneva, Switzerland.

Wright, David (1998) *The Remedial Constructive Trust*, Sydney: Butterworths.

Wright, Shelley (1996), 'Intellectual Property and the "Imaginary Aboriginal"' in Greta Bird, Gary Martin and Jennifer Neilson (eds), *Majah: Indigenous Peoples and the Law*, Sydney: The Federation Press, pp. 129–151.

Wright, Shelley (2001), *International Human Rights, Decolonisation and Globalisation: Becoming Human*, London UK: Routledge.
Young, Alison and Austin Sarat (eds) (1994), *Beyond Criticism: Law Power and Ethics*, London UK: Sage Publishers.
Young, Iris Marion (1990), *Justice and the Politics of Difference*, Princeton USA: Princeton University Press.
Young, Simon (2001), 'The Trouble with "Tradition": Native Title and the *Yorta Yorta* Decision', *The University of Western Australia Law Review*, 30 (1), 28–49.
Yunupingu, Galarrway (1997), 'From the Bark Petition to Native Title' in *Land Rights: Past Present and Future – Conference Papers*, Canberra: Northern and Central Land Councils, 1–17.
Ziff, Bruce and Pratima Rao (1997), *Borrowed Power: Essays on cultural appropriation*, New Jersey USA: Rutgers University Press.

Index